All in One

Information Technology
Code-402

CBSE Class 9

Focused Theory ▪ Practice Exercise ▪ Sample Papers

Recommended by Teachers
Trusted by Toppers

All in One®

Information Technology

Code-402

CBSE Class 9

Focused Theory ▪ Practice Exercise ▪ Sample Papers

Author
Neetu Gaikwad
(B. Tech, MBA)

arihant
SUCCESS AND NOTHING LESS

ARIHANT PRAKASHAN
(School Division Series)

卐 ADMINISTRATIVE & PRODUCTION OFFICES

Regd. Office

'Ramchhaya' 4577/15, Agarwal Road, Darya Ganj, New Delhi -110002
Tele: 011- 47630600, 43518550; Fax: 011- 23280316

卐 *Head Office*

Kalindi, TP Nagar, Meerut (UP) - 250002, Tel: 0121-7156203, 7156204

卐 SALES & SUPPORT OFFICES

Agra, Ahmedabad, Bengaluru, Bareilly, Chennai, Delhi, Guwahati, Hyderabad, Jaipur, Jhansi, Kolkata, Lucknow, Nagpur & Pune.

PO No : TXT-XX-XXXXXXX-X-XX

Published By Arihant Publications (India) Ltd.

For further information about the books published by Arihant, log on to www.arihantbooks.com or e-mail at info@arihantbooks.com

Follow us on

卐 PRICE ₹300.00

PRODUCTION TEAM

Publishing Managers	*Cover Designer*	*Inner Designer*
Mahendra Singh Rawat & Keshav Mohan	Rakesh Rawat	Ankit Tyagi
Project Head	*Page Layouting*	*Proof Reader*
Shruti Aggarwal	Ravinder Kumar	Sumit

Index *cum* Study Planner

One Book- Endless Features

to Help you Succeed

Chapter Checklist

At the start of each chapter, all the topics of the chapter have been listed , so that students may know what they are going to study.

UNIT

01

Communication Skills-I

Chapter Checklist

Communication
Perspective in Communication
Methods of Communication
Writing Skills : Parts of Speech
Parts of a Sentence
Pronunciation Basic

Communication skills are those skills which are needed to speak and write properly. These are important for everyone, these teach us about how we can give and receive information and convey our ideas and opinions to those around us.

We must develop a variety of skills for both communicating to others and learning how to interpret the information received from others.

An effective speaker is the one who is able to speak appropriately whilst maintaining eye contact with the audience, uses different vocabulary and articulate speech to suit the need of audience.

Importance of Communication

Ability to communicate clearly and share thoughts, feelings and ideas help us in all relationships. A good communication makes our personal as well as professional life smooth.

Some of the importance of communication skills are as follows:

I. **Inform** Communication is required to give facts or information to someone. i.e. Communicating the timetable of an exam to a friend.

Simplified Theory

Each chapter contains the necessary study material well supported by Definitions, Facts, Figures, Flow Charts, etc.

Check Point 01

1 The content of the communication is called ....

2 Which among the following is not an importance of communication skills?

(a) Inform (b) Influence (c) Express feelings

3 What is encoding?

4 The choice of channel or medium of communication depends on the ....

Check Point

A set of 3-5 Questions given in between the text, helps students to remain connected with the text while studying. They can instantly assess themselves for their understanding.

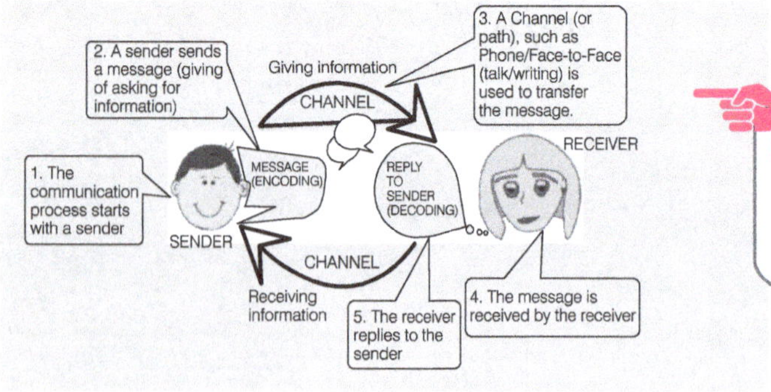

Illustrative Figures

To make the concepts completely visible, illustrative diagrams have been given at various place.

One Book- Endless Features

to Help you Succeed

Box Matter

Information given in the box is related to the explanation of daily life phenamena related to the concept given.

- **Public Speaking** Public speaking means speaking infront of a large group. Often it makes people nervous. To get over the fear and become a confident and effective speaker we must use 3Ps, *viz*, prepare, practice and perform.
- **Prepare** means think about the topic and prepare oneself in the best way to make one's listeners to understand the topic.
- **Practice** means prior practices by oneself before public speaking.
- **Perform** denotes start speaking confidently what one has preponed.

NCERT Folder

Complete explanations of all the questions of NCERT Exercises.

Exam Practice

Exam Practice having all types of questions; MCQs, True-False, Fillers, Matching, VSA, SA & LA.

NCERT FOLDER

Check Your Progress Pg 6-7

A. Multiple Choice Questions

Read the questions carefully and circle the letter (a), (b), (c) or (d) that best answers the questions.

1. What is the purpose of communication?
   (a) Inform (tell someone about something)
   (b) Influence (get someone to do something you want)
   (c) Share thoughts, ideas, feelings
   (d) All of the above

Ans. (d) All of the above

2. Which of the following methods are used to receive information from the sender through a letter?
   (a) Listening (b) Speaking
   (c) Reading (d) Writing

Ans. (c) Reading

3. How do you receive information on phone?
   (a) Listening (b) Speaking
   (c) Reading (d) Writing

Ans. Factors affecting perspectives in communication are given below :

(i) **Language** In this factor, in case of use of incorrect words, unfamiliar language and lack of detail, language can act as a barrier to communicate what a person wishes to convey.
(ii) **Visual Perception** It is the brain's ability to make sense of what we see through our eyes.
(iii) **Past Experience** If the past experience has been bitter, the future communication between them will surely be ineffective.
(iv) **Prejudice** Fixed ideas, such as thinking 'No one in my class likes me' may stop a students from communicating openly in the class.
(v) **Feelings** Our feelings and emotions, such as lack of interest or not trusting the other person affect communication.
(vi) **Environment** Noise or disturbance in the surroundings may make communication difficult.
(vii) **Culture** Signs which have a different meaning in different cultures, such as showing a thumb may mean 'good job' done for some people but may be insulting to others.

Exam Practice

Multiple Choice Questions

1. Communication skills are those skills which are needed to
   (a) Speak properly (b) Write properly
   (c) Think Properly (d) All of these

Ans. (d) All of these

2. The word 'Communication' came from the
   (a) French word (b) Latin word
   (c) Greek word (d) None of these

Ans. (b) Latin word

3. The information can be
   (a) Drawings (b) Words
   (c) Gestures (d) All of these

Ans. (d) All of these

4. Communication involves
   (a) Sender (b) Receiver
   (c) Giver (d) Both (a) and (b)

(a) Verbal Communication
(b) Non-verbal Communication
(c) Visual Communication
(d) All of the above

Ans. (a) Verbal Communication

10. Facial expression, posture, gesture/body language, touch, space etc are types of which method of communication?
    (a) Verbal Communication
    (b) Non-verbal Communication
    (c) Visual Communication
    (d) None of the above

Ans. (b) Non-verbal Communication

11. What is a phrase?
    (a) A group of ideas that form a complete paragraph.
    (b) A group of words which does not make

Chapter Summary

Summary of chapter given at the end of each chapter helps to revise the chapter quickly at the time of examination or routine school tests.

Sample Question Papers

To make students practice of examination in real sense, there are 3 Sample Question Papers at the end. All these Sample Questions Papers are exactly prepared on the latest syllabus & pattern of examination.

SUMMARY

- Communication skills are needed to speak and write properly.
- The word communication derives from the latin word 'Communicane' which means 'to share'.
- Important elements of communication are senders, ideas, channel, receiver, encoding, decoding, feedback, etc.
- Factors which affect perspectives in communication are language, visual perception, past experience, prejudices, feelings, environment, personal factors and culture.
- Methods of communication are of three types, viz, verbal, non-verbal and visual communication.
- In English, sentence is the basic framework of communication.
- There are eight basic parts of speech in the English language, *viz*, noun, pronoun, verb, adjective, adverb, preposition, conjunction and interjection.
- Sentences have subject, verb and object.
- The object in a sentence can be either direct or indirect.
- Sentences can be categorised into declarative, interrogative, exclamatory and imperative sentence.
- In English, words are made of three basic types of sounds, *viz*, vowels, diphthongs and consonants.
- Greetings are of three types, *viz*, formal, informal and greetings according to time.
- In introduction, we need to talk about ourselves. In many situation we need to write about ourselves in a form.
- There are two types of questions, i.e. close-ended questions and open-ended questions. In order to get correct information, we need to ask correct questions.

SAMPLE QUESTION PAPER 1

A Sample Question Paper for CBSE Class 9

Information Technology

General Instructions

1. Please read the instructions carefully.
2. This Question Paper consists of 21 questions in two sections: Section A & Section B.
3. Section A has Objective Type Questions whereas Section B contains Subjective Type Questions.
4. Out of the given (5 + 16 =) 21 questions, a candidate has to answer (5 + 10 =) 15 questions in the allotted (maximum) time of 2 hours.
5. All questions of a particular section must be attempted in the correct order.

Time : 2 hours ***Max. Marks : 50***

Latest Course Structure

	UNITS	No. of Hours for Theory and Practical		Max. Marks for Theory and Practical
Part A	**Employability Skills**			
	Unit 1 : Communication Skills -I	10		2
	Unit 2 : Self -Management Skills -I	10		3
	Unit 3 : ICT Skills -I	10		1
	Unit 4 : Entrepreneurial Skills -I	15		3
	Unit 5 : Green Skills -I	05		1
	Total	**50**		**10**
Part B	**Subject Specific Skills**	**Theory (In Hours)**	**Practical (In Hours)**	**Marks**
	Unit 1: Introduction to IT - ITeS Industry	2	4	4
	Unit 2: Data Entry & Keyboarding Skills	4	10	6
	Unit 3: Digital Documentation	10	26	10
	Unit 4: Electronic Spreadsheet	18	35	10
	Unit 5: Digital Presentation	10	31	10
	Total	**44**	**106**	**40**
Part C	**Practical Work**			
	Practical Examination			15
	Written Test			10
	Viva Voce			10
	Total			**35**
Part D	**Project Work/Field Visit**			
	Practical File/ Student Portfolio			10
	Viva Voce			05
	Total			**15**
	GRAND TOTAL	**200**		**100**

Detailed Curriculum / Topics

PART-A : EMPLOYABILITY SKILLS

S. No.	Units	Duration in Hours
1.	Unit 1: Communication Skills - I	10
2.	Unit 2: Self-Management Skills - I	10
3.	Unit 3: Basic Information and Communication Technology Skills- I	10
4.	Unit 4: Entrepreneurial Skills - I	15
5.	Unit 5: Green Skills - I	05
	Total	**50**

PART-B : SUBJECT SPECIFIC SKILLS

UNIT 1 : INTRODUCTION TO IT–ITeS INDUSTRY

S. No.	Learning Outcomes	Theory
1.	Appreciate the applications of IT	• Introduction to IT and ITeS, BPO services, • BPM industry in India, • Structure of the IT-BPM industry, • Applications of IT in home computing, everyday life, library, workplace, education, entertainment, communication, business, science and engineering, banking, insurance, marketing, health care, IT in the government and public service,

UNIT 2 : DATA ENTRY AND KEYBOARDING SKILLS

S. No.	Learning Outcomes	Theory
1.	Use keyboard and mouse for data entry	• Keyboarding Skills • Types of keys on keyboard, Numeric keypad • Home keys, Guide keys • Typing and deleting text • Typing ergonomics • Positioning of fingers on the keyboard, Allocation of keys to fingers on four different rows • Pointing device – Mouse, Mouse operations

2.	Use typing software	• Introduction to Rapid Typing Tutor, • Touch typing technique, • User interface of Typing Tutor, • Typing text and interpret results, • Working with lesson editor, • Calculating typing speed, • Typing rhythm.

UNIT 3 : DIGITAL DOCUMENTATION

S. No.	Learning Outcomes	Theory
1.	Create a document using a word processor	• Introduction to word processing, • Word processing applications, • Introduction to Word Processing tool • Creating a document, Parts of a Word Processor Window
2.	Apply Editing features	• Text editing – Undo and Redo, • Moving and copying text, • Copy and Paste, • Selecting text, • Selection criteria, • Selecting non-consecutive text items, • Selecting a vertical block of text, • Find and replace option, • Jumping to the page number, • Non-printing characters, • Checking spelling and grammar, • Using Synonyms and Thesaurus.
3.	Apply formatting features	• Page style dialog, • Formatting text – Removing manual formatting, Common text formatting, Changing text case, Superscript and Subscript • Formatting paragraph – Indenting paragraphs, Aligning paragraphs, Font colour, highlighting, and background colour • Using bullets and numbering, Assigning colour, border and background to paragraph • Page formatting – setting up basic page layout using styles, Inserting page break, Creating header/footer and page numbers • Defining borders and backgrounds, Inserting images shapes, special characters in a document, Dividing page into columns, Formatting the shape or image.

4.	Create and work with tables	• Creating table in Word Processor, • Inserting row and column in a table, • Deleting rows and columns, • Splitting and merging tables, • Deleting a table, • Copying a table, • Moving a table.
5.	Use Print Options	• Printing options in Word Processor. • Print preview, • Controlling printing, • Printing all pages, single and multiple pages.
6.	Understand and apply mail merge	• Introduction to mail merge • Concept of data source for mail merge

UNIT 4 : ELECTRONIC SPREADSHEET

S.NO.	Learning Outcomes	Theory
1.	Create a Spreadsheet	• Introduction to spreadsheet application, • Starting a spreadsheet, • Parts of a spreadsheet • Worksheet – Rows and columns, Cell and cell address, • Range of cells – column range, row range, row and column
2.	Apply formula and functions in spreadsheet	• Different types of data, • Entering data – Label, Values, Formula • Formula, how to enter formula, • Mathematical operators used in formulae, • Simple calculations using values and operators, • Formulae with cell addresses and operators, • Commonly used basic functions in a spreadsheet – SUM, AVERAGE, MAX, MIN, COUNT • Use of functions to do calculations.
3.	Format data in the spreadsheet	• Formatting tool, • Use of dialog boxes to format values, • Formatting a range of cells with decimal places, • Formatting a range of cells to be seen as labels, • Formatting of a cell range as scientific, • Formatting a range of cells to display times, • Formatting alignment of a cell range, • Speeding up data entry using the fill handle, • Uses of fill handle to copy formulae.
4.	Understand and apply Referencing	• Concept of referencing, • Relative referencing, • Mixed referencing, • Absolute referencing.
5.	Create and insert different types of charts in a spreadsheet	• Importance of chart in spreadsheet, • Types of chart

UNIT 5 : DIGITAL PRESENTATION

S.NO.	Learning Outcomes	Theory
1.	Understand features of an effective presentation	• Concept of presentation, • Elements of presentation, • Characteristics of an effective presentation
2.	Create a presentation	• Introduction to presentation software, • Starting a presentation tool, • Parts of a presentation tool window, • Closing the presentation tool, • Creating a presentation using template, • Selecting slide layout, • Saving a presentation, • Running a slide show, • Save a presentation in PDF, • Closing a presentation, • Using Help.
3.	Work with slides	• Inserting a duplicate slide, • Inserting new slides, • Slide layout. • Copying and moving slides, • Deleting and renaming slides in presentation, • Copying, moving and deleting contents of slide, • View a presentation, • Controlling the size of the view, • Workspace views – Normal, Outline, Notes, Slide sorter view.
4.	Format text and apply animations	• Formatting toolbar, • Various formatting features, • Text alignment, • Bullets and numbering. • Custom Animation
5.	Create and use tables	• Inserting tables in presentation, • Entering and editing data in a table, • Selecting a cell, row, column, table, • Adjusting column width and row height, • Table borders and background

6.	Insert and format image in presentation	• Inserting an image from a file, • Inserting an image from the gallery, • Formatting images, • Moving images, • Resizing images, • Rotating images, • Formatting using the Image toolbar, • Drawing graphic objects –line, shapes, • Grouping and un-grouping objects
7.	Work with slide master	• Slide masters, • Creating the slide masters, • Applying the slide masters to all slide, • Adding transitions.

Part A

EMPLOYABILITY SKILLS

UNIT

01

Communication Skills-I

Chapter Checklist

Communication skills are those skills which are needed to speak and write properly. These are important for everyone, these teach us about how we can give and receive information and convey our ideas and opinions to those around us.

We must develop a variety of skills for both communicating to others and learning how to interpret the information received from others.

An effective speaker is the one who is able to speak appropriately whilst maintaining eye contact with the audience, uses different vocabulary and articulate speech to suit the need of audience.

Likewise, an effective writer should be able to use words in various style and techniques to communicate their message and ideas to the readers. Thus, good reading, writing, speaking and listening skills are essential for effective communication.

Communication

The word 'communication' derives from the Latin word 'Communicare', which means 'to share'. Communication is the 'sharing' of information between two or more individuals or within a group to reach a common understanding.

The information can be words, drawings, paintings, gestures, music or even sound also.

Communication involves at least two persons, i.e. a sender and a receiver. The sender develops and transmits a message to the receiver and the receiver, receives the message. It is successful only when there is a common understanding between the sender and receiver.

Importance of Communication

Ability to communicate clearly and share thoughts, feelings and ideas help us in all relationships. A good communication makes our personal as well as professional life smooth.

Some of the importance of communication skills are as follows:

I. **Inform** Communication is required to give facts or information to someone. i.e. Communicating the timetable of an exam to a friend.

II. **Influence** Communication is needed to influence or change a person in an indirect but usually important way. e.g. negotiating with a shopkeeper to reduce the price or helping a friend to overcome stress due to examination or any other reason.

III. **Express Feelings** Communication is needed to share and express our feelings to other in a healthy way. i.e. Sharing our excitement about doing well in our examination or sharing our feelings to parents and friends.

Elements of Communication

- Communication is a two-way exchange of information, i.e. giving and receiving.
- Speaking and writing to someone are examples of giving information.
- Reading and listening to someone are examples of receiving information.

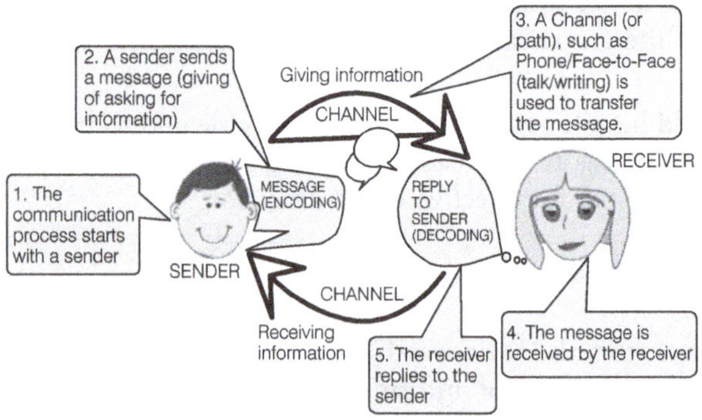

- **Sender** Sender is the person who is first in the process of communication. It decides what the message is, how it will be expressed and sent and how it is to be sent to.
- **Ideas/Message** The message is the actual information that the sender wishes to convey to the receiver.
- **Channel/Medium** Channel is the means by which the message is sent. There can be various forms of media face-to-face communication, letters, radio, television and email etc.
- **Receiver** The person who received the message is called receiver.
- **Encoding** It means to change the message into a form suitable for sending.
- **Decoding** Decoding is the process in which the receiver interprets and understands the message.
- **Feedback** Feedback is the receiver's response to the message. Requesting classification is a part of a good feedback phase of communication cycle.

Check Point 01

1. The content of the communication is called ....
2. Which among the following is not an importance of communication skills?
   (a) Inform (b) Influence (c) Express feelings
3. What is encoding?
4. The choice of channel or medium of communication depends on the ....

Perspectives in Communication

Perspectives are ideas, views, or fixed ways of thinking. These sometimes effect our communication. The perspective of communication is not only checks the way the message transmits information and influences the individual, it also examines the way that the message creates, sustains and changes cultures and communities.

The perspective of communication helps to explore the form, content, medium and pattern of the message and how it influences the way people interpret the meaning and take action.

It also helps to understand how messages are produced, how they are circulated among a group of people and how they are interpreted with an eye on the important consequences of the message.

Factors Affecting Perspectives in Communication

Sometimes, we are not able to communicate clearly because of some barriers that stop us from sharing and understanding messages.

Factor affecting perspectives in communication are as follows :

Language

The process of communication is both verbal and written. Language plays main role in all the types of communication. The same words can have very different meanings depending on how we interpret them.

In case of use of incorrect words, unfamiliar language and lack of detail, language can act as a barrier to communicate what one wishes to convey.

i.e. Language can act as a barrier when an Indian who knows only Hindi and a Chinese who has the knowledge of Mandarin only want to interact with each other.

Visual Perception

Visual perception is the ability to see and interpret (analyze and give meaning to) the visual information that surrounds us. Simply we can say that it is the brain's ability to make sense of what we see through our eyes.

For example, Completing partially drawn pictures with visual perception whereas they may be something else.

Past Experience

Sometime our past bitter experience stop us to communicate properly.

For example, "This shopkeeper cheated me last time. Let me be careful or I scored low marks in my maths exam, so I am scared to ask and answer question in class".

Prejudices

Prejudice means 'prejudgement'. It occurs when we take our past experiences with a person and assume that the same type of experience will happen with all people who are similar to the first. Prejudices are partly due to culture and partly due to personal preferences or experience.

It is used in reference to a preconceived judgement of someone due to their social class, gender, race, ethnicity, disability, age, gender and religion etc.

The problem with prejudices is when they start to influence how or to whom we communicate.

Fixed ideas, such as thinking "No one in my class likes me" may stop a student from communicating openly in class.

Feelings

The process of communication becomes more affective when the sender shows enthusiasm and the receiver is receptive. The mood and feelings of both the parties, affect the process of communication. Our feelings and emotions, such as lack of interest or not trusting the other person affect communication. i.e. "I am not feeling well, therefore, I don't want to talk".

So, when we are not feeling well and uncomfortable, we cannot pay attention to what other are saying.

Environment

There are many environmental factors that hamper the effectiveness of communication. Message may get blocked or interpreted due to environmental factors like location or situation where the situation takes place.

Noise or disturbance in the surroundings may make communication difficult.

For example, Talking to a friend in a function where there is loud music being played by the Orchestra.

Personal Factors

Personal factors include our own feelings, habits and ways of thinking.

For, example, Fear and low confidence may make communication difficult.

Culture

Signs which have a different meaning in different cultures, such as showing a thumb may mean 'good job' done for some people but may be insulting to others.

Check Point 02

1. .... helps to understand how messages are produced.
2. What comes to our mind on seeing something in our perception?
3. Which factors includes our own feelings, habbits and way of thinking?

Methods of Communication

There are different methods of communication, which include non-verbal, verbal and visual.

1. Verbal Communication

Verbal communication is the oldest means of communication. It is most commonly used as a medium for the exchange of information. Verbal communication is the sharing of information by using words.

Types of Verbal Communication

There are mainly two types of verbal communications, *viz*

(a) **Oral or Spoken Communication** It means communication through the mouth (speaking) and the ears (listening). It is also defined as the communication which involves talking.

For example, Face-to-Face conversation, group discussion, talking to family member at home, conversation with public through speeches, talking on phone and classroom teaching etc.

(b) **Written Communication** In this type of communication, the written signs or symbol are used to convey the message. We can say that, it is the communication which involves written typed words.

For example, letters, notes, email, books, newspapers, SMS, documents and files etc.

Advantages of Verbal Communication

- Verbal communication is easy and quick.
- It is more reliable method of communication.
- It is cheaper way of communication and hence saves money.
- It promotes a secure exchange of ideas.

Disadvantages of Verbal Communication

- It has no legal validity and hence will lead to problems in certain situation.
- It has issues when communicating with distant people.
- This form of communication is not suitable for lengthy messages.
- Verbal communication depends on words, sometimes the meaning become confusing and difficult to understand if the right words are not used.

Public Speaking Public speaking means speaking infront of a large group. Often it makes people nervous. To get over the fear and become a confident and effective speaker we must use 3Ps, *viz*, prepare, practice and perform.

- **Prepare** means think about the topic and prepare oneself in the best way to make one's listeners to understand the topic.
- **Practice** means prior practices by oneself before public speaking.
- **Perform** denotes start speaking confidently what one has preponed.

2. Non-Verbal Communication

Non-verbal communication is the message we send to others without using any words. It occurs without using any oral or written words.

We send signals and messages to others, through expressions, gestures and body postures.

Types of Non-Verbal Communication

There are some types of non-verbal communications as follows:

(a) **Facial Expression** Many a times, a facial expression shows the feelings of a person.
For example, when we are happy, we express it through a smile or when we are sad we show a gloomy face.

(b) **Posture** Postures are position of the body. They show our confidence and feelings.

For example, Straight body posture is seen as confidence. Holding your head may be taken as tiredness.

(c) **Gesture/Body Language** Gestures describe movements of parts of the body, especially hands or head, to express an idea or meaning. This includes waving, pointing and using our hands when speaking.

For example, Raising a hand may mean asking a question. Biting nails show nervousness.

(d) **Touch** We communicate a great deal through our touch, such as shaking hands and patting on the back.

For example, A firm handshake shows confidence. Sports coaches pat on the back of the players to encourage the players.

(e) **Space** The space between two persons while communicating, generally depends on the intimacy or closeness between them.

(f) **Eye Contact** Maintaining an eye contact with the person you are talking indicates interest, whereas, looking away can make the other person feel ignored.

(g) **Paralanguage** Paralanguage is the tone of our voice, speed and volume that makes a difference in the meaning of the communication. Speaking too fast may show excitement or nervousness. Speaking too slow may show seriousness, sadness or making a point.

Importance of Non-Verbal Communication

- Non-verbal communication makes our message stronger.
- Using the right gestures while speaking makes our message more effective.
- Non-verbal communication helps us understand our audience's reaction and adjust our behaviour or communication accordingly.
- It is helpful in communicating with illiterate people.
- Using the right gestures and postures helps us to be professional at work.
- If verbal message are blocked by noise or distance, etc, we can use hand movements to exchange our message.

3. Visual Communication

Visual communication involves sending and understanding messages only through images or picture. It is the transmission of ideas and information with the help of symbols and images.

Example of Visual Communication

Visual Communication: Exchanging Information through Images	
Traffic symbol which communicates not to blow horn.	
Sign for ladies and gents toilet.	
Sign for flammable substances.	
Sign used to pause a video or audio file in smartphone or computer.	
Traffic lights - Red for Stop; Yellow for Wait and Green for Go.	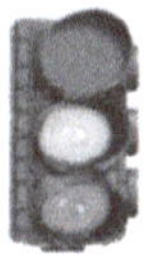
Sign showing railway crossing.	
Sign for slippery surface.	
Sign which communicates that the area is a no smoking zone.	

Advantages of Visual Communication

- The main advantage of this type of communication is that we do not need to know any particular language for understanding it.
- It is simple, easy to understand and remains same across different places.
- The amount of time taken in understanding a visual communication is less as compared to other types of communication.

Check Point 03

1 .... communication is the sharing of information by using words?
2 What is the oldest means of communication?
3 Facial expression is a non-verbal communication. (True/False)

Writing Skills : Parts of Speech

In English, sentences are the basic framework of communication. They are important because unclear sentences create difficulty in understanding the meaning which is to be conveyed.

Sentence

A sentence is a group of words that communicate a complete thought. It always begins with a capital letter, and always ends with either a question mark, a full stop or an exclamation mark.

Phrase

A group of words, which does not make complete sense in itself is known as a phrase.

e.g., (i) Sushmita is a woman of **great intellect**.

(ii) The horse runs **at a good speed**.

In the given examples, the underlined parts are phrases. They do not have any meaning of their own but they contribute to the meaning of the sentence as a whole.

Using Capitals

Capital letters are used at different places. The rules that suggest where a capital letter is to be used is given by MINTS.

MINTS is a set of simple rules that helps an individual to capitalise words correctly. Each letter in the word MINTS refer to one capitalisation rules as given in the table below:

Alphabet	M	I	N	T	S
What it shows	Months	The letter 'I'	Names	Titles	Starting letter of sentences
Rule	Capitalise the first letter in all the names of months.	Capitalise the letter 'I' whenever it is used.	Capitalise the first letter in the names of people, places and days.	Capitalise the first letter in the titles used before people's name.	Capitalise the first letter in every sentence.
Example	I will go to college in June.	I play tennis with him every day.	This Tuesday, Vidya will be in Rajasthan.	Dr Shah and Mr Patel work together.	The cat ran out of the house.

Punctuation

Punctuation refers to the marks like comma, full stop, question mark etc., which help us in separating the parts of a sentence so that its meaning becomes clear. Knowledge of proper use of punctuation marks is necessary for writing and reading English correctly.

Some of the common punctuation marks and their use have been given below:

Punctuation name	Sign	Use	Examples
Full stop	.	Shows the end of a sentence. Also used to show short form of long words. e.g. 'doctor' can be shortened to 'Dr', when we use it as a title before a name.	This is a sentence. This is another sentence. Sanjay is a doctor. His patients call him Dr. Sanjay.
Comma	,	Sometimes, we use a comma to indicate a pause in the sentence. We can also use a comma to separate items when we are listing out more than two items.	After the waiter gave me a menu, I ordered food. I bought apples, oranges and grapes.
Question mark	?	We use a question mark at the end of a question.	What is your name? How old are you?
Exclamation mark	!	We use an exclamation mark at the end of a word or a sentence to indicate a strong feeling, such as surprise, shock or anger.	What a pleasant surprise! You are late!
Apostrophe	(')	We use an apostrophe followed by an s in a word to show that something belongs to someone. We also use an apostrophe to indicate the shortened form of some words in informal speech.	That is Divya's pen. Are these Abdul's books? Let's go. (Instead of Let us go.) He isn't here. (Instead of He is not here.)

Basic Parts of Speech

According to their function in a sentence, a word in the English language can be classified into eight basic parts of speech. These are as follows:

- Noun
- Pronoun
- Adjective
- Verb
- Adverb
- Conjunction
- Preposition
- Interjection

Main Parts of Speech

Main parts of speech indicates how a word functions in producing meaning in a sentence. These are the different types of words used in the sentence. The main parts of speech are given in the table below:

Part of Speech	What they do	Example sentence (Examples are underlined in the sentences)
Noun	Nouns are words that refer to a person, place, thing or idea. These are 'naming words'. They are sometimes used with an article (the, a, an).	Rajiv wrote a very long letter.
Pronoun	A pronoun is a word used in place of a noun.	He went to Rashid and told him the secret of his happiness.
Adjective	Adjectives are words that describe other words specifically nouns and pronouns.	The young boy is very clever.
Verbs	Verbs are words that show action.	Puja wrote a letter.
Adverbs	Adverbs are words that add meaning to verbs, adjectives or other adverbs. They answer the questions—How? How often? When? And Where?	She laughed loudly. Lucy is very tall.
Conjunctions	Conjunctions are words that join two nouns, phrases or sentences. Some common conjunctions are 'and', 'or' and 'but'.	You can have either chocolate or vanilla icecream. Sheela and I went to the market.
Prepositions	Preposition connect one word with another to show the relation between them. They usually answer the questions 'where', 'when' and 'how'. Some common prepositions are 'on', 'at', 'in' etc.	The cat is on the roof. The shop is at the end of the market. Amit is standing under the tree. Raunak lives in Delhi.
Interjections	These words express strong emotions, such as happiness, surprise, anger or pain. They end with an exclamation mark.	Oh God! i don't know what to do in this horrible situation! Wow! it is magnificent.

Supporting Parts of Speech

Alongwith the main parts of speech, there are some other words that are required to make a sentence. These words are supporting words that join the main pairs of speech and add information to the sentences.

The four supporting parts of speech are given in the table below:

Supporting Parts of Speech	Use	Example sentences (examples are underlined in sentences)
Articles	The words 'a', 'an' and 'the' are known as articles. Articles are generally used before nouns. **An** is used before words with a vowel (a, e, i, o, u) sound. **A** is used before nouns with a consonant (all other alphabets) sound. **The** is used to refer to specific or particular words.	The car stopped suddenly because a cat ran in front of it. A book An apple An umbrella The sun

Parts of a Sentence

Almost every sentence in English have two parts, i.e. a subject and a verb. Some sentences also contain a third part called an object.

- **Subject** A subject is a person or thing that does an action.
- **Verb** A verb describes the action performed.
- **Object** An object is a person or thing that receives the action or on which an action is performed.

For example, Dia and Sanjay broke the bottle.

In the given sentence, 'Dia and Sanjay' are the subject as they perform an action, 'broke' is the verb and 'the bottle' is the object as the action is performed on it.

Types of Objects

In a sentence, an object an either be direct or indirect.

- **Direct Object** Direct objects are the ones directly 'acted on' by the verb. In other words, direct object answers the question 'what?'

  For example, Ravi kicked the ball.

  In the given sentence, the action is directly performed on the 'ball'. Hence, 'the ball' is the direct object.
- **Indirect Object** Indirect object identifies the person or the thing for whom the action of the verb is performed. It answers questions such as 'to whom' and 'for whom'.

For example, My mother bought a necklace for me.

Or

My mother bought me a necklace.

In the given sentences, 'necklace' is the direct object and 'me' is the indirect object.

Types of Sentences

Depending upon whether the subject of sentence performs or receivers an action, the sentences are of two types:

1. **Active Sentences** Active sentences are those sentences where the subject does an action.

   For example, She wrote a letter.

   He opened the door.

2. **Passive Sentences** Passive sentences are those sentences in which the subject receives an action.

   For example, A letter was written by her.

   The door was opened by him.

Depending upon the purpose of the sentence, sentences can be categorised into four types:

1. **Declarative Sentences** These sentences provides information or functions to state a fact. They are the most common type of sentences that always ends with a full stop '.'.
   For example, I completed my project.
2. **Interrogative Sentences** These sentences are used for asking questions. Therefore, they always end with a question mark '?'.
   For example, Did you complete project?
3. **Exclamatory Sentences** An exclamatory sentence expresses a strong emotion, such as joy, sadness, fear or wonder. It always ends with an exclamation mark '!'.
   For example, I completed my project!
4. **Imperative Sentences** These sentences show an order, command, request or advice. It can end with a full stop or an exclamation mark ('.' or '!').

   For example, Complete your project.

Paragraphs

A paragraph is a group of sentences dealing with a particular topic. A paragraph must have one common idea.
For example, A paragraph on the 'value of trees' will be written as given below:

Trees are our life line. We cannot live anywhere on the plant without trees. Trees give us food, oxygen and all the luxuries that we enjoy. Trees are not only useful for mankind but nature as well. By producing fresh oxygen it makes the environment pollution free. It prevents soil erosion, droughts and flood. So, man must stop cutting more and more trees, otherwise he will suffer greatly.

Check Point 04

1 Give one example of phrase.
2 What is the use of comma (,) as punctuation mark?
3 A verb describes the action performed. (T/F)
4 A/An ..... is a group of sentences dealing with a particular topic.

Pronounciation Basic

Pronunciation

Pronunciation is the way in which an individual says a word. If a word is not said properly, then other might not understand what is being said. Hence, pronunciation is an important part of English.

Correct pronunciation helps an individual to express his/her views in a clear and confident manner.

Speaking Correctly

In English, there are some words that have similar spellings but are pronounced differently. There also exists, words that have different spellings but they are pronounced in the same way. In such cases, the best way to learn the correct pronunciation of words, one must listen to a language expert carefully.

Phonetics

Each and every word that we speak is made up of one or more sounds. So, we put these sounds together to pronounce words. The study of these sounds that we make when we speak is called phonetics. For example, The word 'dog' is made up of three sounds d + o + g.

In English, there are 26 Alphabets and each of these alphabets are pronounced differently. However, there are more than 26 sounds in English.

For example, The letter 'a' can be pronounced in different ways in different words. Some of them are given in the table below:

Words	Pronunciation of the letter 'a'	Pronunciation in Hindi
cat, apple and back	ऐ	कैट, ऐपल, बैक
car, fast and park	आ	कार, फास्ट, पार्क
call, ball and saw	ऑ	कॉल, बॉल, सॉव्

Types of Sounds

All words in English are made of three basic types of sounds. These are as follows:

1. **Vowels** The English alphabet has 5 vowels - 'a', 'e', 'i', 'o' and 'u'. But there are 12 vowel sounds. This means that most vowels can be pronounced in different ways. We make a vowel sound when we read a vowel is a word.

   For example, The vowel 'i' is pronounced differently in 'bit' and 'bite' (बिट, बाइट).
2. **Diphthongs** When we combine the sound of two vowels, the sound produced is called a diphthong. A Diphthong starts as one vowel sound and go to another.

   For example, The sound of 'ou' n mouse (माउस).
3. **Consonants** All sounds except vowels and diphthongs are consonants sounds.

   For example, The sound of letters 'p' and 't' in the word 'pot'. (पॉट).

Some of the different sounds are given in the table below:

Vowel sounds	Examples
long 'ee' (ी) sound	Sleep (स्लीप) Feel (फील) Keep (कीप)
Short 'i' (ि) sound	Slip (स्लिप) Dip (डिप) Fill (फिल)
Short 'u' (ु) sound	Book (बुक) Put (पुट) Foot (फुट)
Long 'oo' (ू) sound	Boot (बूट) Group (ग्रूप) Two (टू)
Diphthong sounds	**Examples**
'ea' sound (ि + ा)	Near (नियर) Dear (डियर) Hear (हियर)
'ae' sound (े)	Late (लेट) Cake (केक) Game (गेम)
'oa' sound (ो)	Boat (बोट) Loan (लोन) Most (मोस्ट)
'ou' sound (ा + ु)	Mouth (माउथ) Cow (काउ) Cloud (क्लाउड)
Consonant sounds	**Examples**
'p' ('प') sound	Pen (पेन) Report (रिपोर्ट) Stop (स्टोप)
't' ('ट') sound	Train (ट्रेन) Story (स्टोरी) Put (पुट)
Consonant sounds	**Examples**
'k' ('क') sound	Book (बुक) Cold (कोल्ड) Music (म्यूसिक)
'l' ('ल') sound	Look (लुक) Place (प्लेस) School (स्कूल)

Greetings and Introductions

Greetings

Before starting a conversation with someone, we use words like 'Hello', 'Good Morning', 'Good Evening' etc. These words are called **greetings**.

There are many ways in which an individual can greet a person. Generally, a greeting and the reply to a greeting depends upon who we are talking to and also according to the time of the day.

Types of Greetings

There are two types of greetings. They are described below:

- **Formal Greetings** Formal greetings are used when we address a stranger. It is also used to greet a senior, an elder or people with whom we have formal relations like teachers, boss etc. This type of greeting is mostly used in schools, colleges and offices.

  For example,

Greeting	Reply
Good Morning Everyone!	Good Morning, Sir!
Hello Mam. How are you?	I am doing well. Thank You!

- **Informal Greetings** These are used when we talk to our friends, family or a known person.

  For example,

Greeting	Reply
Hey!	Hello/Hi!
Hello. How's everything?	Hi. Everything is good. What about you?

- **Greetings according to time** Formal greeting can change according to the time of the day as show in the table:

Greeting	Reply
Good Morning	From early morning to 11 : 59 am
Good Afternoon	12 pm to 5 pm
Good Evening	5 pm to midnight

It is to be noted here that we do not greet people by saying 'good night' even if it is night. 'Good night' is used at the end of the conversation.

Introducing Yourself and Others

When we tell others about ourselves using sentences that provide basic information about us like our name, our hobbies etc, it is known as **introduction**.

We need to 'introduce' ourselves when we meet someone for the first time or when we want others to know about us.

Introduction generally includes an individuals name, hometown, job, subjects as a student, interests, hobbies etc.

We should smile while introducing ourselves and look towards the other person.

For example, Good Morning. I am Aditi.
I am from Agra and I am a teacher.
I love reading books.

Sometimes we have to introduce someone to others. We can do this by telling their name, their job and how do we know them. We can also add some quality of their personality.

For example, This is my uncle Ramesh.
He is a doctor. He is also a very good guitarist.

Talking About Self

There are many occasions when we have to talk about ourselves. This is especially when we are meeting new people. Also, many a times we have to fill forms with information about ourselves.

Talking About Yourself

When we meet someone for the first time, they may want to know about us. So, we need to introduce ourselves.

Introduction definitely, starts with our name. Then we can tell them other things about us like our age, our interests, the place where we live, our likes, dislikes etc.

We can form these sentences using nouns and verbs.

For example,

- My name is Kavita. (Name)
- I live in Delhi. (Hometown)
- I study in class IX. (Class)
- My favourite subject is English. (Favourites)
- I like to play basketball. (Likes)
- I am a good team player. (Strength)
- I cannot manage my time properly. (Weakness)

Filling a Form

In many situations, we need to write about ourselves in a form. A form is a document, typed or printed with blank spaces to fill in the information.

We have different forms for different purposes. So we should carefully read a form before filling it. The form should be filled in a neat handwriting and with correct spellings. A general form usually asks for personal information as given in the table:

Name	Sometimes we might have to right first name, middle name and surname separately.
Date of birth	It is usually written in DD/MM/YYYY format.
Address	This is the postal address which includes your house number and the details of the street, area and the city.
PIN code	This is a group of numbers used by the post office to identify a region. It is an important part of an address.
Signature (or Sign)	This is your name or initials written by hand, in a specific way (which is difficult for anyone else to copy).

e.g. Harish Sethi was born on 5 December 1999. He lives in Agra, in a house named Sukh Nivas. His house number is 13 in Raja Nagar. His postal code is 282001. Harish filled a form asking for personal information like this.

First Name	Harish
Last Name	Sethi
Date of Birth	5 December 1999 (or 05-12-1999)
Address	Sukh Nivas, No. 13, Raja Nagar, Agra
Pin Code	282001

Asking Questions-I

Need for Asking Questions

A question is a request for any type of information. It could be an answer to a question in the textbook, information about a person or a place or about how to do a task.

For example, Where can I find a coffee shop?
Who is Rahul Dravid?

Asking questions is useful because it helps us to

- gain new knowledge, get information,
- ensure that what we know is correct,
- avoid doubts, confusion, misunderstanding and
- starting conversation with people by asking about them and their ideas.

How We Make Sure We Have Complete Information?

Asking right questions at the right time from the right person is very important. Incomplete or incorrect information will not help us to reach a place or do a certain task.

We can follow the simple method of '5W + 1H' to make sure that we have all the information required to do a task.

The 5W+1H method of asking questions is described in the table given below:

5W+1H Method for Asking Questions

Question Words	Usages	Examples
Who	'Who' is used to ask about people	Who is the new student in the class?
Where	'Where' is used to ask about a place	Where does she live?
When	'When' is used to ask about time	When did she join school?
What	'What' is used to ask about a thing, an idea or an action	What is her favourite subject?
Why	'Why' is used to find the reason	Why is she not talking to anyone in the class?
How	'How' is used to find the method	How can I help her make friends?

Asking Questions-II

A question is a sentence, phrase or word that can also be used to test someone's knowledge. We always use a question mark (?) at the end of a question.

We ask questions in our day-to-day conversations to get information. In order to get correct information we need to ask correct questions.

Types of Questions

There are two types of questions as discussed below

- **Close Ended Questions** Such questions are those which can be answered with a 'yes' or a 'no'. Their answers are limited to a 'yes' or a 'no' and no other detail is required.

  For example, Did he go to the temple?

  Yes.

- **Open Ended Questions** Those questions that requires answer in detail are open ended questions. The option of answers to such questions are unlimited.

  For example, What is your favourite memory from childhood.

The answer to such a question could be unlimited and will be described in detail.

Framing Close Ended Questions

Close ended questions are usually formed by beginning the question with auxiliary verbs like Be, Do and Have. Modal verbs like Can, Shall, May, Should, Could can also be used as these show possibility or necessity.

One way to frame a close-ended question is to take a sentence without the above mentioned words and then adding any one of the words before the subject.

For example, The sentence 'I like it' can become "Do I like it?".

Or

'They talk on the phone everyday' will become "Do they talk on the phone everyday?"

It is important to note here that the helping verb, changes based upon the subject while the main verb remains unchanged.

Another way to frame close ended questions is to exchange the positions of the subject and the verb.

For example, "She can cook dinner." will change into "Can she cook dinner?"

Or

"They were cleaning the room." will become "Were they cleaning the room?".

Framing Open-Ended Questions

The answers to the open-ended questions are not limited or closed. They need to be answered with more information than a simple "yes" or "no".

Open-ended questions can be formed by using the question words (5W+1H) like What, Why, Who, When, Where and How.

For example, For the question "What did you do?" an individual can answer anything relevant to the question such as "I went to the park", "I went to the market", "I went to the temple" etc.

Check Point 05

1. ……… is the way in which an individual says a word.
2. What is greeting?
3. A question is a request for any type of information. (T/F)
4. What symbol do we use at the end of a question?

NCERT FOLDER

Check Your Progress

Pg 6-7

A. Multiple Choice Questions

Read the questions carefully and circle the letter (a), (b), (c) or (d) that best answers the questions.

1. What is the purpose of communication?

(a) Inform (tell someone about something)

(b) Influence (get someone to do something you want)

(c) Share thoughts, ideas, feelings

(d) All of the above

Ans. (d) All of the above

2. Which of the following methods are used to receive information from the sender through a letter?

(a) Listening (b) Speaking

(c) Reading (d) Writing

Ans. (c) Reading

3. How do you receive information on phone?

(a) Listening (b) Speaking

(c) Reading (d) Writing

Ans. (a) Listening

B. Match the Columns

1. Match the following columns.

	Column I (Communication Barriers)		Column II (Examples)
A.	Language	1.	Trying to read a book when somebody else is watching TV in the same room.
B.	Emotional	2.	In some cultures, wearing shoes and walking inside the kitchen is considered rude and disrespectful.
C.	Environmental	3.	Talking in Hindi when others know only Tamil.
D.	Cultural	4.	Parent is not talking to the child.

Ans. A → 3, B → 4, C → 1, D → 2,

C. Short Answer Question

1. Write down the seven factors affecting perspectives in communication.

Ans. Factors affecting perspectives in communication are given below :

(i) **Language** In this factor, in case of use of incorrect words, unfamiliar language and lack of detail, language can act as a barrier to communicate what a person wishes to convey.

(ii) **Visual Perception** It is the brain's ability to make sense of what we see through our eyes.

(iii) **Past Experience** If the past experience has been bitter, the future communication between them will surely be ineffective.

(iv) **Prejudice** Fixed ideas, such as thinking 'No one in my class likes me' may stop a students from communicating openly in the class.

(v) **Feelings** Our feelings and emotions, such as lack of interest or not trusting the other person affect communication.

(vi) **Environment** Noise or disturbance in the surroundings may make communication difficult.

(vii) **Culture** Signs which have a different meaning in different cultures, such as showing a thumb may mean 'good job' done for some people but may be insulting to others.

2. Give an example of the following :

(a) Clear communication

(b) Complete communication

Ans. Examples of Clear communication and Complete communication are given below:

(a) **Clear Communication** In clear communication one should be clear about what s/he wants to say.

(b) **Complete Communication** In complete communication one should deliver his/her message completely which should have all the needed information.

Check Your Progress

Pg 10-11

A. Multiple Choice Questions

Read the questions carefully and circle the letter (a), (b), (c) or (d) that best answers the questions.

1. Choose the correct example of oral communication.

(a) Reports

(b) Newspapers

(c) Face-to-face conversation

(d) Notes

Ans. (c) Face-to-face conversation

2. When we communicate verbally, we should use ....
(a) difficult words (b) simple words
(c) confusing words (d) abbreviations

Ans. (b) Simple words

3. Why do we send emails?
(a) To reach on time.
(b) To share documents and files.
(c) To talk to each others.
(d) To meet each other.

Ans. (b) To share documents and files.

B. Short Answer Questions

1. Write down the different types of verbal communication. Give an example for each type.

Ans. Different types of verbal communication are given below

(a) **Oral or Spoken Communication** It means communication through the mouth (speaking) and the ears (listening). It is also define as the communication which involves talking.

For example, Face-to-face conversation, group discussion, talking to family member at home, conversation with public through speeches, talking on phone and classroom teaching etc.

(b) **Written Communication** In this type of communication the written signs or symbol are used to convey the message. We can say that, it is the communication which involves written typed words.

For example, Letters, notes, email, books, newspapers, SMS, documents and files etc.

Check Your Progress **Pg 16-17**

A. Multiple Choice Questions

Read the questions carefully and circle the letter (a), (b), (c) or (d) that best answers the questions.

1. Which of these is a positive (good) facial expression?
(a) Staring hard
(b) Nodding while listening
(c) Wrinkled forehead
(d) Looking away from the speaker

Ans. (b) Nodding while listening

2. What does an upright (straight) body posture convey/show?
(a) Shyness (b) Fear
(c) Confidence (d) Intelligence

Ans. (c) Confidence

3. Which of these is not an appropriate non-verbal communication at work?
(a) Putting arm around a coworker's shoulder.
(b) Shaking hands firmly.
(c) Looking at the speaker with a smile.
(d) Standing with an upright posture.

Ans. (a) Putting arm around a coworker's shoulder.

4. When you are preparing for a presentation, you should ....
(a) focus on the objectives of the presentation.
(b) practice your speech in front of a mirror or friend.
(c) do rehearsals to time your presentation of slides.
(d) All of the above

Ans. (d) All of the above

B. Put a ✗ mark against the actions below which are incorrect for demonstrating the use of non-verbal communication

(i) Laughing during formal communication.
(ii) Scratching head.
(iii) Smiling when speaking to a friend.
(iv) Nodding when you agree with something.
(v) Standing straight.
(vi) Yawning while listening.
(vii) Sitting straight.
(viii) Maintaining eye contact while speaking.
(ix) Biting nails.
(x) Firm handshake.
(xi) Clenching jaws.
(xii) Looking away when someone is speaking to you.
(xiii) Intense stare.

Ans. The incorrect (✗) for demonstrating the use of non-verbal communication are :

(i), (ii), (vi), (ix), (xi), (xii) and (xiii)

C. Short Answer Questions

1. Give examples of any four common signs used for visual communication.

Ans. Four examples of common signs which are used for visual communication are as follows:

Traffic symbol which communicates not to blow horn.

Sign for ladies and gents toilet.

Traffic lights - Red for Stop; Yellow for Wait and Green for Go.

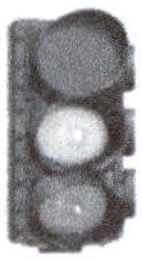

Sign showing railway crossing.

Check Your Progress Pg 24-25

A. Multiple Choice Questions

Read the questions carefully and circle the letter (a), (b), (c) or (d) that best answers the questions.

1. What is a sentence?

(a) A group of ideas that form a complete paragraph.

(b) A group of words that communicate a complete thought.

(c) A set of rules that we must follow to write correctly.

(d) A set of words that contains all the basic punctuation marks.

Ans. (b) A group of words that communicate a complete thought.

2. Which of these sentences use uppercase letters correctly?

(a) I am hungry.
(b) Divya and Sunil are reading.
(c) The bucket is full of water.
(d) She lives in Delhi.

Ans. (b) Divya and Sunil are reading and (d) She lives in Delhi.

3. Which of these sentences are punctuated correctly?

(a) Where are you going.
(b) I have a pen a notebook and a pencil.
(c) I am so happy to see you!
(d) This is Abdul's house.

Ans. (d) This is Abdul's house.

4. Underline the noun, pronoun, adjective, verb and adverb in these sentences.

(a) Sanjay plays football everyday.
(b) Divya gave him new books.
(c) I opened the red box carefully.

Ans. (a) Sanjay plays football everyday.
Noun Verb Noun Adverb

(b) Divya gave him new books.
Noun Verb Pronoun Adjective Noun

(c) I opened the red box carefully.
Pronoun Verb Noun Adverb

B. Fill in the blanks

1. Fill correct nouns and verbs from the box to fill in the blanks given below.

girl, girls, boy, milk, dog, skipping, riding, running, studying, drinking, barking.

(a) The .... is ....

(b) The .... is ....

(c) The .... is ....

(d) The .... are ....

(e) Raju is ....

(f) The .... is ....

Ans. (a) The boy is running. (b) The girl is riding.
(c) The boy is studying. (d) The girls are skipping.
(e) Raju is drinking. (f) Tha dog is barking.

C. Short Answer Questions

1. Identify the conjunctions and prepositions (Remember, conjunctions join two sentences while prepositions help answer the words 'where', 'when' and 'how'.). Choose the conjunctions and prepositions from the box given below and list in the correct box.

Under, And, In, At, Or, Up

Ans.

Conjunction	Preposition
And	Under
Or	In
	At
	Up

Check Your Progress **Pg 31-32**

A. Multiple Choice Questions

Read the questions carefully and circle the letter (a), (b), (c) or (d) that best answers the questions.

1. Identify the subject in the sentence, "The children played football".
   (a) The children (b) Children played
   (c) Played (d) Football

Ans. (a) The children

2. Identify the object in the sentence, "The children played football."
   (a) The children (b) Children played
   (c) Played (d) Football

Ans. (d) Football

3. Which of these sentences has both indirect and direct objects?
   (a) I am watching TV.
   (b) She bought a blue pen.
   (c) The girls played cricket.
   (d) He wrote his sister a letter.

Ans. (d) He wrote his sister a letter.

4. Which of these sentences is in passive voice?
   (a) They are watching a movie.
   (b) The clock was repaired by Raju.
   (c) He is sleeping in the room.
   (d) My pet dog bit the postman.

Ans. (b) The clock was repaired by Raju.

B. Short Answer Questions

1. Write one sentence of each type—statement, question, exclamatory and order.

Ans. **Statement** I live in Delhi.

Question Do you play cricket?

Exclamatory The birthday cake was so good!

Order Shut the door.

2. Which is your favourite festival? Write two paragraphs about your favourite festival. Each paragraph should have a minimum of four sentences. Make sure you follow all the rules about sentences and paragraphs you have learnt.

Ans. My favourite festival is Holi. It is one of the most important festivals in India. Holi is the symbol of celebration of brotherhood. On this day, we all forget our enmities and get into the festival spirit. A day before, a ritual called 'Holika Dahan' is conducted. It symbolises the burning of evil powers. The next day people play with colours. They splash water colours on each other. Children play with water guns.

Holi spreads love and brotherhood. It brings happiness and harmony in the country. Holi symbolises the triumph of good over evil. This colourful festival unites people and removes all sorts of negativity from life. I eagerly wait for Holi every year.

3. Practice speaking correct sentences with your classmates. Try and find the parts of sentences which you use commonly.

Ans. Do it yourself.

Check Your Progress **Pg 36**

A. Multiple Choice Questions

Read the questions carefully and circle the letter (a), (b), (c) or (d) that best answers the questions.

1. What is phonetics?
   (a) It is the study of how we write words in English.
   (b) It is the study of how people understand sentences.
   (c) It is the study of how many words the English language has.
   (d) It is the study of the sounds we make when we speak.

Ans. (d) It is the study of the sounds we make when we speak.

2. What are the different types of sounds used in English pronunciation?
   (a) Vowel sounds (b) Diphthong sounds
   (c) Consonant sounds (d) All of these

Ans. (d) All of these

Check Your Progress
Pg 40

A. Multiple Choice Questions

Read the questions carefully and circle the letter (a), (b), (c) or (d) that best answers the questions.

1. You say 'Good Morning' when it is ....
   (a) 11 am (b) 9 am
   (c) 8 am (d) All of these

Ans. (d) All of these

2. You may say 'Hi' when you meet ....
   (a) your teacher in class
   (b) a senior in the office
   (c) your Principal
   (d) your friends at a shop

Ans. (d) Your friends at a shop

3. You say 'Good Afternoon' when it is ....
   (a) 10 am (b) 11.59 am
   (c) 6 pm (d) 1 pm

Ans. (d) 1 pm

4. You say 'Good Evening' when it is ....
   (a) 11 am (b) 9 am
   (c) 2 pm (d) 7 pm

Ans. (d) 7 pm

B. Short Answer Questions

1. Write two to three lines to you would use to introduce yourself.

Ans. My name is Ayushi.
I live in Agra.
I study in class IX.

Check Your Progress
Pg 44

A. Multiple Choice Questions

Read the questions carefully and circle the letter (a), (b), (c) or (d) that best answers the questions.

1. Use the following words to complete the form given below.
   football and swimming, seven-years-old, Hassan, Yasmin, in Bengaluru.
   (a) My first name is ....
   (b) My surname is ....
   (c) I am ....
   (d) I live ....
   (e) I like ....

Ans. (a) Yasmin
(b) Hassan
(c) Seven-years old
(d) in Bengaluru
(e) Football and swimming

2. A postal code is ....
   (a) a group of numbers or letters used to identify a government building.
   (b) a code used to indicate the door number of a house.
   (c) a group of numbers or letters used by the post office to identify a region.
   (d) a code used to identify different post offices.

Ans. (c) A group of numbers or letters used by the post office to identify a region.

Check Your Progress
Pg 48-49

A. Multiple Choice Questions

Read the questions carefully and circle the letter (a), (b), (c) or (d) that best answers the questions.

1. Raju is the class monitor. He wants to know why Ramesh is coming late every day. Which of the following is a question that Raju can ask Ramesh?
   (a) Do you come on time?
   (b) Are you late?
   (c) Why are you late every day?
   (d) Will it not be easier to complete your work if you come on time?

Ans. (c) Why are you late every day?

2. If you have not understood a task given to you, which question should you ask?
   (a) Where are the reports of this task?
   (b) Can you repeat the instructions for this task?
   (c) Can you give me an example of this task?
   (d) Why are you doing this task?

Ans. (b) Can you repeat the instructions for this task?

3. Sheela does not have time so she decides to delay a task. Which question should she ask before ignoring the task?
   (a) What is this task?
   (b) When does this task need to be completed?
   (c) Is this task important?
   (d) No need to ask any question.

Ans. (b) When does this task need to be completed?

4. Renuka is joining a new school. Which of the following questions will help her become comfortable with her new classmates?
   (a) How along have you been studying here?
   (b) Would you like to share my lunch?
   (c) What do you all do in your free time?
   (d) All the options are correct.

Ans. (d) All the options are correct.

B. Short Answer Questions

1. Re-arrange the words to form questions.

(a) she/like/sing?/Does/to

(b) waiting/What/are/you/for?

(c) play/like/football?/Do/you/to

(d) fighting?/they/are/Why

Ans. (a) Does she like to sing?
(b) What are you waiting for?
(c) Do you like to play football?
(d) Why are they fighting?

Check Your Progress — Pg 52-53

A. Multiple Choice Questions

Read the questions carefully and circle the letter (a), (b), (c) or (d) that best answers the questions.

1. What are close-ended questions?
(a) Questions that can have any answer.
(b) Questions that do not have answers.
(c) Questions with yes/no answers.
(d) Questions that have many answers.

Ans. (c) Questions with yes/no answers.

2. Which of these are open-ended questions?
(a) Where do you live? (b) Are you hungry?
(c) How do you feel? (d) Did you meet him?

Ans. (c) How do you feel?

3. Which of these are question words?
(a) What (b) Want (c) Which (d) How

Ans. (a, c, d) What, Which and How

4. Which of these is the correct way to convert the sentence "You are studying" into a question?
(a) You are studying? (b) Studying you are?
(c) Are you studying? (d) Studying are you?

Ans. (c) Are you studying?

B. Short Answer Questions

1. Make a note of five questions your friends asked you. How many were open-ended questions? Make a list of five close-ended questions you asked other people in one day.

Ans. Five questions my friends asked me :
1. Why did you not come to school yesterday?
2. Did you take medicine?
3. How are you feeling now?
4. Will you be able to play?
5. Do you want to take rest?

Two of these were open-ended questions.
For example, 1, 3.

Close-ended questions
1. Have you completed your homework?
2. Do you play cricket?
3. Can you run 5 kilometres?
4. Is London the capital of England?
5. Did you enjoy the party?

SUMMARY

- Communication skills are needed to speak and write properly.
- The word communication derives from the latin word 'Communicane' which means 'to share'.
- Important elements of communication are senders, ideas, channel, receiver, encoding, decoding, feedback, etc.
- Factors which affect perspectives in communication are language, visual perception, past experience, prejudices, feelings, environment, personal factors and culture.
- Methods of communication are of three types, viz, verbal, non-verbal and visual communication.
- In English, sentence is the basic framework of communication.
- There are eight basic parts of speech in the English language, *viz*, noun, pronoun, verb, adjective, adverb, preposition, conjunction and interjection.
- Sentences have subject, verb and object.
- The object in a sentence can be either direct or indirect.
- Sentences can be categorised into declarative, interrogative, exclamatory and imperative sentence.
- In English, words are made of three basic types of sounds, *viz*, vowels, diphthongs and consonants.
- Greetings are of three types, *viz*, formal, informal and greetings according to time.
- In introduction, we need to talk about ourselves. In many situation we need to write about ourselves in a form.
- There are two types of questions, i.e. close-ended questions and open-ended questions. In order to get correct information, we need to ask correct questions.

Exam Practice

Multiple Choice Questions

1. Communication skills are those skills which are needed to
(a) Speak properly (b) Write properly
(c) Think Properly (d) All of these

Ans. (*d*) All of these

2. The word 'Communication' came from the
(a) French word (b) Latin word
(c) Greek word (d) None of these

Ans. (*b*) Latin word

3. The information can be
(a) Drawings (b) Words
(c) Gestures (d) All of these

Ans. (*d*) All of these

4. Communication involves
(a) Sender (b) Receiver
(c) Giver (d) Both (a) and (b)

Ans. (*d*) Both (a) and (b)

5. Which of the following is the importance of communication skills?
(a) Inform (b) Influence
(c) Express feelings (d) All of these

Ans. (*d*) All of these

6. .... means to change the message into a form suitable for sending.
(a) Decoding (b) Encoding
(c) Feedback (d) Receiver

Ans. (*b*) Encoding

7. Which of the following is the factor affecting perspectives in communication?
(a) Language (b) Visual perceptions
(c) Post experience (d) All of these

Ans. (*d*) All of these

8. Methods of communication includes
(a) Verbal Communication
(b) Non-verbal Communication
(c) Visual Communication
(d) All of the above

Ans. (*d*) All of the above

9. Face to face conversation, letters, notes, emails, books, newspapers, sms etc, are type of which method of communication?
(a) Verbal Communication
(b) Non-verbal Communication
(c) Visual Communication
(d) All of the above

Ans. (*a*) Verbal Communication

10. Facial expression, posture, gesture/body language, touch, space etc are types of which method of communication?
(a) Verbal Communication
(b) Non-verbal Communication
(c) Visual Communication
(d) None of the above

Ans. (*b*) Non-verbal Communication

11. What is a phrase?
(a) A group of ideas that form a complete paragraph.
(b) A group of words which does not make complete sense in itself.
(c) A group of words that communicate a complete thought.
(d) A group of words that contains all the punctuation marks.

Ans. (*b*) A group of words which does not make complete sense in itself.

12. Which of these is a phrase?
(a) I came late.
(b) Reena is singing a song.
(c) In the dark.
(d) The horse runs.

Ans. (*c*) In the dark.

13. Identify the subject in the sentence. "The girls are singing a song".
(a) The girls (b) Girls are singing
(c) A song (d) Singing a song

Ans. (*a*) The girls

14. Which of these sentences has both indirect and direct objects?
(a) I am playing football.
(b) Mother is cooking food.
(c) He gave him a pen.
(d) She came home on time.

Ans. (*c*) He gave him a pen.

15. When do we say 'Good Night'?
(a) 11:00 am
(b) 8 p.m
(c) At the end of the conversation in the evening
(d) 6 p.m.

Ans. (*c*) At the end of the conversation in the evening

16. At 4 p.m, we say
(a) Good Morning (b) Good Afternoon
(c) Good Evening (d) Good Night

Ans. (*b*) Good Afternoon

17. If you want to know the address of a person, which question should you ask?
(a) Where do you live?
(b) Is this your house?
(c) Can you take me to your house?
(d) How can I reach your house?

Ans. (*a*) Where do you live?

18. Which of these is the correct way to convert the sentence "It was a beautiful dress", into a question?
(a) It was a beautiful dress?
(b) What a beautiful dress it was?
(c) A beautiful dress was it?
(d) Was it a beautiful dress?

Ans. (*d*) Was it a beautiful dress?

19. Which of these is a close-ended question?
(a) Where do you live?
(b) Did you have breakfast?
(c) What are your hobbies?
(d) Which is your favourite film?

Ans. (*b*) Did you have breakfast?

20. "Get out of the class". This is a/an
(a) Question
(b) Exclamatory sentence
(c) Statement
(d) Order

Ans. (*d*) Order

21. Raju needs to get out of a building. Which of the following questions will help him?
(a) How many floors does this building have?
(b) Where is the exit?
(c) How many exit gates are there in this building?
(d) How do you people go out of this building?

Ans. (*b*) Where is the exit?

22. Correct arrangement of following words to form a question is this/a/dress/new/is
(a) Is this dress new? (b) This is a new dress?
(c) Is this a new dress? (d) A new dress is this?

Ans. (*c*) Is this a new dress?

23. You may say 'Hello' when you meet
(a) Your elders (b) Your boss
(c) Your seniors in office (d) All of these

Ans. (*d*) All of these

24. Combination vowel sounds are also called
(a) Consonant sounds (b) Vowel sounds
(c) Diphthong sounds (d) None of these

Ans. (*c*) Diphthong sounds

25. 'Pen' is an example of
(a) Vowel sound (b) Consonant sound
(c) Diphthong sound (d) None of these

Ans. (*b*) Consonant sound

26. Which of these sentences is in Active Voice?
(a) The letter delivered by the postman.
(b) The song was sung by her.
(c) They are playing cricket.
(d) The plants are being watered by the gardener.

Ans. (*c*) They are playing cricket.

27. Identify the object in the sentence, "The girls are singing a song."
(a) The Girls (b) Are Singing
(c) A song (d) Singing a song

Ans. (*c*) A song

Fill in the Blanks

1. The word 'Communication' come from the Latin word 'Communicare', which means ....

Ans. To share

2. Communication involves at least two persons viz. a sender and a ....

Ans. Receiver

3. Inform, influence and .... are importance of communication skills.

Ans. Express feelings

4. Prejudice means ....

Ans. Prejudgement

5. .... communication is the oldest means of communication.

Ans. Verbal.

6. A .... is the person on thing that does an action.

Ans. Subject

7. .... are words that join two nouns, phrases or sentences.

Ans. Conjunctions

8. .... are words that add meaning to verbs, adjectives or other adverbs.

Ans. Adverbs

9. .... is a set of marks which help us separate parts of a sentence and explain its meaning.

Ans. Punctuation

10. .... connect one word with another to show the relation between them.

Ans. Prepositions

11. Sentences in which the subject receives an action are known to be in .... voice.

Ans. Passive

True/False

1. Communication is the 'Sharing' of information between two or more individuals or within a group to reach a common understanding.

Ans. True

2. In communication a receiver develops and transmits a message to the receiver.

Ans. False.

In communication a sender develops and transmits a message to the receiver.

3. Sender is the means by which the message is sent.

Ans. False

Channel/medium is the means by which the message is sent.

4. Perspectives are ideas, views or fixed ways of thinking.

Ans. True.

5. Non-verbal communication is the message we send to others without using any words.

Ans. True

6. "He offered me a cup of tea". This sentence has two objects.

Ans. True

7. Sentences where the subject does an action are known to be in the Active voice.

Ans. True

8. Oh, it's so hot is an imperative sentence.

Ans. False

9. Phonetics is the study of sounds that we make when we speak.

Ans. True

10. All English words are made of three basic types of sounds.

Ans. True

11. PIN code is not a part of an address.

Ans. False

Match the Columns

1. Match the following columns.

Column I		Column II	
A.	Sleep	1.	Good Morning
B.	Deer	2.	Consonant sound
C.	Book	3.	Informal Greeting
D.	8:00 am	4.	Diphthong sound
E.	Hi	5.	Vowel sound

Ans. A → 5; B → 4; C → 2; D → 1; E → 3

2. Match the following columns.

Column I		Column II	
A.	Initial written by hand	1.	PIN Code
B.	Important part of an address	2.	Open-ended question
C.	Closed-ended question	3.	Signature
D.	How are you?	4.	Exclamatory sentence
E.	What a lovely picture!	5.	Yes/No

Ans. A → 3; B → 1; C → 5; D → 2; E → 4

Short Answer (SA) Type Questions

1. Who is an effective speaker?

Ans. An effective speaker is the one who is able to speak appropriately whilst maintaining eye contact with the audience, uses different vocabulary and articulate speech to suit the need of audience.

2. Who is an effective writer?

Ans. An effective writer is the one who is able to use written words in various style and techniques to communicate their message and ideas to the readers.

3. State any two importance of communication skill.

Ans. Two importance of communication skills are as follows :

1. **Inform** Communication is required to give fact or information to someone, viz. communicating the timetable about an exam to a friend.
2. **Influence** Communication is needed to influence or change a person in an indirect way and usually important way.

4. What do you understand by feedback in communication?

Ans. Feedback in communication is the receiver's response to the message. Requesting classification is a part of a good feedback phase of communication cycle.

5. State any two advantages and two disadvantages of verbal communication.

Ans. Two advantages of verbal communication :

- Verbal communication is easy and quick.
- It is more reliable method of communication.

Two disadvantages of verbal communication :

- Verbal communication has no legal validity and hence, will lead to problems in certain situation.
- It has issues when communicating with distant people.

6. Write a paragraph on the things you like about your school. The paragraph must contain at least 8 lines and should follow all the rules of punctuation.

Ans. The school is the place that prepares us for a better future. I love my school because it is one of the best schools in the city. The classrooms are wide, large and airy. My school has a very large playground where we play sports. There is a computer lab, science lab and a big library in my school. All of the teachers of my school are kind and cooperative. My school also takes part in various activities like sports, quiz competition, speeches etc. We celebrate all national events with great zeal. My school also offers annual picnics to senior students. I feel greatly honoured and happy to study in such a good school.

7. Introduce your friend in 5 lines.

Ans.
- This is my friend Rajni.
- She is 16-years old.
- She stays at Kalkaji.
- She is a very good dancer.
- She likes to eat Rajma-Chawal.

8. Write three sentences using conjunctions 'and', 'but', 'or' respectively.

Ans. (i) Ramesh saw the dog **and** ran into the house.

(ii) He is poor **but** honest.

(iii) You study hard for the exam **or** you will fail.

9. Rewrite the following paragraph using correct punctuation.

Our solar system includes the Sun and all the planets Moons dwarf planets and asteroids that orbit around it the four planets closest to the Sun includes Mercury, Venus, Earth and Mars these inner planets are made of rock and metals the four outer planets are called gas giants because they are made mostly of gases the outer planets include Jupiter Saturn Uranus and Neptune the most well known dwarf planet in our solar system is Pluto.

Ans. Our Solar System includes the Sun and all the planets, moons, dwarf planets and asteroids that orbit around it. The four planets closest to the Sun include Mercury, Venus, Earth and Mars. These inner planets are made of rock and metals. The four outer planets are called gas giants because they are made mostly of gases. The outer planets include Jupiter, Saturn, Uranus and Neptune. The most well known dwarf planet in our solar system is Pluto.

Self Assessment

Multiple Choice Questions

1. Which of the following sentences does not have an object?
   (a) She came home early.
   (b) Geeta is reading a book.
   (c) Rajesh is watching television.
   (d) He is cleaning.
2. Which of these is an open-ended question?
   (a) Can you dance?
   (b) Did you go to the party?
   (c) Where do you live?
   (d) Do you like chocolates?
3. "What a beautiful picture!" This is an example of
   (a) Exclamatory sentence
   (b) Question
   (c) Statement
   (d) Order
4. 'Game' is an example of
   (a) Vowel Sound
   (b) Diphthong sound
   (c) Consonant sound
   (d) None of these
5. Which of these is the correct way to convert the sentence "It is a remarkable sight", into a question?
   (a) It it a remarkable sight?
   (b) What remarkable sight it is?
   (c) What a remarkable sight is it?
   (d) A remarkable sight it is?
6. 'Quickly' in an example of
   (a) Verb
   (b) Adjective
   (c) Adverb
   (d) Conjunction
7. This shows the end of a sentence.
   (a) Comma
   (b) Full stop
   (c) Question mark
   (d) Exclamation mark

Fill in the Blanks

1. The English alphabet has ……… vowel sounds.
2. We use ……… to speak.
3. The object in a sentence can be either ……… or ……… .
4. ……… express strong emotions such as happiness, surprise, anger or pain.
5. ……… is used to indicate the shortened form of some words.

True/False

1. 'Loan' is an example of a vowel sound.
2. Formal greetings are used when you talk to friends or family.
3. Asking questions help us to gain new knowledge.
4. We can use 'Be', 'Do' and 'Have' to form open-ended questions.
5. A question is a sentence that either asks for information or used to test someone's knowledge.

Match the Columns

1. Match the following columns.

	Column I		Column II
A.	Oof	1.	Diphthong sound
B.	Or	2.	Vowel sound
C.	Put	3.	Conjunction
D.	Cloud	4.	Preposition
E.	Place	5.	Consonant sound

Short Answer (SA) Type Questions

1. Write a paragraph describing your best friend. The paragraph must contain at least 8 lines and should follow all the rules of punctuation.
2. Introduce yourself in 8 lines.
3. Write three sentences using prepositions 'on', 'of' and 'at' respectively.
4. Rewrite the following paragraph using correct punctuation.

   Ice-cream is made from sugar cream milk and all kinds of other ingredients there are so many flavours of ice-cream today that it makes it really hard to choose my favourite ice-cream store always lets me choose three kinds of ice-creams on my cone i love to eat ice-cream.

UNIT

02

Self Management Skills-I

Chapter Checklist

- Self Management
- Self Management Skills
- Strength and Weakness Analysis
- Self-confidence
- Positive Thinking
- Personal Hygiene
- Grooming

Self Management

Self-Management is referred to as 'Self-control' or 'Self-regulation'. It is considered as the ability to regulate one's emotions, thoughts and behaviour effectively in various situations. It includes managing stress and motivating oneself and setting and working towards personal and academic goals. Self-Management involves understanding person's ownself, understanding his interests and abilities, having a positive attitude and grooming oneself in order to develop self-confidence.

Self-Management can help in

- overcoming all challenges and difficulties.
- overcoming bad habits.
- developing good habits.
- reaching your goals.

When individual can manage himself, it helps him to avoid stress and provides opportunities to get involved in fun activities.

Positive Results of Self-Management

Parents, teachers and guardians are not always along the child to guide him/ her. In that case principles of self-management guide the individual day in and day out, on how to respond to the environmental forces. These environmental forces for students can be the class schedule, assignments, competitions, exams, different students and their behavior etc. Students can sail through various situations in life comfortable by taking following benefits from self-management

- It guides individuals to self-monitor their conduct and behavior

  Students, once become aware that they are responsible for their behavior, they become pro-active.

- Prepares individual to complete the task independently.
- Instills ownership to the task and the consequences amongst individuals.

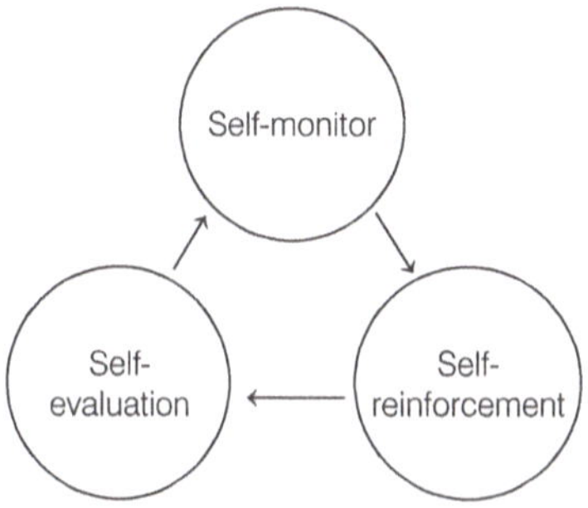

- It helps in self-evaluation
  Self-management makes individuals realize that they need to do course correction by themselves if they do not get desired goals. Once the goals are achieved as desired, it also motivates individuals.
  - Helps in setting individual goals
  - Directs evaluation of performance, objective resetting and enhances self-esteem.
- It leads to self - reinforcement of positive behavior Self-management reinforces appropriate behavior of students as per the time, situation and people involved. It motivates individuals to take up right things and refrains from getting indulged into negative things, keeping long term consequences in focus.
  - Enforces self-learning for goal achievement
  - Self-reliance is enhanced and which reinforces the behavior.

Self Management Skills

Self management skills boost your productivity and performance at work, which helps in achieving professional goals. It is a soft skill that increases your employability and gives you more control over your career path. These skills are essential to showcase that you will be a reliable employee.

For example, Students with strong self-management skill are able to do different activities effectively, including managing their timelines, focusing on their tasks, cooperating with others in school and at home and perform better in their studies. It helps in future studies, work and life.

Various Factors of Self-Management Skills

Self-management skills include the following factors

- **Self-Awareness** Its means knowing yourself as an individual – your values, likes, dislikes, strengths and weaknesses.
- **Self-Control** It is the ability to control your behaviour, discipline etc.
- **Self-Confidence** It means believing in yourself that you can do any task that is given to you and not scared of taking risks.
- **Problem-Solving** Its means understanding a problem and finding a solution using step-by-step method.
- **Self-Motivation** Its mean doing tasks on your own without any external motivation.
- **Personal Hygiene and Grooming** Its mean keeping oneself clean, healthy and smart.
- **Positive Thinking** It means expressing certainty or affirmation even in tough situations.
- **Team Work** It means working together with people to accomplish shared goals.
- **Time Management** It means achieving tasks on time and according to the plan.
- **Goal Setting** It means planning concrete goals to be accomplished within a set of time frame.

Strength and Weakness Analysis

Knowing yourself i.e. what you can do well and what not so well helps you in converting the weakness into strength and strength into an exceptional performance. Strength and weakness analysis begins with knowing yourself.

Knowing Yourself

Knowing yourself means understanding who you are, what you like or dislike, what are your beliefs, what are your opinions, what is your background, what you can do well or not etc. It is very important to know what you are, because only then you can measure your strengths and weaknesses.

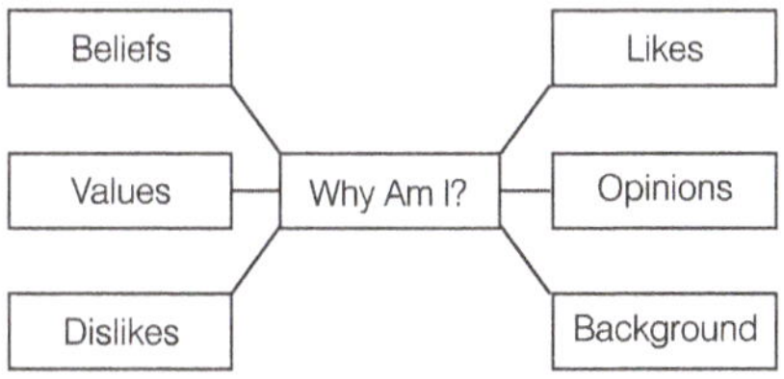

Strength and Weakness Analysis

Being self aware ('Who am I?') means looking outside our usual characteristics like name, qualification, relationship etc. It actually means knowing our inner-strength, hidden talents, skills and even weakness.

Strength

Strengths are what we do well and are good at. Everyone has some strengths.

Examples of Strength

- I play cricket very well.
- I help my parents in household chores.
- I am good at understanding other people's emotion.
- I am confident in dealing with strangers while keeping myself safe from any harm.

Identifying Strengths

You can identify your strengths by following some steps. These include

- Take time to think about what you do well.
- Think of anything that you are always good at.
- Think about what others appreciate about you.

Weakness

Weaknesses are known as 'areas of improvement'. These are what we do not do well and are not good at. Everyone has some weaknesses also.

Examples of Weakness

- I would like to learn more about computers and its application.
- I am unable to resist myself from junk food when my friends suggest.

Identifying Weakness

You have to identify your weakness by following steps. These include

- Point out the areas where you struggle and identify what you find difficult to do.
- Look at the feedback of others that you receive.
- Be open to feedback and accept your weakness without feeling bad. Consider it as an area of improvement.

There are few questions that can help you find your strength and weakness. These are

- How am I different from others?
- What do I do better than others?
- What do other people admire in me?
- What makes me stand out?
- Where do I worry and struggle?
- Where, how and why do others perform better than me?
- What advice for improvement do I often receive from others?

How to Overcome Weakness

There are mainly three steps to overcome weakness

(i) By understanding ourselves we can know what we can and what we cannot do.

(ii) Based on that information, we can plan what and how we can improve ourselves.

(iii) By improving our weakness, we will feel confident about ourselves.

Difference Between Interests and Abilities

Interests are the things that we enjoy doing. These may include

- Activities you like to do at school in your free time which make you happy.
- Activities that make you curious about and you would do even no one asked you to do.
- Activities you want to learn or like to do in the future.

Ability is an acquired or natural capacity that enables an individual to perform a particular job or task with considerable proficiency.

Sometimes interests may not match abilities. In those cases, you can either improve abilities or follow other path. For example, someone may like cricket which is his interest, but he may not be able to play the game due to the absence of his necessary power or skill (ability) required for the game. Thus, it is not necessary to try to become a cricketer in this case.

Check Point 01

1 Name two factors of self-management skill.
2 What is time management as factor of self-management skill?
3 Give one example of strength.
4 Give one difference between interests and abilities.

Self-Confidence

Self-confidence is a sense of trusting own's abilities and self. If a person being intelligent, hardworking and talented, but lacks confidence and avoids taking initiative, then it may be difficult for others to recognise his talent.

Self-confidence can be developed through changes in **attitude** and **practice**.

Self-confidence is regarded as a quality which we build when we believe in our strength to succeed in anything we do in our life.

People who are confident believe that they can do anything given to them in any situation.

Qualities of self-confident people are discussed below

(i) **Self-Belief** It is confidence in our own abilities or judgement.

For example, Thomas Edison made thousands of prototypes of the bulbs, before he could finally invent the bulb. Inspite of struggling with repeated failures, his resilience (the capacity to recover quickly from the difficulties) and self-belief gave the world 'the bulb', an amazing product.

(ii) **Hard Work** Hard work is a great deal of effort done by a person.

For example, Dipa Karmakar, inspite of having a flat foot, worked hard and became the first Indian female gymnast in the Olympic.

(iii) **Positive Attitude** Positive attitude is nothing but focusing on the positives even in the time of adversity. It is a mental attitude that focuses on the bright side of life.

For example, The situation of losing a game can be perceived as losing something or as an opportunity to review the game strategies and improve to win in the future.

(iv) **Commitment** Commitment is the state or quality of being dedicated to a cause, activity etc.

For example, Mahatma Gandhi was highly committed to the cause of making India free from the British Raj by apply his non-violent civil disobedience method.

Factors That Help in Building Self-Confidence

Social

Interactions with family and social environment, like friends, relatives, teachers and media influences self-confidence of individuals. Development of confidence on self is a process which results from the experiences of individuals while interacting with others.

Cultural

Cultural factors comprise of values, beliefs and customs. Indians give higher importance to family values, believe in the philosophy of "Vasudhev Kutumbhkam" and follow custom of celebrating Diwali.

Conforming to cultural values, beliefs and customs enhances self-confidence.

Physical

Physical self-efficacy, physical activity and social physique anxiety are found to be influencing self-confidence of individuals. Physical activity is found to be directly related to self-confidence.

Physical self-efficacy refers to physical potential to complete a given task. Social physique anxiety is a concern amongst individuals about perceived evaluation of one's physical self by the society.

Building Self-Confidence

Three steps to building self-confidence are as follows

(i) **Appreciate Achievement and Accept Failure** The player celebrates the achievements when the team wins a competition and articulates learning when the team loses a competition.

(ii) **Have a Goal and Take Steps Towards** If a player have won bronze at an event, set the goal to win gold medal next time and take action for it.

(iii) **Always Look at the Good Side and be Happy** If a player has lost a match, he celebrates the efforts of those team members who performed well. He will talk to people who are confident and try to gain.

Self-Confidence Building Tips

- **Getting rid of negative thoughts** Going away from negative thoughts takes individuals closer to a peaceful positive mind. To travel away from negative thoughts, individuals need to involve themselves in an activity - take a walk, draw, sing, dance, chat, watch, read or talk.
- **Thinking positively** Positive thinking brings brain to a peaceful stance and increases productivity and performance. When individuals start thinking positively, they feel happy from within and their self-confidence boosts up.
- **Staying happy with small things** An individual who is full of gratitude for every small blessing in his life feels contended. Being thankful towards people and the world, instills confidence in individuals.
- **Staying clean, hygienic and smart** Personal hygiene is the first key to a confident person. Keeping hair, teeth, fingers, body and skin clean and well maintained is an easy and effective way to be at best.

- **Chatting with positive people** Interacting with positive people brings forth a fresh and progressive perspective to life.

  People in similar stages of life go through similar issues. Some positively handle these situations, and interacting with them shall help boost confidence.

Factors That Decreases or Influences Our Self-Confidence

- When we are surrounded by people having negative attitude and their attitude is reflected in their speech.
- When we expect our success at the very first attempt itself and are reluctant to try it again.
- When we do not take lesson from our past mistake, only feel bad about it and keep thinking of it.
- When we think we cannot do a particular work.

Positive Thinking

Positive thinking is a positive approach that looks toward's life's challenges with a positive outlook or finds positivity in everything around us.

A person's attitude may be 'positive' or 'negative'. Positive thinking makes a person to look at the good in things, observe, understand and work towards improving the thing further. But negative attitude makes a person to worry and look for the bad elements in things.

Examples of Positive Thinking

- When a student considers options in other streams rather than science stream after getting poor marks and he thinks this is not the end of his life.
- A player considers to improve the standard of the team for next time after losing the match.

The Importance of Positive Thinking

If an individual has a positive attitude toward's life and its challanges, can overcome them and grow positively in life and work. The benefits of having positive attitude are follows

- It helps to overcome challenges.
- It makes a person an energetic individual who can do well.
- It helps the person to improve his work.
- It makes the person and people around him happy.

How to Keep Persons Thinking Positive?

There are few simple steps to given below to cultivate a positive attitude in life.

S → Start Your Day in a Positive Way

For example, exercising, reading or watching something motivating, talking to people who are positive and make you smile.

M → Manage Time to Relax

For example, sit in a relaxed position and just feel how you are breathing. You can do yoga, meditation or listen to music for relaxation and calmness.

I → Imagine the Best in Any Situation

For example avoid thinking of bad things and instead think how you can make things better.

L → Learn to Take Feedback in a Positive Way

For example, if someone gives you feedback, objectively think how it will help you to improve and start working on it.

E → Express Gratitude

For example, be thankful for all the good things you have, to people who have helped you or pat your back for the good things you have done.

Personal Hygiene

Personal hygiene is the habit or practice of keeping ourselves clean. Cleanliness helps us to maintain our well-being and health. Being healthy helps us to attend school, college and office regularly.

We have to maintain our personal hygiene. For example a beautician takes special care of his dental health as he works closely with customer. He must not have a bad breath which disturbs his customer.

A receptionist at a four-star hotel make sure that his clothes are always clean with no sweat or food stains.

Importance of Personal Hygiene

Personal hygiene is very important as it helps us to

- Stay healthy.
- Create a good image of ourselves.
- Avoid feeling ashamed in public due to our bad breath, body odour etc.

Three Steps to Personal Hygiene

The three main steps of personal hygiene include :

1. Care
2. Wash and
3. Avoid

Care

- Brush your teeth daily.
- Keep your hair free of dandruff.
- Change your toothbrush as soon as it deshapes.
- Rub oil/cream to take care of your skin.
- Cut your nails every week.

Wash

- Take proper bath everyday.
- Wash your hair atleast every second day.
- Wash your clothes regularly.
- Wash your hands frequently.
- Wash your face, feet often.

Avoid

- Keep your feet dry and change socks regularly
- Always blow nose/cough into a handkerchief to avoid spreading germs.

Essential Steps of Hand Washing

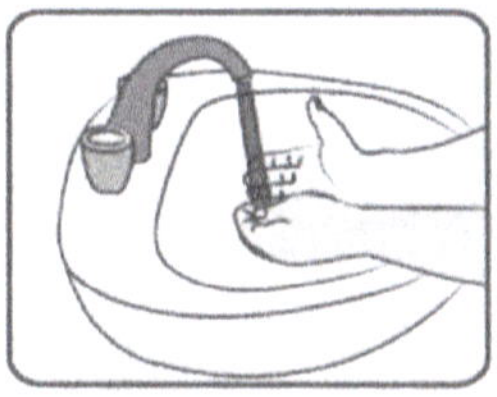

Wet hands with water

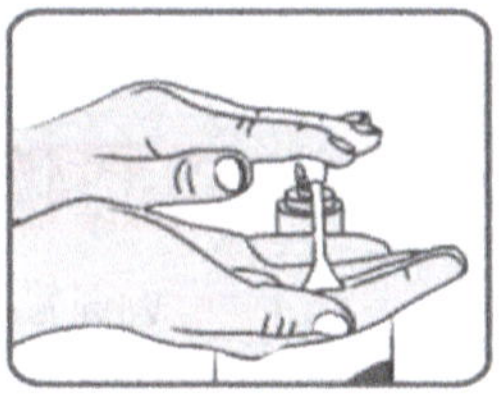

Apply enough soap to cover all hand surfaces

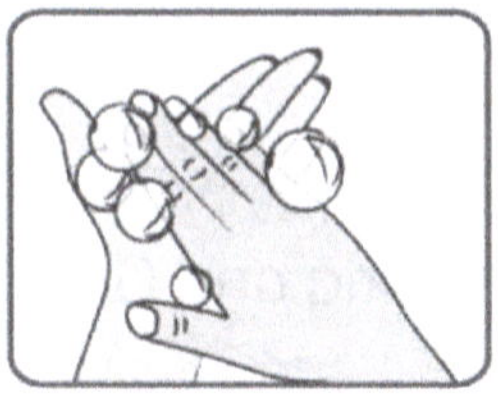

Rub hands palm to palm

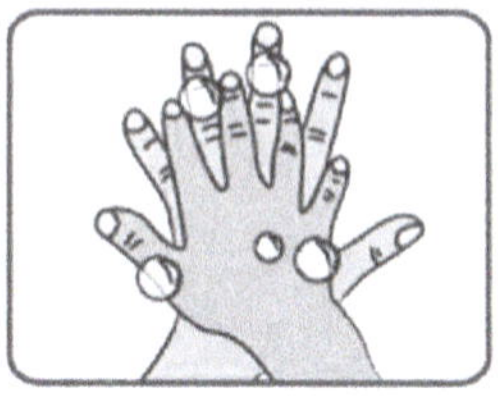

Right palm over left dorsum and vice versa

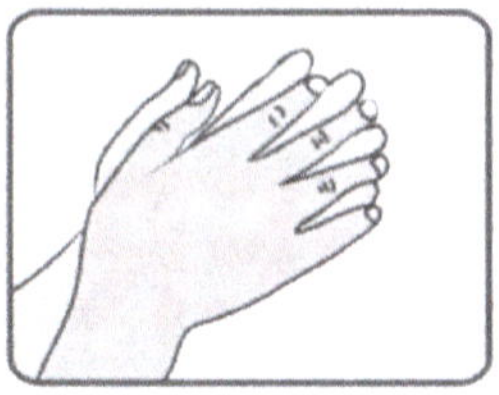

Palm to palm with fingers interlaced

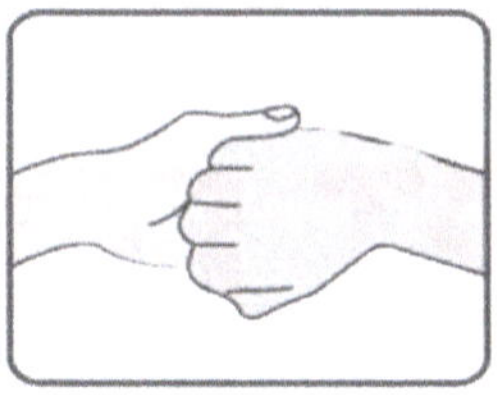

Back of fingers to opposing palms with fingers interlocked

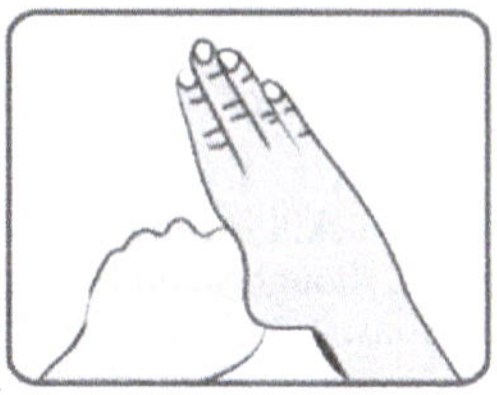

Rotational rubbing of left thumb clasped in right palm and vice versa

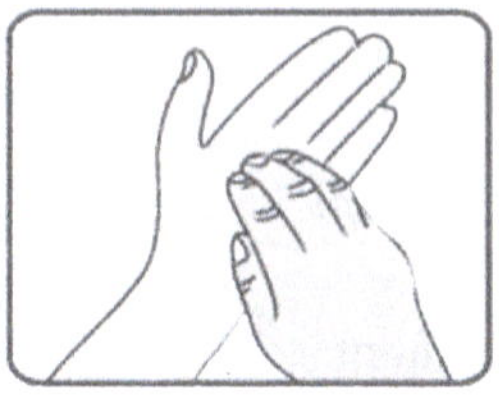

Rub inner surface of palms

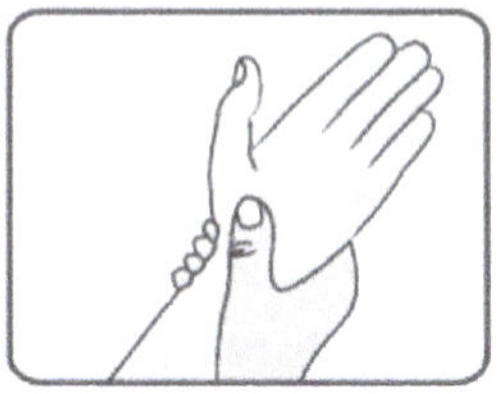

Rub inner surface using the thumb

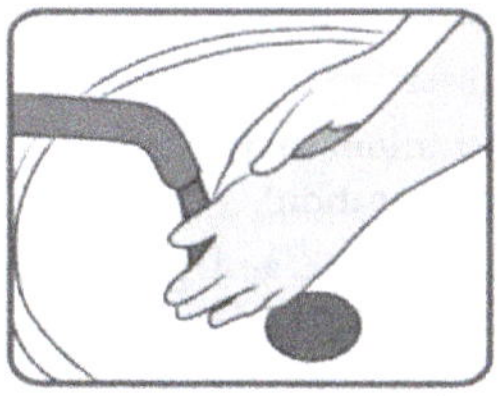

Rinse hands thoroughly with water

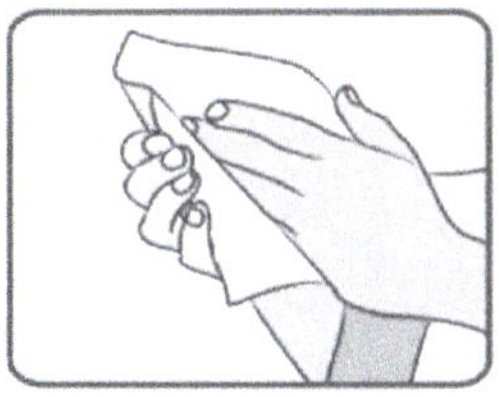

Use towel to dry

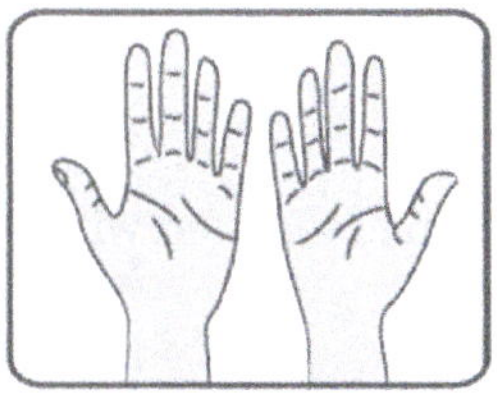

Your hands are now clean.

Grooming

Grooming is the process of making yourself look neat, tidy and smart. Dressing is the action of putting on clothes. Dressing is very important for grooming. The grooming and dressing can either send the message that you are confident, smart and sincere or possess opposite qualities.

The Importance of Grooming and Dressing

Grooming and dressing are important because they help us

- make a good impression of ourselves
- feel confident about ourselves
- look smart

Examples of good dressing and grooming

- Clean face, short hair for boys and neatly tied hair for girls.
- Clean clothes
- Minimum or no flashy things (accessories) in your dress.

Guidelines For Dressing and Grooming

Clothes

- Clothes should be neat, clean and ironed.
- Shoes should be clean and polished.
- Socks should be clean and changed everyday.
- Keep simple accessories like, belts, jewellery etc.
- In certain jobs display of bodily tatoos and piercing is not allowed.

Hair

- Simple hair styles and well combed hair are preferred as these give a smart look.
- Hair should be washed regularly to keep clean.

Face

- Shave regularly, it gives a clean look face.
- Moustache should be neatly trimmed.
- Brush the teeth twice a day to maintain dental hygiene.
- Teeth should be kept clean, without any stains and smell.
- Avoid eating paan or chewing betel leaves.

Check Point 02

1 What is self-belief?
2 Give one example of positive thinking.
3 Name the steps to personal hygiene.
4 What is mean by dressing?

NCERT FOLDER

Check Your Progress

Pg 58

A. Multiple Choice Questions

Read the questions carefully and circle the letter (a), (b), (c) or (d) that best answers the questions.

1. Which of the following is not a self-management skill?
(a) Problem solving
(b) Bargaining
(c) Understanding self
(d) Confidence building

Ans. (b) Bargaining

2. Grooming is a term associated with
(a) time management
(b) problem solving
(c) neat and clean appearance
(d) self-management

Ans. (d) Self-management

B. Short Answer Questions

1. Write a short note on the factors influencing self management.

Ans. Self-management skill is considered as the ability to regulate one's emotions, thoughts and behaviour effectively in various situations.

It includes various factors like :

- **Self awareness** (knowing yourself as an individual)
- **Self control** (ability to control behaviour discipline etc)
- **Self-confidence** (believing in yourself)
- **Problem solving** (understanding and finding a solution)
- **Self-motivation** (doing tasks on your own without any external motivation)
- **Personal hygiene and grooming** (keeping oneself clean, healthy and smart)
- **Positive thinking** (expressing certainly even in tough situation)
- **Team work** (working together to achieve the goal)

- **Time management** (achieving tasks on time and according to the plan)
- **Goal setting** (planning concrete goals within a set time frame).

2. List any five self-management skills.

Ans. Self-management skill are the abilities that allow people to control thoughts, feelings and actions.
Five self-management skills are :

(i) **Self-Awareness** Knowing yourself as an individual. Know your values, likes, dislikes, strengths and weakness.

(ii) **Self-Control** Ability to control your behaviour, discipline etc.

(iii) **Self-Confidence** Believing in yourself that you can do all the tasks given to you and not scared of taking risks.

(iv) **Problem Solving** Understanding a problem and finding a solution using step-by-step method.

(v) **Self-Motivation** Doing tasks on your own without any external motivation.

Check Your Progress

Pg 70

A. Multiple Choice Questions

Read the questions carefully and circle the letter (a), (b), (c) or (d) that best answers the questions.

1. What steps should one take to build confidence?
(a) Set goals in life.
(b) Appreciate oneself for all the achievements.
(c) Always think positively.
(d) Talk to people who are confident.

Ans. (d) Talk to people who are confident.

2. Which of the following is a quality of a self-confident person?
(a) Patient (b) Compassionate
(c) Committed (d) Passionate

Ans. (c) Committed

B. Short Answer Questions

1. What are the factors that affect self-confidence?

Ans. There are some factors that affect or decrease our self-confidence. These one as follows

(i) When we think we can not do a particular work, it affects our self-confidence.

(ii) When we do not take lesson from our past mistake, but keep thinking about it and feeling bad about it. All these disturb our self-confidence.

(iii) When we expect to be successful at the very first attempt itself and do not try again, this attitude affects our self-confidence.

(iv) When we are surrounded by people having negative attitude and negativity in their speech, it affects our self-confidence.

Check Your Progress

Pg 74

A. Multiple Choice Questions

Read the questions carefully and circle the letter (a), (b), (c) or (d) that best answers the questions.

1. What is the best way to start our day positively?
(a) Think about all that can go wrong.
(b) Think about the difficult test you will face during the day.
(c) Think about all your accomplishment so far and feel good about it.
(d) Think about the traffic on the road and feel stressed.

Ans. (c) Think about all your accomplishment so far and feel good about it.

2. Rahul gets feedback on his project work from his class teacher. Which of these options demonstrates positive attitude in this situation?
(a) Rahul ignores the feedback.
(b) Rahul takes the feedback but does not use it.
(c) Rahul tells others that the teacher is wrong.
(d) Rahul learns from the feedback and makes his project work better.

Ans. (d) Rahul learns from the feedback and makes his project work better.

3. What can you do to get rid of negative thoughts or feelings?
(a) Meditate to calm down and feel positive.
(b) Ignore them and move on in life.
(c) Act based on the negative thoughts or feelings.
(d) Talk to a friend and share all your negative feelings.

Ans. (a) Meditate to calm down and feel positive.

Check Your Progress

Pg 78

A. Multiple Choice Questions

Read the questions carefully and circle the letter (a), (b), (c) or (d) that best answers the questions.

1. Do you think people living in hill stations can skip taking a bath for many days?
(a) No, irrespective of the climate, one should take a bath regularly.
(b) Yes, not taking bath for many days is acceptable for people staying in cold climate.
(c) Yes, if they wipe themselves with a wet cloth, then it is fine.
(d) None of the above

Ans. (a) No, irrespective of the climate, one should take a bath regularly.

2. Radha wants to grow her hair and she applies a lot of hair oil. She does not wash her hair for days and sometimes it smells bad too. What would be your suggestion to her?

(a) She can leave the oil in her hair, after all it helps her hair to grow.

(b) She can leave it on at night and wash her hair every day before leaving home.

(c) She should not apply the oil at all.

(d) She can apply the oil and pour a little water on her hair before leaving home to reduce the smell.

Ans. (b) She can leave it on at night and wash her hair every day before leaving home.

B. Short Answer Questions

1. List three things you will do for personal hygiene in each of care, wash and avoid to keep clean.

Ans. Personal hygiene is the habit or practice of keeping ourselves clean. To maintain personal hygiene we must follow some steps in each of care, wash and avoid.These are as follows.

Care

(a) We must keep our hair free of dandruff and dirt.

(b) We brush our teeth daily.

(c) We cut our nails every week.

Wash

(a) We take bath everyday.

(b) We wash our clothes regularly.

(c) We wash our hair at least every second day.

Avoid

(a) We should blow our nose and cough into a handkerchief to prevent spreading of germs.

(b) We keep our feet dry.

(c) We should change our socks every day.

Check Your Progress **Pg 81**

A. Multiple Choice Questions

Read the questions carefully and circle the letter (a), (b), (c) or (d) that best answers the questions.

1. Dressing and grooming are important because they helps us to look ....

(a) smart (b) untidy

(c) shabby (d) All of these

Ans. (a) Smart

2. The following image is an example of .... shirt.

(a) informal

(b) formal

(c) Both of the above

(d) None of the above

Ans. (b) Formal

3. The following image is an example of .... T-shirt.

(a) informal

(b) formal

(c) Both of the above

(d) None of the above

Ans. (a) Informal

SUMMARY

- Self-management is referred to as self-control or self-regulation.
- Self-management skills include self-awareness, self-control, self-confidence, problem-solving, self-motivation, personal hygiene and grooming, positive thinking, team work, time-management and goal setting.
- Our strengths are what we do well and are good at.
- Weakness are known as 'areas of improvement'.
- Interests are the things that we enjoy doing.
- Ability is an acquired or natural capacity that enables an individual to perform a particular job or task with proficiency.
- Self-confidence is a sense of trusting own's abilities and self. It can be developed through change in attitude and practice.
- Positive thinking is a positive approach that looks towards life's challenges with a positive outlook.
- Personal hygiene is the habit or practice of keeping ourselves clean.
- Three main steps of personal hygiene include care, wash and avoid.
- Grooming is the process of making oneself look neat, tidy and smart.
- Proper dressing is very important for grooming.

Exam Practice

Multiple Choice Questions

1. Which of the following is not a self-management skill?
(a) Self motivation (b) Problem solving
(c) Team work (d) Drawing pictures

Ans. (*d*) Drawing pictures

2. Believing in yourself that you can do any task that is given to you is ....
(a) Self-control (b) Self-awareness
(c) Self-confidence (d) Positive thinking

Ans. (*c*) Self-confidence

3. Ability to control your behaviour, discipline etc is regarded as
(a) Self-control (b) Self-awareness
(c) Self-confidence (d) Problem solving

Ans. (*a*) Self-control

4. Expressing certainty or affirmation even in tough situation is known as ....
(a) Self-motivation (b) Positive thinking
(c) Self-awareness (d) Self-confidence

Ans. (*b*) Positive thinking

5. What is self-management?
(a) Self-regulation (b) Self-awareness
(c) Self perseverance (d) Both (a) and (b)

Ans. (*d*) Self-regulation and Self-awareness

6. Which type of people can easily convince others?
(a) Rich people
(b) Self-confident people
(c) Talkative people
(d) Influential people

Ans. (*b*) Self-confident people

7. Which of the following statements about positive thinking is correct?
(a) Positive thinking results in positive circumstances.
(b) Positive thinking helps in focusing on the bright side of an individual's life.
(c) Positive people can easily overcome problems and achieve success.
(d) All of the above

Ans. (*d*) All of the above

8. Suggest the following factor which helps in building self-confidence.
(a) Geographical factors (b) Climate factors
(c) Social factors (d) None of these

Ans. (*c*) Social factors

9. What makes us strong and determined?
(a) Experience (b) Positive thinking
(c) Present environment (d) None of these

Ans. (*b*) Positive thinking

10. I have the power to make my dreams true is an example of
(a) Self-awareness (b) Self-confidence
(c) Positive thinking (d) Self-control

Ans. (*c*) Positive thinking

11. Planning concrete goals to be accomplished within a set timeframe is known as
(a) Time management (b) Goal setting
(c) Problem solving (d) None of these

Ans. (*b*) Goal setting

12. Despite having a flat foot, Dipa Karmakar became the first Indian female gymnast who took part in the Olympics. It is an example of her ....
(a) Time management
(b) Self awareness
(c) Hard work (Self-confidence)
(d) None of the above

Ans. (*c*) Hard work (Self-confidence)

13. What is an example of time management?
(a) The skill of completing a work previously, so as to have leisure time.
(b) The skill of planning and organising time to manage all activities.
(c) The skill of finishing work within 24 hours.
(d) None of the above

Ans. (*b*) The skill of planning and organising time to manage all activities.

14. Personal hygiene is important because it help us
(a) Stay healthy (b) Create good images
(c) Avoid self control (d) Both (a) and (b)

Ans. (*d*) Stay healthy and create good images

15. Arrange serially the essential steps of hand washing.
(i) Apply enough soap to cover the hand.
(ii) Wet hands with water.
(iii) Rinse hands thoroughly with water.
(iv) Rub inner surface of palms.
(a) (ii), (i), (iv), (iii) (b) (i), (iii), (ii), (iv)
(c) (ii), (iii), (iv), (i) (d) (i), (iv), (iii), (ii)

Ans. (*a*) (ii), (i), (iv), (iii)

16. Which of the followings is correct to maintain positivity?
(a) Make time to relax.
(b) Find out the best in any situation.
(c) Criticise the negative things.
(d) Both (a) and (b)

Ans. (*d*) Make time to relax and find out the best in any situation.

17. After losing a game a player considers to improve the standard of the team for next time – it is an an example of
(a) Self-control (b) Self-awareness
(c) Problem solving (d) Positive thinking

Ans. (*d*) Positive thinking

18. Proper dressing helps a person
(a) to make good impression of himself.
(b) to feel confident about himself.
(c) to become famous.
(d) Both (a) and (b)

Ans. (*d*) To make good impression of himself and to feel confident about himself.

19. Which type of hairstyle is giving a smart look?
(a) Trendy hairstyle
(b) Simple hairstyle
(c) Well combed hair
(d) Both (b) and (c)

Ans. (*d*) Simple hairstyle and well combed hair

20. Which way of fashion is not allowed in certain jobs?
(a) Wearing Sandals
(b) Wearing informal dress
(c) Displaying bodily tatoos and piercing
(d) All of the above

Ans. (*d*) All of the above

Fill in the Blanks

1. Self-management means managing your own .... and ....

Ans. Emotions, thoughts and behaviour

2. .... is an acquired or natural capacity that enables an individual to perform a particular job or task with considerable proficiency.

Ans. Ability

3. .... can be developed through changes in attitude and practice.

Ans. Self-confidence

4. My team lost the match because of me - it is an example of ....

Ans. Negative thinking

5. .... help us to create a good image of ourselves.

Ans. Personal hygiene

True/False

1. Self-management helps individual to avoid stress and provides opportunities to get involved in fun activities.

Ans. True

2. Abilities are activities you want to learn or would like to do in the future.

Ans. False

3. Doing tasks on your own without any external motivation is known as self-confidence.

Ans. False

4. Positive thinking makes you happy and people around you happy.

Ans. True

5. Sometimes bad dressing includes bodily tatoos and piercing.

Ans. True

Match the Columns

1. Match the following.

	Column I		Column II
A.	Knowing yourself as an individual	1.	Self-motivation
B.	Doing tasks on your own	2.	Time management
C.	Achieving tasks on time	3.	Goal setting
D.	Planning concrete goals to be accomplished	4.	Self-awareness

Ans. A → 4; B → 1; C → 2; D → 3

2. Match the following.

	Column I		Column II
A.	I can speak many languages	1.	Example of lack of confidence
B.	Gandhiji started non-violent Civil Disobedience Movement	2.	Example of strength
C.	Pooja feared she would not get good marks and actually got poor marks	3.	Example of interest
D.	I like to play cricket	4.	Example of commitment

Ans. A → 2; B → 4; C → 1; D → 3

Short Answer (SA) Type Questions

1. Write any five impacts of self-management skills.

Ans. Self management is considered as the ability to regulate one's emotions, thoughts and behaviour effectively in various situations. Some important impacts of self-management skills are

(i) It helps us have control over negative emotions, behaviours and habits.
(ii) It helps us have control over our actions, so that we do not act in impulse and develop good habits.
(iii) It helps us to be organised.
(iv) It helps us to develop positive attitude.
(v) It helps us to overcome challenges and difficulties.

2. How do we identify our weakness?

Ans. Weaknesses are areas of improvement, where we need to develop and build ourselves. We can identify our weakness in the following ways :

(i) We must look at the feedback we received from others.
(ii) We must point out areas of our difficulty.
(iii) We should open to feedback of others and accept our weakness without feeling bad about it.

3. What is self-confidence? Suggest any two qualities of a self-confident person.

Ans. Self-confidence is a sense of trusting in one's own abilities and self. It tells what we are made up of and how we feel about ourselves.

Two qualities of a self-confident person are :

(i) **Self-Belief** It is confidence in our own abilities or judgement. People learn from their own mistake and achieve success.
(ii) **Positive Attitude** It is focusing an on the positive side of an event in the time of adversily. The situation of losing a game can be perceived as an opportunity to review the game.

4. What do you mean by positive thinking? Write about the importance positive thinking.

Ans. Positive thinking helps in creating a real values in our lives. It requires a person to look at the good in things, observe, understand and works for improving them.

The importance of positive thinking are

(i) It overcomes challenges.
(ii) It makes us do well by making us energetic.
(iii) It help us better at work.
(iv) It make us and people around us happy.

5. What is personal hygiene? Elucidate any four basic habits to maintain personal hygiene.

Ans. Personal hygiene is the habit or practice of keeping ourselves clean. Cleanliness helps us to maintain our well-being and health.

To maintain personal hygiene we should follow some basic habits. These are

(i) **Take a Bath Regularly** Cleaning body and hair is vital for our health.
(ii) **Brush Teeth Daily** We should brush our teeth regularly, at least twice a day.
(iii) **Cut Nails Every Week** We should regularly trim our nails.
(iv) **Use Tissues/Handkerchief While Coughing/Sneezing** It is important to use tissues or handkerchiefs while blowing nose and coughing to avoid spreading germs.

6. What do you mean by grooming and dressing? Write about the importance of dressing and grooming.

Ans. Grooming is the process of making oneself look neat, tidy and smart. Dressing is the action of putting on clothes. The way a person dresses or grooms reveals the confidence, smartness of him or the opposite qualities possessed by him.

The importance of dressing and grooming are as follows:

(a) They help us to look smart.

(b) They make us feel confident about ourselves.

(c) They make a good impression of ourselves.

Self Assessment

Multiple Choice Questions

1. Which of the following is a self-management skill?

(a) Self-control (b) Self-awareness

(c) Self-motivation (d) All of these

2. 'I am unable to resist junk food when someone offers me', is an example of

(a) Weakness (b) Self-control

(c) Positive attitude (d) None of these

Fill in the Blanks

1. People with .... can easily convince others.
2. The best part of self-confidence is that it can be ....

True/False

1. Self management make a person well organised and well equipped.
2. Positivity is accepting things as they are.

Short Answer (SA) Type Questions

1. What is self-management? Suggest atleast two self-management skills.
2. What are strengths and weakness? Why it is important to know our own strengths and weakness?
3. What are interests and abilities? Why is it important for a person to know his interests and abilities?
4. What is self-confidence? Suggest three steps for building self-confidence.
5. Why positive thinking is very important for us?
6. Why personal hygiene is necessary? Explain with examples.

UNIT

03

Basic ICT Skills-I

Chapter Checklist

ICT stands for Information and Communication Technology. It includes a diverse set of technological tools and resources used to communicate, create, disseminate, store and manage information.

ICT includes computers, Internet, broadcasting technologies and telephony. People use technology every day at home and at workplace. ICT tools enable anytime, anywhere access to information and resources. The various ICT tools that are used include computes we use at work, smartphone through which we talk, Internet for getting information, communicating with others through E-mail and social networks, watching movies etc.

For example, to find a job you may have to search the Internet for job openings, create a resume on a computer, use E-mail to send the resume, send messages through your phone to communicate appear for telephonic interview and get your offer letter through E-mail.

ICT skills help us to communicate, run our business and stay connected with our family and friends. Hence, every person needs to acquire ICT skills and build them to stay updated with the latest softwares and applications (apps).

The basic ICT skills that you need are knowing how to

- operate computers.
- browse the Internet for collecting, storing and disseminating information.

ICT at Workplace

ICT has become part of our workplace in all sectors of economy, money transactions through online banking system, development of research papers in educational institutions etc.

At workplace, we used different computer softwares and applications to complete different tasks like making documents, calculations, tables, graphs etc. We can also use applications to do every day work, like buying things, booking train or bus tickets, Internet banking and making online payments.

Modern ICT employs a variety of media forms which includes text, graphics, animation, audio and video. It also involves creating, curating, managing images and documents; gathering and processing data and presenting them; working with audio and video tools to create media rich communications.

ICT at Home

These days most of the people use television for entertainment. New devices, such as smartphones with an Internet connection are now being used to stay connected with family and friends on a regular basis through social media networks, such as Facebook, Instagram and Twitter. We use computers and mobile phones for talking to each other, sending and receiving information, watching videos and news, listening to music and playing games.

You can visit the following sites and know about the ICT activities:

Sector	ICT used for	Website
Agriculture	Various activities related to research, development and training in agriculture and allied fields	http://dare.nic.in/ https://bit.ly/2H3DJfU
Retail	Training programmes in the retail sector	http://rasci.in/
Beauty and Wellness	Training programmes in beauty and wellness sector	http://www.bwssc.in/
Banking and Finance	Training programmes in banking, financial services and insurance sector	http://www.bfsissc.com/
Apparel	Training programmes in Apparel sector	http://sscamh.com/index Home.php
Logistics	Training programmes in Logistics sector	http://lsc-india.com/
Healthcare	Training programmes in Healthcare sector	http://www.healthcare-ssc .in

ICT Tools: Smartphones and Tablets

Smartphones and tablets are becoming more and more important as most people carry them around and use them in daily activities like sending E-mails and messages, sharing pictures etc.

The spreading of an idea or news occurring some where in the world is now possible through social sites on the Internet. Smartphones are now being used to stay connected with social media and exchange information.

Smartphones

Mobile phones are ICT tools for talking to people but smartphones are more advanced. With a simple mobile phone you can only make phone calls and receive calls. With a smartphone, you can make calls and do things that you normally do using a computer, such as browsing the web, sending E-mails, making video calls, playing games, listening to music, watching movies and much more.

Smartphones do not need a telephone line. They use wireless (mobile) networks to make calls and to connect to the Internet. Some of the popular operating systems for smartphones are Android, Apple iOS and Windows Mobile.

Tablets

For some activities, such as reading a book for a longtime, the screen of a mobile may be too small. For such activities, we can use a tablet. A tablet is a mini computer with input, output and processing functions that are all combined into one touchscreen, where you can do various tasks just by touching its screen. It is bigger than a smartphone and you can perform all the functions that one can perform on a computer or a smartphone.

TV and Radio

TV and Radio are being used as an ICT tool since a long time. Radio is used to broadcast audio while TV is used to broadcast audio-visual information to many people. You can hear news, songs, stories, speeches, cricket commentary etc on radio, while TV is used for watching movies, news, weather forcasting, songs, cartoons and educational lectures.

Applications or Apps

Smartphones perform so many functions with the help of software applications (Apps). On the screen of smartphone or Tablet, you see a lot of small pictures (or icons). If you touch these, they start programs or functions required for watching movies, playing games, using camera etc.

Apps are software programs that perform different functions. Some of the apps are already present on the phone or tablet. These are called default apps.

Besides, there are hundreds of other apps that can be purchased or downloaded free of cost from online stores. There are several online stores, including Google Play Store for Android phone and Apple App Store for Apple phone.

Commonly found Applications

Some of the default apps installed on all smartphones/mobiles are given below:

- **Phone** This app is used to make calls. It also stores the contacts and call history.
- **Calendar** It shows a calendar and you can also enter appointments, remainders etc in it.
- **Camera** It is used to take photos and videos.
- **Mail** This app is used to send and receive E-mails using your E-mail account in G-mail, Yahoo, Outlook etc.
- **Gallery** It helps you to store all photos and videos and arrange them into albums.
- **Maps** This app helps you to find directions where you want to go. It uses GPS (Global Positioning System).
- **Browser** It allows you to open a browser to search and visit different websites.
- **Clock** This app shows the time and also sets alarm, timers etc.
- **Messages** This app is used to send and receive SMS messages.
- **Music** This app allows you to play songs and music.

Differences between a smartphone and a tablet are as follows:

	Smartphone	Tablet
(i)	Used as a phone but with some additional features such as camera.	Used as a wireless portable personal computer with a touchscreen interface which makes it more useful than notebook computer.
(ii)	Screen size is small.	Has a big screen.
(iii)	Watching a movie or making changes to a picture is difficult.	Watching videos and making changes to a photo is better and easier due to bigger screen size.
(iv)	Comes with different storage capacities.	Usually have higher storage capacity.

Check Point 01

1. TV and Radio are being used as an ICT tool. (True/False)
2. Commonly found application(s) on phone is/are
   (a) Gallery (b) Browser (c) Clock (d) All of these
3. These days most of the people use television for ....
4. Write any use of ICT at workplace.
5. What is app?

Mobile Device Layout

Some of the basic controls you see on mobile device are as follows:

- **Power button** This is used to start and shut down a mobile device.
- **Screen** A screen on which we perform functions by touching with our fingers.
- **Back button** This is used to go back to the previous screen in an application.
- **Microphone** This is present at the bottom of the mobile and used when we talk to someone.
- **Menu button** This is used to show the options available in a particular app. This may not be present in all mobile devices.
- **Home button** This brings you back to the home screen.
- **Earpiece** This helps you to listen to voice calls.
- **Volume buttons** This helps you to increase or reduce the sound of your mobile.

Basic Features of a Mobile Device

Some of the basic features present in all mobile devices are given below:

- **Bluetooth** It is a short range wireless technology which helps you to connect with other devices. Other device should be within 30 feet of where you are. Once connected, you can share photos, songs etc.
- **Chargeable battery** It is a portable power pack which can be recharged. It allows you to use the mobile device anywhere.
- **Wi-Fi** It is a wireless network technology that helps you connect to the local area network. This is used to connect to the Internet.
- **Cellular network connectivity** It provides the network through which you can make calls.
- **Global Positioning System (GPS)** It is a navigation (direction finding) system that helps you to navigate, find direction and maps to specific locations.

Home Screen of a Mobile Device

The home screen is the first (start) screen of a mobile device. There are three main parts of the home screen as:

(i) **Top** The top part of the screen is called the status bar. It displays icons to show the network signal, battery life, Wi-Fi and Bluetooth connectivity, 3G/4G status etc.

(ii) **Middle** This is the main part of the screen that consists of icons/shortcuts to the applications. These icons can be placed anywhere you want.

(iii) **Bottom** This is the lower part of the screen which is called the Dock. The apps in this area can always been seen even if we move to a different pages.

Basic Gestures Used

Gestures are used to interact with the touchscreen of your mobile device. For example, instead of clicking a mouse to open an App, you tap on the touchscreen.

Some of the gestures are as follows:

- **Tap** Touch the screen with your finger, once, to click.
- **Tap and hold** This is similar to right clicking your mouse.
- **Drag** To tap, hold and move your finger across the screen.
- **Swipe** To slide finger to the right, left, up or down of the screen like turning a page.
- **Double tap** To tap twice quickly-this is to zoom out (increase the size) of something.
- **Pinch** To bring thumb and finger together on the screen to zoom in (reduce the size). e.g. to make a picture appear smaller.

Check Point 02

1 ...... helps you to listen to voice calls.
(a) Earpiece (b) Microphone
(c) Mic (d) Speaker

2 A/An ...... on which we perform function by touching with our fingers on phone.

3 What is the use of bluetooth?

4 Define pinch the basic gesture of mobile device.

5 GPS stands for Global Positioning System. (True/False)

Computer System

A computer system is a programmable machine designed to store and retrieve information and perform arithmetic and logical operations to produce meaningful results in desired format.

The term computer is derived from the Latin word 'Computare' which means 'to calculate'.

The basic functions of a computer system are to accept the input, process the input, display the output and to store data.

Note *The I/O devices that are attached externally to the computer machine are called peripheral devices.*

Parts of Computer System

Parts of a computer are as follows:

(i) Input Devices (Unit)
(ii) Output Devices (Unit)
(iii) Central Processing Unit (CPU)
(iv) Memory Unit

1. Input Devices

An input device is a hardware device that sends data into the computer system. These devices are used to input (or enter) data and instructions into the computer system. All instructions are accepted by the CPU through electrical pulses from various kind of input devices. Some of the input devices are Keyboard, Pointing Devices, Scanner, MICR, OCR, OMR, Barcode Reader, Microphone (Mic), Web Camera, Digital Camera, Biometric Sensor, Smart Card Reader, which described below:

I. Keyboard

It is the most commonly used input device which uses an arrangement of buttons and keys. Both data and program can be entered into the computer through the keyboard. It is an essential device for interactive processing because the user can easily issue commands to receive the data response immediately on the computer screen.

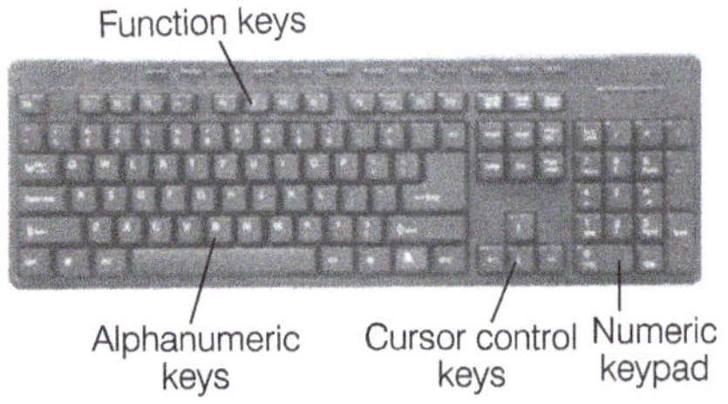

Layout of a Keyboard

Types of Keys on Keyboard

- **Function keys** Keys labelled from F1 to F12 are function keys. You use them to perform functions. Their functions differ from program to program. The function key F1 in most programs is to get help on that program.
- **Control keys** Keys such as Ctrl, Alt, Shift, Tab are special control keys that perform special functions depending on when and where they are used.
- **Enter key** The label on this key can be either Enter or Return depending on the brand of computer that you are using. You use them to move the cursor to the beginning of a new line. In some programs, it is used to send commands and to confirm a task on a computer.

- **Punctuation keys** These include keys for punctuation marks such as colon (:), semicolon (;), question mark (?), single quotation mark (' '), double quotation mark (" ") etc.
- **Navigation keys** Some keys such as the arrow keys, Home, End, PageUp and PageDown are navigation keys. The Home and End keys move the cursor to the left and right end of a line of text, respectively. The PageUp and PageDown keys are used to move one page up and one page down, respectively.
- **Command keys** Some keys such as Insert, Delete and Backspace are command keys. When the Insert key is turned ON, it helps you overwrite characters to the right of the cursor. The Delete key and Backspace key are used to remove typed characters and other objects on the right and left side of the cursor respectively.
- **Windows key** It opens the Start menu.

II. Pointing Devices

A pointing device is used to communicate with the computer by pointing to the locations on the monitor.

It can also be used for

- sending command signals to the computer.
- selecting items on the screen.
- selecting commands from command menu.
- drawing graphics, sketches, etc.

Some commonly used pointing devices are mouse, joystick, light pen, graphics tablet, touch screen and trackball, which described below :

(i) **Mouse** It is a pointing device that allows to control the movement of pointer (also known as **mouse pointer)** on screen. Mouse performs various functions by detecting two-dimensional motion relatively to its supporting surface. Generally, a mouse has two buttons-right button and left button.

Mouse also includes a scroll wheel between these two buttons to scroll down the application window and their contents also. These are three types of mouse as – Wireless mouse, Mechanical mouse, Optical mouse. Some actions or functions of mouse are as follows:

Wired Mouse

Wireless Mouse

- **Roll over/hover** Some actions can be done by simply rolling over or hovering an object. When you bring the mouse over a file, it will show the details of that file.
- **Point and click** As you move the mouse on your desk, a pointer moves correspondingly on your computer's screen. The mouse allows you to select an item on the screen. When you click a particular file, it gets selected.
- **Drag and drop** To move an item, you need to click it, and then holding the mouse button down, move the item to a new location. After you move the item to the new location, you release the mouse button. This is called drag and drop.
- **Double click** It means to quickly click the left mouse button twice. When we double click the file icon, it will open the file.

(ii) **Joystick** It is a pointing device that moves in all directions and controls the movement of the cursor. A joystick is similar to a mouse excepts that the movement of cursor on screen stops working as soon as user stop moving the mouse. But with a joystick, the pointer continuous moving in the previously pointing direction.

Joystick

Commonly, joysticks are used for playing computer games like flight simulators but occasionally used for CAD/CAM systems and other applications.

(iii) **Light Pen** It is a handheld electro-optical pointing device, which is used for making drawings, graphics and for menu selection. It senses the light from the screen when it becomes closer and generates a pulse. Light pen is used especially in Personal Digital Assistants (PDA). It is very useful in identifying a specific location on the screen.

Light Pen

(iv) **Graphics Tablet** A graphics tablet (or digitisers, digitising tablet, or simply tablet) is an input device that consists of an electronic writing area and a special pen that works with it.

It allows artists to create hand-made images and graphical images with motion and action, similar to the way a person draws images with pencil and paper. When user draws anything on the tablet with the special pen, the drawing appears on the screen. Graphics tablet may also be used to capture data or handwritten signatures.

Graphics Tablet

(v) **Touchscreen** It is an electronic visual display that can detect the presence and location of a touch within the display area. The term touch screen generally refers to touching the display of the device with a finger or hand.

The touchscreen sends a signal to the computer. This signal gives the location on the screen, which has been touched. Touchscreen is quick and simple to use. Generally, smartphones have a high-resolution capacitive touch screen.

Touch Screen

There are different types of touchscreens available with electronic devices like capacitive touchscreen, resistive touchscreen and gorilla glass touchscreen, etc.

(vi) **Trackball** It is designed for computers, generally serves as mouse replacement. It is primarily used to move the cursor on the screen. The trackball has a ball on its top. Trackball can be rolled with fingers and the internal rollers sense the motion, which is transmitted to the computer.

Trackballs are common on CAD workstations and sometimes seen on computerised special purpose work stations, such as the radar consoles in an air-traffic control room or sonar equipment on a ship or submarine.

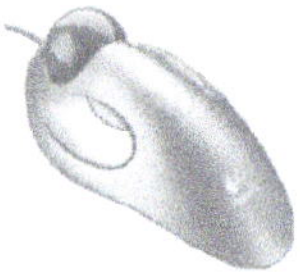

Trackball

III. Scanner

It is an input device that makes copies and reproduces text and images and convert it into a digital file, allowing the computer to read or display the scanned object. Scanners can be used for storing the documents in their original form that can be modified and manipulated later on. It is mainly used to convert a scanned document in a digital format.

Scanner

Scanners come in a variety of sizes from hand held models to desktop models as Handheld scanners, Flatbed scanners and Drum scanners.

IV. MICR (Magnetic Ink Character Recognition)

It is a character recognition technology which is primarily used by the banking industry to facilitate the processing of cheques. This technology allows the computer to read information (such as account numbers) on printed documents.

MICR

MICR can read upto 2400 documents/min. The MICR coding system contains 14 characters (4 special symbols and 10 decimal digits). So, it can recognise these 14 characters only. The type font E-13 B, a standard typographical style, is used to print the characters or identification marks.

V. OCR (Optical Character Recognition)

It is used to translate scanned images of handwritten, type-written, printed text or special type font printed on conventional paper with conventional ink into machine-encoded text. OCR is widely used to convert books and documents into electronic files, to computerise a record-keeping system in an office or to publish the text on a website.

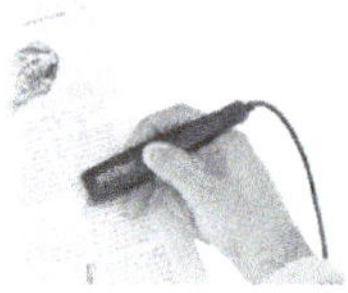

OCR

An optical reader uses photoelectric devices to scan the characters being read and convert the reflected light patterns of the data into binary data suitable for computer input. The normal speed of an OCR is 1500 to 3000 characters per second.

The technology is being developed for greater accurate recognition and is also known as Intelligent Character Recognition (ICR).

VI. OMR (Optical Mark Reader)

OMR is the process of detecting the presence of intended marked responses. OMR is mainly used to detect marks on a paper. It uses a beam of light that is reflected on the paper with marks, to capture presence and absence of data (Marks).

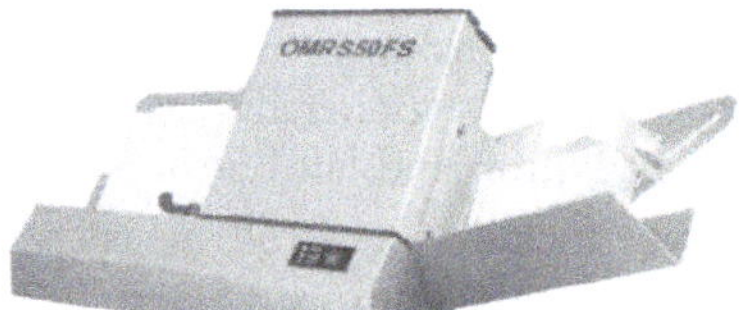

OMR

The OMR reader interprets the patterns of marks into a data record and sends this to the computer for storing, analysing and reporting. OMR is widely used to read the answer of objective type tests, voting applications and other evaluations studies.

VII. Barcode Reader

It is an input device used for reading printed bar codes (Universal Product Code) available on product to be sold. A barcode reader emits a beam of light, which reflects off the barcode image.

A light sensitive detector in the barcode reader identifies the barcode image by recognising special bars at both the ends of the image.

Barcode Reader

Once code is identified, it is converted into a numeric code. A perfect example of a barcode reader is its use in a super market where barcode scanner reads the price of a product.

A barcode is a machine readable representation of information in the form of stripes of dark and light ink.

VIII. Microphone (Mic)

We can send sound to the computer through a special manual input device called microphone or mic. A mic converts the received sound into computer's format, which is called Digitised Sound or Digital Audio. To convert a voice into digital form, an additional hardware is always needed which is known as Sound Card.

Sound is used most often in multimedia, where user can make his/her presentation more attractive using recorded narration, music or sound effects.

A microphone can be attached to a computer to record sound. Now-a-days, microphones are also being used with speech recognition software. This means that you do not have to type the document, rather just have to speak and the spoken words appear in your document.

Microphone

IX. Web Camera (Webcam)

Webcam is a digital camera attached to computers and can be used for video conferencing or online chatting, etc. It is a video capturing device. Webcams are able to capture full motion videos as well. A webcam connected to a computer allows the user to view either a still picture or motion video of a user or other object.

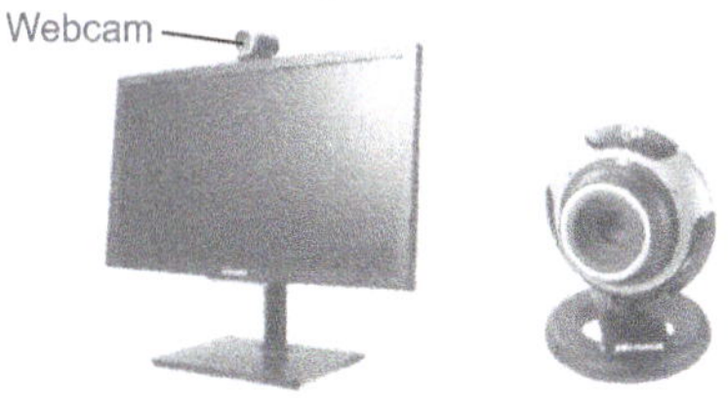

Webcam Attached with Computer

Webcam

Web Camera

Now-a-days, webcams are either embedded into the display with laptops or connected *via* USB or firewire port or Wi-Fi to the computer system. After connecting webcam to a computer, you need to install a required software or drivers.

X. Digital Camera (Digicam)

It is an input device that stores the pictures or videos in an electronic format instead of film. There are several features that make digital camera a popular choice, when compared to film cameras. Most enjoyable feature is the LCD display on the digital camera. This display allows users to view and save photos or videos after the picture or video has been taken, that means, if you take a picture and don't like the results, you can delete it, or if you like the picture, you can save it and easily show it to other people.

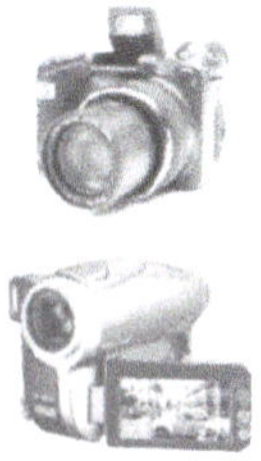

Digital Cameras

XI. Biometric Sensor

It is a device which recognises physical or behavioural traits of an individual. Biometric sensors are mainly used marking attendance of employees/students in organisations/institutions. Biometric sensors are working with accuracy, so these can be widely used in security purpose.

Biometric Sensor

XII. Smart Card Reader

It is a device which is used to access the microprocessor of a smart card. There are two kinds of smart cards. Memory cards the cards which contain only non-volatile memory storage components and some specific security logic. Microprocessor cards contain volatile memory and microprocessor components. The card is made-up of plastic generally PVC. Smart cards are used in large companies and organisation for strong security authentication.

Smart Card Reader

2. Output Devices

An output device is a part of computer hardware equipment, used to communicate the results of data processing which are carried out by the information processing system (such as a computer), to the outside world. Output devices carry the results of various operations performed by the user. Output device makes it possible to view or print data.

Some of the devices, which are used to display the processed result or output are Monitor, Printer, Plotter, Speaker, Headphone, Projector, Speech synthesizer which explained as below :

I. Monitor/VDU

A monitor (called a Visual Display Unit, VDU) is an electronic visual device used to display the output. The rectangular area of the monitor, its refresh rate and dot pitch, all directly affect the resolution of the display.

A monitor is of two kinds : Monochrome display monitor and Color display monitor.

A monochrome display monitor uses only one color to display text and color display monitor can display 256 colors at a time.

An image on the monitor is created by a configuration of dots, also known as pixels.

The clarity of image depends on three factors :

- **Resolution of Screen** Resolution refers to the number of pixels in horizontal and vertical directions. The resolution of monitor is higher when the pixels are closer together.
- **Dot Pitch** It refers to the diagonal distance between two colored pixels. The smaller the dot pitch, the better the resolution.
- **Refresh Rate** The refresh rate of a monitor is the maximum number of times the image on screen can be drawn or refreshed per second.

II. Printer

It is an output device which produces a hard copy of documents that are stored in an electronic form on physical print media such as paper or transparencies. So, printers are the primary output devices used to prepare permanent documents.

The speed of a printer is normally rated either by Pages Per Minute (PPM) or by Characters Per Second (CPS). Printer resolution is a numerical measure of print quality that is measured in Dots Per Inch (DPI).

Printers can be classified into two broad categories as follows :

(i) **Impact Printers** These printers rely on a forcible impact to transfer ink to the print media, similar to the action of a typewriter. There is a mechanical contact between the paper and the print head.

(ii) **Non-impact Printers** These printers are much quieter than impact printers as their printing heads do not strike on the paper. These printers are comparatively faster and produce high quality output. They can be used for printing text and graphics both in black & white and colored.

III. Plotter

It is an output device similar to a printer that uses a pen, pencil, marker or other writing tools to make a design.

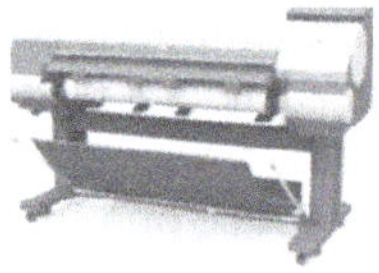

Plotter

Plotters are generally used to generate the map of building and shopping malls. A plotter is a computer printing device for printing vector graphics. In the past, plotters were widely used in applications such as Computer Aided Design (CAD) and other printing jobs. Though, they have generally been replaced with wide-format conventional printers.

IV. Speaker

It is an output device that receives the sound in the form of electric current from the sound card and convert it into sound format. Speakers are used for listening music. Computer speakers (multimedia speakers) are the speakers, which are attached internally or externally to a computer system.

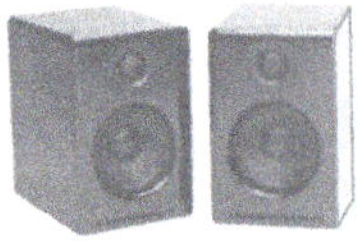

Speaker

V. Headphones

These are a pair of small loudspeakers or less commonly a single speaker, held close to a user's ears and connected to a signal source such as an audio amplifier, radio, CD player or portable media player. They are also known as stereo phones, headsets or cans.

Headphones

VI. Projector

It is an output device which is used to project information from a computer onto a large screen, so it can be viewed by a large group of people simultaneously. Projectors are widely used for classroom training or conference holes with a large audience. It provides a temporary output display.

VII. Speech Synthesizer

It is used to produce sound from a text and can be implemented in software and hardware. A text-to-speech system converts normal language text into speech.

3. Central Processing Unit (CPU)

It is the part of a computer system that carries out the instructions of a computer program, to perform the basic arithmetical, logical and input/output operations of the system.

The CPU is also known as the brain of the computer. The speed of CPU depends upon the type of microprocessor used and it is measured in MegaHertz (MHz).

Two typical components of a CPU are Arithmetic Logic Unit and Control Unit.

I. Arithmetic Logic Unit

In computing, an Arithmetic Logic Unit (ALU) is a digital circuit that performs arithmetic and logical operations. The ALU is a fundamental building block of the central processing unit of a computer. ALU uses registers to hold the data that is being processed. Most ALUs can perform the following operations :

- **Logical Operations** (AND, NOT, OR)
- **Arithmetic Operations** (addition, subtraction, multiplication and division)
- **Bit-shifting Operations** (shifting or rotating a word by a specified number of bits to the left or right, with or without sign extension)
- **Comparison Operations** (=, <, <=, >, >=)

- **Register** It is the internal part of CPU which gives special purpose location to arithmetic logic unit and control unit. These are used to store intermediate results obtained during the execution of instructions.
- **Microprocessor** It is fabricated on a single IC (Integrated Circuit). IC is a piece of silicon, composed by thousands of transistors.
- **Motherboard** The main circuit board contained in any computer is called a motherboard. It is also known as the main board or logic board or system board or planar board. All the other electronic devices and circuits of computer system are attached to this board like, CPU, ROM, RAM, expansion slots, PCI slots and USB ports. It also includes controllers for devices like the hard drive, DVD drive, keyboard and mouse. In other words, motherboard makes everything in a computer work together.

II. Control Unit

It coordinates the input and output devices of a computer system. Control Unit (CU) fetches the instructions which are given in the form of micro-programs. It directs the operation of other units by providing timing and control signals. In general, CU is a central part of the computer that controls its operations and entire processing. The control unit is the circuit that controls the flow of data through the processor and coordinates the activities of the other units within it. Control unit acts like human nerves system, which does not process data but behaves as a central unit for other data manipulating components.

4. Computer Memory

The computer memory is one of the most important elements in a computer system.

It is the internal or external storage area, which holds the data and instructions during processing in the form of binary numbers.

Memory also relates to many devices and components that are responsible for storing data and applications on a temporary or a permanent basis. Computer memory can be classified into two types– Primary memory and Secondary memory/Storage device.

I. Primary Memory

It is also known as main memory. It is the internal memory used by computer to hold data and instructions. The primary memory has limited storage capacity. It holds the data and programs needed at that instant by CPU. Primary memory is volatile in nature i.e. it requires constant power supply to motion the current information.

There are two types of primary memory i.e. RAM and ROM.

(i) **RAM** (Random Access Memory) It is the internal memory that can be read from as well as written to.

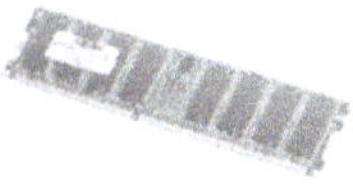

RAM

This memory is often associated with volatile types of memory. It can hold data only on temporary basis because it requires a continuous flow of electrical current. If current is interrupted, data is lost.

(ii) **ROM** (Read Only Memory) In ROM, information once stored remain fixed, i.e. it can not be changed. So, ROM can only be read and used. The contents of ROM remain stored even if power is turned OFF. This memory is often associated with non-volatile types of memory. ROM cannot be altered once the chip has been made.

ROM

Cache Memory

It is a storage buffer that stores the data that is used more often, temporarily and makes them available to CPU at a fast rate.

The data and instructions that are required during the processing of data are brought from the secondary storage devices and stored in the RAM.

Cache memory is a very high speed memory placed in between RAM and CPU. Cache memory increases the speed of processing.

Cache memory is very expensive, so it is smaller in size. Generally, computers have cache memory of sized 256KB to 2MB.

II. Secondary Memory/Storage Device

Secondary memory, also known as Secondary Storage or Auxiliary Memory, is the slower and cheaper form of memory. It is a permanent storage device. CPU does not access the secondary memory directly. The content in it must first be copied into the RAM to be processed. Secondary memory is non-volatile in nature, i.e. the information does not get erased even when the power is switched OFF and data will not be destructed until and unless the user erases it.

Secondary Memory Devices include

Magnetic Disks	Optical Discs	Solid State
Floppy Disk	CD	Pen/Flash Drive
Hard Disk Drive	DVD	
Magnetic Tape	Blu-ray Disc	

(i) **Floppy Disk** (Diskette) A Floppy Disk Drive (FDD) is a computer disk drive that enables a user to save data on removable diskettes. This portable storage device is a rewritable media and can be reused a number of times. It is made of plastic with magnetic coating on it. It is round in shape and is covered by square plastic jacket. Floppy disks are commonly used to move files between different computers. Although 8" disk drives made available in 1971 were the first real disk drives, the first widely used floppy disk drives 4", $5\frac{1"}{4}$, which were later replaced with $3\frac{1"}{2}$ floppy disk drive. However, today these drives are replaced with CD-R and other writable disk drives and flash drives.

(ii) **Hard Disk Drive** A Hard Disk Drive (HDD) is a non-volatile and random access digital data storage device. It is a data storage device used for storing and retrieving digital information using rotating disks (platters) coated with magnetic material. All programs of a computer are installed in hard disk within a particular drive.

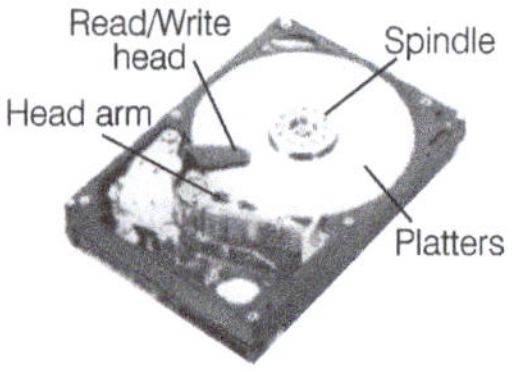

Hard Disk Drive

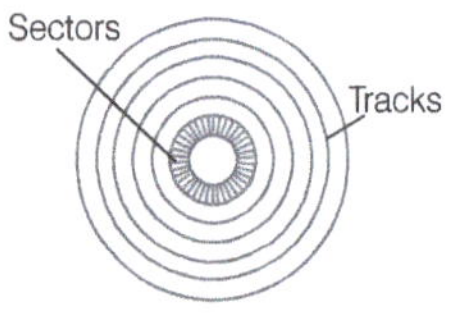

Tracks and Sectors

It consists of a spindle that hold non- magnetic flat circular disks, called platters, which hold the recorded data. Each platter requires two read/write heads, that is used to write and read the information from a platter. All the read/write heads are attached to a single access arm so that they cannot move independently.

The information is recorded in bands, each band of information is called a track. Each platter has the same number of tracks and a track location that cuts across all platters is called a cylinder. The tracks are divided into pie-shaped sections known as sectors.

(iii) **Magnetic Tape** It is a medium of data storage, made up of a magnetic material. It is a storage medium on a large open reel or in a smaller cartridge or cassette (like a music cassette). It is used for those applications that are based on sequential data processing i.e. it is a sequential data access medium.

Due to this (sequential data access) nature, these tapes are not suitable for data files that need to be revised or updated often. They are generally used to store backup data or that type of data, which is not frequently used or to transfer data from one system to another.

(iv) **Compact Disc** (CD) It is an optical media that is used to store digital data. It is relatively cheap, small, portable and round in shape storage medium which is made up of molded polymer. It consists of a circular disc, which is coated with a thin metal that is highly reflective. Laser beam technology is used for recording/reading of data on the disc. It is also known as laser disc or optical laser disc, due to the use of laser beam technology. CD provides random access medium for high capacity secondary storage. The diameter of the CD ranges from 10cms to 30cms. One CD can store 600 MB to 750 MB.

(v) **Digital Video Disc** (DVD) It is also known as Super Density (SD) disc. A DVD is an optical disc storage media manufactured for the first time by Philips, Sony, Toshiba and Panasonic in 1995. DVDs offer higher storage capacity than compact discs while having the same dimensions.

Depending upon the disk type, DVD can store several Gigabytes of data (4.7 GB-17.08 GB). DVDs are primarily used to store music or movies and can be played back on your television or on the computer too. They are not rewritable media.

(vi) **Blu-ray Disc** (BD) It is an optical disc storage medium designed to recapture the data normally in DVD format. Blu-ray discs contain 25 GB (23.31 GB) per layer space. The name blu-ray disc refers to the blue laser used to read the disc, which allows information to be stored at a greater density. Blu-ray can hold almost 5 times more data than a single layer DVD.

(vii) **Pen/Flash/Thumb Drive** A flash drive is a data storage device that consists of flash memory (USB memory/key memory) with an integrated, Universal Serial Bus (USB) interface. USB flash drives are typically removable, rewritable and physically much smaller than a floppy disk. A USB flash drive, thumb drive or pen drive is a portable drive that is same as the size of your thumb that connects to the computer USB port. Today, flash drives are available in various storage capacities as 256 MB, 512 MB, 1 GB, 4 GB, 16 GB, 64 GB, etc. Flash drives are widely used as an easy and small medium to transfer and store the information from the computers.

Pen Drive

(viii) **Memory Stick** It is USB-based flash memory drive. A family of flash memory cards from Sony designed for digital storage in cameras, camcorders and other handheld devices. Capacity of memory stick varies from 4 MB to 256 MB.

Memory Stick

Basic Units of Measurement

When user uses a RAM, ROM, Floppy disk or Hard disk, the data is measured using some units. In computer terminology, they are called Nibble, Bit, Byte, Kilobyte, Gigabyte etc.

Units of Computer Memory Measurements

- **Bit** (Binary digit) The smallest unit of data. It is either 0 or 1.
- **Nibble** A group of 4 bits or half a byte.
- **Byte** A group of 8 bits. A byte can represent 256 (2^8) distinct values, such as the integers from 0 to 255. Each keyboard character is represented through atleast 1 byte.
- **Kilobyte** (KB) It is actually 2^{10} bytes or 1 KB = 1024 bytes.
- **Megabyte** (MB) It is actually 2^{20} bytes or 1 MB = 1024 KB.
- **Gigabyte** (GB) It is actually 2^{30} bytes or 1 GB = 1024 MB.
- **Terabyte** (TB) It is actually 2^{40} bytes or 1 TB = 1024 GB.
- **Petabyte** (PB) It is actually 2^{50} bytes or 1 PB = 1024 TB.
- **Exabyte** (EB) It is actually 2^{60} bytes or 1 EB = 1024 PB.
- **Zettabyte** (ZB) It is actually 2^{70} bytes or 1 ZB = 1024 EB.
- **Yottabyte** (YB) It is actually 2^{80} bytes or 1 YB = 1024 ZB.
- **Brontobyte** It is actually 2^{90} bytes or 1 Brontobyte = 1024 YB
- **Geopbyte** It is actually 2^{100} bytes or 1 Geopbyte = 1024 Brontobyte. Geopbyte is the highest and bit is the smallest memory measurement unit.

Check Point 03

1 1GB equals to
(a) 1024 MB (B) 1024 KB
(c) 1024 Byte (d) 1024 TB

2 MICR stands for ....

3 Name the types of printer.

4 The speed of CPU depends upon microprocessor. (True/False)

5 Give any one difference between RAM and ROM.

Ports and Connections

The slots or channels into which we connect the mouse/keyboard/external hard disk wires are called ports. Thus, ports help us to connect input, output and storage devices in a computer system.

There are several types of ports that you can use to connect a computer to an external devices and networks.These are

- **Universal Serial Bus (USB) port** generally connects peripheral devices, such as a mouse or a keyboard or a printer to a computer using the cable.
- **Display port** connects the monitor or any display unit to the computer using the cable. These can be of different types, like Video Graphics Array (VGA) and High Definition Multimedia Interface (HDMI), depending on the requirement.
- **Audio ports** help to connect microphone, speakers and headphones to a computer system. Often, the speaker and headphone port is called the line out port, i.e. it is meant for sound output.

- **Ethernet port** is used for connecting the system to high speed Internet cable.
- **Power port** is used for connecting the computer system to the power supply.

Basic Computer Operations

Computer Hardware and Software

A computer system consists of two main parts-the hardware and the software.

The physical parts that we can see and touch are called the hardware. It is the machinery of a computer.
e.g. Keyboard, Mouse, Monitor, CPU etc.

The software that we cannot see and makes the hardware work the way we want. It is a collection of computer programs, procedures and related data that provide the instructions for telling a computer what to do and how to do it.

e.g. The monitor is a hardware. When we start a program, it is displayed on the monitor. This is done by the software which displays things on monitor. Hardware would not be of any use without the software.

The most important software in any computer is the Operating System (OS). This is the software that starts working as soon as we switch ON a computer. It displays the desktop on the monitor.

Some of the most commonly used operating systems for laptops and desktop are Ubuntu, Microsoft Windows, Mac OS etc.

Mobile devices also have operating system that helps them perform their functions. Some of the mobile operating systems are Apple iOS and Google Android.

Starting a Computer

When a computer is switched ON, it performs some basic processes or functions, before it is ready to take instructions from the user.

To start a computer, press the Power ⏻ button on the CPU. This will start the Windows operating system and display the windows desktop on the monitor.

Basic Functions Performed when a Computer Starts

A computer automatically runs a basic program called BIOS (Basic Input/Output System) as soon as it is switched ON or the power button is pushed ON.

The BIOS first does a self test. If the self-test shows that the system is fine, the BIOS will load the operating system. This means that the computer's operating system, is now ready to take inputs from the user.

Login and Logout

When multiple users use the same computer, each user has his/her own files and applications. To make sure that nobody else sees other's work, each user should have login-IDs and passwords.

A login and password is like a key to lock which allows them to use the computer.

When user login to the computer with his/her logic-ID and password, the computer knows that they are an authorized user and allows them to work on applications in the computer.

Once they finish working, they must log out or sign out so that no one else can see their work.

Shutting Down a Computer

In Ubuntu operating system, user can shut down the computer by clicking "Systems" at the top right and then click on Shut Down option.

When user clicks Shut Down, the operating system will close all the applications and turn off the computer.

Need to perform basic file operations

Information on a computer is stored in electronic files, which can be put into separate folders. It is easier to manage the electronic files as they can be simply copied, moved, renamed or even deleted.

Files and Folders

All information stored in a computer is kept in files. Different types of files store different types of information. Each file is given a file name and has a file name extension that identifies the file type.

The file name and file name extension are separated by a period or a dot (.).

For example, a document created using Notepad will have extension .txt.

There are other types like .doc, .xls, etc. An image file usually has an extension .jpg, while a sound file usually has .mp3. A folder is a location where a group of files can be stored. A folder within a folder is called sub folder.

Creating a File (Using a Text Editor in Ubuntu)

Let us create a new file using a text editor in Ubuntu :

- To open a text editor, type 'editor' in the search dialog box. Then double click the text editor option. This will open a blank document.

Note *In Windows, you can open the Notepad and type in the text.*

- Here you can add text.
- To save the file click Save. In Save As dialog box, browse to the Desktop folder, type the name and click Save button.

Check Point 04

1 Name any two port.
2 Some commonly used OS is/are
(a) Ubuntu (b) Windows
(c) Mac OS (d) All of these
3 A computer consists of two main parts are ....
4 To start a computer, press the Power button. (True/False)

Communication and Networking

Basics of Internet

The Internet is a huge network of computers around the world. Using the Internet you can get any information that is stored in a web page on the World Wide Web. With the help of the Internet, you can gather a lot of knowledge which is available on it. The knowledge is stored in a big library/storehouse, called the World Wide Web (WWW) or the web.

WWW is a collection of different websites that you can view if you are connected to the Internet. You can also use these websites to buy something, watch movies, read books, learn new skills, educate yourself, find the best colleges to study further etc.

Uses of the Internet

There is no limit to what you can do online,but some of the most common uses of Internet are as follows:

(i) **Search Information** You can get the latest information about anything that is uploaded on the web, whether it is result of any exam, news, a cricket match, election details and many more.

(ii) **Entertainment** You can listen to music, play games, watch movies, share images or videos etc using Internet.

(iii) **E-mail and Chatting** You can receive and send messages to others all around the world in quick and easy manner. G-mail, Outlook etc are used for E-mailing while Facebook messenger, Whatsapp etc are used for chatting.

(iv) **Social Networking** You can share your interests, knowledge and stories with your family, friends, relatives etc around the world. e.g. Facebook, Twitter etc.

(v) **Online Shopping** You can buy and sell things such as books, electronic goods, clothes, shoes etc over the Internet. You can also pay for these things *via* digital modes of payments such as wallets, plastic cards or through e-Banking etc.

(vi) **Online Booking** You can book movie tickets, hotels, bus/train/plane tickets etc using Internet.

(vii) **Online Learning** There is a number of courses available online-some are free while others are paid.

(viii) **Online Banking** You can do banking operations, like checking details of your bank account or transferring money from one account to another through mobile banking/NEFT/RTGS.

Connecting to the Internet

To connect to the Internet, there is need following:

(a) A device, such as a computer, laptop or mobile.

(b) A connecting device, i.e. a modem.

Internet Service Provider (ISP)

It is a company which provides the Internet connectivity using the phone lines or a wireless network.

Types of Connections

There is two types of Internet connection as:

(a) **Wired connections** When our computer is connected to the Internet using a wire or cable, it is called a wired connection. We use Ethernet cables (cables used for connecting to the Internet) to connect to the modem which connects to the ISP using a phone line.

(b) **Wireless connections** Computers can also be connected to the Internet using wireless technology. Laptops need a wireless Internet card to connect to a modem with using any cables. Wi-Fi, WiMAX are the ways to connect the Internet wirelessly.

Bandwidth

It is the amount of data that can be transmitted over a network in a certain amount of time.

e.g, The amount of water flowing through a pipe depends on its thickness.

Similarly, the amount of data that your network can receive or send depends on its bandwidth. In case of digital devices, the bandwidth is usually expressed in bits per second (bps) or bytes per second.

In case of analog devices, the bandwidth is expressed in cycles per second or Hertz (Hz).

Data transfer speed over the networks is calculated in terms of bits per second.

1 Kbps (Kilobits per second) = 1000 bits per second

1 Mbps (Mega bits per second) = 1000 kilobits per second

1 Gbps (Giga bits per second) = 1000 mega bits per second

World Wide Web

The World Wide Web (WWW) or simply the web is a huge collection of information. It was introduced on 13th March 1989. It is a vast network of linked hypertext files, stored on computers throughout the world that can provide a computer user with information on a huge variety of subjects.

Thus, it serves as a platform through which users can use or share information.

It is made up of

- A web page
- A website
- A web browser
- A system to transfer information between the web browsers and the web pages.

Web Page

A web page is a document present on a computer that is connected to the Internet. There are hundreds of web pages. Each web page has a unique address/location like to the address of a house. We can use the address to see a particular web page. To view a web page, you need a web browser on your computer.

Website

A group of web pages that follow the same theme and are connected together with hyperlinks is called a website.

Websites and web pages are written in a coding language that makes it possible to add pictures, sound and interactivity to plain old text, making people's reading experience more exciting. The very first page of a website is called home page of that website.

e.g. http://www.carwale.com is a website while http://www.carwale.com/new/ is a web page.

Internet Browser/Web Browser

To see the information on the various websites, you need an Internet browser. Internet browser or web browser (Commonly referred to as browser) is an application or an application software program on your computer, laptop or mobile which helps to visit the various websites. It is an application for using and sharing information on the World Wide Web.

The most popular web browsers that are used today as Mozilla Firefox, Google Chrome, Internet Explorer, Apple Safari, Opera etc.

Searching for Information

Follow the below steps to search for information on Internet:

Step 1 Open the browser, e.g. Google Chrome.

Step 2 Type the topic about which you want information in the search box and press Enter key.

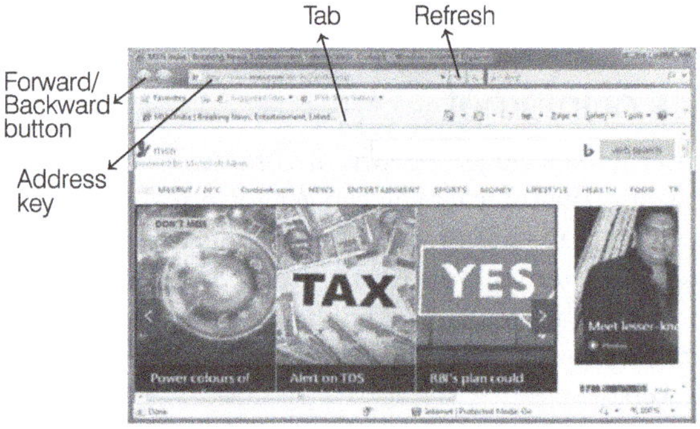

Step 3 The search results having the required information will be displayed.

In Ubuntu

- In Ubuntu operation system, click the Firefox icon from side menu bar to open the Firefox Mozilla browser.
- Search the information which you want.

Hyperlinks

There are hyperlinks present on web pages of browser. If you click a hyperlink, it will take you to another part on the same page or to a different page.

Important Parts of a Web Browser

(i) **Address bar** (Alt+d) You can type the address/URL of a website in the bar and press Enter. The browser will display the page linked to that URL.

(ii) **Tabbed browsing (Ctrl+T)** Tabbed browsing allows a user to view multiple pages in the same window. So, if you want to compare two types of computers for example mainframe and micro, you can open the two different tabs in same window.

(iii) **Backward and forward buttons** (Alt + Left or Right arrow) These buttons allow to go back to the last page viewed or go forward to the next page viewed.

(iv) **Refresh button (F5)** Sometimes, you do not see the complete page correctly. You can reload the page by clicking the Refresh button.

Check Point 05

1 Use(s) of the Internet
(a) Entertainment (b) E-mail chatting
(c) Search information (d) All of these

2 ISP stands for Internet Service Provider. (True/False)

3 What is the use of online learning?

4 Define bandwidth in one line.

5 To reload a page, shortcut key ...... is used.

Introduction to E-mail

Electronic mail or E-mail is a quick way of sending messages to people using Internet. Electronic mail is a message sent over the Internet from one person to another. It consists of lines of text and images. The invention of E-mail has influenced our lives and they have become a popular means of communication.

Files containing videos, documents, spreadsheets etc., can be sent along with the E-mail as attachments. E-mail is fast and easy to use. It can be sent to multiple people at the same time.

Comparing between Postal mail and E-mail

	Postal mail	E-mail
Address	Postal mail address is a street, city etc., of a geographical location.	An E-mail address is a digital location on a mail computer where you can send or receive an electronic message.
Written on	Postal mail is written with paper and pen.	An E-mail is written on a computer or mobile device.
Sent *via*	Postal mail is sent by bus, air, train.	An E-mail travels in a digital format over an Internet connection.
Received in	Postal mail is brought by the postman and dropped into the letterbox outside our house.	E-mail comes into inbox of the receiver's E-mail account.

E-mail ID or Address

An E-mail address is composed of two separate parts :

1. Your personal identity or account name (user name) on that mail server.
2. The domain name of the mail server computer on which you have an E-mail account.

An E-mail address is generally in the form of username@domain name. Some examples of E-mail address are – arihant@gmail.com, webmaster@yahoo.com, etc.

In E-mail address, symbol '@' is used as an separator. It separates your account name and domain name.

Advantages of E-Mail

1. The delivery of messages is very fast.
2. The cost of E-mailing is almost free as it involves negligible amount of telephone and Internet Service Provider (ISP) charges.
3. Multiple copies of the same messages can be sent to a group of people at the same time and can be sent as easily to a single person.
4. Pictures, documents and other files can also be attached to messages.

Disadvantages of E-Mail

1. Viruses attached with an E-mail could seriously affect recipient's computer.
2. E-mails cannot really be used for official business documents. They may be lost and you cannot find them.
3. E-mails may be intercepted by hackers as E-mail, before it is delivered to the recipient, 'bounces' between servers located in different parts of the world.
4. If an E-mail is too long or not drafted properly by the sender, the reader may lose interest to read the mail till the end.

Creating an E-mail Account

There are various web-portals (websites), which allow you to create free E-mail account. e.g. www.gmail.com, www.yahoo.com, www.hotmail.com, www.rediffmail.com, www.msn.com, etc.

Some steps for opening an E-mail account are as follows :

Step 1 Enter the URL address as www.gmail. com. Gmail Homepage will appear.

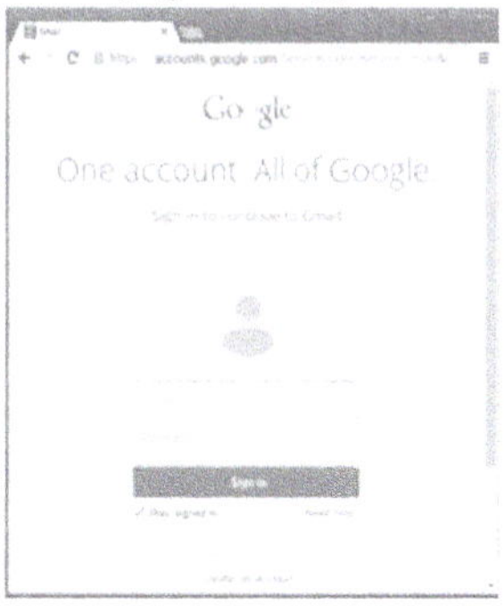

Step 2 Click on Create an account hyperlink. The Registration Form will appear.

Step 3 Fill those details which are mandatory. You can also skip some of the personal details.

Step 4 After completing the registration form, click on Next step button.

Step 5 Create your public Google+ profile page will appear. If you want to create a profile, click on Create your profile button otherwise click on No thanks button.

Step 6 After the creation of an E-mail account, the confirmation information will be given to the user and the following web page will display on the browser.

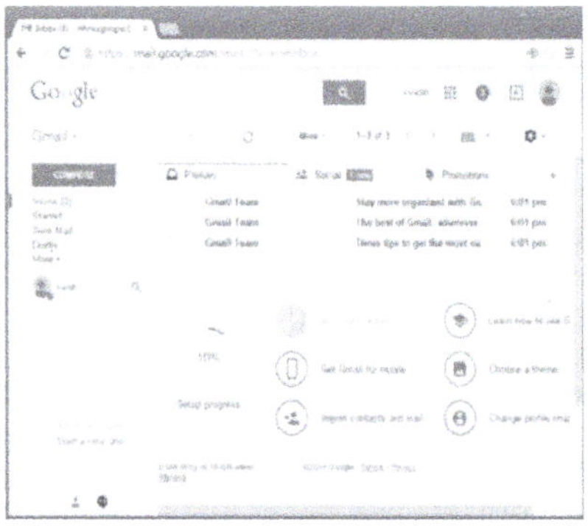

Writing an E-mail

After login, if a user wants to create an E-mail click on COMPOSE button and New Message window will display on the screen.

In this window, **To** text box carries the E-mail address of the recipient, **Subject** carries the heading for E-mail or subject of the E-mail and the **whole body** of text matter comes within the Body option.

For sending an E-mail, click on Send button. E-mail delivers to the recipient's end instantly.

Instead of this, if a user wants to send a file (.doc, .pdf, .jpg, etc.) then click on Attach files for the attachment of files.

There are various options which are accessible within an E-mail like Text Formatting, Cc (Carbon Copy), Bcc (Blind Carbon Copy) etc.

Some of these are as follows :

- **Cc** (Carbon copy) This allows an E-mail to be send to a large number of people by writing their respective addresses separated by commas.
- **Bcc** (Blind carbon copy) This is Cc, except that the recipient does not see the list of people in the Bcc field.
- **Signature** This is one of the basic elements of an E-mail message. By this, you are often able to set a signature, meaning a few lines of text which will be added to the end of the document.

Attaching a file to an E-mail

An attachment is a type of file such as a photo or document that you can send along with your E-mail.

To send a soft copy in the form of attachment, follow these steps :

Step 1 Click on COMPOSE button on Gmail account window. New Message box will display on the screen.

Step 2 Type the E-mail address of the recipient in To: line or you can also select E-mail address from your address book.

Step 3 Type the subject of the E-mail in the subject line.

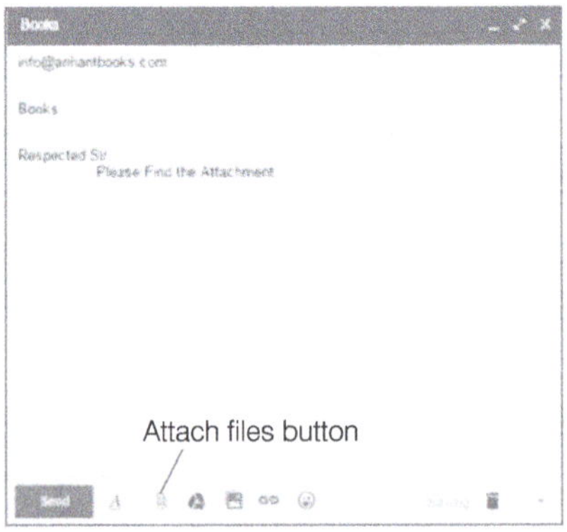

Step 4 To attach any soft copy, click on Attach files button ( ) and the Open dialog box will display on the screen.

Step 5 Select the file which you want to attach. After selecting the file, click on Open button.

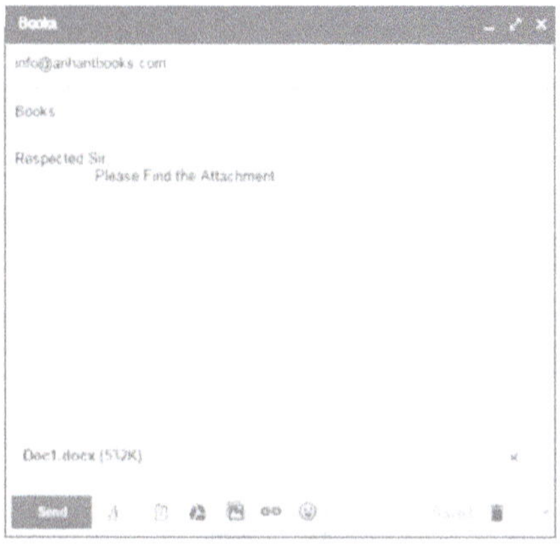

Step 6 When the file gets attached to E-mail, click on Send button.

Managing Folders

There are different folders that could help you manage and organise your E-mails, which describe below:

- **Inbox** A place where E-mail messages are received. The inbox is the default location for all incoming mails unless rules have been setup to forward messages to another program or folder.
- **Outbox** A term used to describe the location or folder where E-mail is stored before being sent. It gives the opportunity to the user to review, edit and delete messages before they are sent.
- **Drafts** This folder contains items that have not yet been sent. An E-mail is saved to the drafts folder when a user composes an E-mail and then click the Save and Close button.
- **Sent Items** This folder contains all items that have been sent but not deleted. It saves all the messages that were successfully sent.
- **Junk/Spam** This folder holds e-mails that may not be useful.
- **Trash** This folder holds E-mails that you no longer need and have deleted. To delete an E-mail, you select an E-mail and then click on the Delete button for it to be moved from inbox to trash folder.

Receiving an E-mail

Receiving mails will appear in inbox. It shows the name of the sender, subject and a title of the main message. It will remain bold till you open it.

Step 1 Click on the mail to open it.

Step 2 Once you have read the E-mail, you can reply, forward or delete the mail.

Step 3 If the message was sent to many people, you get another option, i.e. Reply to All. When you click this, the reply will be sent to all the people who received a copy of this mail.

Replying to an E-mail Message

For replying to an E-mail message, follow these steps :

Step 1 Open the E-mail which you have to answer.

Step 2 Click on Reply option.

Step 3 Click on Reply to all option for answering the all recipients of To and Cc boxes.

Forwarding an E-mail Message

To forward an E-mail message, follow these steps :

Step 1 Open the E-mail which a user wants to forward.

Step 2 Click on Forward option.

Step 3 Enter the names of the recipients in To, Cc and Bcc boxes.

Step 4 Click on Send button.

Forward is used to send a copy of received E-mail to someone else.

Deleting an E-mail

E-mail can be delete by clicking on delete icon. This will remove the E-mail from inbox and move it to the Trash folder. It will remain there for a few days before it is removed from the system.

Check Point 06

1. Name any two attachments that can be sent through E-mail.
2. Write any two disadvantages of E-mail.
3. Bcc stands for ....
4. Spam folder holds E-mails that may be useful. (True/False)

NCERT FOLDER

Check Your Progress **Pg 87**

A. State whether True or False

1. The full form of ICT is Information Commuting Technology.

Ans. False; The full form of ICT is Information and Communication Technology.

2. Live sports and news can only be shown using ICT.

Ans. True; Live sports and news can only be shown using ICT tools such as TV.

B. Short Answer Questions

1. Give any two uses of ICT at home.

Ans. Two uses of ICT at home are as follows:

(i) People uses television for entertainment.

(ii) We use computers and mobile phones for talking to each other, sending and receiving information, watching videos, playing games etc.

2. What are the emerging skills in ICT?

Ans. Emerging skills in ICT are:

(i) Develop knowledge and skills to plan.

(ii) Implement and manage ICT solutions to support emergency response.

3. What are the key skills one should possess to use ICT?

Ans. The basic ICT skills that you need are:

(i) Knowing how to operate computers.

(ii) Knowing how to browse the Internet for collecting, storing and disseminating information.

Check Your Progress **Pg 91**

A. Short Answer Questions

1. Identify the following symbols and write the name in the blank space.

(a)  ....

(b) 

....

(c)  ....

(d)  ....

(e)  ....

(f)  ....

Ans. (a) Phone (b) Calendar (c) Music (d) Gallery (e) Clock (f) Messages

2. Write any two differences between a smartphone and a tablet.

Ans. Differences between smartphone and tablet are:

Smartphone	Tablet
Comes with different storage capacity.	Usually have higher storage capacity.
Watching a movie or making changes to a picture is difficult.	Watching videos and making changes to a photo is better and easier due to bigger screen size.

Check Your Progress **Pg 94-95**

A. Multiple Choice Questions

Read the questions carefully and circle the letter (a), (b), (c) or (d) that best answers to the questions.

1. What is a short-range wireless communication technology called?

(a) Wi-Fi (b) Internet
(c) Bluetooth (d) PS

Ans. (c) Bluetooth is a short range wireless technology which helps you to connect with other devices.

2. Which part of the home screen is visible on all pages?

(a) Status bar (b) Main icon area
(c) Dock (d) Clock

Ans. (c) Dock is the lower part of the screen which can always been seen even if we more to a different page.

3. What does GPS stand for?
(a) Global Positioning System
(b) Global Payment System
(c) Global Program System
(d) Global Pointing System

Ans. (a) Global Positioning System (GPS) is a navigation (direction finding) system that helps you to navigate, find direction and maps to specific location.

Check Your Progress Pg 102

A. Multiple Choice Questions

Read the questions carefully and circle the letter (a), (b), (c) or (d) that best answers the questions.

1. Which of the following units make up the CPU? Choose and tick all the correct options.
(a) Processing Unit (b) Input Unit
(c) Memory Unit (d) Control Unit
(e) Output Unit

Ans. (b, c, e) Input unit, memory unit, output unit

2. Which of the following are names of ports in a computer? Choose and tick all the correct options.
(a) HDMI (b) Input (c) VGA
(d) USB (e) Ethernet

Ans. (b, c, d, e) Input, VGA, USB, Ethernet

3. There is a talent contest in your town. For participating in the audition, you have to send a recording of a song. What would you connect to your computer to record you song?
(a) Keyboard (b) Microphone
(c) Scanner (d) Mouse

Ans. (b) Microphone converts the received sound into computer's format.

B. Short Answer Questions

1. Write the purpose of the I/O devices
(a) Mic/Microphone (b) Scanner
(c) Camera (d) Barcode Reader
(e) Printer (f) Speaker

Ans. (a) **Microphone** is used to record voice on the computer.
(b) **Scanner** is used to scan/capture a paper image, document and converts it to digital file on computer.
(c) **Camera** stores the pictures or videos in an electronic format.
(d) **Barcode Reader** is an input device used for reading printed bar codes available on product to be sold.
(e) **Printer** helps to printout the visual output on the paper.
(f) **Speaker** plays back all the sound based output.

Check Your Progress Pg 109

A. Multiple Choice Questions

Read the questions carefully and circle the letter (a), (b), (c) or (d) that best answers the questions.

1. Which of the following functions are performed using a mouse. Choose and tick all the correct options.
(a) Turn on computer (b) Typing
(c) Right click (d) Drag and drop an icon

Ans. (c, d) Right click and Drag and drop an icon.

2. What is the term used when you press and hold the left mouse key and move the mouse around?
(a) Highlighting (b) Dragging
(c) Selecting (d) Moving

Ans. (b) Dragging the mouse refers to moving its position while holding the mouse button depressed.

3. Rearrange the steps for starting a computer in the correct sequence.
(a) Desktop appears after login
(b) Login screen appears
(c) Power on Self-Test (POST) starts
(d) Operating system starts
(e) Welcome screen appears

Ans. Correct sequence is
(e), (d), (b), (a), (c)

B. Short Answer Questions

1. Describe the functions of at least 5 types of keys.

Ans. Functions of different types of keys:
(i) **Control Keys** They perform special functions depending on when and where they are used.
(ii) **Enter Key** It is used to move the cursor to the beginning of a new line.
(iii) **Navigation Keys** These are used to move up and down, right and left in a document.
(iv) **Windows Key** It is used to open the Start menu.
(v) **Punctuation Keys** These are used for punctuation marks.

2. Describe the functions of a mouse.

Ans. Refer to text on Pg 43.

Check Your Progress Pg 112

A. Multiple Choice Questions

Read the questions carefully and circle the letter (a), (b), (c) or (d) that best answers the questions.

1. Which one of the following shortcut key is used to paste a file? Tick mark the correct answer.
(a) Ctrl + C (b) Ctrl + P (c) Ctrl + V (d) Ctrl + X

Ans. (c) Ctrl + V shortcut key is used to paste a cutted or copied file. Ctrl + C shortcut key is used to copy the text, Ctrl + P is use to print the document and Ctrl + X is used to cut the text.

2. Which of the following is a valid file extension for Notepad file? Tick mark the correct answer.
(a) .jpg (b) .doc (c) .text (d) .txt

Ans. (d) Notepad is the text editor which has file extension .txt. Image file has file extension .jpg and word document has file extension is .doc.

3. Which key do you use to copy something? Tick mark the correct answer.
(a) Ctrl + X (b) Ctrl + C (c) Ctrl + Z (d) Ctrl + T

Ans. (b) Ctrl + C shortkey is used to copy the selected text. Ctrl + X shortkey is used to cut the selected text and Ctrl + Z is used to undo action.

Check Your Progress Pg 116

A. Multiple Choice Questions

Read the questions carefully and circle the letter (a), (b), (c) or (d) that best answers the questions.

1. To connect to the Internet, the computer has to be connected to the
(a) Internet Society
(b) Internet Architecture
(c) Internet Service Provider
(d) Large Area Network

Ans. (c) Internet Service Provider is a company, which provides the Internet connectivity using the phone lines or a wireless network.

2. What is the Internet?
(a) Phone connections
(b) Collection of computer networks
(c) Network of computers in an office
(d) None of the above

Ans. (b) Internet is a huge network of computers around the world.

B. Short Answer Questions

1. Write a short note on the uses of Internet.

Ans. Refer to text on Pg 51.

Check Your Progress Pg 120

A. Multiple Choice Questions

Read the questions carefully and circle the letter (a), (b), (c) or (d) that best answers the questions.

1. What do I need to get information from the World Wide Web?
(a) Computer (b) Browser
(c) Internet Connection (d) All of these

Ans. (d) To get the information from World Wide Web, we need computer, browser and Internet connection.

2. Which of the following is a web browser?
(a) Internet (b) Chrome
(c) Windows (d) None of these

Ans. (b) Web browser is an application for using and sharing information on the World Wide Web e.g. Mozilla Firefox, Google Chrome, Internet Explorer, etc.

B. Short Answer Questions

1. List the steps to search for information using a web browser.

Ans. Refer to text on Pg 52.

Check Your Progress Pg 123

A. State whether True or False

1. E-mail cannot be sent to more than one person at a time.

Ans. False; E-mail can be sent to large number of people by writing their respective addresses separated by commas.

2. E-mail is an electronic message sent over the Internet or a computer network.

Ans. True

3. Pictures, videos, audio files, and spreadsheet files cannot be attached with an E-mail.

Ans. False; Attachment such as picture, video, etc. can send along with your Email.

Check Your Progress Pg 125

A. Multiple Choice Questions

Read the questions carefully and circle the letter (a), (b), (c) or (d) that best answers the questions.

1. Here are the steps to sign in to your Gmail account.
(i) Type username (ii) Go to www.gmail.com
(iii) Click Sign in (iv) Type password

Choose the option with the correct order.
(a) (i) > (ii) > (iv) > (iii)
(b) (ii) > (i) > (iii) > (iv)
(c) (ii) > (i) > (iv) > (iii)
(d) (ii) > (iii) > (i) > (iv)

Ans. (c) (ii) > (i) > (iv) > (iii)

2. Which one of the following statement is false?
(a) You need to create an account before you can send an E-mail.
(b) You should sign out of your account when you are not using the computer.
(c) You do not need an Internet connection to use your Gmail account.

(d) You must not share your password with others.

Ans. (c) You do not need an Internet connection to use your Gmail account.

3. Which of the following in an e-mail service?

(a) WhatsApp (b) WeChat
(c) Gmail (d) Facebook

Ans. (c) Gmail

B. Short Answer Question

1. What characters should the password have in E-mail address, to make it more secure?

Ans. In E-mail, a password should be at least 8 characters long and contain letters, numbers and special characters. This will make it more secure.

Check Your Progress **Pg 129**

A. Multiple Choice Questions

Read the questions carefully and circle the letter (a), (b), (c) or (d) that best answers the questions.

1. What do you type of the "To" field?

(a) The topic of the E-mail

(b) The main message of the E-mail

(c) E-mail address of the person to whom you want to send a copy of the E-mail

(d) E-mail address of the person you are sending the mail to

Ans. (d) E-mail address of the person you are sending the mail to.

2. You want to send an e-mail message to your friend Sushil. In which order will you perform the given steps to write and send an E-mail to him?

(i) Type Sushil's E-mail address, subject and message

(ii) Click on the Compose button

(iii) Click Send

(iv) Open your E-mail account.

(a) (iv)>(ii)>(i)>(iii) (b) (iv)>(i)>(ii)>(iii)
(c) (iv)>(i)>(iii)>(ii) (d) (iii)>(i)>(ii)>(iv)

Ans. (a) (iv) > (ii) > (i) > (iii)

B. Fill in the blanks

1. In "To :" section .... is typed for sending a message through E-mail.

Ans. E-mail id of the receiver

2. The Attach button in E-mail often has a .... as its symbol.

Ans. Paperclip

3. In the .... section of the E-mail, the topic of the mail is written.

Ans. Subject

4. After typing the message in the main body of the E-mail, you need to click on .... button to send the E-mail.

Ans. Send

Check Your Progress **Pg 132**

A. State whether True or False

1. By choosing the "Reply" option, the E-mail address of the sender of the original message will appear in the "To" field.

Ans. True

2. E-mail is an electronic message transmitted over the Internet or computer network from one user to another.

Ans. True

3. You can forward the e-mail by clicking on the delete icon.

Ans. False; Delete icon is used to delete the Email.

SUMMARY

- ICT stands for Information and Communication Technology. It includes a diverse set of technological tools and resources.
- Gestures are used to interact with the touchscreen of your mobile device.
- An input device is a hardware device that sends data into the computer system.
- Output devices carry the results of various operations performed by the user.
- The CPU is also known as the brain of the computer. The speed of CPU depends upon the type of microprocessor used.
- It is the internal or external storage area, which holds the data and instructions during processing in the form of binary numbers.
- The slots or channels into which we connect the mouse/keyboard/external hard disk wires are called ports.
- The Internet is a huge network of computers around the world.
- It is the amount of data that can be transmitted over a network in a certain amount of time.
- A web page is a document present on a computer that is connected to the Internet.
- A group of web pages that follow the same theme and are connected together with hyperlinks is called a website.
- Electronic mail is a message sent over the Internet from one person to another.

Exam Practice

Multiple Choice Questions

1. ……… includes computers, Internet, broadcasting technologies and telephony.
(a) ICT (b) Browser
(c) IT (d) None of these

Ans. (a) ICT stands for Information and Communication Technology that includes computers, Internet, broadcasting technologies and telephony.

2. With a ……… you can only make calls and receive calls.
(a) Smartphone (b) Android phone
(c) Simple phone (d) Tablet

Ans. (c) Simple phone is used to make calls and receive calls.

3. This is used to enter appointments, remainders etc.
(a) Mail (b) Calendar
(c) Phone (d) Clock

Ans. (b) Calendar is a default app in smartphone to enter appointments, remainders, etc.

4. Which of the following is/are features of mobile device?
(a) Bluetooth (b) Wi-Fi
(c) Camera (d) All of these

Ans. (d) There are various features of mobile device such as bluetooth, Wi-Fi, camera, GPS, etc.

5. The top part of the screen is called the ……… .
(a) Status bar (b) Main part
(c) Dock (d) All of these

Ans. (a) Status bar is the top part of screen which displays icons to shows network signal, Wi-Fi, etc.

6. Which of the following device is used to enter information into the computer?
(a) Output (b) Input
(c) Computer (d) Memory

Ans. (b) Input device is a hardware device that sends data or information into the computer system.

7. It is used to record voice on the computer.
(a) Projector (b) Speakers
(c) Microphone (d) Scanner

Ans. (c) Microphone is an input device that used to record voice on computer.

8. Which of the following is a brain of computer?
(a) RAM (b) ROM
(c) ALU (d) CPU

Ans. (d) CPU is Central Processing Unit which also known as brain of computer.

9. The bandwidth is usually expressed in
(a) bits per second (b) bytes per second
(c) Both (a) and (b) (d) None of these

Ans. (c) In digital devices, the bandwidth is usually expressed in bits per second (bps) or bytes per second (Bps).

10. ……… is a document present on a computer that is connected to the Internet.
(a) Web page (b) Website
(c) Browser (d) Server

Ans. (a) Web page is a document present on a computer that is connected to the Internet. There are hundreds of web pages in a website.

11. World Wide Web is made up of
(a) web page
(b) web browser
(c) a system to transfer information
(d) All of the above

Ans. (d) All of the above

12. E-mails can be sent to multiple users along with the
(a) procedure (b) attachments
(c) subjects (d) accounts

Ans. (b) E-mails can be sent to multiple users alongwith the attachments, where attachment is a type of file.

Fill in the Blanks

1. Mobile phones are ……… tools for talking to people but smartphones are more advanced.

Ans. ICT

2. ……… allows you to play and listen to songs and music.

Ans. Music

3. Lower part of the screen which is called the ……… .

Ans. Dock

4. Input and output devices are also called ……… .

Ans. Peripherals

5. .... port is used for connecting the computer system to the power supply.

Ans. Power

6. The BIOS first does a ....

Ans. Self test

7. Keys labelled from .... to .... are function keys.

Ans. F1, F12

8. 1 Mbps is equal to ....

Ans. 1000 kbps

9. To view a web page you need a .... on your computer.

Ans. Web browser

10. .... folder holds all the E-mail you have started writing but not yet sent.

Ans. Drafts

True/False

1. The output display of a mobile device is a touch screen.

Ans. True

2. Drag is similar to right clicking your mouse.

Ans. False

3. Input devices bring information from the computer to the user.

Ans. False

4. Smartphones are now being used to stay connected with social media.

Ans. True

5. Calls app is used to make calls in phones.

Ans. False

6. Processing unit acts like a receiver and a manager of a company.

Ans. False

7. Postal mail is written with paper and pen.

Ans. True

8. E-mail comes into the Inbox of the receiver's E-mail account.

Ans. True

9. The Internet is a huge network of computers around the world.

Ans. True

10. Notepad will have the extension .doc.

Ans. False

Match the Columns

1. Match the following columns.

	Column I		Column II
A.	Input device	1.	Control unit
B.	Output device	2.	Scanner
C.	Memory	3.	Hard disk
D.	CPU	4.	Arithmetic logic
E.	ALU	5.	Projector

Ans. A → 2; B → 5; C → 3; D → 1; E → 4

Short Answer (SA) Type Questions

1. What do you mean by tablet?

Ans. A tablet is a mini computer with input, output and processing functions that are all combined into one touchscreen, where you can do various tasks just by touching its screen.

2. Name any four apps which installed on smartphones by default.

Ans. Phone, Calendar, Camera, Mail

3. What is the difference TV and radio?

Ans. Radio is used to broadcast audio while TV is used to broadcast audio visual information to many people.

4. Name the online stores including for Android phone and Apple phone.

Ans. Google Play Store for Android phone

Apple App Store for Apple phone

5. What is the use of Maps app in phone?

Ans. Maps app helps you find directions to where you want to go.

6. Define the following.

(i) Wi-Fi

(ii) Chargeable battery

Ans. (i) **Wi-Fi** is a wireless network technology that helps you connect to the local area network.

(ii) **Chargeable battery** is a portable power pack which can be recharged. It allows you to use the device anywhere.

7. What is peripheral? Name any two peripheral devices.

Ans. Input and output devices are also called peripherals. Two peripheral devices are keyboard and monitor.

8. Define motherboard.

Ans. Motherboard also referred to as a system board, is the main circuit board inside a computer. It connects input, processing and output devices. It also includes controllers for devices like the hard drive, DVD drive, keyboard and mouse.

9. List any two ports that can use to connect to a computer.

Ans. (i) **Display port** It connects the monitor or any display unit to the computer using cable.

(ii) **Audio port** It helps to connect microphone, speakers and headphones to a computer system.

10. What are the basic functions performed when a computer starts?

Ans. Refer to text on Pg 50.

11. How to create a new file using a text editor in Ubuntu?

Ans.
- To open a text editor, type 'editor' in the search dialog box. Then, double click the text editor option. This will open a blank document.
- Where you can add text.

12. What do you need to connect to the Internet?

Ans. To connect to the Internet, you need
- A device, such as a computer, laptop or mobile.
- A connection device, i.e. a modem.

13. What is World Wide Web?

Ans. Refer to text on Pg 51.

14. Give any two advantages of E-mail.

Ans. (i) The delivery of messages is very fast.

(ii) Pictures, documents and other files can also be attached to messages.

15. Explain file and folder.

Ans. **Files** These are the collection of data stored on auxiliary storage media. The name given to a file or document by the user is called **file name.** Each file has a specific filename and has a file extension that identifies the file type.

Folders These are containers that you can use to store files. Folders can also store other folders, i.e. sub-folders. You can create any number of sub-folders and each can hold any number of files and additional sub-folders.

16. Define social networking.

Ans. Refer to text on Pg 51.

17. List any two important parts of a web browser.

Ans. (i) **Address bar** You can type the address/URL of a web page in this box and press Enter. The browser will display the page linked to that URL.

(ii) **Tabbed browsing** It allows a user to view multiple pages in the same window.

18. How can the E-mail be delete?

Ans. Refer to text on Pg 55.

Self Assessment

Multiple Choice Questions

1. Smartphones can work on following operating system(s)?
   (a) Android (b) Apple iOS (c) Windows (d) All of these
2. Which of the following basic controls help you to listen to voice calls?
   (a) Earpiece (b) Volume button (c) Mic (d) Microphone
3. Which of the following is an input device?
   (a) Printer (b) Plotter (c) Scanner (d) Projector
4. Which memory depands on voltage?
   (a) RAM (b) ROM (c) Hard disk (d) CD
5. It serves as a platform through which users can use or share information.
   (a) Website (b) Web page (c) WWW (d) Browser

Fill in the Blanks

1. A/An .... is a document present on a computer that is connected to the Internet.
2. A password should be at least .... characters.
3. Connects to the .... in the phone and takes photos and videos.
4. The output displays of a mobile device is a ....
5. .... is a primary memory which does not depend on voltage.

True/False

1. 1024 gigabyte make 1 terabyte.
2. Hardware will be useful without the software.
3. Once you finish working, you must not log out the computer.
4. Insert, Delete and Backspace are command keys.
5. E-mail is written only on a computer.

Match the Columns

1. Match the following columns.

	A		B
A.	Input device	1.	Projector
B.	Output device	2.	Floppy
C.	Operating system	3.	Bar code reader
D.	File extension	4.	Android
E.	Storage	5.	.txt

Short Answer (SA) Type Questions

1. What are the uses of ICT?
2. Write any two sectors where ICT used for.
3. Define Global Positioning System.
4. Give any two differences between input device and output device.
5. List any two storage devices.
6. What is online banking?
7. How can hyperlink help to switch next page in website?
8. Write the steps to forward the E-mail.

UNIT

04

Entrepreneurship Skills-I

Chapter Checklist

- Business
- Types of Business Activities
- Entrepreneurship
- Distinguishing Characteristics of Entrepreneurship and Wage Employment
- Types of Business Activities
- Entrepreneurship Development Process

Business

Business is an economic activity related with continuous and regular production and distribution of goods and services for satisfying human needs.

Businesses can be for profit entities or non-profit entity or organisation. Profit entities is one whose main goal is to make money. Non-profit entity or organisation usually have other non business goals, such as helping the community.

But sometimes, there is a gap between what is needed and what is available. This gap is used by some people as an opportunity by providing necessary products and services. Such people are called entrepreneur.

In other words, an entrepreneur is a person who is self-employed, is willing to take a calculated risk and brings in a new idea or method to start a business.

But, all self employed person are not entrepreneurs. A shopkeeper cannot be called an entrepreneur unless he uses a new idea or method in the business.

Types of Business Activities

Broadly a business can belong to one of the following categories:

(a) **Product Business** A business where a seller and buyer exchange an item, which can be seen and touched, is called a product based business. For example, A sports shop.

(b) **Service Business** A business where a seller helps the buyer to finish some work. For example, A cricket coaching centre.

(c) **Hybrid Business** A business in which both product and services are sold is referred as Hybrid business. For example, Restaurants where the food itself is the product sold and the catering is the service provided.

Differences between Product and Service Business

The key differences between product and service business activities can be summarised as follows:

Categories	Product Business	Service Business
Seen and touched	Product can be seen and touched. Customer pays for physical exchange of thing under this business.	Service cannot be seen or touched. Customer pays for an experience under this business.
Stored	Product can be made and stored.	A service cannot be stored.
Mode and transported	Product can be made at home or factory. It can be transported.	A service cannot be made or transported.
Same quantity and quality	The quality and quantity of the product will be same every time.	The quality and quantity of a service can be different at different times under this business.

Types of Product Based Business

There are two types of product based business:

(a) **Manufacturing Businesses** In manufacturing businesses, products are first made in factories and then sold in market.

(b) **Trade Businesses** In trade businesses, products are transported from factory to warehouses and shops near to customers where trade businesses buy and sell a product. Examples of these business include wholesalers, distributors and retail shops.

Types of Businesses in Our Community

Based on size

- **Micro Enterprise** A micro enterprise is a business enterprise where the investment in plant and machinery or equipment is not more than INR 1 crore and turnover does not exceed INR 5 crores.
- **Small Enterprise** A small enterprise is a business enterprise where the investment in plant and machinery or equipment is not more than INR 10 crore and turnover does not exceed INR 50 crores.
- **Medium Enterprise** A medium enterprise is a business enterprise where the investment in plant and machinery or equipment is not more than INR 50 crore and turnover does not exceed INR 250 crores.

Based on legal form

- **Sole Proprietorship** In a sole proprietorship, the ownership and control of the business is with one single person, and the liability of the owner is not separate from the entity.
- **One Person Company** A One Person company also has only one person as a member, who acts in the capacity of both, a shareholder and a director, but an OPC is legally separate from its owners. There is no threat on the owner's personal property in case of unmet liabilities.
- **Partnership** Partnership is a legal form, where at least two people, or more start a business as co-founders or co-owners and divide the share as per agreement. The partners are personally liable for an unlimited amount of liabilities.
- **Limited Liability Partnership** In a Limited Liability Partnership, there are two or more partners. In this, no one single partner or owner is individually responsible for any other partner's or member's negligence or misconduct or liability.
- **Company** A company is defined as a legal entity formed to get engaged in business, by a group of individuals. Usually, these individuals have limited liability, and the capital in units of equal value of a company are called 'shares'. Company can be public or private.

Based on sector

- **Primary Sector** This sector includes businesses that involve extraction, retrieval, harvest and production of raw materials using natural products from the earth. For example, some raw materials include coal, wood, grains, iron, corn etc. Thus, some primary sectors include mining, agriculture, fishing, horticulture etc.
- **Secondary Sector** The main activity of businesses in this sector is transformation of raw materials into finished goods. It takes products from primary sector and organizes all factors of production to make utility as well as luxury products.
- **Tertiary Sector** This sector is defined by provision of services to businesses and customers. It is completely based on a service and there is no production of goods involved.

Check Point 01

1. Name any two business activities.
2. Give the example of hybrid business.
3. How many types of product based business are there?
4. Name one sector of primary, secondary and tertiary.

Entrepreneurship

The process of developing a business plan, launching and running a business using innovation to meet customer needs and to make profit is known as entrepreneurship.

Ideas created by an entrepreneur can be of many kinds; new types of products, new services e.g. home delivery, credit services, new marketing ideas, cost reduction ideas, etc.

An **enterprise** is a project or undertaking that is bold and fulfills need and wants of the society which no longer has ever addressed.

Entrepreneurship Development

It involves enabling entrepreneurs through institution-building learing & development programs and structured training. Largely, the objective of these programs is to empower budding entrepreneurs to start and run their business effectively and efficiently. These programs cover aspects of entrepreneurial skills, business planning, fundraising, setting up of a new venture and growth & development strategies.

Role of Entrepreneurship

- **Capital Formation** Entrepreneurship leads to value addition and creation of wealth, because entrepreneurs promote capital formation by mobilising the idle savings of public.
- **Employment Generation** There is potential for increase in large-scale employment opportunities with increase in entrepreneurial activity. As more enterprises, offices, factories, businesses, trading entities etc. are set up, numerous job opportunities are created for skilled, unskilled and unemployed people, especially in developing countries.
- **Balanced Regional Development** Entrepreneurship helps to remove regional disparities through setting up of industries in less developed and backward areas. Micro businesses and cottage industries also play a role in increasing entrepreneurial activity in many specific cultural regions.
- **Value Creation** Value creation occurs when the worth of products and services increases for a customer base and a business earns profit by selling the product or service to fulfil customer needs and wants. Value is created when outputs are more valuable than inputs. Value creation is the foundation of every entrepreneurial activity or business.
- **Wealth Distribution** Wealth and income are distribution across people and geographies due to entrepreneurship and transaction-based activities. Employees are paid salaries, vendors are paid for their supplies, goods are sold in multiple markets, services are provided at large scale etc. This stimulates distribution of wealth to larger sections of society.
- **Industrialization and Development** Establishment of even a single enterprise can lead to beginning of a new industry. In a specific region, if a business is set up and seen to be a profitable opportunity, it is likely that others will get motivated to set up similar businesses. Additionally a business might require certain inputs, which leads to setting up of businesses that can supply those inputs. Hence, entrepreneurship catalyses industrialization in almost a chain reaction form, which in turn contributes positively to economic and infrastructural development.

Rewards of Entrepreneurship

- **Economic Development** Some features of economic development include optimal use of resources, creation of new ideas, wealth generation, continuous flow of money, skill building etc. All these factors are enabled due to entrepreneurship and are essential for economic development of a nation.
- **Enterprise and Business Creation** Business creation is a direct result of entrepreneurship. Many types of enterprises can be created by coordinating and combining different types of resources such as physical, financial, human, intellectual and entrepreneurial skills such as risk taking, innovation, leadership, resource planning etc.
- **Capacity Building** Skilled development and training is a significant reward of entrepreneurship as an entrepreneur invests in training employees and building their managerial capabilities. Similarly, an entrepreneur also develops his/her own capabilities by solving problems, making decisions, embracing failures, experimenting with alternative approaches etc.
- **Improved Standard of Living** With entrepreneurship, customers have many options of choosing from different products and services to solve the same purpose. This variety and availability of improved goods and services offered by enterprises leads to higher standards of living.

Qualities of a Successful Entrepreneur

An entrepreneur needs to have the following set of qualitites:

(a) **Patience** Success may not be achieved quickly. It is important for an entrepreneur to have patience while running the business.

(b) **Positivity** When people starts a business, they may face lots of difficulties and failure. An entrepreneur should stay positive and continue to work hard to achieve this goal.

(c) **Hardworking** Every new business goes through failures and therefore, an entrepreneur needs to work hard till he becomes successful.

(d) **Never Giving up and Perseverance** It is necessary for an entrepreneur to continuously work hard towards his own and company's goals. The entrepreneur must not give up even he/she suffers failure. He/she must demonstrate perseverance and work hard to achieve his/her goal.

(e) **Confidence** An entrepreneur needs to be very confident while taking decisions about his business. He/she also needs to communicate confidently with the customers.

(f) **Open to Trial and Error** Entrepreneur needs to be open to new ideas and try them without fear of failure. Entrepreneur will have to use trial and error method while starting a business. He/she should also experiment with different ideas in order to become successful.

(g) **Creativity and Innovation** An entrepreneur should come up with original and creative solution to a problem after analysing it with various prospective. They should also be able to recognise an opportunity in a problem and find an innovative solution.

(h) **Risk Bearing** An entrepreneur should be willing to take a calculated risk and is always open to new idea to make his/her business grow.

Distinguishing Characteristics of Entrepreneurship and Wage Employment

Entrepreneurship means, organising, developing and managing a business venture along with any of its risks in order to make profit.

- **Profit** The profit earned is the excess of earning. It is calculated by deducting all expenses from earning.
- **Risk** A risk is situation where result is unknown and may lead to a loss in future. Entrepreneurship is not without risks but entrepreneurs are not afraid of taking calculated risks. Risk may result in failure, however, entrepreneurs continue their courses of action till they succeed.

Characteristics of Entrepreneurship

Some of the distinguishing characteristics of entrepreneurship are:

- Risks taking nature.
- Believe in hard work and discipline.
- Entrepreneurs show adaptability and flexibility in achieving the goals and customer satisfaction.
- Knowledge of the product and services as per demand in market.
- Financially literate and has money management skills.
- Effective planner and executes efficiency.

Wage Employment

Wage employment is always consist of two parties. One is known as the employer and other is the employee. The continuity of the service in case of wage, employment depends on the terms and conditions laid down in the contract between these two parties. Continuity of service also depends upon the relationship between these two parties.

Difference between Entrepreneurship and Wage Employment

- An entrepreneur is the business owner and an employee is the worker and get a salary.
- An entrepreneurs are self-employed while the employees are wage earner.
- An entrepreneur work for self but wage earners work for others and get a salary for his work.
- The wage employment does not involve too much risk but entrepreneurship involves taking certain amount of calculated risks.

A Comparison between Entrepreneurship and Employment

Activities	In Entrepreneurship	In Employment
Allows a person to make money.	Yes	Yes
Finding solutions for a community problem by himself/herself.	Yes	No
The job done by the person is decided by himself/herself.	Yes	No
Use personal knowledge and interest to make money for oneself.	Yes	No
Use innovation and creativity to attract clients.	Yes	No
Keep most of the money, i.e., profit made for a product/service.	Yes	No
Take risk to make profit.	Yes	No

Benefits of Entrepreneurship

The various benefits include the following:

(a) **Do What You Are Interested In** Entrepreneurship allows to start something according to choice. These choice depend upon hobbies and skills of entrepreneur.

(b) **Work for Yourself, and Not for Other** Entrepreneur work for own and not for someone else. An entrepreneur decide the kind of work and how to do it.

(c) **Make Profits for Yourself** The principle focus of entrepreneurship is earning money. An entrepreneur decide how much money to earn and how to earn.

(d) **More Risk, More Profit** There are risks in entrepreneurship. It allows entrepreneur to decide how much risk to take. Usually, the larger the risk, the bigger could be profit.

Entrepreneurship Development Process

It is the process of enhancing the knowledge and skills of entrepreneurs with help of various training programme. Entrepreneurship development process can take place through formal and informal learning system.

- **Formal Learning System** In the formal learning system, training programmes are conducted to bring about awareness, knowledge and skill related to entrepreneurship.
- **Informal Learning System** It is a spontaneous process of learning through conversation, exploration and enlargement of the experience.

Steps of Starting a Business

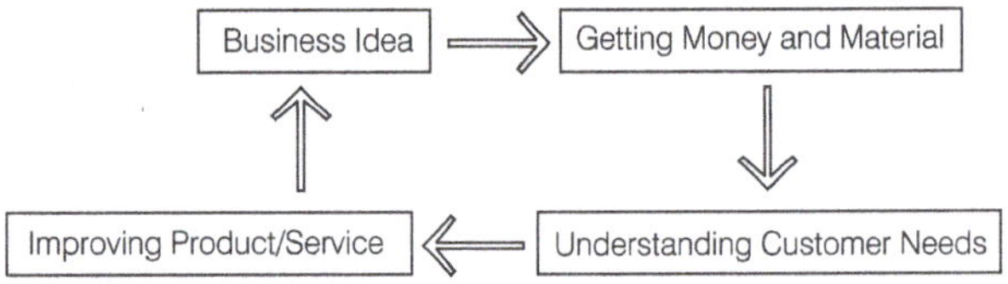

1. **Business Idea** The first step while starting a business is to come up with an idea. A business idea is based on
   (a) Interest of individual (b) Market need
2. **Getting Money and material** Second steps of starting business is the use of idea to start on a small scale with some money. It helps in buying basic material.
3. **Understanding Customer Need** Once entrepreneur starts selling, he/she will find out the likes and wants and also dislikes of customers.
4. **Improving Product/Service** He/she can use this knowledge of what your customer likes and does not likes to improve their product.

Check Point 02

1. What is enterprise?
2. Write the role of entrepreneurship as wealth distribution.
3. Wage employment is always consists of how many parties?
4. What is the importance of patience for successful Entrepreneur?

NCERT FOLDER

Check Your Progress Pg 138-139

A. Multiple choice questions

Read the questions carefully and circle the letter (a), (b), (c) or (d) that best answers the question.

1. Business is a (an) .... activity.
(a) social
(b) economic
(c) hazardous
(d) selling

Ans. (b) economic

2. What is the aim of entrepreneurship?
(a) Earn a profit
(b) Solve customers' need innovatively
(c) Both of the above
(d) None of the above

Ans. (c) Both of the above

B. Short Answer Questions

1. List three businesses seen around you. Share details of what the business does and how they run it?

Ans. Three businesses I have seen in my locality are:

(a) **Dolma Aunty, The Momo Seller** One aged lady, Dolma Aunty from Manipur has a small stall in our locality.

She is making vegetarian and chicken momos which she sells from 12 noon to 8 pm at night. Her momos are very popular among young generation. By selling momo, she is surviving in Delhi.

(b) **Naresh, The Burgerwala** A young man, named Naresh has a small stall nearby a park, where he sells fresh aloo tikki burger. As his food is very tasty, everybody likes it.

He sells burger from 4 pm to 9 pm at night and earns a good amount of money.

(c) **Pooja, The Beautician** Pooja is an enterprising girl who has taken a beautician course and also has marked for sometimes in a beauty parlour. Now, she is doing the business independently.

She has good contacts with her customers and charges less than the beauty parlour. Her service is satisfactory to like customers, thus she is doing well in her business.

C. Read the following statement and write 'Yes' or 'No' as to whether the person is an entrepreneur or not.

	Statement	Yes/No
1.	Ravi made tea for his friends in the office. Everyone liked the tea very much and told him that he is very good at making tea.	
2.	Savita, a house wife, needs extra money for her kids' tuition. She notices that in the afternoon, the children coming out of a nearby college look tired and hungry. She makes refreshing *Neembu Pani* and *samosas* and sells them to the students.	
3.	Rahul loves dogs. He plays with dogs of his friends' family. One day when they were going out-of-station, they asked Rahul to take care of their dog. Rahul thought that this was a good idea, 'taking care of dogs when the owner is traveling'. He started his own company which is like a 'hotel for dogs'. When the dog-owners travel, they leave their dogs at this hotel and pay the company money for each day, they take care of the dog. Is Rahul an entrepreneur?	
4.	Monica noticed that her neighbours used to face a problem. They had to leave their young baby behind when they went for work. Monica started going to this house in the evening to take care of the baby for them. Her neighbours were very happy and used to give her chocolates for doing that.	

Ans. 1. No, 2. Yes, 3. Yes, 4. No

Check Your Progress Pg 141-142

A. Short Answer Question

Answer the following questions in your own words.

1. Gulab lives in a small village in Rajasthan. She noticed that all the women in her village were good at making paintings and handicraft product. She collected money and started a business. Gulab would help the women to get material from cities and support them in making latest designs. She would then arrange for these paintings and handicraft products to be sold in big cities. How do you think Gulab, is helping her society as an entrepreneur?

Ans. Gulab helps like poor women in her village by supply them raw material and modern designs. She has made arrangement for selling of this product. This helps the women to be economically independent. By helping the women, he directly helps the community. In this way, by his business idea, she has helped her society a lot.

2. Give examples of three entrepreneurs you know who live around you. Write how they are helping your city?

Ans. Do it yourself.

Check Your Progress Pg 147

A. Short Answer Questions

1. Identify qualities of the following entrepreneurs. Also write why you think this person has this quality or the qualities.

(a) Anil wanted to do something very different and something no one has thought of before. He decided to start a special travel services for old people/senior citizens.

(b) Rakesh loves playing outdoors. He used to spend his evenings with his friends, playing games. But, he had seen that many of his friends didn't like playing outdoors because they didn't feel safe. He decided to open a playground for children of all ages, with proper security. He found an unused playground, got permission to use it and asked his friends to help him clean it. He hired a security guard for the playground. He charged a small fee for people who wanted to play. Both parents and children liked his idea, and started playing there regularly. His business helped children who would not play outdoor before.

(c) Radhika was a cook in a small restaurant in her area. She made enough money to support her husband and children. She decided to start her own food stall to sell Punjabi food. She would make special parathas. A few days after starting her business, the police came and told her that she was not allowed to run her stall in the area. Radhika did not give up. She started a Tiffin service through which she would deliver fresh food to people.

Ans. (a) Anil has decided to start a special travel services for senior citizens. There are lots of travelling agencies who entertained general people, but none of them has realised the need of senior citizens. Anil thought some special facilities like special travel discounts, specified medical facilities, healthy and light foods etc. are to be given by his travelling agency. Thus, Anil has the quality of an entrepreneur who thinks different.

(b) Rakesh is a sport person. He has changed his passion into business. He has knowledge of outdoor games. With this knowledge he has made the effective planning and extended it. Thus, he is a real entrepreneur.

(c) Radhika has started food service as she has like special attitude for cooking and ambition to do something big in life. She is a true entrepreneur as she does something she is interested in. By applying her cooking skill she has started the new business, i.e. tiffin service through which she would deliver fresh food to people.

2. Do you think you have the qualities of an entrepreneur in you? If yes, give examples when you have shown these qualities.

Ans. Do it yourself.

3. Read the story of Sushma, the toy maker once again and fill in the boxes mentioning the various qualities that Sushma might have possessed as an entrepreneur.

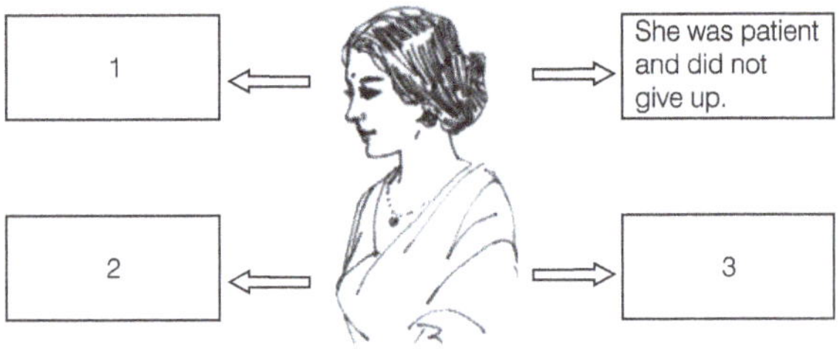

Ans. 1. She made huge efforts to persuade her customers to buy her toys.
2. She was thinking positively and improved her product.
3. She became partner with different toy shops and created a website to sell online.

Check Your Progress Pg 152

A. Fill in the blanks

1. State whether the person engaged in the activity mentioned below is an Entrepreneur or an Employee.

(a) Rahul starts a shop to sell Chaat and special Paani Puri. He is an ....

(b) Shahid becomes the manager of a dealership selling food products. He is an ....

(c) Ritu leaves the company she worked for and starts catering food for marriage programmes. She is an ....

Ans. (a) Entrepreneur (b) Employee (c) Entrepreneur

B. Short Answer Questions

1. List any four characteristics of entrepreneurship.

Ans. Four characteristics of entrepreneurship are
(i) Risks taking nature.
(ii) Believe in hard work and discipline.
(iii) Financially literate and has money management skills.
(iv) Effective planner and executes efficiency.

2. List any two characteristics of wage employment.

Ans. Two characteristics of wage employment are

1. Allows a person to make money (get a salary).
2. Wage employment work for others.

3. Name any one factors that is common to both entrepreneurship and wage employment on contract basis.

Ans. Aim of earning money is common to both entrepreneurship and wage employment on contract basis.

Check Your Progress Pg 155

A. Fill in the blanks

State the type of business–product, service or hybrid

1. Arun bakery, which makes and sells bread to people. ....

Ans. Product business

2. Ram's repair shop, which repairs motorcycle. ....

Ans. Service business

3. Hari's hair-salon, where he cuts hair for women and men. ....

Ans. Service business

B. Short Answer Question

1. What are the three types of business activities? Explain with examples?

Ans. The three types of business activities are

- **Product Business** A business where a seller and buyer exchange an item, which can be seen and touched, is called a product-based business. For example, A Sports Shop.
- **Service Business** A business where a seller helps the buyer to finish some work. For example, A cricket coaching center.
- **Hybrid Business** A hybrid is the one where the business is doing both selling product and selling services. For example, Rahul starting a sports academy for coaching and selling sports equipment.

Check Your Progress Pg 158-159

A. Fill in the blanks

1. Write P-Product, S-Service and H-Hybrid for the following businesses.

(a) Ice-cream seller: ....

(b) Restaurant/Cafeteria owner: ....

(c) Car-driving/School owner: ....

Ans. (a) P-Product (b) H-Hybrid (c) S-Service

B. Short Answer Questions

1. What are the key differences between product and service-based businesses?

Ans. Key differences between product and service-based businesses are as follows

Product Business	Service Business
Product can be seen and touched. Customer pays for physical exchange of things.	Service cannot be seen or touched. Customer here pays for an experience.
A product can be made and stored in a shop or a warehouse (usually).	A service, for example, cutting hair, cannot be stored. Service is provided when a customer asks for it.

2. If you had a choice to start a business of your own, which business will you start (include in your reply the product or service that you would like to take up)? Why do you want to start this type of business?

Ans. If I have a choice to start my own business then I will start a cricket sports academy for coaching and selling. The business will follow the hybrid type of business model, where both selling products (sports item) and services (coaching) will be provided. I love to play cricket. I have participated in many state level matches. I have enough experience of playing cricket. Applying my experience and passion, I want to start this business.

3. What is the meaning of manufacturing and trading based business?

Ans. Manufacturing businesses are the businesses that make a product and sell it. Products are usually made in factories. Trading based businesses buy a product and sell it. They transport the product from the factory to warehouse and then wholesalers, distributors and retail shops.

Check Your Progress Pg 162

A. Match the following

1. Match the following columns.

	Column A		Column B
1.	Business idea	A.	Arun goes to the bank to get loan for the shop.
2.	Get money	B.	Arun and Shyam are thinking about selling tea in front of their school.
3.	Customer needs	C.	Arun and Shyam decide to sell tea along with free biscuits.
4.	Attract customers	D.	Shyam takes his tea samples to customers to understand their taste preferences.

Ans. 1 → B, 2 → A, 3 → D, 4 → C,

B. Short answer questions

1. My customers are not buying my food product because they do not like the flavour of it. What step of the business should I follow next?

Ans. If my customers are not buying food products due to its flavour, I will try to improve the product/services in next steps. I will try to know their preferred taste and flavour and make product accordingly.

2. Write the four steps of entrepreneurship development. Give one example.

Ans. Four steps of entrepreneurship development are

1. Business idea
2. Getting money and material
3. Understanding customer needs
4. Improving product/service.

For example,

(i) Rakesh wants to open a small food stall near a railway station.

(ii) He asked his father and uncle for a small loan to set up the stall.

(iii) After establishing the stall he found that his customers like tasty and cheap foods.

(iv) By applying his experience in a South Indian food stall, Rakesh has started to make Dosas and Idlis for his customers, which are both pocket friendly and delicious.

SUMMARY

- An entrepreneur is a person, who is self-employed, is willing to take a calculated risk and brings a new idea to start a business.
- Patience, positivity, hard working, never giving up and perserverance, confidence, open to trial and error, creativity and innovation, risk bearing are the different qualities of a successful entrepreneur.
- Entrepreneurship means organising, developing and managing a business venture alongwith any of its risks in order to make profit.
- Wage employment consists of employer and employee.
- Generally, business activities are of three types, *viz*, product business, service business and hybrid business.
- There are mainly two types of product based business, i.e. manufacturing business and trade business.
- Entrepreneurship development process can take place through formal learning system and informal learning system.
- There are mainly four steps for starting a business, *viz*, business idea, getting money and material, understanding customer need and improving product and services.

Exam Practice

Multiple Choice Questions

1. Business is an activity for satisfying
(a) entrepreneur (b) owner
(c) new idea (d) human needs

Ans. (*c*) new idea

2. Businesses cater to the need of the
(a) area (b) society
(c) market (d) village

Ans. (*b*) society

3. An entrepreneur is a self employed person and is willing to take a
(a) product and service
(b) satisfying human need
(c) calculated risk
(d) regular production

Ans. (*c*) calculated risk

4. The role and benefits of entrepreneurship are
(a) Social development
(b) Improved standard of living
(c) Optimal use of resources
(d) All of the above

Ans. (*d*) All of the above

5. Creation of more job by entrepreneur is
(a) Economic development
(b) Social development
(c) Living standard development
(d) Service development

Ans. (*b*) Social development

6. Entrepreneurs uses optimal ways of using the resources to
(a) reduce cost (b) increase profit
(c) Both of these (d) None of these

Ans. (*c*) Both of these

7. Qualities of entrepreneurs are
(a) hardworking (b) never giving up
(c) perseverance (d) All of these

Ans. (*d*) All of these

8. Experiment with different idea is the quality related to
(a) perseverance (b) confidence
(c) trial and error (d) creativity

Ans. (*c*) trial and error

9. The quality of creativity and innovation of entrepreneurs is related to
(a) patience (b) positivity
(c) hardworking (d) solution

Ans. (*d*) solution

10. Ability to take up risks is a
(a) role of entrepreneur
(b) quality of entrepreneur
(c) characteristics of entrepreneurship
(d) None of the above

Ans. (*c*) characteristics of entrepreneurship

11. The employees are
(a) self employed (b) wage-earner
(c) take risk (d) self job decider

Ans. (*b*) wage-earner

12. A risk may lead to a
(a) excess of earning (b) loss in future
(c) human needs (d) growth

Ans. (*b*) loss in future

13. Wage employment is always consists of
(a) one party (b) two parties
(c) three parties (d) four parties

Ans. (*b*) two parties

14. The wage employment does not involve too much
(a) salary (b) opportunity
(c) innovation (d) risk

Ans. (*d*) risk

15. Entrepreneurship allows to start something according to
(a) market (b) choice
(c) need (d) innovation

Ans. (*b*) choice

16. The principle focus of entrepreneurship is
(a) more risk (b) more work
(c) more profit (d) more job

Ans. (*c*) more profit

17. Product and services both are sold in
(a) Product business (b) Service business
(c) Hybrid business (d) General business

Ans. (*c*) Hybrid business

18. Product can be seen and touched in
(a) Product business
(b) Service business
(c) Hybrid business
(d) General business

Ans. (*a*) Product business

19. Manufacturing businesses are the types of
(a) Trade businesses
(b) Product based business
(c) Hybrid based business
(d) Service based business

Ans. (*b*) Product based business

20. Which one is not steps of starting a business?
(a) Business idea
(b) Getting money and material
(c) Understanding customer needs
(d) Trade services

Ans. (*d*) Trade services

Fill in the Blanks

1. Entrepreneurs sell products like a tractor, a mobile phone or a mobile service. It come under the role of entrepreneurship of ....

Ans. Improved standard of living.

2. Ramesh is chai wala selling tea near a busy bus stop. He is a ....

Ans. Business man

3. Sushma kept working for two years before success came her way. This quality of Sushma came under ....

Ans. patience

4. Raja was confident about the quality and effective use of her toys. It is sign of (quality of) ....

Ans. Confidence

5. The .... earned is the excess earning after deducting all expenses.

Ans. profit

6. Pragya, the delivery girl is in the type of business called ....

Ans. Service business

7. Sports academy is ....

Ans. Hybrid business

8. Continuity of service of wage employment depends upon the relationship between ....

Ans. Employer and employee

True/False

1. Innovation is necessary for entrepreneurship.

Ans. True

2. Business can be for profit entities or non-profit entities.

Ans. True

3. All self employed person are entrepreneurs.

Ans. False

4. A business started by an entrepreneur is usually a very large business.

Ans. False

5. More benefits at lower prices products and services at competitive prices.

Ans. True

6. An entrepreneur needs to be very confident while taking decisions about his business.

Ans. True

Match the Columns

1. Match the following.

Column A		Column B	
1.	Economic Development	A.	Quality of a successful Entrepreneur.
2.	Confidence	B.	Role of Entrepreneurship.
3.	Risks taking nature	C.	Benefits of Entrepreneurship.
4.	More risk, more profit	D.	Characteristics of Entrepreneurship.
5.	Product business	E.	Types of business Activities.

Ans. 1 → B; 2 → A; 3 → D; 4 → C; 5 → E

2. Match the following.

Column A		Column B	
1.	Stationary shop	A.	Salary
2.	Plumbing shop	B.	Product business
3.	Hair cut Barbar shop	C.	Economic activity
4.	Wage employment	D.	Service business
5.	Business	E.	Hybrid business

Ans. 1 → B; 2 → E; 3 → D; 4 → A; 5 → C

Short Answer (SA) Type Questions

1. What are the key differences between entrepreneurship and enterprise?

Ans. The process of developing a business plan, launching and running a business and also using innovation to meet customer needs for making profit is known as entrepreneurship.
An enterprise is a project or undertaking that is bold and fulfills a need and wants of the society. The need previously unfulfilled.

2. What are the key differences between patience and Hardworking?

Ans. Success may not be achieved quickly. It is important for an entrepreneur to have patience while running the business. Every new business goes through failures and therefore, an entrepreneur needs to work hard till it becomes successful. It is necessary for an entrepreneur to continuously work hard to achieve his company's goal.

3. List any two difference between entrepreneurship and wage employment.

Ans. The two differences between entrepreneurship and wage employment are

(a) An entrepreneur is the business owner and an employee is the worker and get a salary.

(b) The wage employment does not involve too much risk but entrepreneurship involves taking certain amount of calculated risks.

4. List any two comparison of activities between entrepreneurship and employment.

Ans. Two comparison of activities between entrepreneurship and employment are

(a) The job done by the person is decided by himself or herself. But in employment, the job done by the is decided by employer.

(b) Use personal knowledge and interest to make money for oneself is possible in entrepreneurship not in employment.

5. Explain any two steps of entrepreneurship development.

Ans. Two steps of entrepreneurship development are

(a) **Business Idea**

The first step while starting a business is to come up with an idea. A business idea is based on

- Interest of individual
- Market need.

(b) **Getting money and material**

Second steps of starting business is the use of idea to start on a small scale with some money. It helps in buying basic material.

Self Assessment

Multiple Choice Questions

1. A shopkeeper cannot be called an entrepreneur unless he uses a new
   (a) risk (b) idea (c) project (d) customer
2. Prices of products come down when the entrepreneurs complete in the
   (a) economy (b) resources (c) market (d) method
3. It is necessary for an entrepreneur to continuously work
   (a) deal (b) idea (c) use (d) hard
4. An entrepreneur is always open to new idea to make his/her business
   (a) grow (b) method (c) duration (d) risk
5. Profit is calculated by deducting all expenses from
   (a) earning (b) future (c) risk (d) method

Fill in the Blanks

1. .... can be for profit entities or non profit organisations.
2. An .... is a project or under taking that is bold and fulfills a need first time of the society.
3. An .... complete in the market, price of products come down.
4. An .... come up with original and creative solutions.
5. The .... does not involve too much risk.

True/False

1. Entrepreneurship involves taking uncertain amount of risk.
2. A business where a seller and buyer exchange any kind of item is called a product-based business.
3. There are three types of product based business.
4. Understanding customer needs is the steps of starting a business.

Match the Columns

1. Match the following

	Column A		Column B
1.	Seen and touched	A.	Product Business
2.	Money in circulation	B.	Social Development
3.	Creation of job	C.	Money in Circulation
4.	First step of business	D.	Trade Business
5.	Wholesales	E.	Idea

Short Answer (SA) Type Questions

1. What are the key differences between creativity and Innovation?
2. Give Distinguished characteristics of entrepreneurship and wage employment.
3. List any two benefits of entrepreneurship.
4. List any two difference between Manufacturing businesses and Trade businesses.

UNIT

05

Green Skills-I

Chapter Checklist

- Introduction to Environment
- Natural Resources
- Ecosystem and Factors Causing Imbalance
- Effect of Environmental Imbalances
- Saving the Environment : What Can You Do?
- Reduce, Reuse, Recycle
- Conserving Natural Resources
- Sustainable Development and Green Economy
- Biodiversity
- What is Sustainable Development?
- Green Growth
- Green Economy
- Skill Development for Green Economy
- Green Skills
- What are Green Jobs?
- Green Projects

Introduction to Environment

Everything around us forms our environment. It affects all aspects of our life, likewise our day to day activities also affect the environment.

We depend on different environmental resources, like; Forests, Grasslands, Rivers, Plants etc for our food and other needs.

Over the years with economic development there has been an increase in environmental pollution that threatens the stability of environment. We need to plan the maintenance of the environment in a sustainable manner, so that we can enjoy the good environment, it may be sustainable agriculture, developing eco-fashion design, manufacturing of solar panel, etc.

Relationship Between Society and Environment

The society constitutes of group of people living together in a community, a village, a city, a town, a states or a country. It is these group of people with their own set of ideologies and beliefs that affects the environment. If a group of people believe that rivers are sacred, then all people belonging to that group will resonate the practices that support their belief.

If a group of people believe that killing of animals is a heinous crime, the people in that community will reflect it in their behaviour shaping their relationship. But, if a group of people is greedy and is concerned to accumulate wealth, their actions will echo their mind-set and will have adverse effect on the environment.

As said every action have an equal and opposite reaction. So, is this true in case of the Society and Environment. To fulfil our greed, we are exploiting the resources nature has given us, while nature has its own way to show its fury.

Issues like Global Warming, Climate change, other man-made disasters are a few that have a directly implication of man's activities. Natural Disasters like earthquakes have a direct impact on the economy hence affecting the society. Hence, it may be concluded that both society and environment are interdependent and cannot exist in isolation.

Natural Resources

A resource is any natural or artificial substance, energy or organism which is used by humans for its welfare.

Natural resources are the resources that are available freely in nature such as water, land, soil, rocks, forests, animals, fossil fuels and minerals. They are the basis of life and all life forms depend on them.

Natural resources are used to survive and to function properly.

Natural resources can be consumed directly or indirectly. Humans depend on forest directly for food, biomass, health, recreation etc. Indirectly forests help in climate regulation, prevention of floods, storm protection etc.

Artificial Resources

Resources developed by humans during the growth of civilisation are called artificial resources. For example, biogas, thermal electricity, plastics etc.

Natural resource can be in solid, liquid or gas form. They can be organic, inorganic, metallic or non-metallic.

Different forms of natural resources are given below:

(i) Land Resource

Land as a resource is used for food production, for residence and recreation. It is a finite (limited) resource, used for agriculture and non-agriculture such as developing infrastructure.

(ii) Forest Resource

A forest is a natural, self sustaining community characterised by the presence of trees. Wood from forest is used in making furniture, tool handles, railway sleepers, matches, ploughs, bridges, boats etc. Wood is also used as an energy source for cooking and keeping warm.

Flora and fauna of forests provide other resources like tannins, gums, drugs, spices, waxes, honey, horns, musk, ivory, hides etc.

(iii) Water Resource

Water covers about three quarter of Earth's surface which includes water in rivers, lakes, oceans, underground aquifers etc. It is a necessary element for life and vital in agriculture, industry, household, recreation (activities like swimming, fishing) and in environmental activities.

(iv) Mineral Resource

Mineral deposit is a concentration of naturally occurring solid, liquid or gaseous material. They are present in or on the Earth's crust in such form that their extraction and conversion into useful materials are profitable now or in future. Minerals are non-renewable. They can be metals like iron, copper, aluminium or non-metals like salt, gypsum, clay, sand phosphates. Some minerals consist of a single element such as gold, silver, diamond, sulphur etc.

(v) Food Resources

Resources that are used as food or provide food for organisms are called food resources, e.g. plants. Agriculture is main source of plant food for human. Plants serve as food resource for herbivores and omnivores. They are eaten by animals and birds who become the food for carnivores and omnivores.

(vi) Energy Resources

Resources that produce heat, power that can be used as energy to produce electricity or to move objects are called energy resources.

Different types of energy resources are given below:

- Nuclear fusion e.g. solar energy.
- Gravity generated by Sun and Moon.
- Nuclear fission (atomic energy).
- Energy in the interior of the Earth.
- Energy stored in chemical bonds, e.g. fossil fuels.

Fossil Fuels

It provide huge amount of energy but they have harmful effects on the environment. They are also non-renewable.

Categories of Natural Resources

Natural resources can be categorised as follows

- **Inexhaustible Resources** The resources which cannot be exhausted by human consumption are called inexhaustible resources, e.g. solar radiation, wind power, water power, tidal power etc.
- **Exhaustible Resources** Resources that are available in limited quantities and are going to be exhausted due to continuous use are called exhaustible resources e.g. stock of coal. It is in limited quantity and it's continuous use will exhaust this resource.
- **Renewable Resources** Resources that are constantly available (like water) or can be replaced or recovered (like vegetative land) are called renewable resource. Some resource can be replaced but the process may take many years. They are not counted as renewable.

  Some exhaustible resources are naturally regenerated, e.g. forest trees and plants. They are renewable. But if the forest is totally cut down to get land for construction of buildings, then the forest cover is lost forever.
- **Renewable Energy Systems** Renewable resources that are constantly replaced and are less polluting, are used to produce energy such as hydropower (energy from moving water), solar, wind, geothermal (energy from the heat inside the Earth).
- **Non-Renewable Resources** The resources that cannot be easily replaced once they are destroyed or used up are called non-renewable resource, e.g. fossil fuels, minerals.

  It takes thousands of years for minerals to form again in a process called rock cycle, so it is a non-renewable resource.

  Some non-renewable resources are called **Inorganic Resources** as they come from non-living things like minerals, they come from rocks, land, soil etc.

Non-Renewable and Renewable Resources

Non-renewable Resources	Uses	Renewable Resource	Uses
Coal (Cheapest source of fuel)	Cooking, heating, used as fuel in power houses and factories	Water (2.5% fresh water on Earth)	Hydroelectricity from river water, sea tides and ocean tides
Petroleum (Petrol, diesel, mineral oil)	Run motor vehicles, furnaces and power houses	Sun	Solar energy in calculators, light street lamps, room heaters, water heaters
LPG (Liquified Petroleum Gas)	Cooking and running vehicles	Wind	Wind energy for running wind mills, grinding grains, pumping water
CNG (Compressed Natural Gas)	Running vehicles	Biomass (produced from plant and animal wastes)	Produce electricity and heat for cooking, lighting
Minerals	Gold, bauxite, mica, iron-ore, etc. have lot of uses	Soil	Provide shelter, agriculture
Nuclear Plants	Source of electricity	Forests	Preserve ecological balance, give clean air and forest products like wood, fuel, medicines

Ecosystem and Factors Causing Imbalance

Ecological imbalance is caused when natural or a man-made disturbance disrupts the natural balance of an ecosystem. Human activities have direct implication in causing ecological imbalance.

Following are the man-made disruption that causes ecological imbalance:

Over Exploitation

It takes place when harvesting of resources is more than their reproduction or replenishment (recovery). It means that a particular species or a resource is used up or taken away much faster than its natural population can recover or replace it.

For example, Removal of wild medicinal plant at a much faster rate than it can be replaced naturally. Over hunting, over fishing also makes a species extinct. Excessive grazing, destruction of forests, water acquifers and natural habitats are overexploitation of natural resources.

Mining

Mining takes place when mines are dug below the Earth's surface to get ores. The ores are then refined to extract valuable elements like metals, gems, minerals.

The environmental impacts of mining are erosion, formation of sinkholes and loss of biodiversity. Chemicals from the mines also cause contamination of soil, ground water and surface water.

Deforestation

Clearance of forest or stand of trees to convert that land to non-forest use for agriculture, construction etc. is deforestation. It causes loss of habitat for plant and animal species living in the forest and may lead to their extinction.

Pollution

The word is derived from the Latin word 'Polluere' meaning 'to soil' or 'defile (contaminate)'. Pollution is caused by pollutants which are unwanted solid, liquid or gaseous in nature.

Pollutants are produced due to human activity. They bring undesirable changes in our surroundings that have harmful effects on plants, animals and human beings.

For example, Factories release harmful chemicals in air, land and water thus contaminating the atmosphere and causing water pollution.

Fossil fuel emissions pollute the air as they emit carbon dioxide, methane and nitrous oxide on burning.

Types of Pollution

	Land Pollution	Water Pollution	Air Pollution
Definition	Damage to land due to presence of harmful substances on it.	Addition of harmful substances, disease causing germs to water bodies like rivers, lakes, sea, ocean.	Addition of harmful gases, particles, smoke in air.
Effects	• Diseases-dysentry, Cholera, Typhoid. • Contamination of land. • Less availability of land for agriculture, forest and houses.	• Diseases-dysentry, Diarrhoea, Jaundice, Typhoid • Less availability of clean drinking water. • Loss of local earning opportunities like fishing, tourism etc.	• Heart and breathing problems, cancers. • Lack of clean air. • Climate change, droughts, famines, floods.
Cause	• Deforestation, mining. • Use of excessive chemicals, (pesticides, fertilisers) in agriculture. • Release of sewage, toilet waste, waste from factories/houses • Dumping of chemical wastes, plastics.	• Release or leakage of sewage from sewer lines. • Throwing human waste/household waste in water. • Dumping of chemical wastes from factories and farms. • Dumping of plastics like water bottles. • Accidental oil leakage from ships.	• Burning of fossil fuels from vehicles, factories that include emissions like CO_2, methane, nitrous oxide, CFCs etc. • Burning crop residue and wastes. • Smoke from factories. • Dust from construction. • Emissions from pesticides and fertilisers.
Prevention	• Reduce waste. • Segregate (separate) waste before dumping. • Use more biodegradable products. • Adopt natural and organic methods of farming. • Plant trees.	• Do not throw waste, chemical into water bodies. • Do not throw chemicals, medicines, oils in drain. • Avoid use of pesticides, fertilisers. • Ensure proper treatment of sewage and factory waste. • Use water wisely.	• Use renewable sources of energy. • Avoid fuels and vehicles that create lot of pollution. • Stop people from burning wastes, crop residues. • Avoid pesticides, fertilisers that release harmful gases.

Types of Pollutants

	Biodegradable Pollutants	Non-Biodegradable Pollutants
Definition	Pollutants that can be broken down into simpler, harmless substances naturally by the action of moisture and bacteria.	Pollutants that cannot be broken down into simpler, harmless substances.
Examples	Vegetable/Fruit waste, sewage waste, paper, wood, cattle dung, agricultural waste from organic farms.	Plastics, insecticides, pesticides, chemicals like mercury or lead, aluminium, glass

Effects of Environmental Imbalances

Environmental degradation disrupts the delicate balance in nature. It changes the Earth in many ways. The ill-effects of environmental imbalances are described below :

Climate Change

Frequent changes in climate is the result of global warming and green house effect.

Global Warming

Global warming is the heating up of the Earth. This happen when the burning of fossil fuels like coal, petrol, diesel produce gases that trap and prevent Earth's heat from escaping.

Green House Effect

The Earth becomes hotter due to global warming which is caused by emission of gases that trap heat. This is called the **green house effect.**

Forest convert carbondioxide into carbon and oxygen. But the loss of forest cover and increasing release of green house gases through industrialsation contributes to green house effect.

Green House Gases

Green house gases occur naturally through decomposition of organic matter and through human activity like agriculture, burning of fossil fuels. These gases are water vapour, Carbondioxide (CO_2), Methane (CH_4), Nitrous Oxide (N_2O) and Ozone (O_3).

Some green house gases have no natural sources but are side products of industrial processes or specially manufactured for various purposes such as clearing agents, refrigerants and electrical insulators.

These are fluorinated gas : Chlorofluorocarbons (CFCs), Hydro Chlorofluorocarbons (HCFCs), Hydrofluorocarbons (HCFCs). These gases causes snow to melt very fast.

arbondioxide gas has increased by 31% since pre-industrial times. It causes more heat to be trapped in the lower atmosphere resulting in frequent floods, changes in climate, damage to crops and animal life.

Harmful Radiation

The atmosphere protects us from the harmful radiations from the Sun. It is done by the Ozone layer, a layer of gas all around the Earth in the atmosphere.

Cleaning chemicals, coolants in refrigerators and air-conditioners release substances such as chlorofluorocarbons that deplete the ozone layer. These chemicals destroy the ozone layer by making holes in it through which harmful radiations reach earth. The radiations cause increased incidence of health disorders such as skin cancer.

Natural Disasters

These include floods, earthquakes, landslides, storms etc. Human actions in exploiting natural resources for making dams, buildings aggravates the impact of natural calamities and disasters.

Saving the Environment : What can you do?

For saving the environment, there is need to educate people. Education gives people the knowledge and skills that they need to perform.

Educating people about the environment, through the environment and for the environment will enlighten them in utilising their knowledge and skills for saving the environment.

Education help in saving the environment in three ways :

1. Learning About The Environment

Learning about the environment focuses mainly on acquisition of knowledge and understanding of our surroundings and related issues.

2. Learning Through The Environment

It refers to the processes of learning while being engaged with environment inside and outside the classroom. Learning processes like observation, hands on experience, learning by doing, problem solving are focussed here. Direct contact with environment, helps in acquiring knowledge, skills, aesthetic appreciation (admiring nature) and practical experience of learning.

Damage to the environment can be reduced by developing skills and knowledge needed for efficient resource utilisation, green processes and technologies. Integrating this knowledge into businesses and daily activities reduce damage to environment.

3. Learning For the Environment

It aims at the development of an informed response and responsibility towards the environment.

Check Point 01

1. Name the artificial resources.
2. What is inorganic resource?
3. Earthquakes, landslides etc are which type of disasters?
4. Which type of gases deplete the ozone layer?

Reduce, Reuse, Recycle

Three Rs can be applied for saving the environment. They are Reduce, Reuse and Recycle. It is a modern waste management concept.

Reduce

It refers to 'do not use what you do not need'. Reduction at source will have lesser chances of waste generation. This will reduce the pressure on our natural resources also.

People can reduce the use of unnecessary items while shopping, buy items with minimum packaging, avoid buying disposable items and avoid asking for plastic carry bags. Using reusable cloth or jute bag is better than plastic bags.

Reuse

It refers to reuse the materials for other purposes such as making pillow covers or rags out of used shirts or ladies suits.

Recycling

It refers to reusing some components of the waste that may have some economic value. Recycling helps in conservation of resources, reduction in energy used for manufacturing and reducing pollution. Metals, paper, glass, plastics are recyclable. Aluminium and steel can be recycled many times.

Wet waste from kitchen (fruit, vegetable peels) are also recyclable as it can be utilised to make compost and used as an organic fertiliser. For this, every house should segregate (separate) waste into dry and wet garbage.

Kitchen waste are wet garbages that can be turned into vermicompost. Dry garbages are also mostly recyclable. Break through technologies have developed recently to recover useful materials from industrial wastes.

Non-toxic solid waste should also be segregated. They should be properly disposed in **landfills** that are sealed to avoid any leakage and contamination of surrounding land and groundwater.

Example of Reduce, Reuse, Recycle

Material	Reduce : Use less things	Reuse : Use things for longer time	Recycle : Use things in new/different ways
Paper	• Reduce wastage of paper. • Do not leave too much spaces while writing.	• Use both sides of paper for writing. • Give old books/ notebooks to someone needy.	• Recycle to make paper again. • Make papier mache products by using paper pulp, glue, starch or wall paper paste.

This will help in reducing cutting of trees from which paper is made.

Actions for Saving The Environment

	Avoid	Prefer
Air pollution	• Burning material, e.g. wheat, rice straw in farms.	• To use natural ventilation or fans instead of AC.
Energy Use	• Leaving electrical lights or appliances on when not in use.	• To use public transport like bus, metro and cycles instead of cars. • To use solar and wind energy.
Water pollution	• Throwing wastes in rivers and lakes.	• Using recycled water or water harvested through rains wherever possible, e.g. watering garden plants.
Waste	• Using plastic bags.	• To segregate waste before throwing to separate biodegradable waste.

	Avoid	Prefer
Chemicals in food	• Using chemical pesticides and fertilisers.	• To use and promote organic foods and farming methods.
Forest plants	• Avoid over use of paper.	• Reuse paper wherever possible.
Water	• Avoid over use of water.	• Reduce water usage, e.g. bathing by using bucket filled with water instead of shower.

Conserving Natural Resources

Conservation

It refers to the proper management of natural resources to prevent their exploitation, destruction or degradation. Conservation is the sum total of activities where natural resources are used efficiently to derive benefits but at the same time preventing their excessive use to avoid any destruction, degradation or wastage.

To conserve a resource, first step is resource audit which examines the way of consumption of resources, then to take conservation measures accordingly is the next step.

Example

1. For energy use audit, examine the use of AC system, ventilation system, light system and entry of sunlight into the room/building.
2. Plan energy saving measures by cleaning dust from tubelights for better lighting, regular servicing and maintenance of home appliances. Switching off lights, fans, devices when not in use.

This helps to conserve energy which ultimately saves money and fossil fuels.

Conservation of the natural resources are described below

Soil Conservation

It refers to adopting various methods to check soil erosion and to improve soil fertility. Soil conservation can be done by the following ways :

- **Maintenance of Soil Fertility** Fertility can be maintained by adding manures and fertilisers regularly and by crop rotation (growing of different crops in succession).
- **Control on Grazing** Grazing uproots the grasses therefore it should be allowed in specific areas only.
- **Reforestation** Planting of trees and increasing vegetation cover to reduce soil erosion.
- **Terracing** A farming practised in hilly areas. It is done by dividing a hill slope into several flat fields. This controls rapid run of water.
- **Contour Ploughing** Ploughing at right angles of the natural slopes. This allows the furrows to trap water and check soil erosion caused by rain water.

Water Conservation

Water conservation and its management is essential for the survival of mankind, plants and animals. This can be done by following ways:

- **Growing Vegetation** Vegetation in the catchment areas (land areas from which water flows into river) help in holding water in the soil. The water then percolates into deeper layers and forms or increases ground water.
- **Construction of Dams and Reservoirs** This helps in two ways– regulate water supply to the fields and enables the generation of hydroelectricity.
- **Sewage Treatment** Treating of sewage water and then releasing the clear water into the rivers.
- **Prevent Water Pollution** By treating industrial wastes (effluents) prevents chemicals from entering water sources. Thermal pollution of fresh water should also be prevented.
- **Rainwater Harvesting** This should be done by storing rainwater and recharging groundwater.
- **Watershed Management** Watershed is a single unit of land with its water drainage system. Its management includes soil and water management which increases vegetative cover in the area.

Energy Conservation

Human use a lot of non-renewable sources of energy for their needs. Since these resources are limited, their conservation is essential. Energy conservation refers to efficient use of the energy sources and save them wherever possible. Some of the ways of conserving energy are as follows:

- Switch off lights, fans, TV, electrical items when not in use.
- Use tube lights and energy efficient bulbs that save energy.
- Remove dust from tubes and bulbs and keep them clean to improve lighting levels by 10-20%.
- Some electric items like AC, geysers, heaters, dryers use lot of electrical power, use them when necessary.
- Use pressure cooker and keep vessels covered while cooking to save energy and for faster cooking.

- Do not keep the door of refrigerator open for a long time and cool down the hot foods before putting in refrigerator.
- Use cooking methods that use less energy like use a pressure cooker or solar cooker.
- Travelling in a bus or in a group in a carpool also saves energy.

Food Conservation

Conserving food and its storage have been practiced by people to feed mankind during shortage. Food is stored in warehouses to feed people on large scale. At home food is stored in refrigerators.

There are various other ways of food preservation to prevent its spoilage from harmful bacteria and other micro-organisms.

Forest Conservation

It refers to the retention of existing forest or the creation of new forest at the levels prescribed by the state or local authority.

For this, forest conservation programs are initiated but participation of the local community living in and around the forest is important for their success.

Sustainable Development and Green Economy

The current way of economic development is using up resources of the world rapidly. The future generation would have to face serious environmental problems that are much worse than present situation.

The increase in population and income has increased the consumption of goods. This has led to rise in production for which natural resources are used rapidly.

This is unsustainable so the society must change its development strategy to a form which will not destroy the environment. This new form of sustainable development can be brought if people practice a sustainable life style and ensure judicious utilisation of resources.

Biodiversity

Biological diversity is variety and richness of different plants and animal species found locally in a region, in the country and the world. It exists in different type of ecosystems-both terrestrial (land) and aquatic.

Biodiversity is essential for the following purposes:

- Preserving ecological processes such as fixing, recycling of nutrients
- Soil formation
- Circulation and cleansing of air and water
- In maintaining global life support systems such as plants giving out O_2 and absorbing CO_2
- Maintaining the water balance within ecosystems
- Watershed protection
- Maintaining stream and river flows throughout the year
- Erosion control
- Local flood reduction

What is Sustainable Development?

As per World Commission on Environment and Development, 1987, Sustainable development is defined as 'development that meets the needs of the present without compromising the ability of future generations to meet their own needs'.

It guarantees the balance between economic growth, care for the environment and social well-being.

The concept appeared for the first time in 1987 with the publication of the Brundtland Report. The report warned about negative environmental consequences of economic growth and globalisation. Sustainable development includes the following:

- Reducing excessive use of resources and enhancing resource conservation.
- Recycling and reuse of waste material.
- Scientific management of renewable resources, especially bio-resources.
- Planting more trees.
- Planting green grassy patches between concrete buildings.
- Using more environment friendly material or biodegradable material.
- Use of environment friendly technologies that are based on efficient use of resources.

Sustainable Development Goals

Sustainable Development Goals (SDGs) also known as Global Goals are a universal call to action to end poverty, protect the planet and ensure that all people enjoy peace and prosperity.

They were launched at the United Nations Sustainable Development Summit held in New York in September 2015, forming the 2030 agenda for sustainable development. The agenda with its 17 SDGs was adopted by world leaders in 2015. Main idea is to develop a roadmap for progress that is sustainable and leaves no one behind.

Objectives For Making SDGs

The SDGs are framed with the objective to address vital issues facing businesses, governments and society about poverty, gender equality, water use, energy, climate change and biodiversity. Aim is to provide secure, affordable and sustainable economy for which countries are framing policies and regulations.

Green Growth

It refers to the aims for achieving economic growth that is socially inclusive and environmentally sustainable. The **Ministry of Environment, Forest and Climate Change,** Government of India recognised green growth in its vision, wherein 'poverty eradication' along with green growth is important for green economy.

As per the **Finance Commission of India,** green growth is "rethinking growth strategies with regard to their impacts on the environmental sustainability and the environmental resources available to poor and vulnerable groups". Extent of economy to grow green is on two things–ability to reduce the quantity of resources required and support economic growth that leads to social equality and job creation.

For sustainable development, any activity for economic growth must also consider its environmental impacts. e.g. Vehicles on road that leads to traffic jam, waste of time for commuters, emission of harmful gases should be slowly replaced with an efficient public transport system.

Green Economy

Green economy was coined in 1989 in a report titled 'Blue Print for a Green Economy' made for the Government of United Kingdom by leading environmental economists.

According to United Nations Environment Program (UNEP) 2011, "green economy is one that results in improved human well-being and social equity, while significantly reducing environmental risks and ecological scarcities". It is low in carbon, resource efficient and socially inclusive.

Importance of Green Economy

A green economy is a system which helps in economic growth at the same time, taking care of the environment. It is beneficial from three aspects which are shown in the figure below

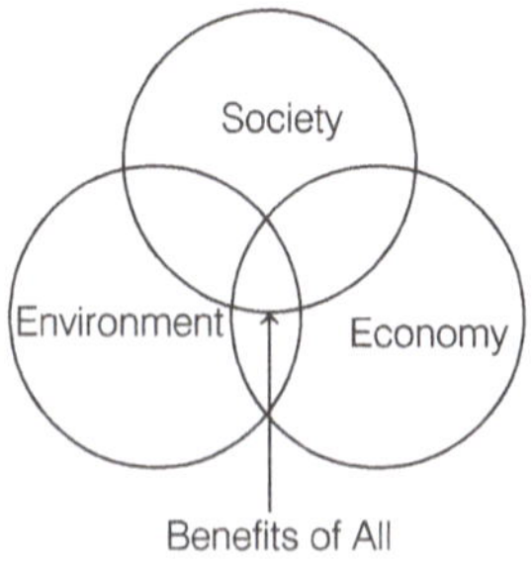

Green Economy

The figure shows that green economy is beneficial for all, i.e., **environment, economy** and **society.**

Building factories, using chemicals for more crops harm the environment. But if farmers do not use fertilisers, then it will harm the economy of the farmers.

But both, the environment and economy are part of society. As people become aware of serious health hazards caused by fertilisers and pesticides in their food, they will put pressure on farmers to reduce the use of chemicals.

People will use more of green products made by ecosensitive industries and products that cause severe damage to the environment may not be used. In this way green economy is beneficial from three aspects, i.e. environment, economy and society.

Green Consumer

A green consumer is very concerned about the environment and therefore only purchases products that are environment friendly and eco-friendly. Eco-friendly products are those that have very little packaging, made from natural ingredients and their making do not causes pollution.

Components of a Green Economy

Green economy uses less resources, causes less pollution and provides growth for everyone. The components are as follows:

Renewable Energy

- Energy from renewable sources like wind, water, Sun, Earth, biomass etc. These are available in large quantities and cause less pollution.

- India is amongst the top 10 countries for production of renewable energy through solar, wind and biomass.

Green Building

- Buildings that cause minimum damage to the environment during their construction and operation.
- Green buildings use energy, water and other resources wisely with minimum waste.

Well-Managed (Sustainable) Transport

- Sustainable means what is good for the economy as well as the future of the environment.
- Sustainable transport cause less or no damage to the environment.
- It costs less and help more people move quickly.

Water Management

- Need to avoid wastage of water.
- Need to reduce water pollution.
- Need to recycle water for various purposes.

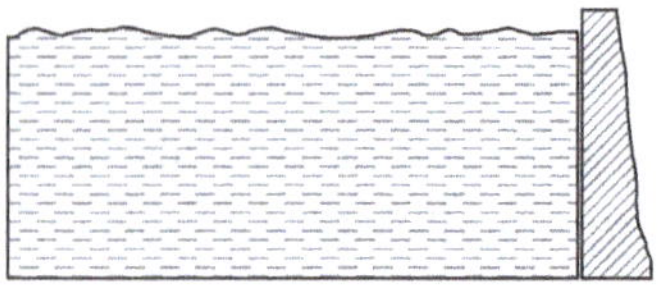

Waste Management

- Waste materials increase land, water and air pollution and causes loss of resources for cleaning the waste.
- Waste can be managed by separating it before throwing.
- Using 3R-Reduce, Reuse and Recycle will help in waste management.

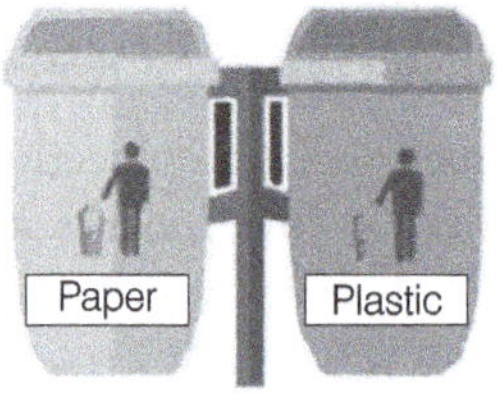

Land Management

- Land is needed for many purposes like farming, forests, factories, homes, roads etc.
- Land management is when land is used in a way that it meets the requirements of people without causing damage to the environment.

Skill Development For Green Economy

India is facing a major challenge of expanding access to food, energy, water, essential goods and services to its growing population. Therefore, it needs to work towards the objective of alleviating poverty and facilitating sustainable development.

Skill development for a green economy ensures an efficient transition from unsustainable to a green economy. This is done by matching supply with the demands needed for skill development.

For example, An organic farmer needs to have knowledge and skills for growing organically certified crops. Similarly, solar technicians or engineers should possess the knowledge and skills for design, installation and maintenance of solar panels and appliances. Green job can be with business, non-profit organisations, government or education.

Some green jobs may not require specific skills.

For example, A graphic designer or a cashier working for a green organisation will not require specific skill development.

But they will be contributing to the development of green growth and economy.

Green Skills

Green skills are skills used to promote green economy. They are needed in areas similar to renewable energy, sewage water treatment, developing climate resilient cities, green construction, solid waste management etc. Green skills are also known as skills for sustainability.

According to **Green Skills Agreement**, "skills for sustainability, also known as green skills, are the technical skills, knowledge, values and attitudes needed in the workforce to develop and support sustainable social, economic and environmental outcomes in business, industry and the community".

> Green skills are those skills required to adapt processes, services and products to climate change and the environmental rules and necessities related to it. They embrace the information, abilities, values and attitudes required to live in, develop and support a sustainable and resource-efficient society.

Areas of Green Skills

Some of the areas in which green skills contribute to the sustainable development are as follows:

- Using renewable energy (e.g. solar power, wind energy)
- Water and waste management
- Rain water harvesting
- Conserving energy
- Reducing pollution

Importance of Green Skills

Green skills are crucial for making a transition from an economy based on energy and emissions to cleaner and greener production and services.

It prepares people for green jobs that contribute to preserving or restoring the quality of the environment, while improving human well-being and social equality.

For this, technologies to make use of solar energy such as solar lights, solar cooker, solar water heaters etc. are developed.

Green skills contribute to preserving or restoring environmental quality for sustainable future. Therefore, it include jobs that protect ecosystems and biodiversity, reduce energy and minimise waste and pollution.

In future green skills are going to be more important as all countries will move towards a greener economy.

National Skill Development Mission

The mission was officially launched by Government of India in 2015. It is developed to create convergence across sectors and states in terms of skill training activities including green skills.

The knowledge and skills needed for managing resources and supporting efficiency are as follows:

Purpose	Knowledge and Skills Needed For Green Economy
Manage natural resources	• To assess environmental impact. • To design and adopt technologies to reduce consumption of natural resources. • To understand legislation and guidelines for sustainable use of natural resources.
Support climate resilience	• To develop models for interpreting climate change projections. • To develop risk management strategies for future resource availability. • To adopt technologies that improve resilience (flexibility) to climate change.
Support resource efficiency	• To develop business models that are resource efficient. • To develop and adopt technologies that maximises resource utilisation and reduce wastage.
Support low-carbon industry	• To develop technologies that promote renewable energy sources. • To design and adopt technologies and products that minimise carbon emission.

Green Skill Development Programme

The Ministry of Environment, Forest and Climate Change has taken the initiative for skill development in environment and forest sector. It enables India's youth to get gainful employment and/or self-employment. This program is called Green Skill Development Programme.

The programme aims to develop green skilled workers having technical knowledge and commitment to sustainable development to attain the sustainable development goals.

Green skills thus aim to balance economic development with environmental conservation, so that needs of the society, economy and environment are efficiently met with minimum damage to the environment.

Green Consumer Day

The Green Consumer Day is celebrated globally on 28th September of every year. On this day people celebrate Earth by bringing about awareness on how small actions can help Earth to remain green and clean.

People wear the colour green to express to the world their feelings regarding the universe and mother nature. People tend to recycle more than usual on that day.

What are Green Jobs?

Green job is employment in any industry that contributes to preserving or restoring environmental quality in that sector and allowing for sustainable development. The jobs that help protect ecosystems and biodiversity as well as aim to reduce energy, materials and water usage are included in green jobs. They can be in any sectors such as agriculture, manufacturing, research and development activities etc. They can bring transition from high carbon to low carbon economy by promoting environment friendly technologies. Sectors with potential to green jobs are as follows:

Sectors With Potential to Green Jobs

Sector	Areas/Field	Green Jobs
Agriculture	• Organic farming • Watershed management • Rain water harvesting	• Water quality technician • Rain water harvesting professional and technician • Solar pump technician • Greenhouse or polyhouse professional and technician
Construction	• Planning, design and manufacturing of energy efficient lighting appliances and equipments • Planning, design and construction of green buildings • Increasing efficiency of existing buildings through energy audits • Green plumbing, using sensor based equipments	• Green builders • Green design professionals • Green workers
Energy	• Research, construction and monitoring of power plant including plant efficiency and carbon sequestration (removal of carbon) • Increased power plant efficiency	• Solar cell technicians and engineers • Wind energy professionals • Wind energy workers • Wave energy producers • Biofuel professionals
Forestry	• Reforestation and afforestation projects • Agroforestry and vertical farming (growing crops on vertical stacks/layers)	• Natural scientists
Manufacturing	• Pollution control • Energy efficiency • Recycling waste materials	• Recyclers
Retail	• Greener products and specially targeted green stores	• Green salesperson • Accountants • Cashiers • Sales associates
Automotive and transport	• Research and design on more fuel efficient vehicles and on public transport systems • Manufacture of alternatively fuelled vehicles	• Clean car engineers
Tourism and hospitality	• Eco-friendly practices such as centralised lighting and air conditioning systems for saving electricity • Eco-tour guides	• Eco-tour guides • Green tour guides
Education	• Research and development activities for promoting green growth and economy • Teaching environmental education • Research and development in conservation of natural resources	• Teachers teaching environmental education • Green scientist • Conservation biologists

Green Projects

Green projects are implemented by people and organisations concerned and motivated to do something for saving the environment. Green projects are implemented in areas like waste management, energy conservation, green sanitation, biofuel use, green buildings etc.

Examples of Green Projects

1. **Solid Waste Management by 'Swachh Cooperative'** Swachh cooperative is in Pune and is wholly owned by waste pickers.

   These people are engaged in door step collection of waste. The cooperative has successfully integrated informal waste picking with Pune city's solid waste management system.

   They now work with dignity and ensure efficient disposal of wastes. Wet waste is used for regeneration of biogas and solid waste is recycled.

2. **Modern Chulha of Society of Development and Environment Protection** In this project, modern chulhas are developed which are energy efficient cooking stoves.

   These stoves help the movement of air through it, so that wood burns easily and efficiently. Chulha uses biomass that reduces consumption of wood by 50% and reduction in smoke by 80%. The chulhas are developed by the society of development and environment protection and named as 'Modern DEEP (Development and Environment Protection).

   This project trains masons and welders to produce these chulhas thereby increasing employment and entrepreneurship opportunities. Project was first started in 1995 in 35000 households of solan district in Himachal Pradesh.

3. **Bio-toilet by 'Green Solution Foundation'** Bio-toilet project is initiated by Green Solution Foundation (GSF). It provides hygienic sanitation in villages and slums of cities that lack in sewage systems. This eco-friendly toilet has a biodigester tank that uses aerobic bacteria and converts human waste into environment standard compatible water. This can be used for flushing and irrigation.

   The GSF provides training on toilet use and servicing, which increases employment and entrepreneurship opportunities. The bio-toilets are funded by users and donors.

   Benefits of Bio-toilets

   - Efficient sewage system
   - Water conservation due to less flushing
   - Decrease in soil and water contamination
   - Decrease in diseases due to hygienic sanitation

Check Point 02

1 What is energy conservation?

2 When does green consumer day celebrate?

3 Give two benefits of Bio-toilets.

4 Give two examples of green skills that you can start learning from now.

NCERT FOLDER

Check Your Progress

Pg 177

A. Multiple Choice Questions

Read the questions carefully and circle the letter (a), (b), (c) or (d) that best answers the questions.

1. What are some of the environmental changes caused due to modern methods of agriculture?
   (a) Chemical pollution due to fertilisers
   (b) Improvement in the environment
   (c) Lower air pollution due to crops
   (d) Decrease in forest areas

Ans. (a) Chemical pollution due to fertilisers

2. How can we conserve our health and environment? (Choose all the correct options)
   (a) Grow organic crops
   (b) Use natural fertilisers
   (c) Manage waste water
   (d) Use more air conditioning

Ans. (b) Use natural fertilisers

3. A steel factory burns firewood and charcoal for heating and melting the steel? What are the possible effects on the environment? (Choose all the correct options)
   (a) Increase in global temperature
   (b) Decrease in global temperature
   (c) Increase in air pollution
   (d) Decrease in air pollution

Ans. (c) Increase in air pollution

B. Short Answer Questions

1. What are the five sources of energy available to us? Give two examples of each source?

Ans. Five sources of energy available to us are
   (i) Nuclear fusion, e.g. Solar energy (Sun)
   (ii) Gravitational energy, e.g. Gravity generated by Earth and Moon
   (iii) Nuclear fission, e.g. Nuclear energy
   (iv) Energy in the interior of the Earth, e.g. Geothermal energy
   (v) Energy stored in chemical bonds, e.g. coal, petrol

2. What are the sources of pollution?

Ans. Sources of pollution are as follows:
   (i) Excessive use of chemicals in agriculture (like fertilisers, insecticides) affect the alkalinity of the soil causing land pollution.
   (ii) Dangerous gases like chlorofluorocarbons or CFCs, methane, carbon dioxide from industrial processes causes air pollution.

3. Classify the following under the three respective categories of natural resources :
   Air, iron, sand, petroleum, wind, clay, fish, forest, gold, pearls

Inexhaustible	Renewable	Non-renewable
...	...	...

Ans.

Inexhaustible	Renewable	Non-renewable
Wind Air Sand Clay	Fish Forest Pearls	Iron Petroleum Gold

Check Your Progress

Pg 181

A. Multiple Choice Questions

Read the questions carefully and circle the letter (a), (b), (c) or (d) that best answers the questions.

1. What does conservation of energy mean? (Choose all options that apply)
   (a) Saving energy
   (b) Producing energy
   (c) Using energy efficiently
   (d) Creating energy sources

Ans. (a, c) Saving energy and using energy efficiently.

2. Which of the following are non-renewable resources? (Choose all options that apply)
   (a) Coal
   (b) Diesel
   (c) Sun
   (d) Water

Ans. (a, b) Coal and diesel

3. Which of the following is an example of renewable resources?
   (a) Coal
   (b) Solar energy
   (c) CNG
   (d) Petroleum

Ans. (b) Solar energy

B. Short Answer Questions

1. Write any three actions which you can take to conserve energy.

Ans. Three actions that can be taken to conserve energy are as follows:
(a) Switch off lights, fans when not in use.
(b) Use energy efficient bulbs that use less energy.
(c) Travel in a public transport or carpool instead of going alone in a car.

2. Describe any three methods of water conservation.

Ans. Three methods of water conservation are as follows:
(a) Growing vegetation in catchment areas to hold in the soil.
(b) Rainwater harvesting to store rainwater.
(c) Prevention of throwing industrial wastes into sources of water.

3. What is the purpose of soil conservation?

Ans. The purpose of soil conservation is to maintain soil fertility. Soil may loose its fertility due to soil erosion, heavy use of chemicals in agriculture and deforestation. Soil fertility can be maintained by adding manure, rotation of crops and planting trees.

4. State any three ways by which we can save energy.

Ans. The ways to save energy are as follows:
(a) Use pressure cooker to save energy required for cooking.
(b) Using electric items like AC, geyser only when necessary as they use lot of electricity.
(c) Use renewable sources of energy wherever possible like using solar cooker, solar heater etc.

Check Your Progress Pg 193

A. Multiple Choice Questions

Read the questions carefully and circle the letter (a), (b), (c) or (d) that best answers the questions.

1. Which of the following options describe a green economy correctly? A green economy
(a) uses less resources (b) uses more resources
(c) wastes less items (d) wastes more items

Ans. (a) uses less resources

B. Short Answer Questions

1. What are green skills?

Ans. Green skills are those skills required to adapt processes, services and products to climate change and the environmental rules and necessities related to it. These skills are used to promote green economy.

2. Give two examples of green skills that you can start learning from now.

Ans. Two examples of green skills that can be learnt:
(a) To reduce use of non-renewable sources of energy and use renewable sources wherever possible, e.g. to study in daytime use more of natural light instead of tubelight.
(b) To segregate household waste for proper waste management, e.g. keeping two separate dustbins for collection of dry and wet waste.

SUMMARY

- People live together and form societies which interact with the environment to cause changes in it.
- Natural resources are available freely in nature like land, forest, water, mineral, food and energy resources.
- Natural resources are exhaustible, inexhaustible, renewable and non-renewable.
- Factors causing imbalances in environment are over-exploitation, mining, deforestation and pollution of land, water and air.
- The ill-effects of environmental imbalances are climate change, global warming, green house effect, harmful radiation and natural disasters. Environmental education can help in learning about through and for the environment.
- Three 'R'– Reduce, Reuse and Recycle are three ways of saving the environment.
- Conservation of soil, water, energy, food and forest are also essential for saving the environment.
- Sustainable development, green growth and green economy is preferred for environmental conservation and economic growth at the same time.
- Components of green economy includes developing more of renewable energy, green buildings, sustainable transport, water management, waste and land management.
- Skill development for a green economy ensures sustainability alongwith development.
- Green skills are the technical knowledge, values and attitude needed to support sustainable and resource efficient society.
- National Skill Development Mission was launched in 2015 and the initiative for skill development is taken by Ministry of Government, Forest and Climate.
- Green job is employment in any industry that contributes to preserving or restoring environmental quality in that sector such as agriculture, construction, etc.
- Green projects are for saving the environment and implemented in areas like waste management, energy conservation etc.

Exam Practice

Multiple Choice Questions

1. Which is an example of a natural resource?
(a) Natural gas (b) Copper
(c) Fertile land (d) All of these

Ans. (*d*) All of these

2. Which type of resources can be replenished?
(a) Non-renewable resources
(b) Exhaustible resources
(c) Renewable resources
(d) Mineral resources

Ans. (*c*) Renewable resources

3. Which is an artificial resource?
(a) Plants (b) Dams
(c) Water (d) Air

Ans. (*b*) Dams

4. Biomass and liquified petroleum gas are examples of
(a) Renewable resources
(b) Non-renewable resources
(c) Energy resources
(d) Inexhaustible resources

Ans. (*c*) energy resources

5. Which is not an effect of mining?
(a) Extinction of a species
(b) Formation of sinkholes
(c) Loss of biodiversity
(d) Contamination of groundwater

Ans. (*a*) Extinction of a species

6. Which of the following is not an example of forest resource?
(a) Tannins (b) Horns and hides
(c) Wood (d) Gypsym

Ans. (*d*) Gypsum

7. Fossil fuel emissions cause which of the following?
(a) Air pollution (b) Water pollution
(c) Land pollution (d) Noise pollution

Ans. (*a*) Air pollution

8. Which of the following is a biodegradable pollutant?
(a) Lead (b) Plastic
(c) Cattle dung (d) Insecticide

Ans. (*c*) Cattle dung

9. Which is not a naturally occurring green house gas?
(a) Nitrous Oxide (b) Hydrofluorocarbons
(c) Ozone (d) Methane

Ans. (*b*) Hydrofluorocarbons

10. Learning about the environment, mainly focuses on
(a) learning by doing
(b) direct contact with environment
(c) aesthetic appreciation
(d) acquiring knowledge about environment

Ans. (*d*) acquiring knowledge about environment

11. If you are starting to use jute bags instead of plastic bags, then which 'R' you are doing?
(a) Reduce (b) Reuse
(c) Recycle (d) All 3R

Ans. (*a*) Reduce

12. To reduce wastage of any kind you should first
(a) avoid overuse of paper
(b) segregate waste before throwing
(c) prefer using recycled water
(d) All of the above

Ans. (*d*) All of the above

13. Sustainable development goals are also known as
(a) Green goals (b) Global goals
(c) Energy saving goals (d) Scientific goals

Ans. (*b*) global goals

14. Which of the following is not a component of green economy?
(a) Organic farming
(b) Intensive agriculture
(c) Biomass and Biogas
(d) Waste management

Ans. (*b*) Intensive agriculture

15. Which among the following job do not require any green skill?
(a) Organic farmer (b) Solar engineer
(c) Graphic designer (d) Wind mill mechanic

Ans. (*c*) Graphic designer

16. An area in which green skills contribute to sustainable development
(a) rain water harvesting
(b) automotive manufacturing
(c) building factories
(d) None of the above

Ans. (*a*) rain water harvesting

17. Green project 'Swachh Cooperative' is about
(a) teaching hygenic habits
(b) efficient sewage system
(c) disposal and management of waste
(d) providing energy efficient chulhas

Ans. (*c*) disposal and management of waste

Fill in the Blanks

1. In every locality, city, state or country there is constant interaction between .... and environment.

Ans. Society

2. .... is an organic resource.

Ans. Wood/biogas/coal/petrol

3. .... is buried under lakes and oceans and is found above the oil in the oil wells.

Ans. Natural gas

4. Hunting more of a particular animal species leading to its extinction is ...... of resources.

Ans. Over exploitation

5. Clearance of trees for agriculture and non-agriculture uses is ....

Ans. Deforestation

6. Pollutants that cannot be broken down into simpler and harmless substances are called ....

Ans. Non-biodegradable pollutants.

7. The very first step to prevent land pollution and waste management is to .... the waste.

Ans. Segregate

8. Heating of the Earth because of burning of fossil fuels is due to ....

Ans. Global warming

9. .... happens when gases trap and prevent the Earth's heat from escaping leading to its warming.

Ans. Green house effect

10. Due to release from cleaning chemicals and coolants .... layer has developed holes in it.

Ans. Ozone

True/False

1. A natural resource can be termed as something that you do for a living.

Ans. False

2. Air and water are inexhaustible, renewable resources of the Earth.

Ans. True

3. Discarded electronic items, clothes, food and metals are known as metal waste.

Ans. False

4. Methane gas does not aid to green house effect.

Ans. False

5. Utilising kitchen wastes to make vermicompost is an example of recycling.

Ans. True

6. Sustainable developmental strategies are very helpful in the preservation of biodiversity.

Ans. True

7. Growth that is socially exclusive and caters to environment stability is green growth.

Ans. False

8. Green Consumer Day is celebrated on 28th September every year.

Ans. True

9. Green jobs can be developed in traditional areas also like in construction, manufacturing.

Ans. True

10. National Skill Development Mission was adopted in 2012.

Ans. False

Match the Columns

1. Match the following columns.

Column I		Column II	
A.	Water pollution	1.	Chemicals in agriculture
B.	Air pollution	2.	Improper disposal of sewage
C.	Land pollution	3.	Exhaust fumes from vehicles

Ans. A → 2; B → 3; C → 1

2. Match the following columns.

Column I		Column II	
A.	Food conservation	1.	Warehouses and refrigerators
B.	Energy conservation	2.	Local community participation
C.	Forest conservation	3.	Contour ploughing
D.	Soil conservation	4.	Keep tubelights clean

Ans. A → 1; B → 4; C → 2; D → 3

3. Match the following columns.

Column I		Column II	
A.	Agriculture	1.	Clean car engineers
B.	Transport	2.	Biofuel professionals
C.	Energy	3.	Solar pump technician
D.	Education	4.	Environmental education teachers

Ans. A → 3; B → 1; C → 2; D → 4

Short Answer (SA) Type Questions

1. What is environment? Which Article of Indian Constitution safeguards environmental protection?

Ans. Environment is defined as everything that surrounds us which includes flora, fauna, air, water, land etc. The environment affects all aspects of our life.
Article 48-A of the Constitution of India safeguards environmental protection. It contains specific provisions for the protection and improvement of environmental quality.

2. Write three ill-effects of pollution.

Ans. Pollution of land, air and water is not good for the environment. The ill-effects of pollution are as follows:

1. **Land pollution** through contamination of soil may cause various diseases in human like dysentry, cholera, typhoid.
2. **Air pollution** through greenhouse effects causes many changes in climate leading to floods, famines, droughts etc.
3. **Water pollution** through dumping of industrial wastes makes the water unfit for drinking, kills aquatic life and affects tourism adversely.

3. How education can help in saving the environment?

Ans. Education is very important in saving the environment. It helps in three ways:

1. **Learning About the Environment** Education about the environment helps in acquiring knowledge and understanding of the surroundings and related issues.
2. **Learning Through the Environment** It helps in establishing direct contact with the environment through observation, learning by doing, exposure to the environment. This helps in developing the skills for efficient use of resources.
3. **Learning for the Environment** It aims at development of an informed response and responsibility towards the environment. This makes people more aware towards conservation of the environment.

4. What is sustainable development? Mention two strategies of sustainable development.

Ans. Sustainable development is defined as the development that meets the needs of the present without compromising the ability of future generation to meet their own needs. It aims to bring economic growth alongwith care for the environment and social well-being.

Strategies of sustainable development are as follows:

1. Scientific management of renewable resources especially bio-resources.
2. Reducing excessive use of non-renewable resources alongwith reusing and recycling of waste materials.

5. Define Green economy. Explain its two components.

Ans. Green economy is defined as the one that results in improved human well-being and social equity while significantly reducing environmental risks and ecological scarcities.

Two components of green economy are as follows:

1. Using the land resources to meet the requirement of people without causing damage to the environment.
2. Develop sustainable transport system that will cost less, help more people to move quickly and cause less or no damage to the environment.

6. How can green jobs be developed in construction and forestry?

Ans. Green jobs include jobs that help protect the ecosystem and diversity.

In construction the areas in which green jobs can be developed are in planning, design, manufacturing of buildings, lighting appliances etc. Green jobs in this sector are green builders, green design professionals, green workers.

In forestry the areas in which green jobs can be developed are in reforestation, afforestation projects, agroforestry and vertical farming. Green jobs in this sector are of natural scientists.

Self Assessment

Multiple Choice Questions

1. Natural resource like forest are consumed directly when

(a) they prevent soil erosion (b) they cause rainfall
(c) they are used for eco-tourism (d) they regulate the climate

2. Which of the following is a finite resource?

(a) Land (b) Gold (c) Kerosene (d) All of these

3. Ecological imbalances are created when there is

(a) afforestation (b) recycling (c) green growth (d) heat radiation

4. Deterioration of our natural environment takes place when

(a) average temperature rises (b) glacier melt
(c) water is contaminated (d) All of these

5. Main source of water pollution is

(a) rainwater pollutants (b) sewage water
(c) atmospheric pollutants (d) melting of snow

6. Which of the following are essential for green economy?

(a) Conservation of wildlife (b) Employment creation
(c) Energy efficiency (d) Both (a) and (c)

7. Which of the following agency is responsible for the creation of GSDP?

(a) UNICEF (b) Central Government
(c) WHO (d) State Government

Fill in the Blanks

1. Everything around us forms part of our ……… .

2. Taking less time in shower or bathing with one bucket full of water helps in ……… conservation.

3. Designs and scientific knowledge to adopt the energy of wind, Sun and tides is ……… energy.

4. ……… are required to adapt processes, services and products to climate change and the environmental rules and necessities related to it.

5. Modern DEEP are energy efficient ……… developed in the Solan district of Himachal Pradesh.

True/False

1. Human activities change the environment in a big way.
2. All minerals are non-renewable and exhaustible natural sources.
3. Say no to polythene is an initiative to save the environment.
4. Crop rotation helps in retaining the fertility of the soil.
5. It is possible to change the unsustainable development practices by following the concept of green economy.

Short Answer (SA) Type Questions

1. Write two actions and two precautions that can be taken for saving the environment.
2. With the help of an example, explain how reduce, reuse and recycle can protect the environment from degradation.
3. Discuss how industrial affluents are the main cause of climate change.
4. Sustainable development and green growth are ways to conserve the environment along with development. Discuss.

Part B

SUBJECT SPECIFIC SKILLS

UNIT

01

Introduction to IT-ITeS Industry

Chapter Checklist

- Information and Communication Technology
- Information Technology enabled Services (ITeS)
- BPO Services
- IT Applications

Information Technology (IT) means creating, managing, storing and exchanging information. IT includes all types of technology used to deal with information, such as computer hardware and software technology used for creating, storing and transferring information. Now a days, IT is an integrate part of business.

Information and Communication Technology

An extended synonym for Information Technology (IT) is Information and Communication Technology (ICT). ICT covers any product that will store, retrieve, manipulate, transmit or receive information electronically in a digital form. ICT includes any communication device or application including radio, television, cellular phones, computer, satellite system, etc. alongwith the various services and applications provided by them such as video conferencing, E-learning, E-banking etc.

Advantages of ICT

- **Communication** Speed/time and money can be saved because ICT much quicker to move information.
- **Availability** ICT has made it possible for businesses to be automated giving clients access to a website.

- **Education** Computers alongwith their programs and Internet have created interesting learning.
- **New Jobs** ICT has been creation of new and interesting jobs.

Disadvantages of ICT

- **Privacy** Through information technology may have made communication easier and more convenient, it has also brought privacy issues.
- **Job Loss** People have to lose their jobs due to the come of new technology.
- **Expensive** Too expensive to afford for most of people.

Information Technology enabled Services (ITeS)

Information Technologies that enable the business by improving the quality of services are called Information Technology enabled Services (ITeS).

It is defined as outsourcing of processes that can be enabled with information technology and covers diverse areas like finance, HR, administration, health care, telecommunication, manufacturing etc. ITeS is also called web-enabled services or remote services.

E-enabled services radically reduce costs and improve service standards. ITeS offers different services integrated in a single delivery mechanism to end users. The services may include :

- Medical transcription
- Customer relationship management
- Data entry and data processing
- Software development
- Data warehousing
- IT help desk services
- Enterprise resource planning
- Telecommunication services

BPO Services

Business Process Outsourcing (BPO) services means performing business operations through an outside service provider. BPO also comes under IT services as IT plays a very useful role in optimising the business performance.

The BPO industry is highly organised and hence various kind of jobs are outsourced in India.

Some of the BPO services are as follows:

- Financial and Accounting Services
- Taxation and Insurance Services
- e-Publishing and Web Promotion
- Legal Services and Content Writing
- Multimedia and Design Services
- Document Management Services
- Software Testing Services
- Healthcare Services

BPM Industry in India

The IT-BPM (Business Process Management) industry has been fueling India's growth.

The growth of IT-BPM industry has provided India with a wide range of economic and social benefits to contribute in GDP (Gross Domestic Product) and exports. This includes raising income levels, creating employment and improving exports.

This industry has approximate doubled in terms of revenue and contribution to GDP of India over the last ten years (2008-2018).

BPO services industry is doing exceptionally well in India because of the following advantages :

(i) In India, BPO service providers invest in hi-tech hardware and software to deliver the best services. These providers follow quality checks to ensure error free and exceptional services.

(ii) Government of India is encouraging the BPO industry by providing necessary infrastructure.

(iii) In India, BPO industry is highly developed and capable of delivering numerous types of BPO services in exceptional quality.

Structure of the IT-BPM Industry

The organisations within the IT-BPM industry are categorised along the following parameters :

- Sector that the organisation is serving.
- Type as well as range of offering the organisation provides.
- Geographic spread of operations.
- Revenues and size of operations.

A broad structure of the industry based on parameters represented as follows :

(i) **Multinational Companies (MNCs)** Multinational corporations are firms with headquarters outside India. These firms would have their branch offices and/or subsidiaries in India that cater to global customers (external clients).

e.g. IBM, Accenture, HP, DELL, Microsoft, Genpact, Convergys, Intel, Synapse Techno Design Innovations and Pvt. Ltd., etc.

(ii) **Indian Service Providers (ISPs)** These are firms with their headquarters in India. These may cater to domestic or international customer base.

e.g. TCS, Infosys, Wipro, HCL, Mahindra Satyam, SASKEN Technologies, Tata Technologies, KPIT Technologies (Birlasoft Limited) and so on.

(iii) **Global In-house Centres (GICs)** GICs include both MNC owned units that undertake work for the parent's global operations and ISPs owned units of domestic companies.

e.g. Barclays Technology Center India, EMC, Ford, Boeing, Honeywell, UTC Aerospace and so on.

Check Point 01

1. Which of the following is/are disadvantage(s) of ICT?
   (a) Privacy (b) Job loss
   (c) Expensive (d) All of these
2. BPO also comes under .... services.
3. IT BPM includes raising income levels and improving exports. (True/False)
4. Write the full form of ITeS.
5. Give any two examples of Multinational Companies (MNCs).

IT Applications

IT has applications in almost all aspects of our life. Some of important ones are :

(i) IT in Home Computing

A Personal Computer (PC) is a general purpose, cost effective computer that is designed to be used by a single end-user. At home, we use PC to do household related accounts, watching online movies, listening music, playing games, searching information etc. We can also watch movies which are stored in CD (Compact Disc) by CD-ROM drive. We can learn many things or take online classes from computer at home. Computers and digital services are also used to do online shopping at home.

(ii) IT in Everyday Life

In our daily life, we use washing machines, microwave oven and many other products which have embedded software. We can store all the information about our important work, appointments schedules and list of contacts in a computer. Computers are playing a very important role in our lives and now we cannot imagine the world without computers.

(iii) IT in Library

Now a days, all work in libraries are done with computer. It is easy to keep record of all books in computers. Many work are done in libraries, such as keep the record of books subjectwise or department wise, book's issue record, book's return record and many more are done with the help of computers. All these work can be done easily with library software.

Many libraries software are launched in market, which maintain the record of books. Each book in the library has magnetic strip which is detected by barcode reader that help to find the detail of book.

(iv) IT at Workplace

In the office environment, computers and computer applications are used to perform office work more effectively. In assembly line industries, where attention to detail, speed and efficiency are important, automation is becoming more and more common. Internet and office applications form the basis of modern business.

(v) IT in Education

Computer and Information Technology has been proved to be very much beneficial in the field of education. Computers are used actively in education to improve the quality and learning outcomes. Teachers can use audio, video and graphics aids through computer to prepare lesson plans.

(a) ICT in the Classroom

There are many ways in which the ICT is used for education in the classroom, such as

- e-Learning classrooms
- Smart board presentations
- Videos on experiments
- Creation of images and video
- Desktop publishing of magazines, letters and documents
- Educational games
- Learning using the CD-ROM media
- Gathering educational information on the Internet

(b) Education- Anywhere Anytime

Any student in India can access the NCERT book online through the website www.epathshala.nic.in or mobile app. Apart from this, there are a variety of websites and mobile apps to access educational resources on any topic.

You can also contact a teacher or a trainer *via* Internet to use WBT (Web Based Training). In this way, education has reached the far flung areas by reaching the unreached.

(c) Learning Management System (LMS)

It allows to create, deliver and report on training courses and programs. LMS also provides an instructor with a way to create and deliver content, monitor student participation and access student performance. Students and teachers can register on LMS website and access many services delived by LMS, as it can be used to

- access content anywhere and anytime.
- use interactive features such as discussion forums, video conferencing etc.
- monitor the progress of children.

(d) Teaching Aids and Media

- Teachers can create interactive classes by making the lessons more interested.
- Students find images and graphical representation of concept more interesting as compared to the theoretical knowledge.
- Using ICT, teachers can explain most complex concept in a very simplified manner using graphics, videos and animations.

(vi) IT in Entertainment

Information Technology had a major impact on entertainment industry. Importance of IT in entertainment defined in many ways as:

(a) In Movies

Computers are widely used to create special effects in big budget movies. They are also extensively used behind the scenes to edit movie during the production process. Movies are developed using computer graphics, animations etc.

(b) In Games

Computer games is a quickly growing market. Computers have access to many peripheral devices such as keyboard, mouse, joystick and more. Computers are absolutely necessary for programming any sort of new video game.

(c) In Animation

Animation can be used to make cartoons, animated movies etc. The computer can create outerspace, alien characters and so on without the need of creating their physical models.

(vii) IT in Communication

Communication is simply the act of transferring information from one place, person or group to another. Every communication involves one sender, a message and recipient. Communication through computers can be done in many ways as e-Mailing, chatting, video conferencing, protocols etc.

(viii) IT in Business

In context of business, IT has been proved to be most beneficial. Some of the benefits are as follows :

- With the help of IT, business can maximise employee engagement and productivity using different technology because an employee can work from anywhere at anytime.
- IT can help a company in knowing the customer mindset and hence can deliver them quality product services accordingly.
- Better and simpler organisation of data can be done by using computer.
- It provides better and enhanced job opportunities.

(ix) IT in Science and Engineering

Computers are widely used in engineering purpose. One of major areas is CAD (Computer Aided Design), that provides creation and modification of images. Computers help in planning towns, designing buildings, determining a range of buildings on a site using both 2D and 3D drawings. Computers deal with design, implementation and improvement of integrated systems of people, materials and equipments.

(x) IT in Banking

In modern banking system, computer is an essential part. Every activity of a bank is now online. All the work of bank like record the customer's data, transaction etc, done by computers. Recurring deposits (e-RD), Fixed deposits (e-FD), money transfer from one account to another (NEFT, RTGS), online transactions etc, are done using Internet.

Capital market transactions, financial analysis and related services are also available in online platforms. Bank customers use ATM (Automated Teller Machines) for cash deposits, withdrawal or to view current balance.

(xi) IT in Insurance

Insurance companies keep all records up to date with the help of database which are stored in computers. In insurance companies, procedures for continuation of policies, starting date, date of next installment, maturity date, interest dues, survival benefits, bonus etc. are declared and saved by using computers.

Many online policies are also available on internet which can be purchased by customers using the website of insurance companies.

(xii) IT in Marketing

In marketing, computers are used for advertising of products. These advertising are done using arts and graphics facility on computer. With the help of interesting advertisements of various products, we can achieve the goal of selling. Using e-Commerce websites, people can purchase items even sitting at home.

(xiii) IT in Healthcare

Computers and ICT technologies are making healthcare for all patients more efficient and accurate. ICT is used in the healthcare sector in numerous ways. Hospital management system is used to maintain and manage patient's records as well as various activities, pertaining to hospital administration. The computerised machines are used for ECG, EEG, ultrasound and CT scan. A variety of measuring instruments and surgical equipment are used to monitor's patient condition during complex surgery. Expert system is used for diagnosis. Healthcare manufacturing companies use computers to aid the production of diagnostic tools and instruments.

Computers are an integral part of laboratories and dispensaries.

Use of ICT in Diagnosis

With the advancements in computer technology, various high tech machines are used in the diagnosis and treatment of critical diseases. Using expert system, diseases can be diagnosed at the early stages and patients can be given treatment according. Some of these machines are :

(i) **Computerised Axial Tomography (CAT) Scan** CAT scanning is a painless X-ray test in which a computer generates three dimensional (3D) images of different parts of body. These images are helpful in the diagnosis of diseases. It can identify normal and abnormal structures. CAT scan is also known as CT (Computerised Tomography) scan.

(ii) **MRI (Magnetic Resonance Imaging) Machine** MRI machines are used to give the digital impression of internal organs of the body by using strong magnetic fields and radio waves. The digital images are very helpful in the detection and in deciding the treatment of diseases.

(iii) **Electrocardiogram (ECG) Machine** The ECG machine is used to monitor the heartbeat. When the heart pumps blood to different parts of the body, some electrical impulses are produced. This machine records the electrical impulses and shows it in the form of graph.

(iv) **Cardiac Screening Machine** This machine displays the physiology of the heart and it displays the movements inside the heart. Through this machine, it is possible to diagnose problems of the heart such as thinning of veins and then recommend treatment.

(v) **EEG (Electro-encephalography) Machine** This machine is used to record the activities of the brain. For this, a small electrical probes attached to the head. It receives the electrical impulses of the brain and display them on a computer screen. This device can retrieve the data in both states when a patient is awake or asleep.

(vi) **Blood Sugar Testing Machine** This device analyses a sample of blood and determines the glucose level in blood.

(vii) **Blood Pressure Measuring Machine** This device worn as a wrist band, can measure the blood pressure of person at rest as well as in some physical activity.

(xiv) IT in the Government and Public Service

The government uses large-scale computer applications in its daily operations and is actively encouraging e-Governance practices. By using Internet, government can offer services in an efficient and easy manner.

Digital India and e-Governance initiative of Government of India are best examples of this. Government and Non-Government Organisations (NGOs) as well as International Government agencies use ICT applications to communicate and provide various services to the people and is called as **e-Governance**.

Computers are used in income tax department, sales tax department, preparations of voters list, preparation of PAN card etc. Many government services are available online, even electricity bills can now be paid online. The government uses electronic voting for elections, by replacing the traditional voting slip and ballot box.

Check Point 02

1. Communication through computers can be done with
(a) e-Mailing (b) chatting (c) video conferencing (d) All of these
2. Using .... websites, people can purchase items even sitting at home.
3. Expert system is used for diagnosis. (True/False)
4. Write the full form of EEG machine.
5. What is the use of computers in library?

NCERT FOLDER

Check Your Progress

Pg 14

A. Give an example of the use of IT in the following areas. Avoid already discussed examples.

Teacher Practice	Example
1. Classroom content transaction	
2. Assessment of students	
3. Library management	
4. Student record management	

Ans. 1. Creation of images and video.
2. Keep the student database.
3. Keep the record of books subjectwise.
4. Edmatrix

B. Short Answer Questions

1. What do you understand by the term IT and ITeS?

Ans. Refer to text on Pages 99 and 100.

2. What are the pros and cons of using ICT?

Ans. Refer to text on Pages 99 and 100.

3. What precautions are required to ensure that ICT use is safe?

Ans. The precautions may be

- By keeping the use of ICT safe, we need to make sure that we do not overuse it.
- One should install protective softwares which can help to reduce any damage to the data present in the computer, from malware function, data erasing etc.
- Almost every type of content is available on the Internet these days, but we need to avoid getting manipulated with violent, pornographic or harmful content and make best use of useful content.

4. What are the four main sub-sectors in the IT-BPM industry?

Ans. Refer to text on Page 100.

5. Give examples of use of IT in everyday life.

Ans. In our daily life, we use washing machines, microwave oven and many other products which have embedded software. We can store all the information about our important work, appointments schedules and list of contacts in a computer. Computers are playing a very important role in our lives and now we cannot imagine the world without computers.

6. How is IT used in libraries?

Ans. Refer to text on Page 101.

7. What are the various processes of education where IT is used?

Ans. Refer to text on Pages 101 and 102.

8. Which softwares are used in digital communication?

Ans. Communication is used to convey messages and ideas, pictures or speeches. There are many softwares developed to facilitate the digital communication between peoples some of them are

- **Skype** It is a software that enables the individuals or businesses to make free video and voice one-to-one and group calls, send instant messages and share files with other people.

- **Dropbox** IT is one of several popular cloud storage services that enable you to store and share your files online in the cloud.
- **Slack** It is a group messaging communication software with real-time messaging, archiving and search for team.
- **Google drive** It is another popular web based sharing platform. With a google drive connector, users can readily access folders and files to boost productivity.

9. For what purpose is IT used in business?

Ans. Refer to text on Page 102.

10. Which are the prominent areas where IT is used in science and engineering?

Ans. Refer to text on Page 102.

11. List the various uses of IT in a banking system.

Ans. In modern banking system, computer is an essential part. Every activity of a bank is now online. All the work of bank like record the customer's data, transaction etc, done by computers. Recurring deposits (e-RD), Fixed deposits (e-FD), money transfer from one account to another (NEFT, RTGS), online transactions etc, are done using Internet.

Capital market transactions, financial analysis and related services are also available in online platforms. Bank customers use ATM (Automated Teller Machines) for cash deposits, withdrawal or to view current balance.

12. Which are different areas of health care where IT is used? And how?

Ans. Refer to text on Page 103.

13. List any five websites of the Indian government which provide IT enabled services to the people.

Ans. Five websites of the Indian government which provide IT enabled services to the people are:

- **https://uidai.gov.in** This website provides the facility for applying new adhaar card, to view status of adhaar card etc.
- **https://www.indiapost.gov.in** This website provides the services related to postal.
- **https://portal1.passportindia.gov.in** This website provides the services related passport such as apply new passport, some changing in passport etc.
- **https://www.epfindia.gov.in** This website provides all services related to provident funds.
- **https://www.irctc.co.in** This website provides all services related to Indian railway such as rail ticket booking, check ticket status, check seat availability etc.

SUMMARY

- Information Technology (IT) means creating, managing, storing and exchanging information.
- ITeS is defined as outsourcing of processes that can be enabled with information technology and covers diverse areas like finance, HR, administration, healthcare, telecommunication, manufacturing etc.
- BPO (Business Process Outsourcing) services means performing business operations through an outside service provider.
- IT-BPM (Business Process Management) industry has been fueling India's growth.
- The use of computer and Information Technology can be observed at home, workplace, in modern service industry and in all aspects of our life.
- A computer can be used to study a wide range of online training courses from home.
- The software and hardware technology is used for creation and transmission of information in various forms including still pictures, audio, video and animation to the learners.
- Communication is used to convey messages and ideas, pictures or speeches.
- Hospital management system is used to maintain and manage patient's records as well as various activities pertaining to hospital administration.
- Government and Non-Governmental Organisations (NGOs) as well as International Government Agencies use ICT applications to communicate and provide various services to the people and is called as e-Governance.

Exam Practice

Multiple Choice Questions

1. Which of the following means creating, managing, storing and exchanging information?
(a) IT (b) ITeS (c) BPO (d) KPO

Ans. (a) IT

2. ITeS offers different service(s)
(a) medical transcription (b) data warehousing
(c) IT help desk services (d) All of these

Ans. (d) All of these

3. .... are firms with their headquarters in India.
(a) MNCs (b) GICs
(c) ISPs (d) None of these

Ans. (c) ISPs

4. What is the full form of CAD?
(a) Computer Aided Design
(b) Computer Added Design
(c) Computer Aided Digital
(d) Computer Added Digital

Ans. (a) Computer Aided Design

5. In banking system, customer's data and transactions are recorded by
(a) computers (b) ATM
(c) scanner (d) fax

Ans. (a) computers

Fill in the Blanks

1. .... is also called web-enabled services.

Ans. ITeS

2. BPO stands for Business Process ....

Ans. Outsourcing

3. BPO services follow .... to ensure error free and exceptional free.

Ans. quality checks

4. .... is used to issue and return the book.

Ans. Computer software

5. Students can also contact a teacher or a trainer *via* Internet to use ....

Ans. Web Based Training (WBT)

True/False

1. ICT has been creation of new and interesting jobs.

Ans. True

2. Government of India is encouraging the BPO industry by providing necessary infrastructure.

Ans. True

3. Through online discussion forums, students cannot share knowledge.

Ans. False

4. CAT stands for Computer Axial Tomography.

Ans. False

5. ECG machines record the electrical impulses and show it in the form of graph.

Ans. True

Match the Columns

1. Match the following columns.

Column I		Column II	
A.	IT-BPM industry	1.	DELL, HP, Accenture etc.
B.	MNCs	2.	Include both MNCs and ISPs
C.	EEG machine	3.	Fueling India's growth
D.	ISPs	4.	HCL, Mahindra Satyam etc.
E.	GICs	5.	Record the activity of brain

Ans. A → 3; B → 1; C → 5; D → 4; E → 2

Very Short Answer (VSA) Type Questions

1. What is the extended synonym for Information Technology?

Ans. An extended synonym for Information Technology (IT) is Information and Communication Technology (ICT).

2. What do you mean by Indian Service Providers?

Ans. Indian Service Providers (ISPs) are firms with their headquarters in India. These may cater to domestic or international customer base.

3. Write any two Global In-house centres.

Ans. Barclays Technology Center India, Honeywell

4. What is flipped classroom model?

Ans. Flipped classroom model is where students watch lectures at home on the computer.

5. How to explain entertainment in one line?

Ans. Entertainment is something that holds the attention and interest of an audience or give pleasure and delight.

Short Answer (SA) Type Questions

1. Explain the difference between IT and ICT.

Ans. Difference between IT and ICT are as follows :

IT	ICT
IT stands for Information Technology.	ICT stands for Information and Communication Technology.
It is used in more complex and bigger organisations such as companies and large corporations.	It is mainly used in the academic setup.

2. What do you mean by BPO services?

Ans. BPO (Business Process Outsourcing) services means performing business operations through an outside service provider. BPO also comes under IT services as IT plays a very useful role in optimising the business performance. BPO categories are front office customer services.

3. What is the use of learning management system?

Ans. Refer to text on Page 102.

4. Describe the use of IT in games?

Ans. Refer to text on Page 102.

5. List the various use of IT in insurance.

Ans. Refer to text on Page 103.

6. Write the difference between IT and ITeS.

Ans. Difference between IT and ITeS are as follows :

IT	ITeS
IT stands for Information Technology.	ITeS stands for IT enabled Services.
It is the study of design, management, development, implementation and support of computer based information systems.	It is the study of outsourced service which has arisen due to involvement in various fields of IT.
It includes hardware and software industry and even IT telecom.	It includes call center, BPO, KPO, RPO, etc.

7. What is the ICT?

Ans. Refer to text on Page 99.

8. Define the services which are included by ITeS.

Ans. Refer to text on Page 100.

9. What are the uses of IT at workplace?

Ans. In the office environment, computers and complex applications are used to perform office work more effectively. In assembly-line industries, where attention to detail, speed and efficiency are important, automation is becoming more and more common. Internet and office application from the basis of modern business.

10. Define the ICT in the classroom.

Ans. Refer to text on Page 101.

Long Answer (LA) Type Questions

1. What is BPM industry? Also, explain the structure of the IT-BPM industry.

Ans. Refer to text on Pages 100 and 101.

2. What is the use of IT in entertainment? Explain.

Ans. Information Technology had a major impact on entertainment industry. Importance of IT in entertainment defined in many ways as:

(i) **In movies** Computers are widely used to create special effects in big budget movies. They are also extensively used behind the scenes to edit film during the production process. Movies are developed using computer graphics, animations etc.

(ii) **In games** Computer games is a quickly growing market. Computers have access to many peripheral devices such as keyboard, mouse, joystick and more. Computers are absolutely necessary for programming any sort of new video game.

(iii) **In animation** Animation can be used to make cartoons, animated movies etc. The computer can create outerspace, alien characters and so on without the need of creating their physical models.

3. Write about any five machines that are used in diagnosis.

Ans. Refer to text on Page 103.

4. Describe the examples of use of IT in education.

Ans. Refer to text on Pages 101 and 102.

Self Assessment

Multiple Choice Questions

1. C in ICT stands for

(a) Communication (b) Computer (c) Control (d) None of these

2. Which field has been benefitted using the Information Technology?

(a) Education (b) Health (c) Governance (d) All of these

3. Which of the following software is/are used for science and engineering?

(a) CAD (b) CDA and CAM (C) CAM (d) Both (a) and (c)

4. What is the full form of MRI?

(a) Magnetic Resource Imaging (b) Magnetic Resonance Imaging
(c) Magnetic Resource Image (d) Magnetic Resonance Image

5. Which of the following is/are advantage(s) of ICT?

(a) Communication (b) Availability (c) New jobs (d) All of these

Fill in the Blanks

1. .... is a tightly integrated part of business.

2. In library, each book has .... which detect by barcode reader.

3. .... can be used to make cartoons, animated movies etc.

4. CAD stands for Computer Aided ....

5. CAT scan is also known as ....

True/False

1. Computers and information systems are an essential part of every business today.
2. India has the expertise in reducing costs with firm control on the quality of service.
3. MNCs has their headquarters in India.
4. Computers are now used for online shopping.
5. ECG machine is related to Health.

Match the Columns

1. Match the following columns.

	Column I		Column II
A.	ECG machine	1.	Money transfer
B.	CAD	2.	Used in engineering
C.	NEFT	3.	Monitor the heartbeat
D.	e-RD	4.	Used for communication
E.	FTP	5.	Recurring deposits

Very Short Answer (VSA) Type Questions

1. Write any two example of Indian Service Providers.
2. What is the use of ITeS?
3. Write the full form of IT-BPM.
4. Where is/are personal computer used?
5. What do you mean by e-Commerce?

Short Answer (SA) Type Questions

1. What is e-Governance?
2. Define the multinational companies. Also, give its example.
3. What is the use of IT in animation?
4. What is the purpose of Cardiac Screening machine?
5. Write any two differences between ICT and ITeS.
6. Write some of the BPO services.
7. For what purpose is IT used in science and engineering?
8. List the uses of IT in marketing.
9. What are the difference between MNCs and ISPs?

Long Answer (LA) Type Questions

1. What is IT-BPM industry? Also, write some advantages for which BPO services industry is doing exceptionally well in India.
2. Define ICT. Also, give its advantages and disadvantages.
3. Describe the uses of IT in government and public service.

UNIT

02

Data Entry and Keyboarding Skills

Chapter Checklist

- Keyboarding Skills
- Pointing Devices
- Typing Ergonomics
- Successful Keyboarding Tips
- Introduction to RapidTyping Tutor
- View and Analyse Statistics

Data entry is the process of inputting data or information into the computer using devices such as keyboard, scanner, microphone etc. This process is done by data entry operators who have complete knowledge regarding data entry. In general, data entry work includes all kind of data to be entered in the digital format from the source file which can be either in paper form or any other medium.

In order to enhance operational skills in the use of computers, knowledge of efficient and effective keyboarding skills and typing ergonomics is highly required with consistent, sincere efforts and controlled environment, we can master keyboarding skills and acquire high speed.

In this chapter, we will discuss various types of keys, typing ergonomics and positioning of fingers on the keyboard according to touch method of typewriting and use of typing software for learning keyboarding skills.

Keyboarding Skills

Keyboard is one of the most common text based input devices. The user can type text and command using this device. The layout of the keyboard was borrowed from the regular typewriter with some additional keys.

Keyboard is used to enter data or information in a computer system, which may be in numeric form or alphabetic form. When a key is pressed, an electrical signal is formed. These electrical signals are transmitted to a micro-controller in a coded form to the computer describing the character which corresponds to that key.

A keyboard generally has more than 100 keys. Each key of a keyboard corresponds to a single symbol. Some symbols require pressing and holding several keys simultaneously or in sequence. Simultaneous key press can produce actions or computer commands. Keyboards are also used for computer gaming either with regular keyboards or by using keyboards with special gaming features.

There are different types of keyboard such as QWERTY, DVORAK and AZERTY.

Keyboarding skills are a set of skills required to operate a keyboard smoothly while typing.

Types of Keys on Keyboard

The keys are categorised under the following groups:

1. **Alphanumeric keys** These include the alphabet keys (A, B, C, ..., Z) and number keys (0, 1, 2, 3, ..., 9).
2. **Punctuation keys** All of the keys associated with punctuation, such as the comma (,), period (.), semicolon (;), brackets ([]), parenthesis ({}) and so on.
3. **Alt key** It is short for Alternate key. It is used to change the function of other pressed keys.
4. **Arrow keys** There are four arrow keys to move the cursor (insertion point) Up (↑), Down (↓), Right (→) or Left (←). Arrow keys can also be used in conjunction with the Shift or Alt key.
5. **Shift key** Some keys on the keyboard like numeric keys have a symbol printed on their upper portion. Shift key is used to print these symbols. This key is also called combination key.
6. **Backspace key** It is used to erase anything typed.
7. **Caps Lock key** It is used to type the alphabet in capital letters. It enables or disables all the letters from being typed in capital letters. When this key is enabled, the alphabet would be in capital letters and when it is disabled, the alphabet would be in small letters.
8. **Control key** It performs a special operation with the combination of other keys.
9. **Delete key** It is used to erase information from the computer's memory and characters on the screen.
10. **Enter key** It is used to finish an entry and begin the new entry in a document. Enter key is an alternative to press ok button.
11. **Escape key** (Esc) It allows a user to cancel or abort operations, which are executing at present. It opens Start menu with the combination of Ctrl key.
12. **Function keys** These are the programmable keys, i.e. the programs can assign some specific actions. They are numbered from F1 to F12.
13. **Cursor control keys** Above the arrow keys there are four more keys to control the cursor. These are as follows :
    (i) **Home** It is used to return the cursor to the beginning of the line or the beginning of a document.
    (ii) **End** It moves the cursor to the end of line.
    (iii) **Page Up** When it is pressed, the page view will be moved up on page and cursor goes to the back page.
    (iv) **Page Down** When it is pressed, the page view will be moved down one page and cursor goes to the next page.
14. **Numeric keys** These are located at the right hand side of the keyboard. They consist of digits and mathematical operators.
15. **Num Lock key** It is used to enable and disable the numeric keypad.
16. **Windows key** It is used to open the Start menu.
17. **Spacebar key** It provides a space between two words. It is the longest key on the keyboard.
18. **Tab key** It is used to move the cursor over to the right to a pre-set point. In word document, tab is used to indent a paragraph.

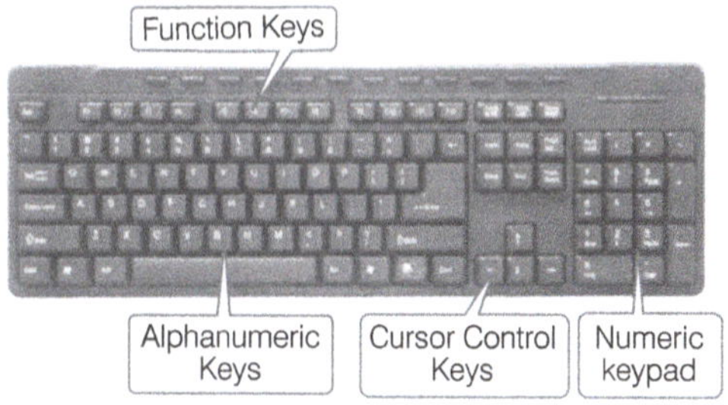

Keyboard

Numeric Keypad

It is used when enormous numeric data is to be entered. This keypad is just like a simple calculator. It is normally located on the right hand side of computer keyboard.

Numeric keypad contains numbers 0 to 9, addition (+), subtraction (–), multiplication (*), division (/), a decimal point (.) and Num Lock and Enter keys. Some of the keyboards of laptop do not have a numeric keypad. Numeric keypad may also work on dual mode like: numeric mode and cursor control mode. In numeric mode, it represents numbers and in cursor control mode, it contains various keys like: Arrow, Page Up, Page Down keys etc.

Home Keys

Home keys are also known as home row keys. Alphabets A, S, D and F are home keys for the left hand and; (semicolon) L, K and J for the right hand. The fingers are trained to make the correct movement to other keys and each finger returns immediately to its respective home key after it has pressed the corresponding key in any other row.

Position on Home Row

Guide keys

On a computer keyboard, keys F and J are called guide keys for left and right hand, respectively. Both contain a small raised tangible mark with the help of which the touch typist can place the fingers correctly on the home keys. Above figure shows the position of fingers of both hands on the home row.

Typing and Deleting Text

After opening a document, user starts typing. Cursor inserts a character at its current position, forcing all characters past it one position further. After typing the text in the document, the user can edit that text as per his/her requirement.

To add some text in the document, click the pointer on the correct position and then start typing, the all typed text will add to the right hand side of the cursor.

For typing numbers in a document, you should use the numeric keypad or the numbers on the second row of keys on keyboard.

For deleting text in a document, you should use the Backspace key or the Delete key. Backspace key deletes text to the left of the cursor. Delete or Del key deletes text to the right of the cursor.

Typing Capital Letters

To type capital letters, switch ON the Caps Lock by pressing the key before typing. A light will shine on the top right side corner of the keyboard that shows Caps Lock is ON. To switch it OFF, again press the Caps Lock key before typing.

Typing Symbols

Press and hold the Shift key and then press the key with the required symbol. There are two Shift keys on the keyboard–to the bottom left and right of the letters. The Shift key is used to type the top symbols that are one of the key with two characters.

Typing Sentences

To get the space between typed words, press the space bar once and then type the next word.

Creating New Lines and Space between Paragraphs

The Enter key is used to create new lines and spaces between paragraphs. Make sure that the cursor is blinking from a new line.

Check Point 01

1. What is meant by data entry?
2. Which of the following is a alphanumeric key?
   (a) B (b) 3
   (c) Both (a) and (b) (d) AB
3. Write the name of modifier keys.
4. Which key is used to delete the text?

Pointing Devices

A pointing device is used to communicate with the computer by pointing to the locations on the monitor. Movements of the pointing device are echoed on the screen by movements of the pointer. Some commonly used pointing devices are mouse, trackball, joystick, light pen, trackball, touch screen, etc.
Here we will discuss about only mouse:

Mouse

It is a pointing device used to point a particular place on the screen and select to perform one or more actions. It can be used to select menu commands, resize windows, selecting actions from screen icons etc.

A mouse primarily comprises of three parts : the buttons, handling area and the rolling object. By default, the mouse is configured to work for the right hand. The left handed persons can change the settings as per the needs.

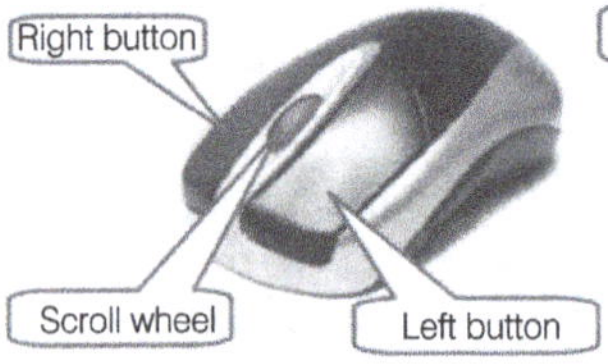

Mouse Buttons

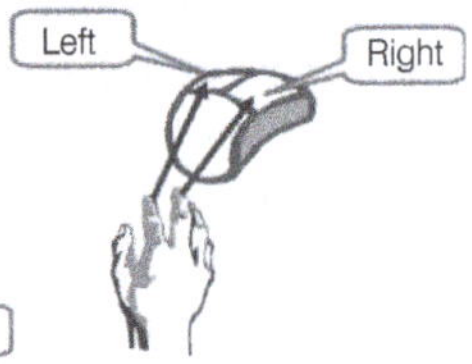

How to Hold the Mouse

Put the right hand on the mouse, the index finger goes on the left button and the middle finger goes on the right button.

Mouse Pointer

The mouse pointer allows to point on the screen. The pointer changes as shown below :

(i) ↖ This mouse pointer will appear as you move it around the screen. It will appear as you move it around the screen.

(ii) I This mouse pointer can be seen when you are about to type text.

(iii) While working on a web browser, the pointer change to a symbol (Pointing finger symbol) as moved it over the page. This identifies a hyperlink. Click the left mouse button once to follow the hyperlink to another page.

Mouse Operations

All mouse do not use the same mechanical operations but all of them accomplish the same task. Some of them use a tracking ball at the bottom and some of them use a type of light beam to detect the motion of mouse. Laptops are equipped with a small flat surface or sometimes with a very short stick for performing same job as mouse.

Mouse has two or three buttons on its top. These buttons are used for different actions. With the left button of mouse, we can use different operations like: selection, dragging, moving, pasting etc. With the right button, we can open a context menu for an item.

The common mouse actions are as follows:

1. **Click or Left Click** It selects an item on the screen.
2. **Double Click** It is used to open a document or program.
3. **Right Click** It displays a list of commands on the screen. Right clicking is used to access the properties of selected object.
4. **Drag and Drop** It is used to move an item from one location to another on the screen.
5. **Scrolling** Many applications provide scrollbars on right side of screen, if the page length is more than the screen length. It is used to view the whole active window. There are two types of scroll bars, i.e., horizontal scrollbar and vertical scrollbar. Move the mouse pointer to the desired position, your middle finger on the right mouse button, keeping the mouse still, click lightly with the middle finger on the right button.
6. **Blocking** It is another way of selecting text. It is used to select text that needs to be edited or formatted. Click at the beginning of the word or sentence and hold down the left button of mouse, then drag along the text and see it being highlighted in block. At the end of the text or sentence release the left button.

Position the mouse on an object, hold down the left button of the mouse and drag the object.

Typing Ergonomics

Typing ergonomics provides the logistic support for efficient and effective typewriting. They are important to attain and maintain accuracy and speed. Some of these factors included are as below :

1. Sitting Posture

While operating the computer keyboard, sit straight, slightly bending your neck forward. Check your comfort and sitting position of body. Touch the lower portion of your back to the lower portion of the back rest of the chair. Touch both the feet to the floor. While typing, you should not cross your legs. There should be a distance of approx 15 cm between two knees.

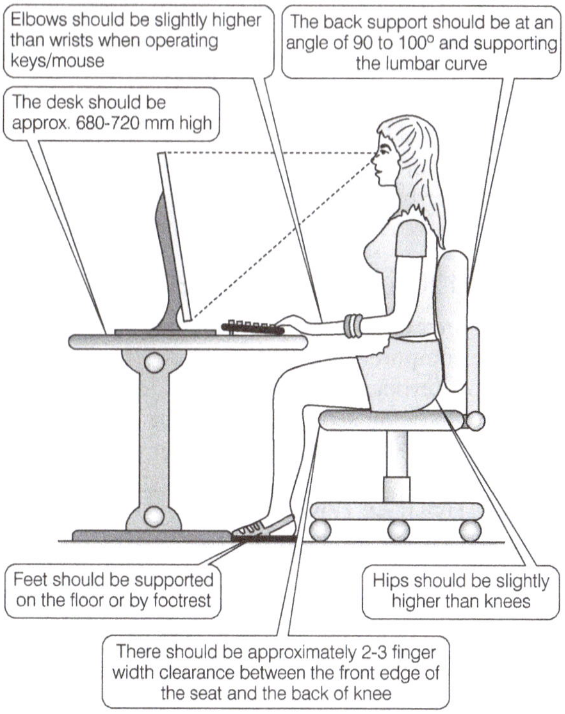

2. Position of Hands

A good position of hands is either parallel or slightly below the elbow. Your forearms should be at level with the keyboard and palms down. Keep your wrists straight.

The shoulders and elbows should hang naturally. The elbows should neither touch the body nor be too far away from the body. Elbows should also be bent at 90° angle.

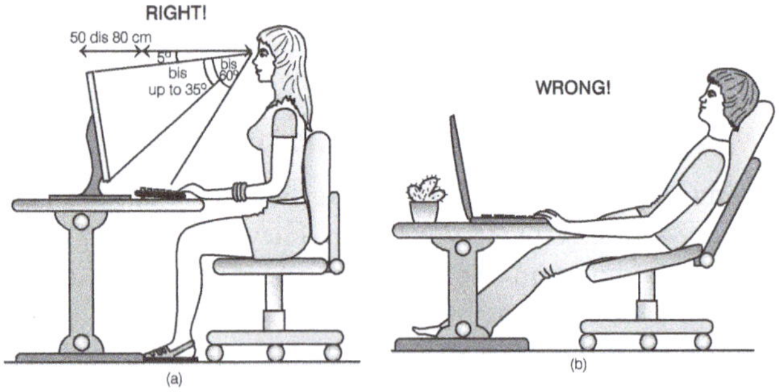

(a) Correct Screen Angle View

(b) Wrong Way Of Sitting

3. Monitor Placement

Do not bend your neck while working on the monitor and keep the upper border of screen at eye level. The distance of screen from the user depends on the size of the screen. Keep an approximate distance of about 60-65 cms for 17 inches screen.

4. Mouse and Keyboard Placements

Keep the keyboard and mouse together at an approximate distance of 20 cm, which will help in smooth and effortless operation of keyboard. Same height of keyboard, mouse and elbows help the users to work comfortably.

5. Chair and Table Placement

Adjust computer chair and table to an optimal height. The chair of the computer user must be supportive to his/her lower back. Keyboard and vibrating devices, such as printers should be on separate tables. The computer table should also have sufficient space for your legs.

6. Placement of Matter to be Typed

Place the matter for typing to the left or right side of the keyboard preferably on a copy holder which has a sloping surface.

Positioning of Fingers on the Keyboard

As typing is equivalent to pen or pencil now-a-days, mastery of computer keyboard has become obvious. Mastery typewriting skills means to attain necessary knowledge and skill of keyboard operation by correct positioning of fingers.

In the home row, all the eight fingers of both the hands rest on home keys during the keyboard operation. The fingers are trained to make the correct movement to other keys in such a way that each finger returns immediately to its home key after it has pressed the corresponding key in any other row. The thumb of the right hand is used to operate the space bar.

Allocation of Keys to Fingers

The keyboard learning process starts from the second row (home row) followed by the third row (upper row), first row (bottom row) and the fourth row (number row). The fingers of both of hands have to operate the keys allotted to them on each row. It must be remembered that each finger has to operate only the key allotted to it. The process of allocation of different keys to different fingers on different rows in given below :

Allocation of Keys to Fingers on the Second Row (Home Row)

Place four fingers of each hand on home row (second row). The remaining two keys G and H on the second row are operated by the forefingers (index finger) of left and right hand, respectively. Finger allocation is given below :

Home row - Left hand				
Lf	Rf	Mf	If	If
A	S	D	F	G

Home row - Right hand				
If	If	Mf	Rf	Lf
H	J	K	L	;

where, If - Index Finger, Mf - Middle Finger
Rf - Ring Finger, Lf - Little Finger

Allocation of Keys to Fingers on the Third Row (Upper Row)

The next step is learning the key-reaches from the home row to the row above it. The learning begins with the reaches from A to Q by left hand little finger and from; (semicolon) to P by right hand little finger. This is followed by the placement of the third fingers (ring finger) to the adjoining keys W and O and so on. In the third row, the allotment of fingers is explained below:

Upper row - Left hand				
Lf	Rf	Mf	If	If
Q	W	E	R	T

Upper row - Right hand				
If	If	Mf	Rf	Lf
Y	U	I	O	P

While typing on the upper row, keep fingers on home row. Lift fingers of left hand and strike upper row key one by one and type Q, W, E, R and T. Now, again lift the fingers of right hand and strike upper row keys one after another and type P, O, I, U and Y. You should ensure that one finger should move at a time, while other fingers should remain on home row.

Allocation of Keys to Fingers on the First Row (Bottom Row)

After learning how to operate keys on home row and third row, the next step is to learn how to operate keys on the first row. Keys Z, X, C, V, B, N, M, comma (,), full stop (.) and forward slash (/) are located on this row. In the first row, the allotment of fingers is explained below:

Bottom row - Left hand				
Lf	Rf	Mf	If	If
Z	X	C	V	B

Bottom row - Right hand				
If	If	Mf	Rf	Lf
N	M	,	.	/

Allocation of Keys to Fingers on the Fourth Row (Number Row)

In this row, type 1, 2, 3 with little, ring and middle fingers of the left hand respectively, and 4 and 5 with the index finger (forefinger). Similarly, type 0, 9, 8 with little, ring and middle fingers of right hand respectively, 7 and 6 with index finger. In the fourth row, the allotment of fingers is explained below :

Number row - Left hand				
Lf	Rf	Mf	If	If
1	2	3	4	5

Number row - Right hand				
If	If	Mf	Rf	Lf
6	7	8	9	0

Using Numeric Keypad

Efficient and effective use of numeric keypad is important in numeric data entry. The numeric keypad has four columns and five rows. The row which has 4, 5, 6 and + is called home row. This is the row which is initially practiced by a touch typist.

On a numeric keypad, the number 5 is the guide key. It has a small raised tangible mark which serves as a guide for the touch typist in the placement of fingers on other keys. Allocation of rest of the keys on numeric keypad 0 is to be pressed by the right hand thumb.

Check Point 02

1. How do you use drag and drop?
2. What is typing ergonomics?
3. Write the position of hands while typing.
4. Name the third row keys.

Successful Keyboarding Tips

The following points may be kept in mind for successful keyboarding techniques :

- Press the keys with feather touch and do not put undue pressure.
- Rest your fingers on home row while typing.
- Allow your fingers to all naturally on the keys so that each rests on top of the next key along the same horizontal row.
- While typing, release the key immediately as soon as you press it. Holding the key for long time, will repeatedly type the same character.
- Do not look at the keyboard while practicing.
- Press the keys with equal intervals of time in rhythm.
- Press the keys only with the fingers allotted for them.
- Do not take any mental stress while typing.
- Maintain a balance between speed and accuracy, as both are equally important. Do not sacrifice accuracy for speed.
- To gain Mastery of computer keyboard, undertake repeated practice of typewriting words, sentences, passages and figures without looking at the keyboard.

Using Typing Software

There are many software available which are free of cost and are customised to learn typing efficiently and effectively.

Introduction to RapidTyping Tutor

RapidTyping tutor is a Free and Open Source Software (FOSS) designed to learn typing skills on the computer. It is free to use and share with others, but only by using the original distribution package. It is efficient typing software that teaches typing through fun and interactive typing game.

Touch Typing Technique

Touch typing improves typing speed and accuracy. A touch typist never looks at the keyboard. The fingers hit the right keys by habit. The typist is entirely focused on the text being typed, reading the words and phrases as the fingers type the text reflexively.

There are three stages involved in touch typing technique:

- **Stage 1** This stage of the process begins with learning the home row of the keyboard (the row beginning with the Caps Lock key). Looking at the keyboard is strictly forbidden. This is followed by learning the lower and upper rows, the number row, uppercase letters and special symbols.
- **Stage 2** In this stage, a touch typing learner starts memorising frequently used syllables and typing words containing these syllables.
- **Stage 3** This stage involves typing actual text to perfect the skills acquired.

Touch Typing Rules

Before we actually start working on the RapidTyping software, it is good to learn about the basic rules that one should keep in mind in order to learn the touch typing skill in a proper manner. The following are some points that you should keep in mind while typing :

(i) The F, D, S, A and J, K, L, ; keys (on a QWERTY keyboard) represent the base position. Keyboards usually have small protrusions on the F and J keys. They help your fingers locate the base position without looking at the keyboard. Try to return your fingers to the base position after each keystroke.

(ii) Color coding of the RapidTyping tutor keyboard shows which finger should press each key. The left index finger is reserved for all the red keys. The right index finger is reserved for green keys and so forth. See the given figure for the color coding:

Keyboard Layout for Learning Typing

Use the thumb of whichever hand is more convenient for you to press Space key.

(iii) The base position on the numeric pad is the 5 number key for the middle finger, 4 for index finger and 6 for ring finger.

(iv) Uppercase letters and symbols appearing on keys in the number row are typed by one hand with the little finger of the other hand holding down the Shift key.

(v) At the time of typing do not look the keyboard. Try to locate the right key with your fingers.

User Interface of Typing Tutor

Open the RapidTyping software by any of the steps mentioned below :

Double click on the shortcut icon of the RapidTyping software.

Or

Click on the Start button → All Programs → RapidTyping 5.

The following RapidTyping window will appear.

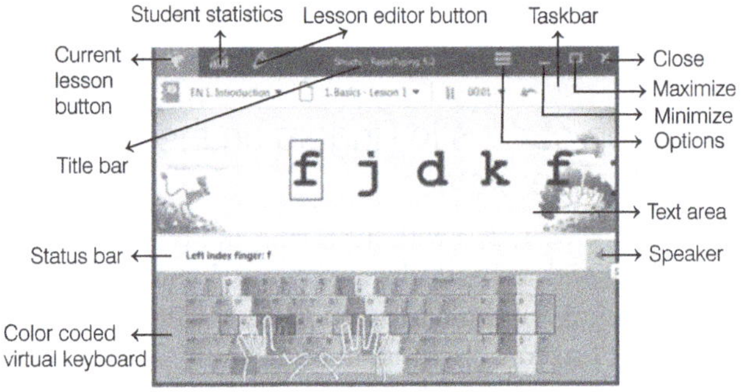

RapidTyping Interface

The different components of the RapidTyping window are as follows :

(i) **Title bar** It shows the name of the application program. It also has buttons for different tasks such as accessing Lesson editor, Current lesson, Student statistics alongwith the minimize, maximize and close buttons.

(ii) **Current lesson button** This button is used to check the current lesson in which a user is working at present.

(iii) **Student statistics button** This button is used to check the statistics of the user's typing skills.

(iv) **Lesson editor button** This button is used to open the Lesson editor to edit the lesson settings.

(v) **Options button** This button is used to set the appearance settings of the typing tutor such as language, keyboard, text color, background color, font, theme etc.

(vi) **Minimize button** This button is used to minimize the RapidTyping window.

(vii) **Maximize button** This button is used to maximize the RapidTyping window.

(viii) **Close button** This button is used to close the RapidTyping window.

(ix) **Select course button** This button is used to select the course type in which a user wants to work, i.e. Introduction, Beginner etc.

(x) **Select lesson button** This button is used to select the lesson type in which a user wants to work.

(xi) **Start/Pause lesson button** This button is used to start/pause the lesson.

(xii) **Current lesson time button** This button shows the elapsed time and remaining time when a user is working with a lesson.

(xiii) **Restart the lesson button** This button resumes or restarts the lesson.

(xiv) **Text area** This area displays the practice text to be typed by a user while practicing with a lesson.

(xv) **Status bar** This is also known as Lesson control panel. This displays the tips to be used to improve the typing skills while working with RapidTyping. It also contains the speaker button to control the sound volume and enable/disable sounds.

(xvi) **Color coded virtual keyboard** This keyboard highlights the keys to be pressed when a user is working with a lesson in the RapidTyping software.

(xvii) **Taskbar** It allows to set or change some basic options to start a lesson (keyboard layout, level, lesson and background).

(xviii) **Keyboard** It is the virtual keyboard that will help you to learn touch typing with all 10 fingers.

Begin Lessons

To start your first lesson in typing tutor, select the keyboard layout, level and lesson category on the taskbar. There are three drop-down lists in the top left corner of the screen. Perform the below mentioned steps to start the touch typing lesson :

(i) Open the RapidTyping software by clicking on its icon. Main window of RapidTyping software will appear.

(ii) By default, the first course is the Introduction course will be shown. Start the Introduction course only by clicking on the Select course button.

(iii) Click on the Select lesson → Basics → Lesson 1 button to select the first basic lesson of the introduction course to start the typing practice.

(iv) Place your fingers on the home row keys as shown in the Color coded virtual keyboard. Notice that the status bar is showing the tip to put the fingers in the base position. Put your fingers in the base position that are shown in the text area. Use your thumbs to press the Spacebar key.

(v) The Current lesson time button displays the lesson time when you are typing.

(vi) To start a lesson, click the '▶' button in the taskbar.

(vii) You can press the || (Pause) button to stop the lesson in case you want to take a break.

(viii) To restart the current lesson, click the ↻ (Restart) button.

(ix) To enable/disable sounds in the current lesson, click the 🔊 button and set the sounds volume using the vertical slider.

Note *You can also set the background image for the Text panel by choosing an option (Animation, Wallpaper or Plain) from the dropdown list on the taskbar in top right corner of the window.*

(x) Continue typing, notice that the status bar keeps on guiding at the time you are pressing the keys on the keyboard. The status bar also displays two progress bars, i.e. yellow and green.

The yellow progress bar shows the acceptable time for typing a single character and the Green progress bar shows the completion status for the Current lesson. When the yellow progress bar runs out atleast once, Typing Tutor records that you have broken the rhythm at this character.

How to Interpret your Results

Each time you complete a lesson, the Results window displays your achievements in this lesson. You can use this window to assess your performance alongwith the progress that you are making.

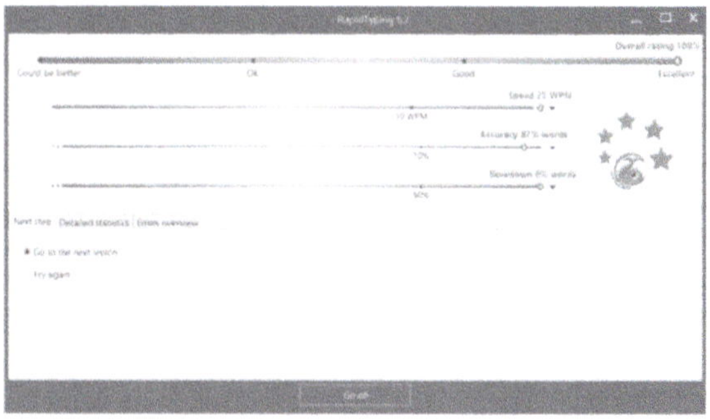

Results Dialog Window for your Achievements

The upper part of the Results window displays overall rating and is known as Rating pane. The lower part has different tabs named Next step, Detailed statistics and Errors overview. Each tab has a different purpose.

The Results window has the following parts :

(i) The Rating pane displays overall rating alongwith the typing speed and typing accuracy. You can view Rating pane to evaluate your typing skills.

(ii) The topmost bar of the Rating pane shows the overall rating scale. It also shows the progress ranging that Could be better, OK, Good and Excellent.

(iii) The second bar of the Rating pane shows the typing speed in terms of WPM (Words Per Minute).

(iv) The third bar of the Rating pane shows the accuracy of your typing lesson.

(v) The last bar of the Rating pane shows the slowdown of your lesson.
Thus, the Rating pane helps in monitoring the progress while practicing with the lessons of the RapidTyping software.

(vi) The lower part of the Results window has following three tabs.

Next step By default, this tab will be activated. It has following two options:

(i) **Go to the next lesson** This option will let you move to the next lesson after finishing a lesson in the RapidTyping.

(ii) **Try again** This option will take you back to the recent lesson in which you were working.

Detailed Statistics The Detailed statistics option shows the detailed statistics analysis of your typing lesson. This option/tab has following two pane :

(i) **Speed pane** The pane shows the statistics based on the typing speed. You can click on Select unit of typing speed button for measuring the speed. By default, the speed will be KPM (Keystrokes Per Minute).

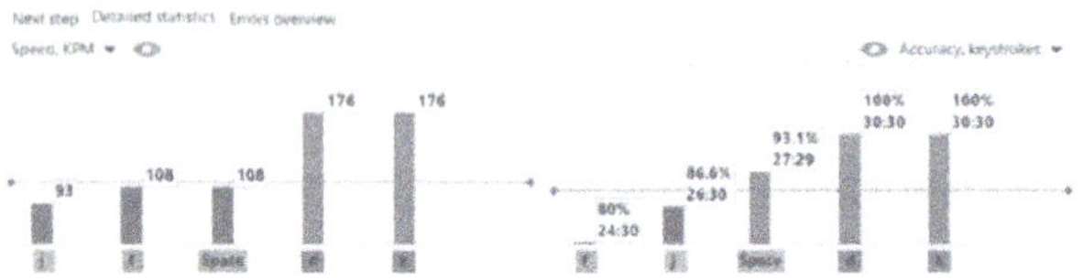

(ii) **Accuracy pane** This pane shows the statistics based on the accuracy of the lesson such as accuracy while pressing the keystrokes or errors while pressing the keystrokes, etc. You can click on the Select unit of typing accuracy button for observing the typing accuracy. By default, the accuracy will be calculated on the basis of keystrokes.

Errors Overview The Errors overview tab can be used to see the errors that were being made while practicing the typing lesson. The color coding used by these tabs are as follows :

(i) **Red color** letters denote wrong inputs within the acceptable timeframe.

(ii) **Green color** letters denote right inputs within the acceptable timeframe.

(iii) **Yellow color** letters stand for right inputs exceeding acceptable timeframe.

(iv) **Orangle color** letters indicate wrong inputs that also exceed the acceptable timeframe.

Check Point 03

1. RapidTyping tutor is a free software. (True/False)
2. Write the use of Current lesson button.
3. To start a lesson, click the .... button in the taskbar.
4. How many colors are used in Errors overview?

View and Analyse Statistics

To view the results of all the lessons that you have already completed. Click on the Student statistics btton, present on the Title bar to open the Student statistics section. The Student statistics window will appear :

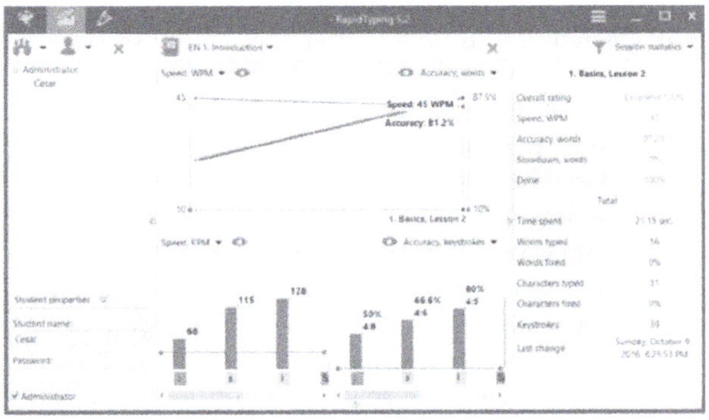

Overall Statistics and Progress of Your Typing

Here, you can review your overall statistics and progress both in graphical and table view. To view and analysis statistics in RapidTyping software, we have to follow the below steps :

Step 1 Click the CPM statistics button in the top-left corner of the window (or press Ctrl +1 shortkey on keyboard) to see your CPM (characters per minute) speed progress.

Step 2 Click the WPM statistics button (or press Ctrl + 2 shortkey on keyboard) to see your WPM (words per minute) speed progress.

Step 3 Click the Accuracy statistics button (or press Ctrl + 3 shortkey on keyboard) to see how your typing accuracy changes in the different lessons.

Step 4 To remove a metric from your statistics, select a lesson in the right table and click the button (or press Delete shortkey on keyboard).

Step 5 On the taskbar in the upper part of the window, you can choose keyboard layout, level and course for which you would like to see statistics.

Step 6 You can also switch between the Lesson Group and Day Group options in the far right drop-down on the taskbar.

Working with Lesson Editor

Lesson Editor allows us to set our own targets in terms of speed, number of errors, slowdown etc. Lesson Editor makes all the lessons fully customisable. You can add, insert, change and delete lessons, group them in courses and review the corresponding metrics.

To open Lesson Editor, click on the Lesson Editor button present on the title bar of the RapidTyping software. The Lesson Editor window will appear.

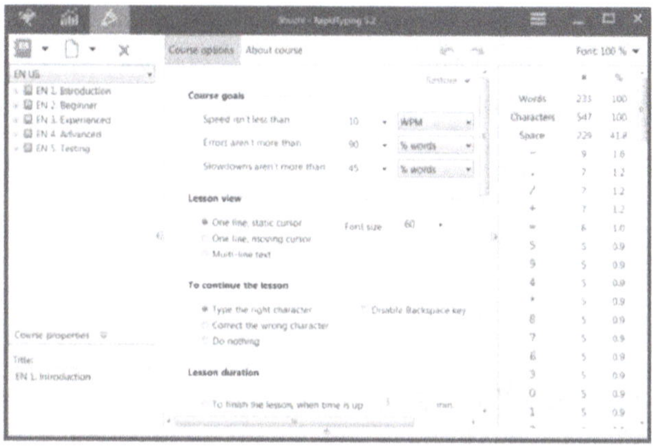

Adding a New Lesson

Perform the following steps to customise a new lesson in the Lesson Editor:

Step 1 Click on the Lesson menu button on the taskbar, a drop-down menu will appear. Select the Create new lesson option from the menu.

Step 2 Select a course in the Navigation tree in which you want to add the lesson such as Beginner.

Step 3 Click on the Lesson type option, a drop-down menu will appear. Click on the main pad option to select the lesson types.

Step 4 Type the text in the text area that you want to add in the lesson.

Step 5 After typing the text, go to the Lesson properties pane.

Step 6 Click in the text box under the Title section and give the lesson a name such as My Lesson.

Saving a Lesson

Perform the following steps to save a lesson in the Lesson Editor:

Step 1 Select the lesson created by you in the Navigation tree.

Step 2 Click on the Save selected lessons option from the Lesson menu.

Step 3 The Save As dialog box will appear. Select the location where you want to save the lesson. Type the name for the lesson in the File name section and click on the Save button to save the lesson.

Deleting a Lesson

Perform the following steps to delete a lesson:

Step 1 Select the lesson that you want to delete in the Navigation tree.

Step 2 Click on the Remove selected lesson or Course button to delete the lesson. The selected lesson will be deleted.

Adding a New Course

Perform the following steps to add a new course in the Lesson Editor:

Step 1 Click on the Course menu button on the taskbar.

Step 2 Click on the Create new course option from the menu.

Step 3 You can select the Course options as per your requirement in the Course options area.

Step 4 After customising the course, go to the Course properties pane.

Step 5 Click in the text box under the Title section and give a name to course such as My Course. The course will be added.

Deleting a Course

Perform the following steps to delete a course:

Step 1 Select the course that you want to delete in the Navigation tree.

Step 2 Click on the Remove selected lesson or Course button to delete the course. The selected course will be deleted.

Calculating the Typing Speed

The typing speed can be measured with different accuracies, such as

- How many **words** are typed for a certain time period (the least accurate)?
- How many **characters** are typed for a certain time period?
- How many **keystrokes** are made for a certain time period (the most accurate)?

Also, there are

- Simple speed (Gross speed)
- Net speed (takes into account the errors)

The following table lists the detailed descriptions for typing speed types:

Types	Description	Formula
WPM	The number of words typed in a one minute period of time.	WPM = (Words without errors + Words with errors)/Time spent in minutes
Net WPM	The WPM without words with errors.	Net WPM = WPM – (Words with errors/Time spent in minutes)
CPM	The number of characters typed in a one minute period of time.	CPM = (Characters without errors + Characters with errors)/Time spent in minutes

Types	Description	Formula
Net CPM	The CPM without characters with errors.	Net CPM = CPM – (Characters with errors/Time spent in minutes)
KPM	The number of keystrokes in a one minute period of time.	KPM = (Keystrokes without errors + Keystrokes with errors)/Time spent in minutes
Net KPM	The KPM without keystrokes with errors.	Net KPM = KPM – (Keystrokes with errors/Time spent in minutes)

e.g. A student typed 240 characters per 2 min with errors in 20 characters

Simple speed = 240 characters / 2 min = 120 CPM

Net speed = 120 CPM – (20 errors/2 min) = 100 Net CPM

Calculating the Typing Accuracy

Typing accuracy is defined as the percentage of correct entries out of the total entries typed. The following table lists, the different formulas for the typing accuracy calculation.

Description	Formula
Accuracy in the words, percent	Accuracy = (100% – Words with errors * 100%) / total number of words
Accuracy in the characters, percent	Accuracy = (100% – Characters with errors * 100%)/ Total number of characters
Accuracy in the keystrokes, percent	Accuracy = (100% – Incorrect keystrokes * 100%)/total number of keystrokes

Sometimes it's convenient to evaluate the typing accuracy in the errors (percentage errors). See table below :

Description	Formula
Errors in the words, percent	Errors % = Words with errors * 100% / Total number of words
Errors in the characters, percent	Errors % = Characters with errors * 100% / Total number fo characters
Errors in the keystrokes, percent	Errors % = Incorrect keystrokes * 100% / Total number of keystrokes

Calculating the Typing Rhythm

In the touch typing techniques, the typing rhythm is very important. This means that keystrokes should come at equal intervals. To control the constant typing speed, the slowdown indicator is used.

The following table shows the different formula for the Slowdown (percentage slowdowns) calculation.

Description	Formula
Slowdown in the words, percent	Slowdown % = Words with delay * 100% / Total number of words
Slowdown in the characters, percent	Slowdown % = Characters with delay * 100% / Total number of characters
Slowdown in the keystrokes, percent	Slowdown % = Keystroke delay * 100 % / Total number of keystrokes

Overall Rating Calculation

Overall rating (%)

= (Net speed / Course goal : Speed) * 100%

where,

- Net speed is Net WPM, Net CPM or Net KPM, the value depends on the Current options.
- Course goal : Speed is customised in the options for each course.

Good Typing Speed

An average professional typist types usually in speeds of 50 to 80 WPM, while some positions can require 80 to 95 and some advanced typists work at speeds above 120 WPM.

The fastest typing speed on an alphanumeric keyboard, 216 words in one minute was achieved by Stella Pajunas in 1946. As of 2005, writer Barbara Blackburn was the fastest alphanumerical English language typist in the world, according to The Guinness Book of World Records. Using the Dvorak Simplified keyboard, she maintained 150 WPM for 50 minutes, and 170 WPM for shorter periods. Her top speed was 212 WPM.

Check Point 04

1. How to open Student statistics in RapidTyping?
2. Write the steps to save a lesson in the Lesson Editor.
3. Write the formula to calculate the WPM.
4. What do you mean by typing rhythm?

NCERT FOLDER

Check Your Progress

Pg 42-44

A. Multiple Choice Questions

Read the questions carefully and circle the letter (a), (b), (c) or (d) that best answers the questions.

1. Which of the following is not a key for punctuation marks?
   (a) Comma (,) (b) Period (.)
   (c) Semicolon (;) (d) Equal sign (=)

Ans. (d) Equal sign (=) is not a key for punctuation marks. All of the keys associated with the comma (,), period (.), semicolon (;), brackets ([]), parenthesis ({}) are called punctuation keys.

2. Which of the following is not an arrow key?
   (a) Top (^) (b) Down (↓)
   (c) Right (→) (d) Left (←)

Ans. (a) There are four arrow keys to move the cursor - Up (↑), Down (↓), Right (→) or Left (←)

3. Which of the following operation is not performed by a mouse?
   (a) Left click (b) Right click
   (c) Middle click (d) Double click

Ans. (c) The common mouse operations are click or left click, right click, double click, drag and drop.

4. In the RapidTyping tutor, which of the following is not true?
   (a) Green letters denote right inputs.
   (b) Yellow letters stand for right inputs in extra time.
   (c) Red letters denote wrong inputs within time.
   (d) Orange letters indicate wrong inputs with in time.

Ans. (d) In the RapidTyping tutor, orange letters indicate wrong inputs that also exceed the acceptable timeframe.

5. The lesson control panel can be used for
   (a) animation
   (b) enable / disable sounds
   (c) plain
   (d) background

Ans. (b) The lesson control panel can be used for enable/disable sounds and control the sound volume.

B. Fill in the blanks

1. A touch typist knows the location on the keyboard through .... memory.

Ans. muscle

2. The typing speed is measured in ....

Ans. Words Per Minute (WPM)

3. Alphabets (A-Z) and numbers (0-9) are known as .... keys.

Ans. alphanumeric

4. Delete key deletes the character at the .... cursor position.

Ans. current

5. A standard keyboard has .... function keys.

Ans. 12

6. Numeric keypad is used to enter .... data.

Ans. numeric

7. Page Up key is used to shift the .... one page up.

Ans. cursor

8. Pressing the End key moves the cursor to the .... character of the line.

Ans. last

9. On numeric keypad '0' is to be pressed by the .... thumb.

Ans. Right hand

10. The numeric keypad has .... columns and .... rows.

Ans. four, five

C. State whether the statements given below are True or False.

1. The Alt key is always used with the other key.

Ans. True; The Alt key is always used with the other key to change the function of other pressed keys.

2. There are 5 arrow keys on the keyboard.

Ans. False; There are four arrow keys on the keyboard such as Up (↑), Down (↓), Right (→) or Left (←).

3. The Backspace key is used to delete the character on the right to the cursor.

Ans. False; The Backspace key is used to delete the character on the left to the cursor.

4. Caps Lock key is a toggle key.

Ans. True; Caps lock key is a toggle key, which when activated causes all alphabetic characters to be uppercase.

5. The Ctrl key is used in conjunction with other keys.

Ans. True; The Ctrl key is used in conjunction with other keys to produce control characters. The meaning of each control character depends on which program is running.

6. Enter key is also known as Return key.

Ans. True; Enter key is also known as Return key, which is used to enter commands or to move the cursor to the beginning of the next line.

7. The function keys have different meaning in different softwares.

Ans. True; Function keys are the programmable keys, i.e. the program can assign some specific actions.

These keys have different meanings in different softwares.

8. The keys 'F' and 'J' are known as guide keys.

Ans. True; On a computer keyboard, keys 'F' and 'J' are called guide keys for left and right hand, respectively.

9. There are two Caps Lock keys on the keyboard.

Ans. False; There is only one Caps Lock key on the keyboard, which is used to type the alphabet in capital letters.

10. The mouse has two scroll buttons.

Ans. False; The mouse has two buttons - right button and left button and one scroll button or wheel between these two buttons.

11. PageDown key is used to move the cursor on next page.

Ans. True; When PageDown key is pressed, the page view will be moved down one page and cursor goes to the next page.

12. Pressing the Home key, moves the cursor to the first character in the document.

Ans. True; Home key is used to move the cursor to the first character of the line or first character of a document.

13. On a numeric keypad, number 8 is the guide key.

Ans. False; On a numeric keypad, number 5 is the guide key. It has a small raised tangible mark, which serves as a guide for the touch typist in the placement of fingers on other keys.

14. In RapidTyping tutor, the right input entered is denoted by yellow color.

Ans. False; In RapidTyping tutor, the right input entered is denoted by green color.

15. In RapidTyping tutor, the right input entered in exceeding time frame is denoted by red color.

Ans. False; In RapidTyping tutor, the right input entered in exceeding time frame is denoted by yellow color.

D. Short Answer Questions

1. Discuss the various types of keys available on a computer keyboard.

Ans. Refer to text on Page 111.

2. Differentiate between Home key and Guide key.

Ans. Differences between Home key and Guide key are as follows :

Home key	Guide Key
A, S, D and F are home keys for the left hand and ; (semicolon), L, K and J for the right hand.	On a computer keyboard, keys F and J are guide keys for left and right hand, respectively.
On a numeric keypad, keys 4, 5, 6 and + are home keys.	On a numeric keypad, number 5 is the guide key.
The fingers are trained to make the correct movement to other keys and each finger returns immediately to its respective home key after it has pressed the corresponding key in any other row.	It has a small raised tangible mark which serves as a guide for the touch typist in the placement of fingers on other keys.

3. What do you understand by Guide keys? Name the Guide keys of a

(a) computer keyboard

(b) typewriter

Ans. Guide keys contain a small raised tangible mark with the help of which the touch typist can place the fingers correctly on the home keys.

(a) On a computer keyboard, keys F and J are called guide keys for left and right hand, respectively. On a numeric keypad, the number 5 is the guide key.

(b) On a typewriter, the two keys a and; (semicolon) are called guide keys which are pressed with left and right hand little fingers, respectively. Initially we place the little finger on these keys thus guiding the placement of rest of the fingers on home keys.

4. Explain the role of typing ergonomics.

Ans. Refer to text on Pages 113 and 114.

5. Why the use of various typing software is common now-a-days?

Ans. Now-a-days, there are uses of various typing softwares the main reason behind this is the situations where people are getting their confidential credentials stolen when they type anything on the keyboard because those keystrokes are recorded and after that is used for hacking. Typing software improves typing speed and accuracy. Typing softwares also provide typing games, multi-user support, method of finding errors and their rectification etc.

6. Mention the finger allocation of keys of the Bottom row of computer keyboard.

Ans. Refer to text on Page 115.

SUMMARY

- Data entry is the process of inputting data or information into the computer using devices such as keyboard, scanner, microphone etc.
- Keyboard is a text based input device. The user can type text and commands using this device.
- Numeric keypad is used when enormous numeric data is to be entered. It contains numbers 0 to 9, addition (+), subtraction (–), multiplication (*), division (/), a decimal point (.), Num lock and Enter keys.
- A pointing device is used to communicate with the computer by pointing to the locations on the monitor.
- Mouse is a pointing device used to point a particular place on the screen and select to perform one or more actions.
- Typing ergonomics provides the logistic support for efficient and effective typewriting. They are important to attain and maintain accuracy and speed.
- As typing is equivalent to pen or pencil now-a-days, Mastery of computer keyboard has become required. Mastery typewriting skills means to attain necessary knowledge and skills of keyboard operation by correct positioning of fingers.
- RapidTyping tutor is a free and open source software designed to learn typing skills on the computer.
- The status bar of RapidTyping tutor also displays two progress bars, i.e. yellow and green. The yellow progress bar shows the acceptable time for typing a character and the green progress bar shows the completion status for the current lesson.
- The Errors overview tab can be used to see the errors that were being made while practicing the typing lesson.
- Lesson Editor allows us to set our own targets in terms of speed, number of errors, slowdown etc. Lesson Editor makes all the lessons fully customisable.
- Typing accuracy is defined as the percentage of correct entries out of the total entries typed.

Exam Practice

Multiple Choice Questions

1. Which of the following is a type of keyboard?
(a) QWERTY
(b) DVORAK
(c) AZERTY
(d) All of the above

Ans. (*d*) There are different types of keyboard such as QWERTY, DVORAK, AZERTY etc.

2. Which key is used to enable and disable the numeric keypad?
(a) Windows key
(b) Num Lock key
(c) Shift key
(d) Ctrl key

Ans. (*b*) Num Lock key is used to enable and disable the numeric keypad.

3. Which of the following mode of numeric keypad represents numbers?
(a) Numeric mode
(b) Cursor control mode
(c) Both (a) and (b)
(d) None of the above

Ans. (*a*) Numeric mode of numeric keypad represents numbers while cursor control mode contains various keys like Arrow keys, Page Up, Page Down etc.

4. Which of the following mouse pointer can be seen when you are about to type text?
(a) ↖ (b) ☝
(c) I (d) None of these

Ans. (*c*) I mouse pointer can be seen when you are about to type text.

5. In which of the following factor, you should not cross your legs?
(a) Position of hands
(b) Sitting posture
(c) Monitor placement
(d) Mouse and keyboard placement

Ans. (*b*) In sitting posture factor, you should not cross your legs at the time of typing.

6. The keyboard learning process starts from
(a) second row
(b) fourth row
(c) first row
(d) third row

Ans. (*a*) The keyboard learning process starts from the second row (home row) followed by the third row (upper row), first row (bottom row) and the fourth row (Number row).

7. Which of the following stage of touch typing technique involves memorising frequently used syllables and typing words containing these syllables?
(a) Stage one
(b) Stage three
(b) Stage two
(d) None of the above

Ans. (*c*) Stage two involves memorising frequently used syllables and typing words containing these syllables.

8. The left index finger is reserved for all the
(a) green keys (b) red keys
(c) blue keys (d) orange keys

Ans. (*b*) The left index finger is reserved for all the red keys.

9. Which of the following buttons shows the elapsed time and remaining time when a user is working with a lesson?
(a) Pause the lesson button
(b) Current lesson time button
(c) Time lesson button
(d) None of the above

Ans. (*b*) Current lesson time button shows the elapsed time and remaining time when a user is working with a lesson.

10. Which shortkey is used to see WPM speed?
(a) Ctrl + 1 (b) Ctrl + 3
(c) Alt + 2 (d) Ctrl + 2

Ans. (*d*) Press Ctrl + 2 shortkey on keyboard is used to see WPM (Words Per Minute) speed.

Fill in the Blanks

1. .... is used to open the Start menu.

Ans. Windows key

2. To get the space between typed words, press the .... once and then type the next word.

Ans. Space bar

3. Do not hit the keyboard keys very ....

Ans. hard

4. .... of touch typing technique involves typing the actual text to perfect the skills acquired.

Ans. Stage 3

5. The .... window displays the result every time you finish a typing lesson.

Ans. Results

6. The .... shows that detailed statistics analysis of your typing lesson.

Ans. Detailed statistics

7. The .... button is used to open the Lesson Editor to edit the lesson settings.

Ans. Lesson Editor

True/False

1. Keyboard is used to select data or information in a computer system.

Ans. False; Keyboard is used to enter data or information in a computer system.

2. Shift, Ctrl and Alt keys are also known as modifier keys.

Ans. True; Shift, Ctrl and Alt keys are also known as modifier keys.

3. The numeric pad covers only the numeric keys on the keyboard.

Ans. True; The numeric pad covers only the numeric keys on the keyboard. This keypad is just like a simple calculator.

4. Left click is used to open a document.

Ans. False; Double click is used to open a document or program.

5. In the home row, all the eight fingers of both the hands rest on home keys during the keyboard operation.

Ans. True; In the home row, all the eight fingers of both the hands rest on home keys during the keyboard operation. It must be remembered that each finger has to operate only the key allotted to it.

6. In number row, keys 1, 2, 3, 4 and 5 are reserved for left hand.

Ans. True; In number row, keys 1, 2, 3, 4 and 5 are reserved for left hand. Similarly, keys 6, 7, 8, 9 and 0 are reserved for right hand.

7. The RapidTyping software is not a free typing software.

Ans. False; RapidTyping software is a free and open source software designed to learn typing skills on the computer.

8. A touch typist looks at the keyboard while typing.

Ans. False; At the time of typing do not look the keyboard. Try to locate the right key with your fingers.

9. Maximize button is used to maximize the RapidTyping window.

Ans. True; Maximize button is used to maximize the RapidTyping window.

10. KPM stands for keystrokes per second.

Ans. False; KPM stands for keystrokes per minutes.

Match the Columns

1. Match the following columns.

Column I		Column II	
A.	Pointing device	1.	shows the name of the application program
B.	Drag and drop	2.	(Net speed/Course goal : Speed) *100%
C.	Title bar	3.	is used to select the items on the screen
D.	Yellow progress bar	4.	is used to move an item on the screen
E.	Overall rating (%)	5.	shows the acceptable time for typing

Ans. A → 3; B → 4; C → 1; D → 5; E → 2

Very Short Answer (VSA) Type Questions

1. What is the use of keyboard?

Ans. Keyboard is used to enter data or information in a computer system, which may be in numeric form or alphabetic form.

2. How will you type the capital letters?

Ans. To type capital letters, switch ON the Caps Lock by pressing the key before typing. A light will shine on the top right side corner of the keyboard that shows Caps Lock is ON. To switch it OFF, again press the Caps Lock key before typing.

3. Explain the mouse and keyboard placement in typing.

Ans. Keep the keyboard and mouse together at an approximate distance of 20 cm, which will help in smooth and effortless operation of keyboard. Same height of keyboard, mouse and elbows help the users to work comfortably.

4. Why are the home row keys called by this name?

Ans. The home row keys are called by this name because we are always at typing using these keys and always return to them.

5. What is meant by touch typing?

Ans. The method of typing fast and in a fluent manner, without even looking at the keyboard is known as touch typing.

6. What does the status bar display?

Ans. The status bar displays the tips to be used to improve the typing skills while working with Rapid typing. It also contains the speaker button to control the sound volume and enable/disable sounds.

7. What is the use of the Lesson Editor?

Ans. The Lesson Editor is used to customise the courses as per our requirement. It allows us to set our own targets in terms of speed, number of errors, slowdown etc.

Short Answer (SA) Type Questions

1. What do you mean by keyboarding skills?

Ans. In order to enhance operational skills in the use of computers, knowledge of efficient and effective keyboarding skills and typing ergonomics is highly required. With consistent, sincere efforts and controlled environment, we can master keyboarding skills and acquire high speed. Keyboarding skills are a set of skills required to operate a keyboard smoothly while typing.

2. Explain the mouse pointer.

Ans. Refer to text on Page 113.

3. What are the base positions of your fingers on keyboard?

Ans. The F, D, S, A and J, K, L, ; (semicolon) keys represent the base position on a QWERTY keyboard. Keyboards usually have small protrusions on the F and J keys. They help your fingers locate the base position without looking at the keyboard. Try to return your fingers to the base position after each keystroke.

4. Write the steps to start the touch typing lesson.

Ans. Refer to text on Page 117.

5. How can you calculate the typing rhythm.

Ans. Refer to text on Page 120.

6. Explain the allocation of keys to fingers on the upper row.

Ans. The learning begins with the reaches from A to Q by left hand little finger and from; to P by right hand little finger. This is followed by the placement of the third fingers to the adjoining keys W and O and so on.

While typing on the upper row, keep fingers on home row. Lift fingers of left hand and strike upper row key one by one and type Q, W, E, R and T. Now, again lift the fingers of right hand and strike upper row keys one after another and type P, O, I, U and Y. You should ensure that one finger should move at a time, while other fingers should remain on home row.

7. What are various stages of touch typing technique?

Ans. Refer to text on Pages 115 and 116.

8. Explain the Detailed statistics in brief.

Ans. The Detailed statistics option shows the detailed statistics analysis of your typing lesson. This option has following two pane :

(i) **Speed pane** This pane shows the statistics based on the typing speed. You can click on Select unit of typing speed button for measuring the speed. By default, the speed will be KPM (Keystrokes Per Minute).

(ii) **Accuracy pane** This pane shows the statistics based on the accuracy of the lesson such as accuracy while pressing the keystrokes or errors while pressing the keystrokes, etc. You can click on the Select unit of the typing accuracy button for observing the typing accuracy. By default, the accuracy will be calculated on the basis of keystrokes.

9. How can you remove a lesson in the RapidTyping software?

Ans. Perform the following steps to delete a lesson:

Step 1 Select the lesson that you want to delete in the Navigation tree.

Step 2 Click on the Remove selected lesson or Course button to delete the lesson. The selected lesson will be deleted.

Long Answer (LA) Type Questions

1. Write some of the factors which are included in typing ergonomics.

Ans. Refer to text on Pages 113 and 114.

2. What is RapidTyping tutor? Write the steps to start the RapidTyping software.

Ans. RapidTyping tutor is a Free and Open Source Software (FOSS) designed to learn typing skills on the computer. It is free to use and share with others, but only by using the original distribution package. It is efficient typing software that teaches typing through fun and interactive typing game.

We perform the below mentioned steps to start the RapidTyping software:

Double click on the shortkey icon of the RapidTyping software.

Or

Click on the Start button → All Programs → RapidTyping 5.

3. Explain the various components of RapidTyping window.

Ans. Refer to text on Pages 116 and 117.

4. Discuss the rules of touch typing.

Ans. Before we actually start working on the RapidTyping software, it is good to learn about the basic rules that one should keep in mind in order to learn the touch typing skill in a proper manner. The following are some points that you should keep in mind while typing :

(i) The F, D, S, A and J, K, L, ; keys represent the base position on a QWERTY keyboard. Keyboards usually have small protrusions on the F and J keys.

They help your fingers locate the base position without looking at the keyboard. Try to return your fingers to the base position after each keystroke.

(ii) Color coding of the RapidTyping tutor keyboard shows which finger should press each key. The left index finger is reserved for all the red keys. The right index finger is reserved for green keys and so on. Use the thumb of whichever hand is more convenient for you to press space key.

(iii) The base position on the numeric pad is the 5 number key for the middle finger, 4 for index finger and 6 for ring finger.

(iv) Uppercase letters and symbols appearing on keys in the number row are typed by one hand with the little finger of the other hand holding down the shift key.

(v) Do not look the keyboard at the time of typing. Try to locate the right key with your fingers.

5. Write the steps to interpret your results in RapidTyping software.

Ans. Refer to text on Pages 117 and 118.

Self Assessment

Multiple Choice Questions

1. Which of the following key consist of digits and mathematical operators?
   (a) Alphanumeric key (b) Cursor control key
   (c) Numeric key (d) None of these
2. Which of the following keys are called guide keys on a typewriter?
   (a) F (b) A (c) ; (d) Both (b) and (c)
3. Which scroll bar is used to view that whole active window?
   (a) Horizontal (b) Vertical (c) Both (a) and (b) (d) None of these
4. Which of the following keys are used for left hand in bottom row?
   (a) Z (b) X (c) C (d) All of these
5. Which of the following button is used to set the appearance settings of the RapidTyping tutor?
   (a) Cursor control (b) Options (c) Select course (d) Current lesson time

Fill in the Blanks

1. Keyboarding skills are a set of skills required to operate a .... smoothly while typing.
2. .... key moves the cursor to the end of line.
3. Cursor inserts a character at its ...., forcing all characters past it one position further.
4. On a numeric keypad, the number .... is the guide key.
5. .... allows to set or change keyboard layout, level, lesson and background.

True/False

1. When a key is pressed, an analog signal is formed.
2. Shift key is also called combination key.
3. Mouse can be used to select menu commands, resize windows, etc.
4. Guide keys has a small triangle mark.
5. Text area displays the practice text to be typed by a user while practicing with a lesson.

Match the Columns

1. Match the following columns.

Column I	Column II
A. Home key	1. is used to type the top symbols.
B. Shift key	2. click the '▶' button in the task bar.
C. Blocking	3. is used to return the cursor to the beginning of the line.
D. Lesson Editor button	4. is used to select text that needs to be edited or formatted.
E. To start a lesson	5. is used to open the lesson editor to edit the lesson settings.

Very Short Answer (VSA) Type Questions

1. What do you mean by Function keys?
2. How can you type the sentence?
3. What is the use of double click?
4. Explain any two keyboarding tips.
5. How can you enable/disable sound in the current lesson?

Short Answer (SA) Type Questions

1. Explain the numeric keypad in brief.
2. How can you create new lines between paragraphs?
3. What do you understand by scrolling?
4. Explain the allocation of keys to fingers on the first row.
5. How can you add a new course in the RapidTyping software?
6. Explain the table that lists the detailed description of typing speed types.

Long Answer (LA) Type Questions

1. Explain the steps to start the touch typing lesson.
2. How can you view and analyse statistics?
3. How will you calculate the typing accuracy of RapidTyping software?

UNIT

03

Digital Documentation

Chapter Checklist

- Typewriter
- Word Processing Software
- LibreOffice
- Opening and Closing Documents
- Cursor Movement
- Editing the Document
- Formatting a Document
- Creating and Managing Tables
- Print Preview and Printing a Document
- Protection of Password in Document
- Mail Merge

In earlier days, manual typewriters were used for typing a document, which was replaced by electronic typewriter and now a computer is used for this purpose.

Word processing, spreadsheet and presentation are most common activities performed in an office.

OfficeSuite software is used to perform these activities effectively.

A document is a paper with written contents and the process of preparing a document is called documentation. Documentation is required to preserve the contents for a long period or to be used as evidence. A document can be letters, reports, thesis, manuscripts, legal documents, books etc.

A data entry operator should possess the skills to use the office productivity tools with a good typing speed. Although typing skill is the essential criteria for data entry operator, a little care has to be taken while using the Word processing software.

Typewriter

It is a hand operated mechanical device with which on typing keys can produce printed characters on paper. There are several limitations to use a typewriter as in case of any typing error, the whole sheet is required to be type again, multiple typing efforts are required to send same letter to different persons with different addresses, typewriter does not have all the required characters or symbols.

In the year 1974, Xerox company had introduced an electronic typewriter, as an attempt to solve the problems of the manual typewriter.

In electronic typewriter, it is possible to make changes in the content, make multiple copies with minor changes.

Word Processing Software

It is used for the creation of text based documents. A Word processor is a software package that process textual matter and creates organised documents.

There are many software packages available to do the job of Word processing. Some examples of Word processing software are: AppleWorks, Microsoft Word, StarOffice, WordPerfect, OpenOffice.org Writer, LibreOffice Writer etc.

The modern Word processors take advantage of a GUI (Graphical User Interface) providing some form of what you see is what you get (WYS/WYG) editing.

Word processing software not only provides basic ability to enter and modify the text but also provides efficient text manipulation functions that can be used for documentation.

Some of the features provided by popular Word processors are as listed below:

- Create, edit, save, retrieve and print the document.
- Select and move the text from one place to another in the document.
- Copy the text to other places within the document.
- Move or copy a selected text from one document to any other document.
- Change the font size, font style of the text in the document.
- Format paragraphs as well as pages.
- Check spelling and grammar.
- Create table, modify the size of the selected rows, columns or cells.
- Combine one or more documents.
- Insert pictures or graphs within the document.
- Print the selected text or selected pages of the document.

Word processors are being used in the business, home and education, i.e. in schools and colleges for preparing letters, reports and many other different types of documents.

OfficeSuite is a collection of programs which are useful for Word processing, spreadsheet preparation, presentation and database management. There are several office suits. We will be using LibreOffice.

LibreOffice

It is a Free and Open Source Software (FOSS), fully featured office productivity suite. Currently, the version of LibreOffice is 6.0 and above are available. It is available free for downloading from the website www.libreoffice.org. This suite is available in many languages and runs on many platforms (such as Windows, Mac and Linux).

The components of LibreOffice are: Writer for word processing, Calc for spreadsheet preparation, Impress for presentation, Base for database management, Draw for drawing and others.

LibreOffice includes support for opening and saving files in many common formats including Microsoft Office, HTML, WordPerfect, PDF etc.

LibreOffice Writer Word Processor

LibreOffice Writer is the free and open source word processor component of the LibreOffice software package you can use it to type letters, newsletters, reports and other documents.

It provides tools for editing, formatting and printing of documents. In LibreOffice Writer, all features of a typewriter are available and there are many additional features which make the task of Word processing much simpler and documents look more attractive and presentable.

Starting LibreOffice Writer

In general, you will find a shortcut of LibreOffice on the desktop or on the Quick Launch Taskbar. The process may slightly differ according to the operating system you are using (Windows or Linux).

In Windows

Click on Start button → All Programs → LibreOffice 6.2 → LibreOffice Writer.

Or

Using the Search command, type the word 'Writer' in the search field and select LibreOffice Writer from the offered results.

In Ubuntu Linux

Find the LibreOffice Writer icon on the application launcher or search it by clicking on 'Show Applications'.

It opens LibreOffice Writer with a blank document. By default, the name of the blank document is Untitled 1 and file extension of LibreOffice Writer is .odt.

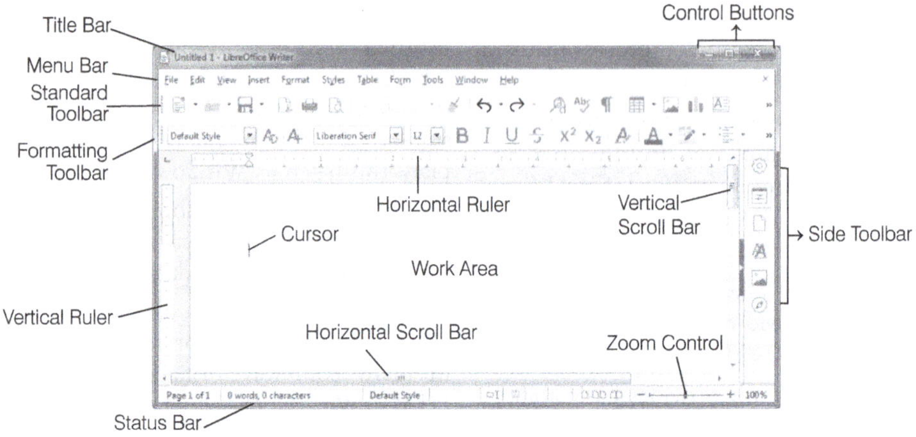

The major components of LibreOffice Writer are shown in the given figure. These parts are introduced below :

Title Bar

It is located at the top of the window and displays the document name. The format of the name displayed on the title bar is document name - LibreOffice Writer.

Menu Bar

It is located just below the title bar. When you select one of the menus, a sub menu drop down to show further options. Different types of bars/tabs are as follows :

- **File Tab** It is found in the top-left corner of LibreOffice Writer window. It is used to open existing document, create new document, save, export, send, close, print, etc.
- **Edit Tab** It is used to cut, copy, paste, redo, find, select all, etc.
- **View Tab** It is used for web layout, text boundaries, data sources, navigator, etc.
- **Insert Tab** It is used to insert header, footer, bookmark, frame, page break, chart, movie and sound, footnote/ endnote, etc.
- **Format Tab** It is used to bullets and numbering, page, title page, wrap, alignment, arrange, flip, rotate, group, etc.
- **Styles Tab** It is used to insert bullet list, number list, etc.
- **Table Tab** It is used to insert table, delete, select, formula, etc.
- **Form Tab** It is used to insert text box, check box, option button, list box, combo box, image control, table control, design mode, etc.
- **Tools Tab** It is used to spelling and grammar, language, word count, bibliography database, macros, etc.
- **Window Tab** It is used to new window, close window, etc.
- **Help Tab** It is used to allow users to search and find any topic about that program, send feedback, know about license information, etc.
- The sub menu item which shows three dots '...' just after the sub menu name, means, clicking on it will open the dialog box.
- The sub menu item which shows right hand side arrows '▶' just after the sub menu name, means clicking on it will open another sub menu.

Toolbars

LibreOffice Writer displays toolbars in different ways : docked (fixed in place) or floating. Docked toolbars can be moved to different locations or made to float and floating toolbars can be docked.

Standard Toolbar It is located just below the menu bar. Standard toolbar consists various options which are showing in below figure :

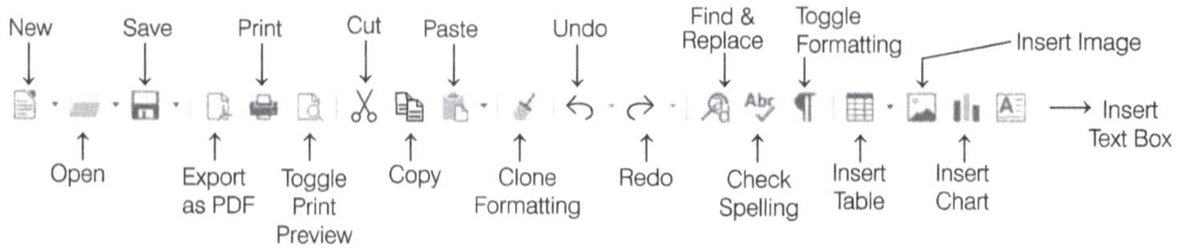

Formatting Toolbar It is located just below the standard toolbar. When we work with text, formatting toolbar is displayed. Formatting toolbar consists of various options which are showing in below figure:

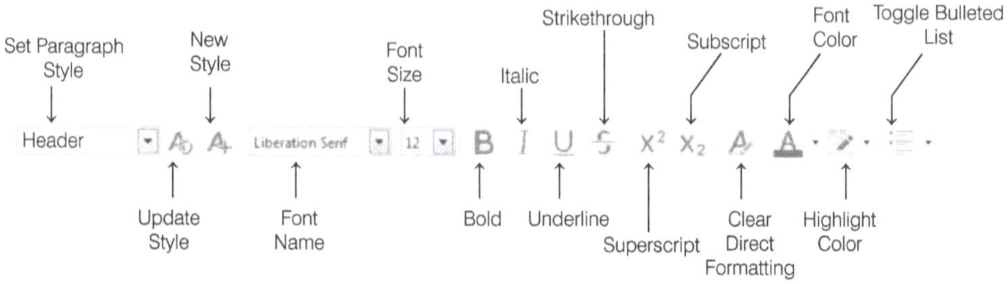

Status Bar

It is displayed on the bottom of the window and used to view the information such as page number, current page, current template, etc.

Scroll Bar

It is used to view the whole active window. There are two types of scroll bars, i.e. horizontal scroll bar and vertical scroll bar.

Zoom Control

Lets you zoom in for a closer look at your text. The zoom control consists of a slider. You can slide it left or right to zoom in or out, to increase or decrease the zoom factor.

Check Point 01

1. Edit tab contains option(s) as
   (a) Cut
   (b) Copy
   (c) Paste
   (d) All of the above
2. LibreOffice is open source software. (True/False)
3. A word processor is a .... package.
4. How to start LibreOffice Writer in Linux?
5. How many types of scroll bar are there in Writer?

Opening and Closing Documents

To prepare a document in the LibreOffice Writer, we have first to open it. We can open either an old document or a completely new document. These are described in following :

Creating a New Blank Document

Each time when you open LibreOffice Writer, a new blank document appears. However, you will also need to know how to create new documents while an existing document is open.

Steps to create a new blank document are as follows :

Step 1 Click on the File tab.

Step 2 Select New, a sub menu will appear.

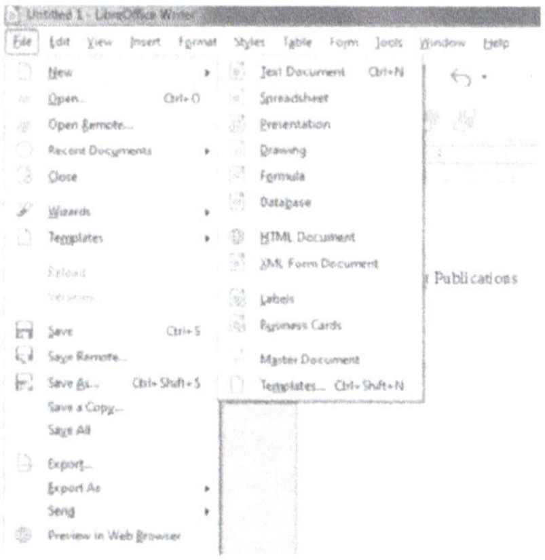

Step 3 Select Text Document or press Ctrl+N shortkey on keyboard.

Step 4 A new blank document will appear.

Saving a Document

To permanently store a document on hard disk, you must save the document and assign a name to it. Saving is one of the most basic features of any application. To save a document, click on File tab, in which various save options are available. There are different types of saving as : Save, Save Remote, Save As, Save a Copy, Save All, etc.

Save

Steps to save a document using Save command are as follows :

Step 1 Click on File → Save on the menubar.

Or

Press Ctrl + S shortkey on keyboard.

Or

Click on Save icon on the standard toolbar.

Step 2 Save the document in its current location with the same file name. But if the file has not been saved previously, a Save As dialog box will appear. Enter the document name and fill the type and click Save button.

Save Remote

This option allows you to setup a connection to an FTP (File Transfer Protocol), Google Drive and several other services. Use this option, when your document is already stored on a remote server or you want to store it on a remote server. For this, follow the given steps :

Step 1 Choose File tab → Save Remote option. Remote Files window will appear.

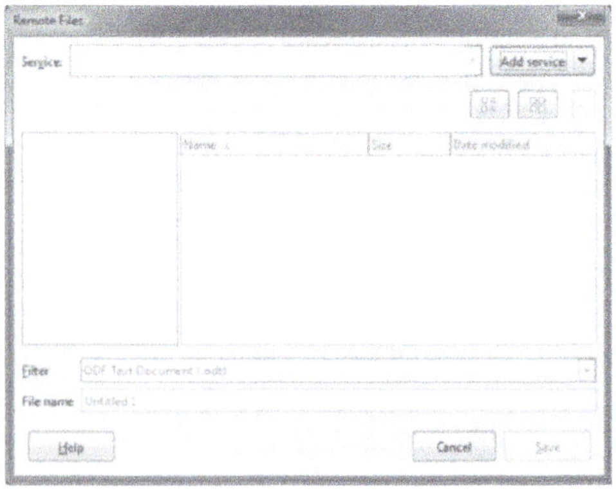

Step 2 Click on Add service button, File Services dialog box will appear.

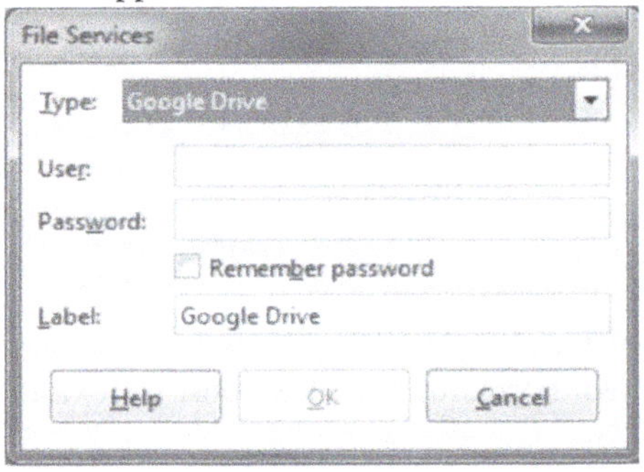

Step 3 User have to enter user name and password to save a file on remote server.

Save As

Save As is a way to create duplicate document that will look exactly the same if opened by LibreOffice, but can be edited without changing the original. You can choose this option, when you want to save same document but with different file name or file type.

Steps to save a document using Save As command are as follows :

Step 1 Click the File tab.

Step 2 Click Save As option or press Ctrl + Shift + S shortkey on keyboard. The Save As dialog box will appear.

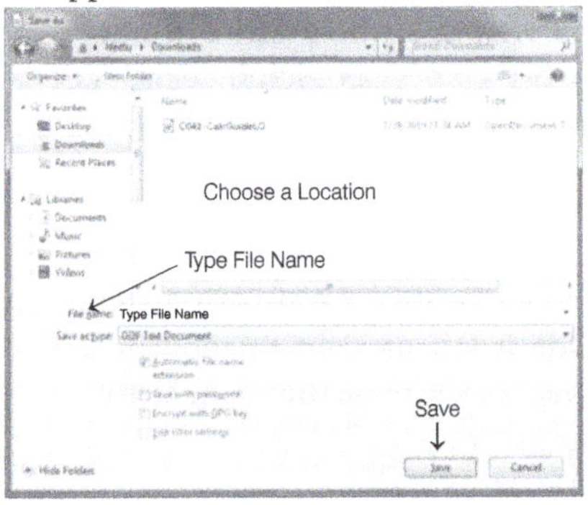

Step 3 Select the location where you want to save the document using the drop down menu.

Step 4 Enter the name and type of document in File name and Save as type boxes respectively.

Step 5 Click the Save button.

Save a Copy

Save a Copy is almost an identical function to Save As. It opens the Save a Copy dialog box and lets you save it in the folder and format of your choice.

It however, cannot overwrite the original file, if you perform Save a Copy and do not change the File name or the folder where it is located.

The Save As function would replace the original file.

Save a Copy won't change the active file like Save As will.

For this, follow the given steps:

Step 1 Select File tab.

Step 2 A drop down menu will appear, Choose Save a Copy option.

Step 3 Save a Copy dialog box will appear.

Step 4 Enter File name and Save as type.

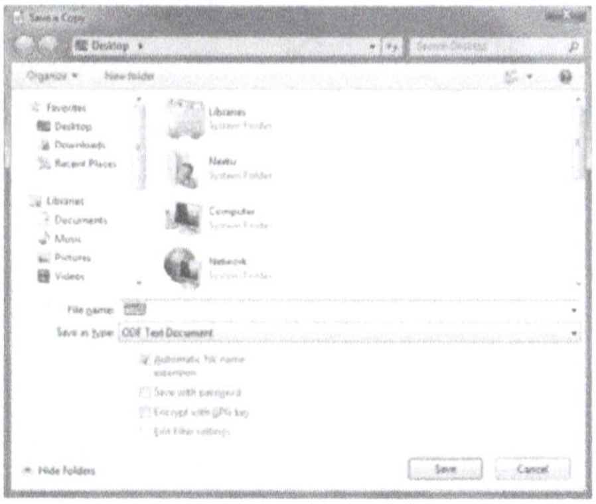

Step 5 Click on Save button.

> **'Save' and 'Save As'**
>
> 'Save' means the file gets saved under its current name, in whatever folder it was saved before or in the default folder of that computer. Whereas 'Save As' gives you the opportunity to save the file under a different name and in another folder. 'Save As' allows you to save the updated version with a new name while at the same time preserving the old version.

Save All

This function is only active when more than one document is open and need to be saved.

For this, choose File→ Save All. All open files will be saved without change the name, type or location.

Closing a Document

Steps to close an active document are as follows :

Step 1 Click the File tab.

Step 2 Select Exit LibreOffice option from drop down menu that will appear.

Or Press Ctrl + Q shortkey on keyboard.

Cursor Movement

(a) Text Cursor Movement

- Observe the location of the 'Text Cursor'.
- Press the different cursor control keys on keyboard and watch how the 'Text Cursor' moves around.

> The 'Text Cursor' is a flashing vertical line in the body of the text. The four arrow keys ← ↑ ↓ → on the keyboard are called cursor control keys.

There are two keys above the cursor control keys marked as Home and End.

- Pressing the Home key jump to the beginning of the line.
- Pressing the End key jump to the end of a line.

These keys can be pressed in combination with Ctrl key as :

- To jump to the beginning of a document, press the Ctrl key, hold it down, then press the Home key (Ctrl + Home).
- To jump to the end of a document, press the Ctrl key, hold it down, then press the End key (Ctrl + End).

(b) Mouse Pointer

This is the mouse pointer. It takes the pointer shape while moving it around the screen.

The mouse pointer changes to I shape, when moved over the text in a document.

Moving the 'I' shaped mouse pointer over the text and clicking on the desired text, helps to get the text cursor while editing the document. Thus, the mouse is used to control the 'Text Cursor' location.

Editing the Document

(a) Undo and Redo

- **Undo** When you want to undo a task due to some reason, then either press Ctrl + Z shortkey on keyboard or click Undo option from standard toolbar.

  By this the last operation done by you will be undone and the file will become as it was before that operation. By giving Undo command repeatedly you can undo many operations done earlier.

- **Redo** To do an operation again, which was reversed by Undo command, you can use Redo command. Press Ctrl+Y shortkey on keyboard or click Redo button from standard toolbar. By giving Redo command repeatedly you can redo many operations undone earlier.

(b) Selecting Text

It is necessary to select the text to perform copy and paste operations. The selected text will be highlighted. For editing the text, you must first select the required text. The editing can be done on the selected text.

(c) Selection Criteria

To select the text in Writer, swipe the mouse cursor over text. There are several selection tricks to speed up the selection process as below:

To Select a Letter(s)	Drag the Mouse Across the Letter(s)
To select a single word at a time	Position the mouse pointer anywhere on that word and double click.
To select a complete sentence at a time	Position the mouse pointer anywhere in the sentence and triple click.
To select a complete paragraph at a time	Position the mouse pointer anywhere in the paragraph and quadruple (four times) click.
A document	Press Ctrl + A shortkey on keyboard. Drag the mouse pointer till you see a right arrow which is white. Then click it thrice (three times).

(d) Selecting Non-consecutive Text Items

The above process shows the selection of continuous (consecutive) text. But suppose if the text is not continuous (consecutive) which you want to select, it is done in Writer. Writer provides a way to select the non-continuous text using the keyboard and mouse.

By using the mouse :

- Select the first word of the document (text).
- Hold down the Ctrl key and use the mouse to select the next word of text.
- Repeat as often as need.

By using the keyboard :

- Select the first word of the document (text).
- Press Shift + F8. This puts Writer in "Adding Selection" mode.
- Use the Arrow keys to move the start of the next text to be selected. Hold down the Shift key and select the next word of text.
- Repeat as often as need.

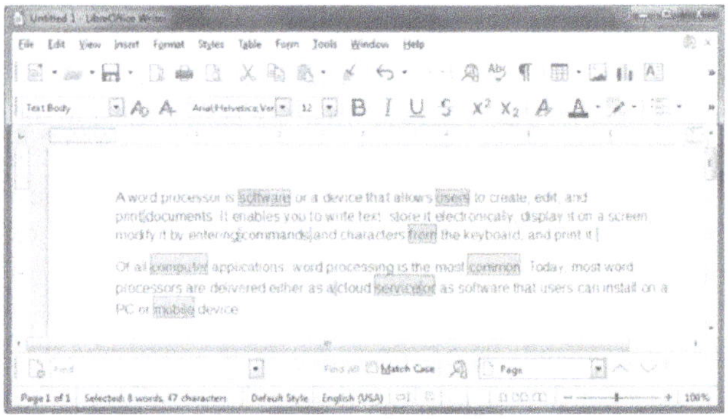

(e) Selecting a Vertical Block of Text

It is also possible to select a vertical block or column of text that is separated by spaces or tabs.

To select the vertical block of text, select from menu:

Edit tab → Selection Mode → Block Area.

Or

Press Ctrl + F8 shortkey on keyboard.

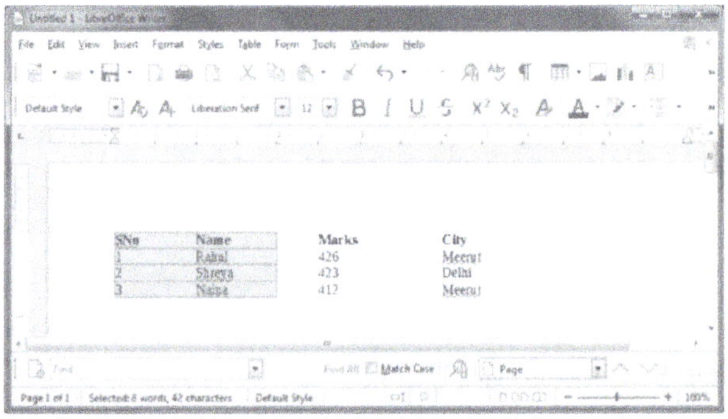

(f) Moving and Copying Text

Cut option is used to move some content from one place to another. While Paste option is used to paste some pre selected content at a new or desired place. To move some text from one place to another, both the options are used. Following steps are used to move some content in Writer document :

Step 1 Select a portion of the text using any one of the text selection methods.

Step 2 Next, with the help of various options available to cut the selected text and put it in clipboard. Just use any one of them :

- Use mouse right click and select Cut option.
- Using Cut option from standard toolbar.
- Using Ctrl+X shortkey from keyboard.

Step 3 Click at the place where you want to move the selected text and use any one of them :

- Use mouse right click and select Paste option.
- Using Paste option from standard toolbar.
- Using Ctrl+V shortkey from keyboard.

(g) Copy and Paste

It is used to make a duplicate copy of selected text.

Following steps are used to copy some content in Writer document :

Step 1 Select a portion of the text using any one of the text selection methods.

Step 2 Next, with the help of various options available to copy the selected text and put it in clipboard. Just use any one of them :

- Use mouse right click and select Copy option.
- Using Copy option from standard toolbar.
- Using Ctrl + C shortkey from keyboard.

Step 3 Click at the place where you want to copy the selected text and use any one of them :

- Use mouse right click and select Paste option.
- Using Paste option from standard toolbar.
- Using Ctrl + V shortkey from keyboard.

(h) Find & Replace

It is the act of searching some text and replace it with other text.

The Find and Replace option helps you to search a particular letter, word, phrase or sentence in your document and then replace it, if you want.

Steps to find the text are as follows :

Step 1 Click Edit tab → Find & Replace. A Find & Replace dialog box will appear.

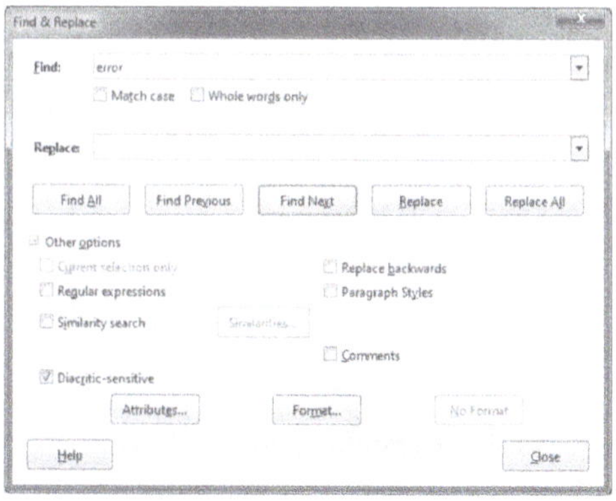

Step 2 Enter the text to find in the Find text box.

Step 3 Either click Find Next or Find All.

Steps to find the text and replace with another word, are as follows :

Step 1 Click Edit tab → Find & Replace. A Find & Replace dialog box will appear.

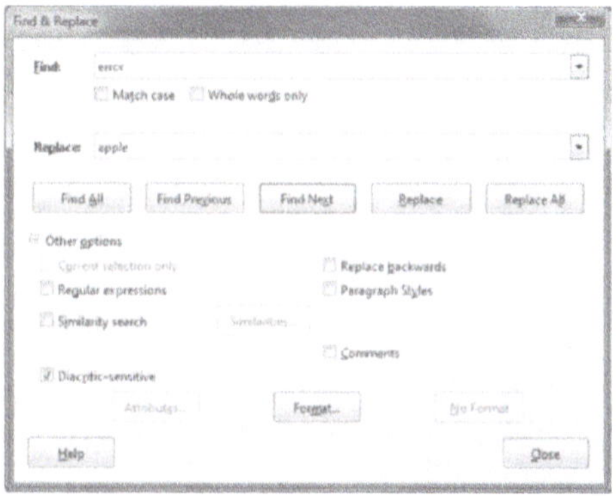

Step 2 Enter the text to search in the Find text box.

Step 3 Enter the text to replace the found text in the Replace text box.

Step 4 Either click Replace or Replace All.

(i) Jumping to the Page Number

Sometimes we may require to jump to a particular page number. It becomes difficult to scroll down if it is a large document with several page. For this, 'Go to Page' feature of Writer is useful.

To do this, select the Edit tab → Go to Page option.

Go to Page dialog box will appear.

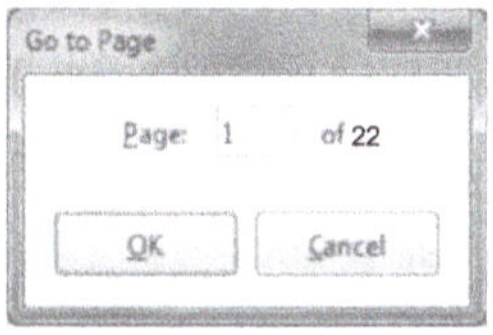

Specify the page number in Page : text box and click on OK button.

We will move first character of the specific page number directly.

(j) Non-printing Characters

In computer data entry, anything entered is treated as a character. We can see the characters like alphabets, numbers, punctuation marks on the computer screen.

But when we press some keys like Enter, Spacebar and Tab that do not appear on the screen, we are actually entering these characters in the document.

To display the non-printing character, use Ctrl + F10 shortkey from keyboard.

The tab space is shown by → sign and spacebar is shown by dot (.).

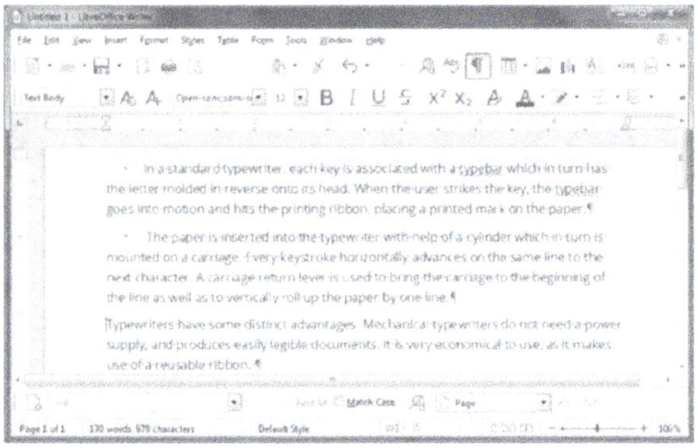

(k) Checking Spelling and Grammar

- **Spelling** Spelling mistake is the most common type of mistakes that can occur while typing a document. Writer provides a spelling checker, which checks to see if each word in the document is in the installed dictionary. Also provided a grammar checker, which can be used separately or in combination with the spelling checker.
- **Automatic Spell Checking** It checks each word as it is typed and displays a wavy red line under any unrecognised words. Right click an unrecognised word to open a context menu. You can click one of the suggested words to replace the underlined word with the one selected.

  If list does not contain the word you want, click Spelling to open a dialog. When the word is corrected, the line disappears.

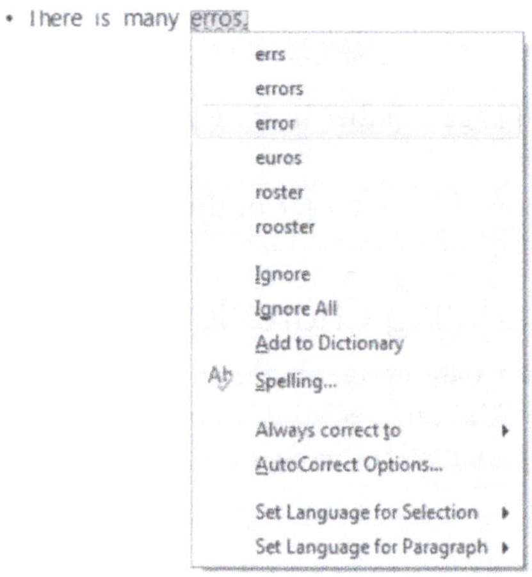

The spell check starts at the current cursor position or at the beginning of the text selection. Steps to check the spelling are as follows :

Step 1 Click the document or select the text that you want to check.

Step 2 Select Tools → Spelling, Spelling: English (USA) dialog box will appear.

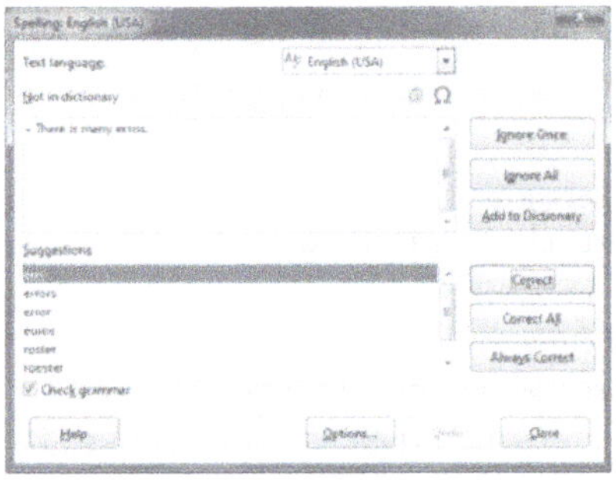

Step 3 When a possible spelling error is encountered, the spell check dialog opens and LibreOffice offers some suggested corrections.

Step 4 Do one of the following :

- To accept a correction, click the suggestions and then click Correct.
- Edit the sentence in the upper text box and then click Correct.
- To add unknown word to a user-defined dictionary, click Add to Dictionary.
- If you know the word is correct entered by you then click Ignore Once or Ignore All.
- **Grammar** By default, check grammar as you type is enabled in Tools → Options → Language Settings → Writing Aids → Options. Automatic spell checking must be enabled for this to work. If any errors are detected, they are shown underlined by a wavy blue line. Right click on this line brings up a context menu.

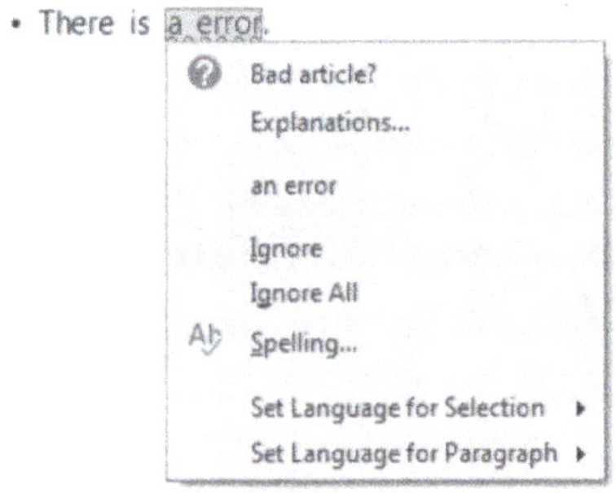

Steps to check the grammar are as follows :

Step 1 Click the document or select the text that you want to check.

Step 2 Select Tools → Spelling.
Spelling: English (USA) dialog box will appear.

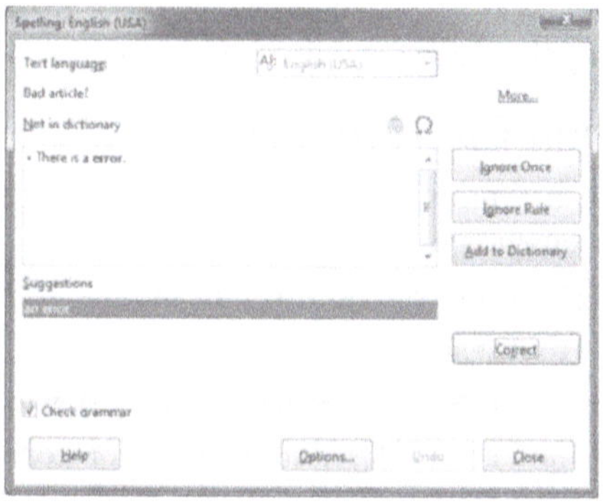

Step 3 When a possible grammar mistake is encountered, the spellcheck dialog opens and LibreOffice offers some suggested corrections.

Step 4 Do one of the following :

- To accept a correction, click the suggestions and then click Correct.
- Edit the sentence is the upper text box and then click Correct.
- To add unknown sentence to a user-defined dictionary, click Add to Dictionary.
- If you know the sentence is correct entered by you then click Ignore Once or Ignore Rule.

(I) Using Synonyms and the Thesaurus

Some times you search for a word having a similar in meaning to the word you have in mind. A Word processor helps to look up synonyms (different words with the same meaning) and antonyms (words with the opposite meaning) in the thesaurus.

To access the synonyms, follow below steps:

Step 1 Right click on a word and a context menu will appear.

Step 2 Point to Synonyms on the context menu.

Step 3 A sub menu of alternative words and phrases are displayed.

Step 4 Click on a word or phrase in the sub menu to replace it with the highlighted word or phrase in the document.

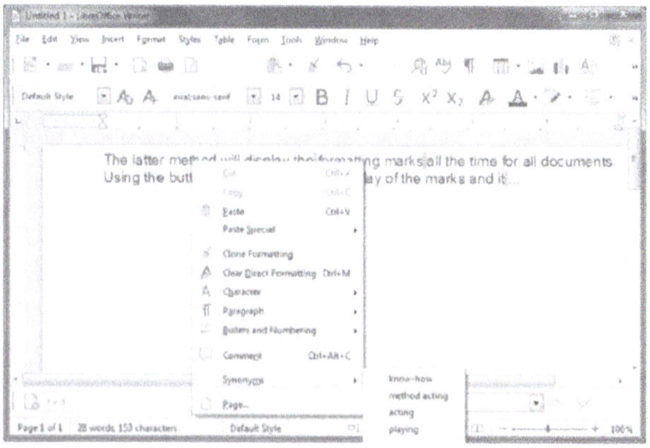

Synonyms are different from a dictionary. A dictionary contains definitions and pronunciations, whereas thesaurus will have words with similar meaning or opposite meanings.

Check Point 02

1. What is the use of Undo command?
2. What shortkey is used to open Block Area?
   (a) Ctrl + F8 (b) Ctrl + F7
   (c) Ctrl + F5 (d) Ctrl + F6
3. Tab space is shown by ↑ sign. (True/False)
4. .... provides a spelling checker.
5. How to select the whole document in Writer?

Formatting a Document

The first step in document preparation is to use page setup. The page formatting is explained in the next section. But for the document preparation, Page Setup is taken here.

To setup a page, follow the below steps :

Step 1 Click on the Format tab, a menu will appear.

Step 2 Select the Page option, and Page Style : Default Style dialog box will appear.

Step 3 In dialog box, select the Page tab.

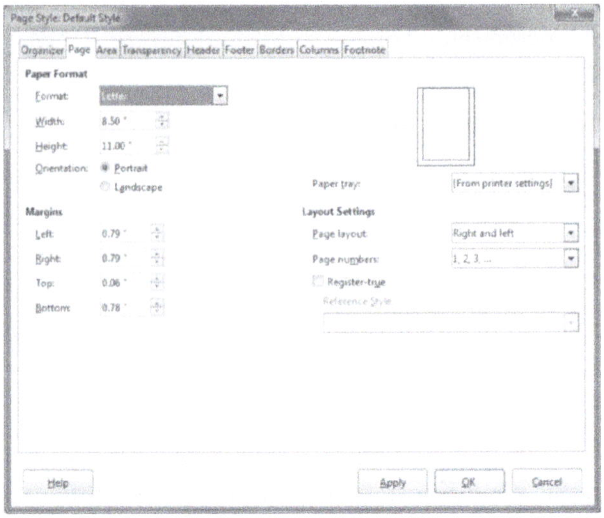

It allows to select Paper Format as Format (A4, A5, B4, Letter). You can also adjust Width, Height, Orientation as Portrait or Landscape and set the Margins (Left, Right, Top, Bottom) and Layout Settings (Page layout, Page numbers).

Formatting Text

It refers to the formatting of paragraphs and characters. To do the formatting, first select the text and then apply the required text formatting features.

There are various methods of formatting text. We can apply any one method as per the suitability. These methods are use

- menu options from menu bar.
- readily available buttons on the formatting toolbar.
- context menu. The context menu appears by right clicking on the selected text.
- shortkey from keyboard.

(a) Removing Manual Formatting

To see the effect of formatting the text, first remove manual formatting. For this, follow below steps:

Step 1 Choose Format tab by which a drop down menu will appear.

Step 2 Select Clear Direct Formatting option from menu bar.

Or

Click on the Clear Direct Formatting button on the formatting toolbar.

Or

Use Ctrl + M shortkey from keyboard.

It will clear the existing formatting on the text and then you can apply the fresh formatting features.

(b) Common Text Formatting

Some of the common text formatting features generally used have been shown below:

- Changing font size - by selecting font size.
- Changing font style - bold, italic, underline.
- Changing font type - by selecting font drop down.
- Changing font color - by selecting font color icon.

On the formatting toolbar, you will find the buttons representing the letter in Bold, Italic and Underline. These buttons are toggle buttons. To apply these, follow below step :

First select the text then press the desired button (Bold, Italic and Underline) which you want to apply on formatting toolbar.

Or

Use the shortkeys Ctrl + B for bold, Ctrl + I for italic and Ctrl + U for underline from the keyboard.

(c) Changing Text Case

While formatting an article, sometimes you need to change the font case in order to emphasise the texts sentences.

Writer has been developed a change case option, which can be used to change the case of text.

Steps to change the text case i.e. lowercase, uppercase etc.

Step 1 Select the text that you want to modify.

Step 2 Click the Format tab and then select Text option. A drop down menu will appear, in which below change case options are available.

Command Tab	Description
Sentence case	Changes the first letter of every sentence in uppercase.
lowercase	Changes the whole selected text in lowercase letters.
UPPERCASE	Changes the whole selected text in uppercase letters.
Capitalize Every Word	Changes first letter of every word in capital.
tOGGLE cASE	It toggles whole selected text i.e. changes each capital letter into lowercase and each small letter into uppercase.

Step 3 Select one of the case options from the list.

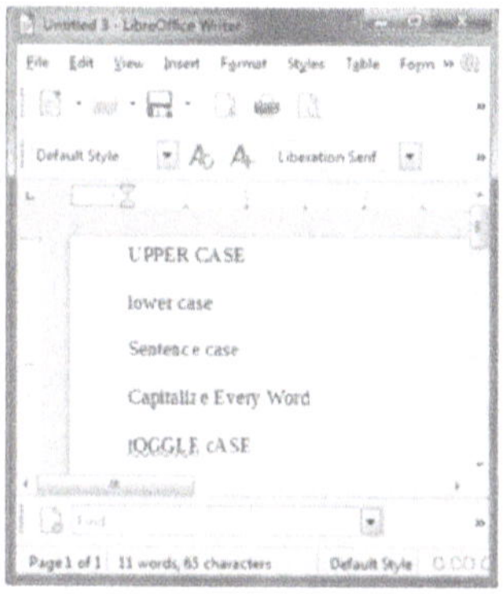

(d) Superscript and Subscript

A superscript is a number or symbol that appears slightly above a word or a letter.

A subscript is a number, figure or symbol that appears slightly below a word or a letter.

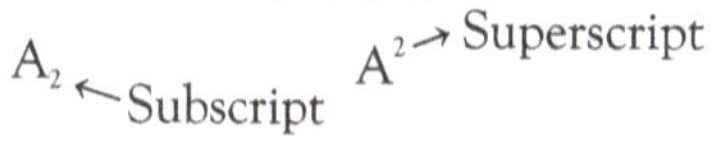

- **To apply superscript** Select the text and then choose Format → Text → Superscript.
- **To apply subscript** Select the text and then choose Format → Text → Subscript.

Paragraph Style

A paragraph in a document can have several sentences, a single sentence, a single word or no words at all. In LibreOffice Writer document, every paragraph has a paragraph style. The paragraph style settings have a pop down window. One can change the paragraph style by clicking on the pop down window.

(a) Indenting Paragraphs

Indents are the white space added to the margins and decreasing the text area for paragraph.

So, when you have a "right margin" and you want to add a right indent of 1.0, your text will be printed 2.0" from the right edge of the paper.

The first line of each paragraph can be indented differently from other lines in the paragraph. The first line can be shorter than the others.

To indent a paragraph, follow these steps :

Step 1 Select the paragraph.

Step 2 Use Increase Indent or Decrease Indent option according to your need from the formatting toolbar.

Indentation can also be done with the help of horizontal ruler. On horizontal ruler, these appears one small triangle in the right side and two small triangles on one another left side.

These all are known as marker. These left and right indent markers are used to indent the selected paragraph. User can move and set the paragraph by using these markers in left or right.

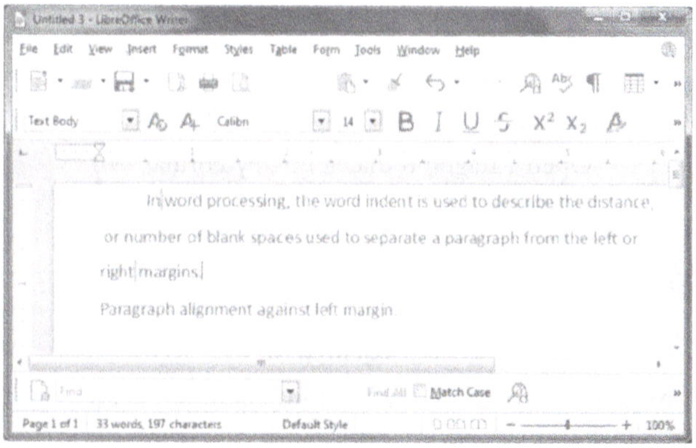

(b) Aligning Paragraphs

The paragraph can be aligned as Left, Right, Center and Justified. In LibreOffice Writer, the default alignment for paragraph is left aligned.

Steps to change the text alignment in a document are as follows:

Step 1 Select the text which you want to modify.

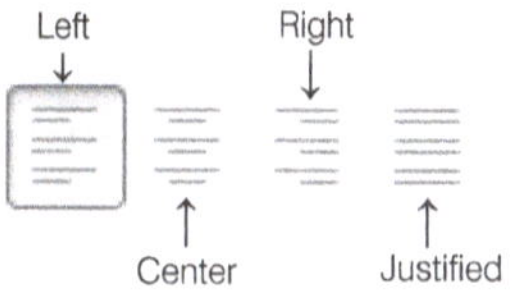

Step 2 Select one of the four alignment options from the formatting toolbar.

You can also use shortkeys for alignment as

- Ctrl + L   Align Left
- Ctrl + R   Align Right
- Ctrl + E   Align Center
- Ctrl + J   Justified

Note *Justified option makes both the left and right sides of the paragraph line up with the margins.*

To change the paragraph style, follow below steps:

Step 1 First select the paragraph by paragraph selection method.

Step 2 Select the drop down arrow of paragraph style.

Step 3 Select Text Body from the pop down menu.

Step 4 Move the mouse pointer to outside the selected text and click the left mouse button once to de-select the text.

To explore more paragraph formatting features, follow below steps :

Step 1 Select the paragraph.

Step 2 Click on the required tools on formatting toolbar.

Or

Open Paragraph dialog box by Format → Paragraph.

Step 3 Select the appropriate tools.

Step 4 Click OK button.

(c) Font Color and Highlighting

Font Color Steps to format the font color of text are as follows :

Step 1 Select the text that you want to modify.

Step 2 Click the drop down arrow next to the Font Color box from the formatting toolbar. The Font Color menu will appear.

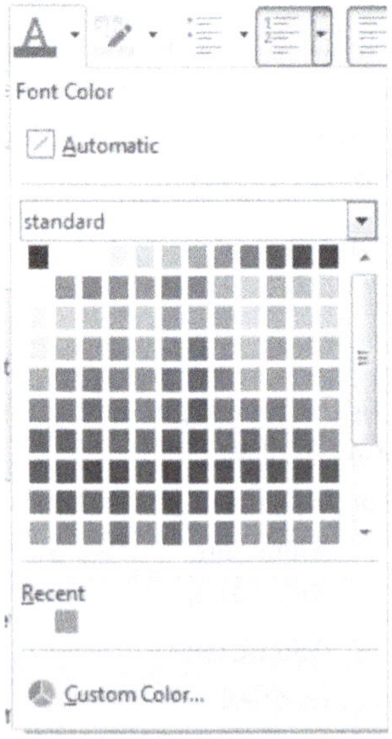

Step 3 Choose the font color that you want to use.

Highlighting Text Following steps are used to highlight the text :

Step 1 Select the required text.

Step 2 Go to the formatting toolbar and click on the Highlight Color option arrow, a color box will open.

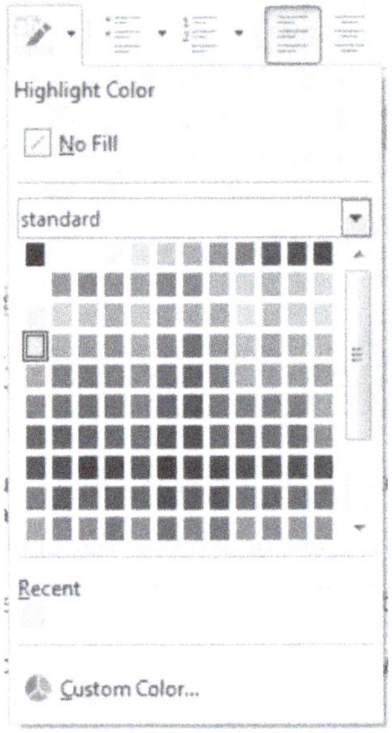

Step 3 In this color box, select the required color. To finish the effect of highlighting, reopen the highlight option and select No Fill.

(d) Using the Bullets and Numbering

While working in a document, sometimes we need to highlight some areas of text in the form of lists for summarising key points. To achieve this purpose, we can use bullets. A bullet could be an asterisk, black dot, circle or any other mark that is found before the text and identifies key items or other important text.

A bulleted list or bullet list is a list of items preceded with bullets or pictures instead of numbers or other objects. You can create a list within a list in your document.

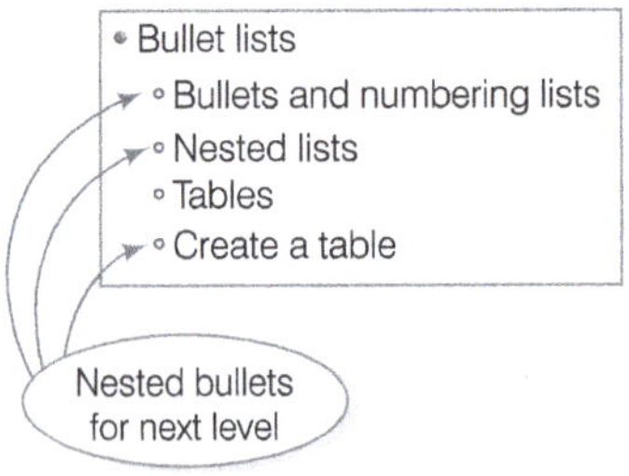

Numbering or number list or order list is a listing order that is done with numbers, often used with a checklist or a set of steps that are to be performed in a particular order.

Bullets and Numbering lists can be used in your documents to arrange and format text to emphasise and to draw the attention of the viewer.

Creating Lists To create a list in Writer, follow the below steps :

Step 1 Select all list items.

Step 2 Click the Toggle Bulleted List or Toggle Numbered List button on the formatting toolbar.

e.g.

Bullet List	**Number List**
• Computer	1. Computer
• Keyboard	2. Keyboard
• Mouse	3. Mouse
• Scanner	4. Scanner
• Printer	5. Printer

To remove bullets or numbering select the list items and click again on the Toggle Bulleted List or Toggle Numbered List button to disable the list formatting.

Format Bullets or Numbers To change format of the bullets or numbers in a list, follow the given steps :

Step 1 Select first all list items and click the arrow on the Toggle Bulleted List or Toggle Numbered List icon. A drop down menu will appear.

Step 2 In the drop down panel, choose the new format for bullets or numbers.

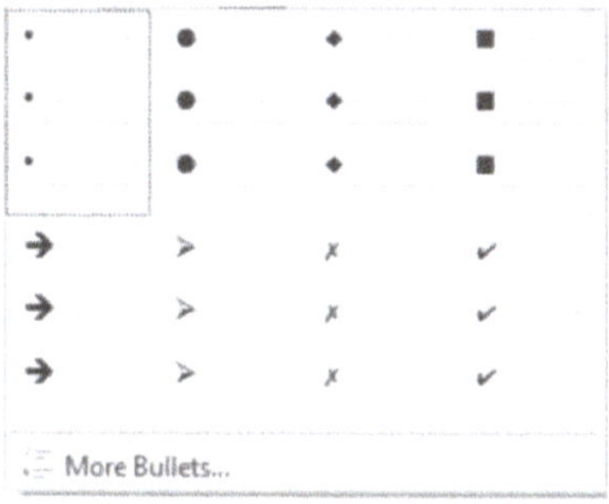

Bulleted List Format

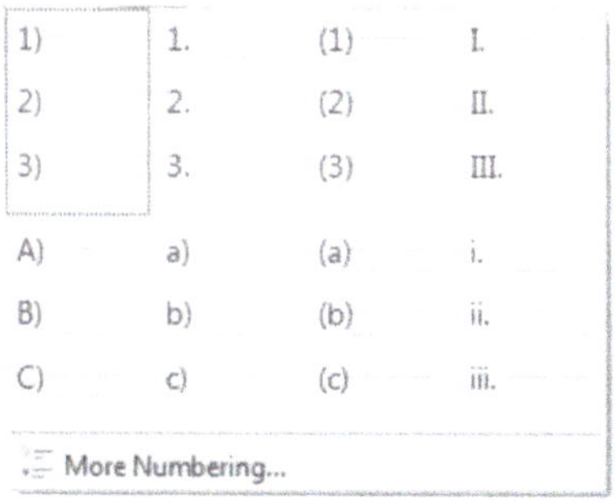

Numbered List Format

(e) Assigning Color, Border and Background

To assign background color to the paragraph, follow the below steps :

Step 1 Select the paragraph.

Step 2 Select the Format tab, a drop down will appear.

Step 3 Choose Paragraph option by which Paragraph dialog box will appear.

Step 4 Choose Area tab, then select Color button. Now select the appropriate color from Colors.

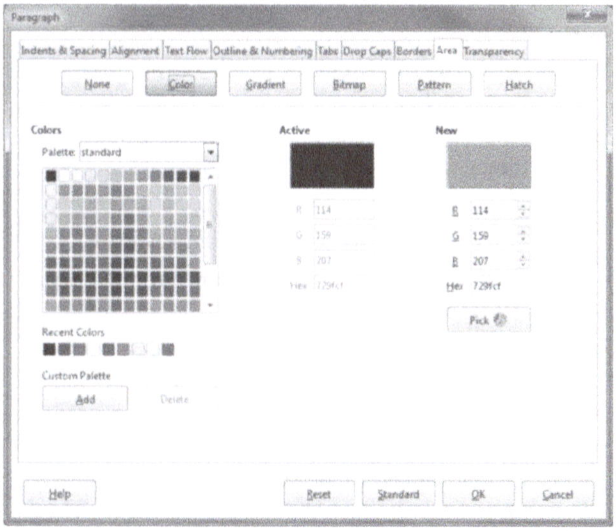

To add border to the paragraph, follow the below steps :

Step 1 Select Format tab → Page option. A Page Style: Default Style dialog box will appear.

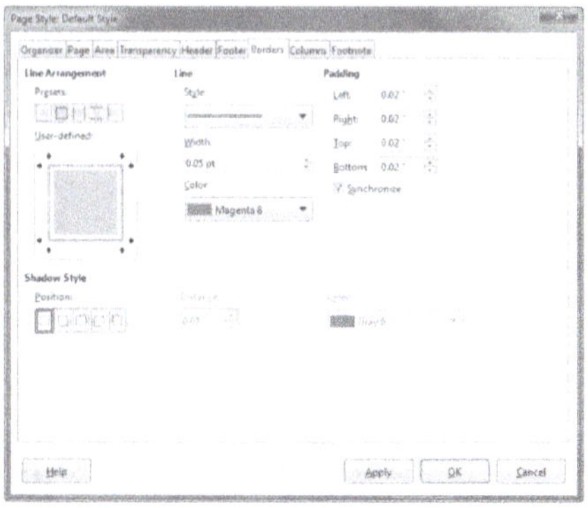

Step 2 In this dialog box, select Line Arrangement, Line, Width and Color for border. For shading, do the modification in Shadow Style.

Step 3 Click OK button.

Note *Border is an outer edge of a document or a separator which is used to divide the whole document in several sections.*

Page Formatting

(a) Inserting a Page Break

In multi-page documents the text flows from one page to the next as you add information. In certain cases, we may require to break the current page and move the next heading or next chapter to the new page in the same document. In such cases, we have to break the page forcefully and take the cursor to the next page to insert the new heading. This is called as a page break.

To break the current page and start the new page, follow below steps:

Step 1 Select the Insert tab, by which a drop down menu will appear.

Step 2 Choose Page Break option from the drop down menu.

Or

Use Ctrl + Return shortkey from keyboard.

The page break can also be narrowed down to the line and column, follow the below steps :

Step 1 Select the Insert tab then choose More Breaks option from drop down menu that will be appear.

Step 2 A sub menu will appear, from where choose Manual Break. Insert Break dialog box will be open.

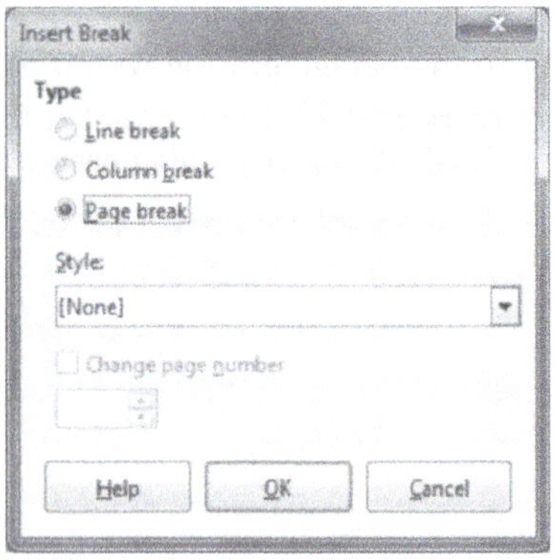

Step 3 Do appropriate setting and click OK button.

(b) Creating Header/Footer and Page Numbers

You can make your documents professional and polished by utilising the header and footer sections. The header is a section of the document that appears at the top margin, while the footer is a section of the document that appears at the bottom margin.

Header and footer generally both contains information such as page number, date, document name, company logo, image etc., which are specified by page styles. Therefore, when inserted, all pages with the same page style will display same header and footer.

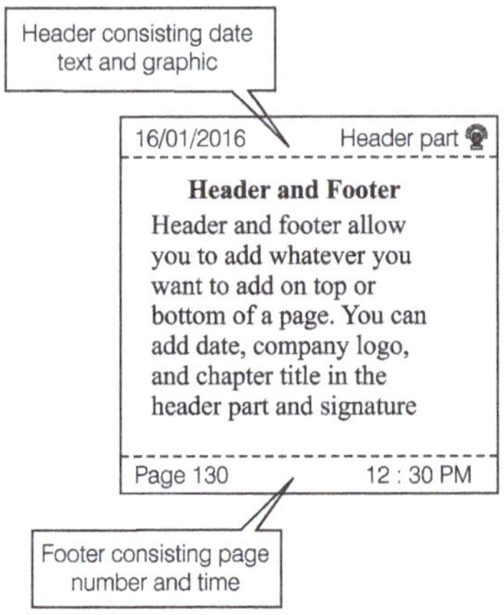

Header and Footer areas

To format the header and footer, follow the below steps :

Step 1 Click Format tab → Page option. A Page Style : Default Style dialog box will appear.

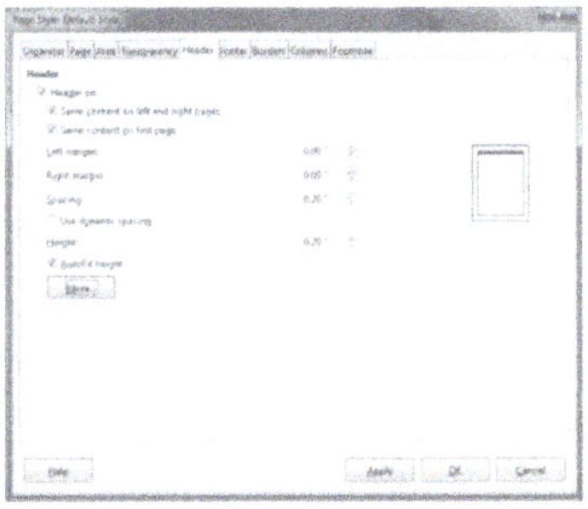

Step 2 Select Header or Footer tab.

Step 3 Set the spacing and margins options that you want to use.

Step 4 To add a border/background to the header or footer, click More button.
The Border/Background dialog box will appear.

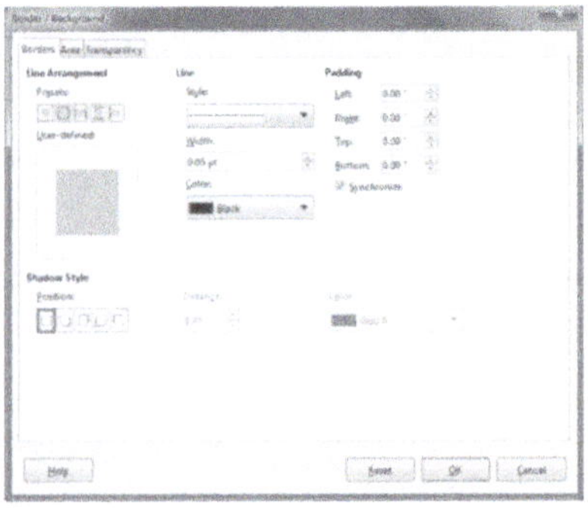

Step 5 In this dialog box, select Line Arrangement, Shadow Style, Line and Padding settings.

Step 6 Click OK button.

Step 7 Click OK button in Page Style: Default Style dialog box.

You can give the document name or chapter name in the header section and page number in the footer section.

To enter page numbers in the footer section, place the cursor in the footer section and select Insert → Page Number.

(c) Inserting Images, Shapes, Special Characters in a Document

The regular text in the document can be made attractive and more informative by inserting the various elements as image, shape and special characters.

(i) **Inserting image** To include any picture or image in document, the image file should be stored in hard disk or external storage, such as pen drive. To insert an image, follow the below steps:

Step 1 Position the cursor where you want to insert the image.

Step 2 Select Insert tab and then choose Image option. Insert Image dialog box will appear.

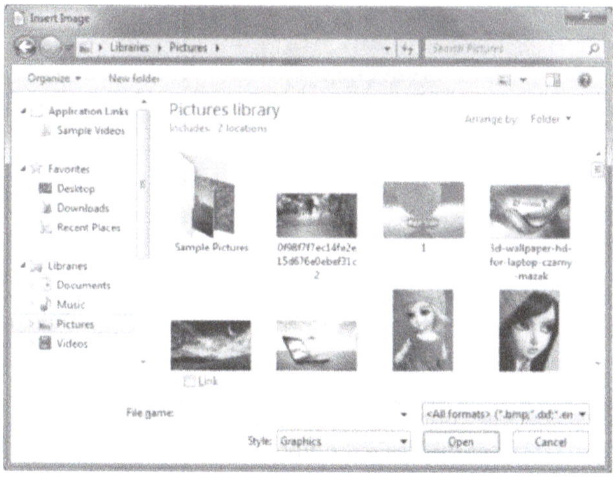

Step 3 Choose the image and then click on Open button. Image will add in document.

(ii) **Inserting shapes** It is possible to insert various shapes in your document. The variety of shapes consists of Lines, Arrows, Symbols, Stars, Callouts, Flowcharts. To insert a shape follow the below step:

Select Insert tab → Shape and then choose the further element you want to insert.

(iii) **Inserting special characters** Sometimes we may require to enter the special character, such as ¶ or which cannot be typed by using the keyboard. LibreOffice Writer provides a feature to enter the number of special characters.

To enter the Special Characters, follow given steps :

Step 1 Select the Insert tab, a drop down menu will appear.

Step 2 Choose the Special Character by which Special Characters dialog box will appear.

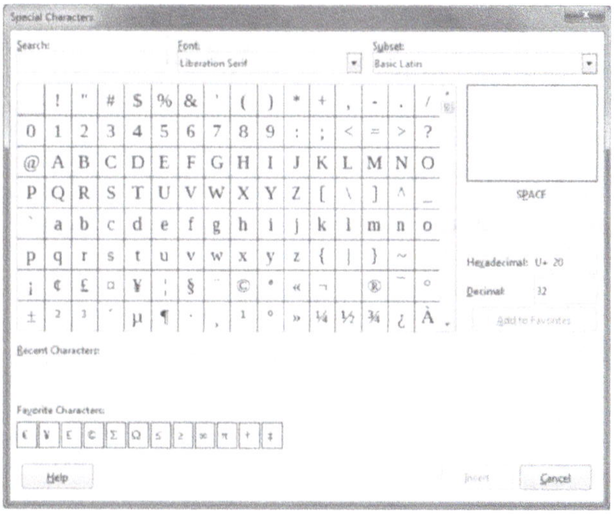

Step 3 Choose the character which you want to use and then click on Insert button.

(d) Formatting the Shape or Image

User can format the space or image inserted in the document. For instance, user can change its size, color, add borders, change its positions etc.

First, select the shape or image by clicking on it. Then make use of the toolbar to perform the required changes.

(e) Dividing The Document Page into Columns

You may have seen some documents where its page is divided into two or three columns. It is used in magazines and newspapers. It is possible to arrange the regular text into columns before or after adding the text.

To divide the page into columns, follow the below steps :

Step 1 Select the Format tab, a drop down menu will appear.

Step 2 Choose Columns option by which Columns dialog box will appear.

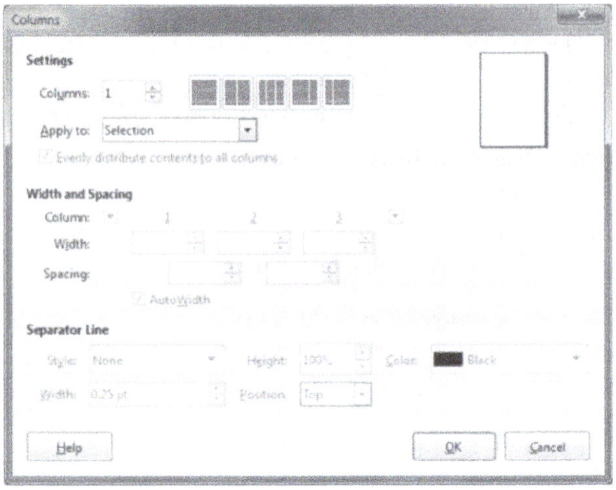

Step 3 Enter the number of columns in the Columns entry box.

Step 4 Give the value for spacing between the columns and click OK button.

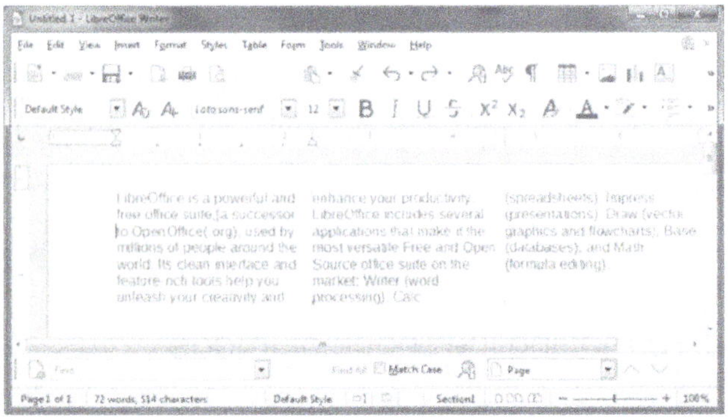

Check Point 03

1. Name the font styles that are available in Writer.
2. What is the use of lowercase text case option?
3. .... can be aligned as left, right, center and justified.
4. You can insert following in a document
   (a) image (b) shape
   (c) symbol (d) All of these
5. Image can be insert with the help of Insert tab. (True/False)

Creating and Managing Tables

In a document, it is normally seen that some data are represented in tabular form. So we collect the similar data and keep it under one heading. The representation of data in a tabular format is called as table. A table has a number of rows and columns. It is possible to have a table with one row and one column.

LibreOffice Writer provides a very rich tool for creating and managing a table.

The various features of table are :

(a) Creating a Table

Steps to draw a blank table in a document are as follows :

Step 1 Place your insertion point in the document where you want to insert the table.

Step 2 Click the Insert Table icon from the standard toolbar.

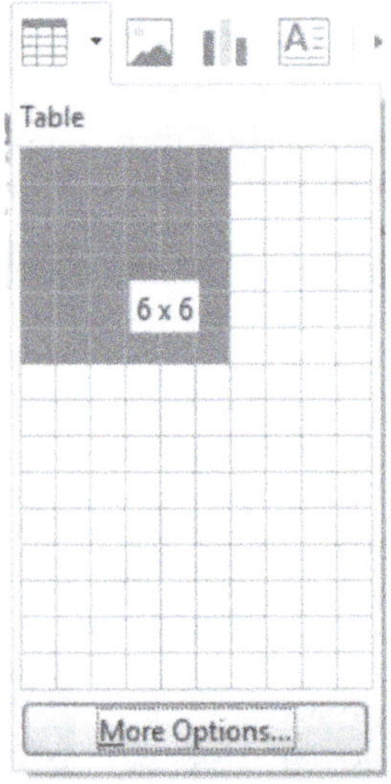

Step 3 Drag your mouse over the squares diagram to select the desired number of columns and rows in the table.

Step 4 Click your mouse and then a table will appear in the document.

Step 5 Now, you can enter text into the table.

You can also insert table into document by using following steps :

Step 1 Select Table tab → Insert Table.

Or

Click Insert Table icon from the standard toolbar. Select More Options button.

Or

Insert Table dialog box will appear. Press Ctrl + F12 shortkey on keyboard.

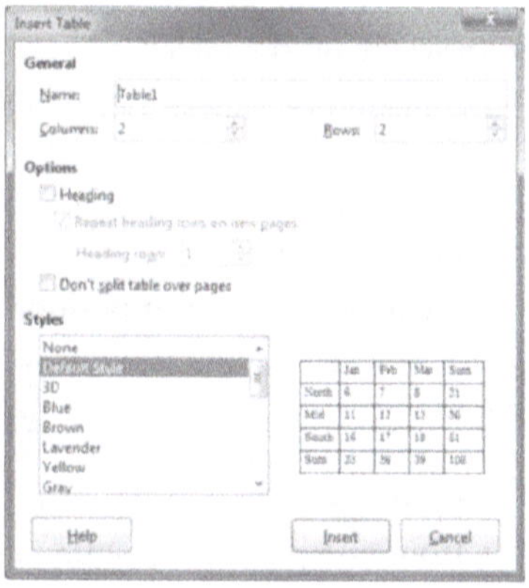

Step 2 Enter table name and number of columns and rows.

Step 3 Select style from the Styles option.

Step 4 Click Insert button.

(b) Inserting Row and Column

Insert Row at the End of Table To insert the row at the end of the table, place the insertion point in the last cell and press the Tab key, a new row will be inserted.

Insert a Row in the Table To insert a row in the table, follow the given steps :

Step 1 Place the insertion point in a column adjacent to the location where you want to add a new row.

Insertion point is in FIRST row so we can add a new row ABOVE it.

Jim M.	$10,252
Beth W.	$5,550
Luiz D.	$8,547
Alice S.	$13,578

Sample Table

Step 2 Right click the mouse. A context menu will appear.

Step 3 Select Insert option, a drop down list will appear.

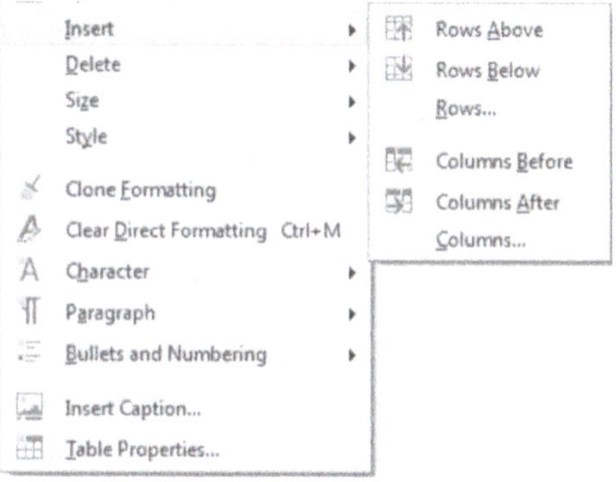

Step 4 Select Rows Above or Rows Below option.

Step 5 A new row will appear.

Jim M.	$10,252
Beth W.	$5,550
Luiz D.	$8,547
Alice S.	$13,578

Sample Table with New Row

Rows Above For inserting a row above the insertion point.

Rows Below For inserting a row below the insertion point.

Insert a column in the table To insert a column in the table, follow the given steps :

Step 1 Place the insertion point in a column adjacent to the location where you want to add a new column.

Step 2 Right click the mouse. A context menu will appear.

Step 3 Select Insert option, a drop down list will appear.

Step 4 Select Columns Before or Columns After option.

Step 5 A new column will appear.

(c) Deleting Rows or Columns

Steps to delete rows or columns from a table are as follows :

Step 1 Select the row or column which you want to delete.

Step 2 Right click the mouse. A context menu will appear.

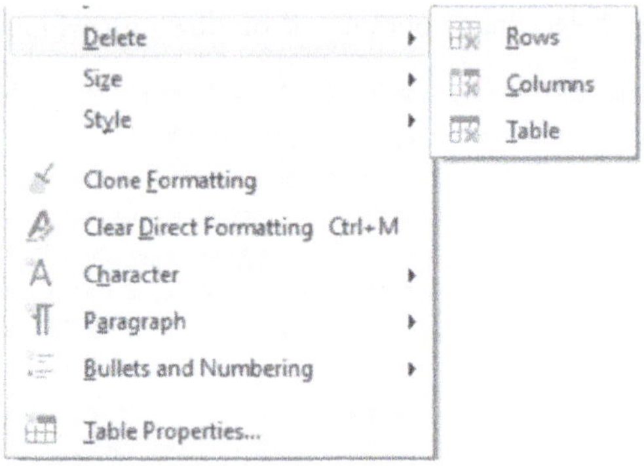

Step 3 Select Delete option, a drop down list will appear.

Step 4 Select Rows or Columns.

Step 5 Rows or Columns will be deleted.

(d) Splitting and Merging Tables

One table can be split into two tables and two tables can be merged into a single table. Tables can only be split horizontally.

(i) To split a table, follow the given steps :

Step 1 Place the cursor in a cell that will be in the top row of the second table after the split.

Step 2 Choose Table tab → Split Table from the menu bar.

Step 3 A Split Table dialog box will appear.

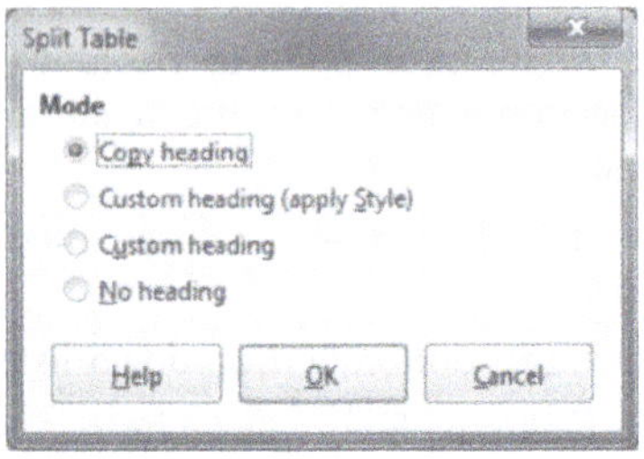

Step 4 You can select No heading or an alternative formatting for the heading.

Step 5 Click OK button.

The table will then split into two tables separated by a blank paragraph.

(ii) To merge two tables, delete the blank paragraph between the tables. You must use the Delete key (not the Backspace key) to do this.

(e) Deleting a Table

To deleting a table, follow the given steps :

Step 1 Click anywhere in the table.

Step 2 Choose Table tab → Delete option → Table.

Or

Select from the end of the paragraph before the table to the start of the paragraph after the table.

Step 3 Press the Delete key or Backspace key.

(f) Copying a Table

To copy a table from one part of the document and paste onto another part, follow the given steps :

Step 1 Click anywhere on the table.

Step 2 From the menu bar, choose Table → Select → Table.

Step 3 Press Ctrl + C or click the Copy icon on the standard toolbar.

Step 4 Move the cursor to the target position.

Step 5 Press Ctrl + V or click the Paste icon on the standard toolbar.

(g) Moving a Table

To move a table from one part of a document to another part, follow the given steps :

Step 1 Click anywhere in the table.

Step 2 From the menu bar, choose Table → Select → Table.

Step 3 Press Ctrl + X or click the Cut icon in the standard toolbar.

Step 4 Move the cursor to the target position.

Step 5 Press Ctrl + V or click the Paste icon on the standard toolbar (this pastes the cells and their contents and formatting).

Step 6 Return to the original table, click somewhere in it and then choose Table → Delete → Table from the menu bar.

Print Preview and Printing a Document

Print Preview

It is a feature that allows a user to view how a printed version of the document would look like on the screen before printing a hard copy.

Steps to preview the document before printing are as follows :

Step 1 Click the File tab, a drop down menu will appear.

Step 2 Select Print Preview or press Ctrl + Shift + O shortkey on keyboard.

The document will open in the Print Preview format.

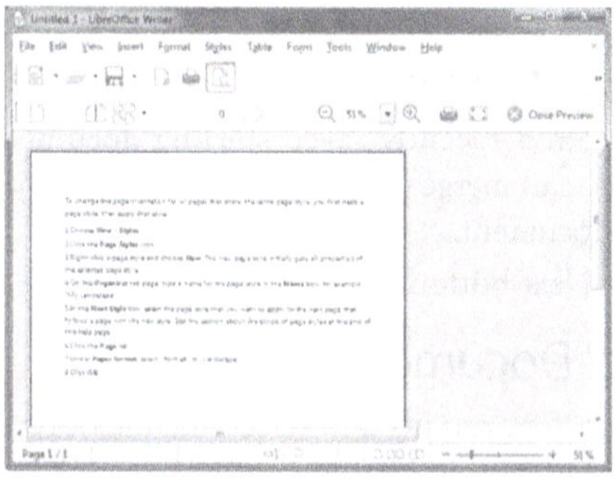

Step 3 Click the Print option to print the document or Toggle Print Preview from standard toolbar to exit the preview format of the document.

In Print Preview format, you can do many tasks :

- Change the page size
- Zoom in and Zoom out to view various parts of the document
- View multiple pages
- Jump to specific page

Printing a Document

Once you complete all the modifications in your document, you may want to print it for various reasons. Steps to print a document are as follows:

Step 1 Click the File tab or press Ctrl+P shortkey on the keyboard.

Step 2 Select Print option, Print dialog box will appear.

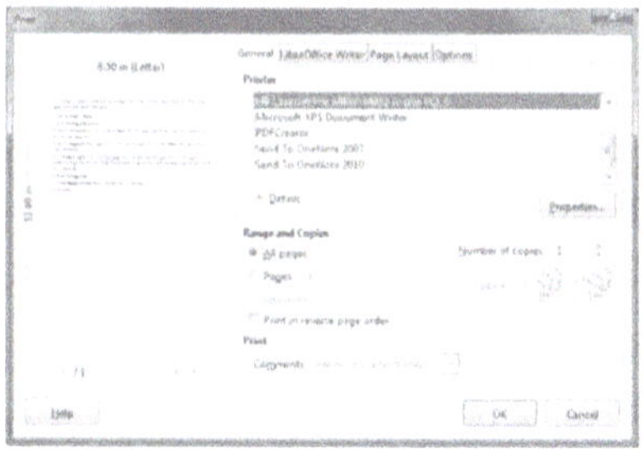

Step 3 Select the pages range you would like to print, either All Pages or Pages.

Step 4 Select the Number of copies.

Step 5 Check the Collate box, if you are printing multiple copies of a multi-page document.

Step 6 Select a printer from the Printer drop down list.

Step 7 Click OK button.

Protection of Password in Document

Password is very important in the document for proper authorisation. Only authorised users can open their accounts or can access their documents using the password option. LibreOffice Writer provides the feature to protect the document.

Here the steps to protect the document :

Step 1 Select the document which you want to protect with password.

Step 2 Find the File button and select Save As option from the drop down menu. Save As dialog box will appear.

Step 3 In the Save As dialog box, select the location where you want to save it and enter the file name.

Step 4 Put a tick the box with labeled Save with password.

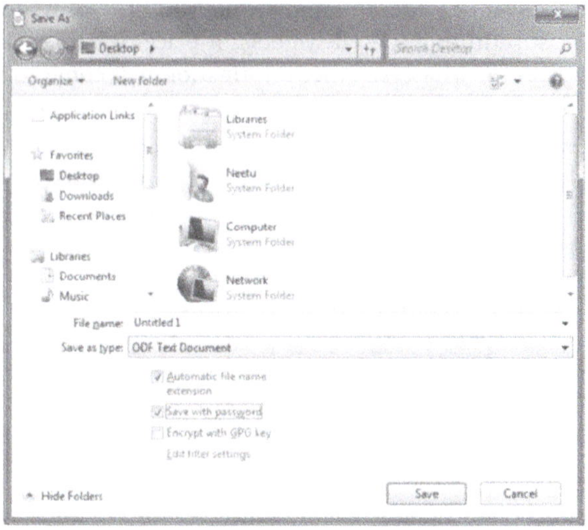

Step 5 Press Save button and a new Set Password window will be displayed.

Step 6 Enter the password in the Enter password to open and confirm your password to enter in Confirm password text field.

Step 7 Click OK button.

Note *Password protection topic is not a part of syllabus.*

Mail Merge

Sometimes you may need to send similar letter to a large number of people. But, each version of letter is not exactly same so, you may need to sit for hours to draft each letter individually. Normally, the mail content of such letters remains the same and only the specific information changes, such as name and address of the recipients. LibreOffice Writer Mail Merge feature can be proved to be a very useful tool in such a situation.

Mail Merge feature enables you to generate a set of forms, letters etc., containing similar information that can be sent to a group of people. To use a Mail Merge system, you have to first store a set of information like a list of names and addresses in one file. In another file, you have to write a letter, substituting special symbols in place of names and addresses (or whatever other information will come form the first file).

Steps to start the mail merge wizard to create letters or send e-mail messages to many recipients are as follows:

Click on Tools tab → Mail Merge Wizard option. Mail Merge Wizard dialog box will appear.

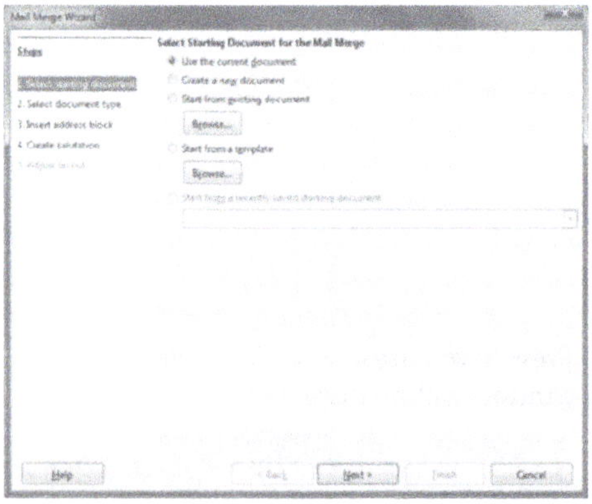

Here is given many steps in above window. We will discuss all steps one by one as follows :

1. Select Starting Document

(i) Click one of the following options :

- **Use the current document** Uses, the current Writer document as the base for the mail merge document.
- **Create a new document** Creates a new Writer document to use for the mail merge.
- **Start from existing document** Select an existing Writer document to use as the base for the mail merge document.
- **Start from a template** Select the template that you want to create your mail merge document with.
- **Start from a recently saved starting document** Use an existing mail merge document as the base for a new mail merge document.

(ii) Click Next button.

2. Select Document Type

(i) In this step, you need to select document type that you want to create.

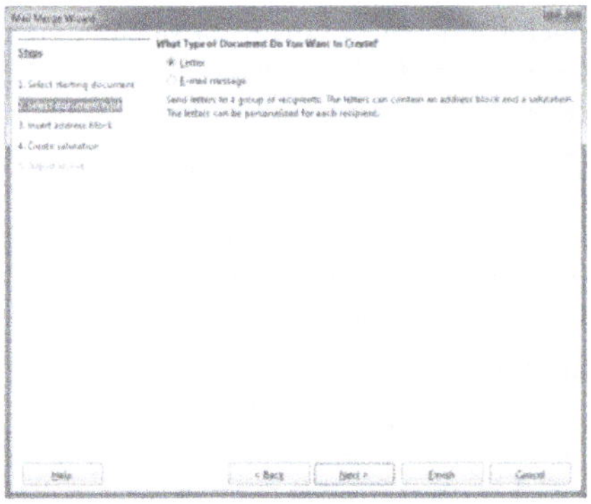

- **Letter** Creates a printable mail merge document that allows you to send letters to a group of people and personalise the results of the letter that each person receives.
- **E-mail message** Creates mail merge documents that you can send as an e-mail message or an e-mail attachment.

(ii) Click Letter and then select Next button.

3. Insert Address Block

It specifies the recipients for the mail merge document as well as the layout of the address block.

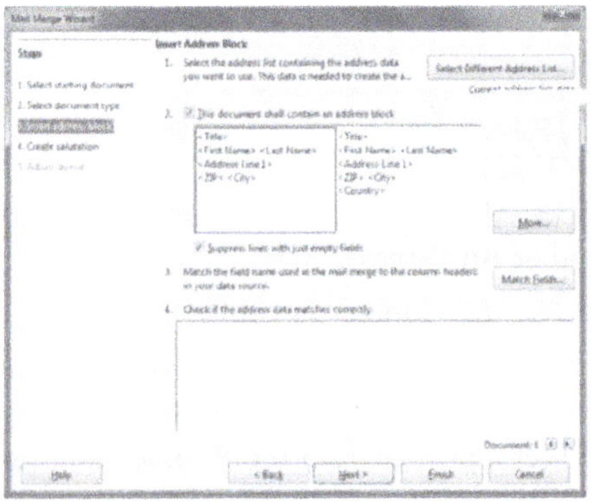

(i) Click on Select Address List button which will open Select Address List dialog box.

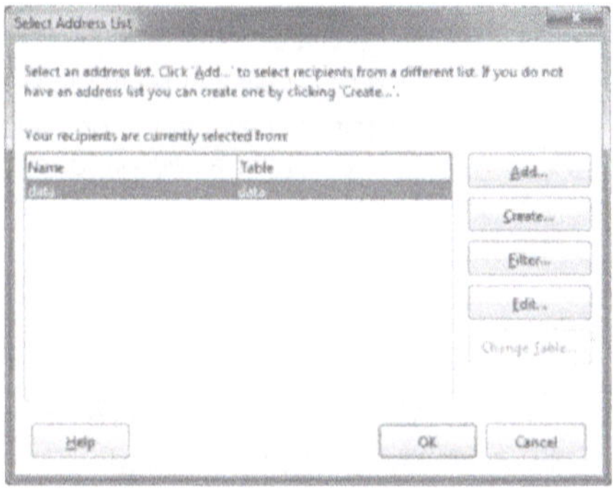

(ii) Click on the Create button. After clicking on the Create button a New Address List window will appear. In this window, under the Address Information section you can enter the information of the recipient.

(iii) If you want to fill the data of the recipient as per the default fields, then enter the data.

(iv) If you want to customise the fields of recipient information, click on Customise button. A Customise Address List window will appear.

(v) Now you can add, delete or rename any field name. You can also change the order of appearance of the fields using up/down arrow button.

- Add (for a new field)
- Delete (to delete unnecessary field)
- Rename (to change the name of the field)

(vi) After entering the data of first recipient, click on the New button to enter the information of the next recipient.

(vii) After entering the information of the entire recipient, click on the OK button to close the list.

(viii) After clicking OK button, the Save As dialog box will appear, which allow to save the list of recipient in .CSV format.

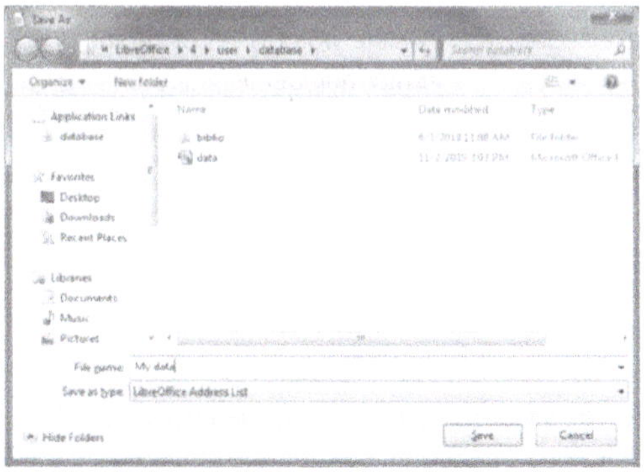

(ix) After saving the list a window will appear which display the various recipients list created till now. You can select any of the created list and click on OK button.

(x) You will move to step 3 of Mail Merge Wizard, a window which will show you the address block.

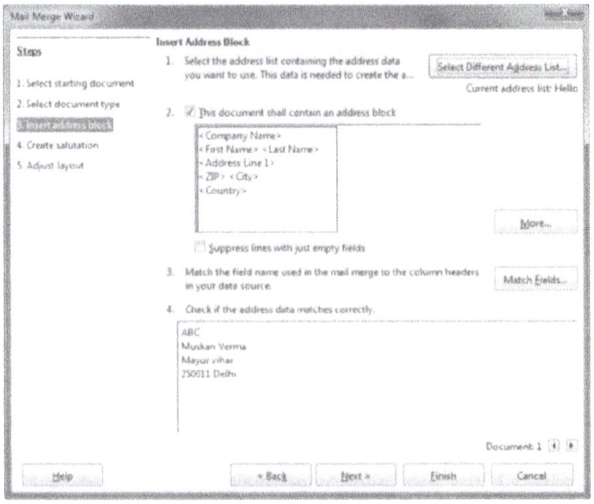

(xi) Click OK button.

4. Create Salutation

Specify the properties for the salutation. If the mail merge database contains gender information, you can specify different salutations based on the gender of the recipient.

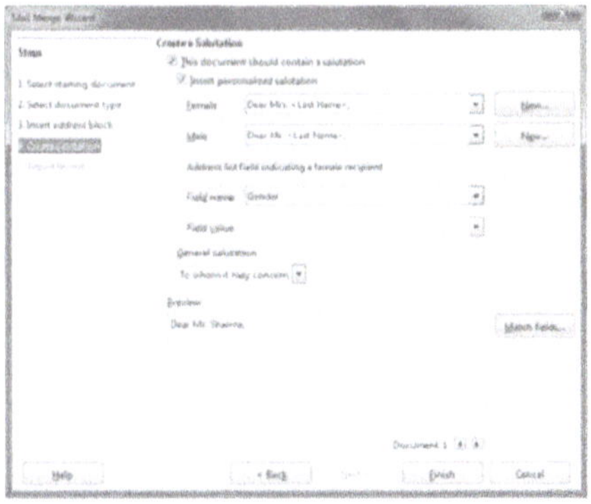

It has many options as follows :

- **Insert personalised salutation** Adds a personalised salutation to the mail merge document. To use the default salutation, clear this check box.
- **Female** Select the personalised greeting for a female recipient.
- **Male** Select the personalised greeting for a male recipient.
- **Field name** Select the field name of the address database field that contains the gender information.
- **Field value** Select the field value that indicates the gender of the recipient.
- **General salutation** Select the default salutation that is used when you do not specify a personalised salutation.

5. Adjust Layout

Specify the position of the address blocks and salutations on the documents.

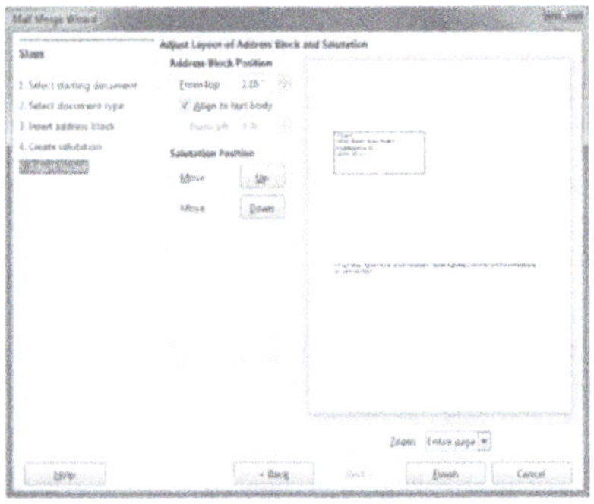

It has many options as follows :

- **Align to text body** Aligns the frame that contains the address block to the left page margin.
- **From left** Enter the value of space to leave between the left edge of the page and the left edge of the address block.
- **From top** Enter the value of space to leave between the top edge of the page and the top edge of the address block.
- **Up** Moves the salutation up.
- **Down** Moves the salutation down.
- **Zoom** Select the magnification for the print preview.

Edit Document

Minimises the wizard so that you can edit the main mail merge document for all recipients. To return the wizard. Click to Mail Merge Wizard button.

Exclude this Recipient

Excludes the current recipient from this mail merge.

Save, Print and Send

Specifies the output options for mail merge documents. The appearance of this page depends on the option that you select. After you specify the settings. Click Finish to exit the wizard. Select Print Merged Documents option to send the merged document directly to the printer. Select Save Merged Documents option to save the document and send E-mail messages to send the document.

Shortkeys for LibreOffice Writer

Shortkeys	Effects
Ctrl+A	Select All
Ctrl+J	Justify
Ctrl+E	Centered
Ctrl+H	Open Find & Replace dialog box
Ctrl+Shift+P	Superscript
Ctrl+L	Align Left
Ctrl+R	Align Right
Ctrl+Shift+B	Subscript
Ctrl+Y	Redo last action
Shift+Enter	Line break without paragraph change
Alt+Enter	Inserting a new paragraph directly before or after a section, or before a table.
Arrow Left	Move cursor to left
Shift+Arrow Left	Move cursor with selection to the left
Ctrl+Arrow Left	Go to beginning of word
Arrow Right	Move cursor to right
Shift+Arrow Right	Move cursor with selection to the right
Ctrl+Arrow Right	Go to start of next word
Arrow Up	Move cursor up one line
Shift+Arrow Up	Selecting lines in an upwards direction
Ctrl+Arrow Up	Move cursor to beginning of the previous paragraph
Arrow Down	Move cursor down one line
Shift+Arrow Down	Selecting lines in a downward direction
Ctrl+Arrow Down	Move cursor to beginning of next paragraph
Home	Go to beginning of line
Shift + Home	Go and select to the beginning of a line
End	Go to end of line
Shift + End	Go and select to end of line
Ctrl+Home	Go to start of document
Ctrl+B	Make letters bold
Ctrl+U	Makes letters underline
Ctrl+I	Makes letters italic
Ctrl+C	Copy the selected text
Ctrl+X	Cut the selected text
Ctrl+V	Paste the copy/cut text
Ctrl+]	Increase the font size by 1 point
Ctrl+[	Decrease the font size by 1 point
Ctrl+S	Save a document
Ctrl+Shift+S	Open Save As dialog box
Ctrl+Delete	Delete word to right of cursor
Ctrl+Backspace	Delete word to left of cursor
F12	Enter number list
Shift+F12	Enter bullet list

Check Point 04

1. Which shortkey is used to redo last action?
   (a) Ctrl + R (b) Ctrl + Y
   (c) Ctrl + X (d) Ctrl + D
2. Mail Merge feature enables you to generate a set of letters. (True/False).
3. .... delete the blank paragraph between tables.
4. What is print preview?
5. How to form a cell in table?

NCERT FOLDER

Check Your Progress

Pg 88-93

A. Multiple Choice Questions

Read the questions carefully and circle the letter (a), (b), (c) or (d) that best answers the questions.

1. Which of the following is not a component of the OfficeSuite?
   (a) Writer (b) Impress
   (c) Internet Explorer (d) Base

Ans. (c) Internet Explorer

2. The most widely used Word processing software in late 1970s was ....
   (a) WordPerfect (b) Word
   (c) WordStar (d) Writer

Ans. (c) WordStar

3. We can change the mistakes noticed in which of the following?
   (a) Electronic typewriter
   (b) Word processor software
   (c) Both (a) and (b)
   (d) Simple typewriter

Ans. (b) Word processor software

4. Header and Footer is available in which of the following menus?
   (a) File Menu
   (b) Format Menu
   (c) View Menu
   (d) Edit Menu

Ans. (b) Format Menu

5. To hide or view ruler we should go to which of the following menus?
   (a) Tools Menu (b) Insert Menu
   (c) View Menu (d) Edit Menu

Ans. (c) View Menu

6. To check the grammar we should go to which of the following menus?
   (a) Tools Menu (b) Insert Menu
   (c) View Menu (d) Edit Menu

Ans. (a) Tools Menu

7. To replace a word Bombay with Mumbai, we should go to which of the following menus?
   (a) Tools Menu (b) Edit Menu
   (c) View Menu (d) Language Menu

Ans. (b) Edit Menu

8. To close an opened document, we should to go to which of the following menus?
   (a) File Menu (b) Insert Menu
   (c) View Menu (d) Edit Menu

Ans. (a) File Menu

9. Which of the following is the default extension of the Writer file?
   (a) .obt (b) .doc
   (c) .odt (d) .docx

Ans. (c) .odt

10. Which of the following technique selects a sentence in Writer?
    (a) Single click (Pressing left button of mouse)
    (b) Double click
    (c) Triple click
    (d) None of the above

Ans. (c) Triple click

11. Which of the following is a shortkey to Redo any operation?
    (a) Ctrl + R (b) Ctrl + Y
    (c) Ctrl + X (d) Ctrl + Z

Ans. (b) Ctrl + Y

12. To find a word in a document we can use which of the following function key?
    (a) F5 key (b) F8 key
    (c) Fl key (d) None of these

Ans. (d) None of these

13. Spellings are corrected automatically in Writer because of which of the following features?
    (a) AutoText (b) AutoCorrect
    (c) AutoComplete (d) All of these

Ans. (b) AutoCorrect

14. The default table size is ....
    (a) 1 column, 1 row (b) 2 columns, 1 row
    (c) 2 columns, 2 rows (d) 1 column, 2 rows

Ans. (c) 2 columns, 2 rows

15. What is the shape of the mouse pointer when drawing a table?
(a) Pencil
(b) White pointing arrow
(c) Black pointing arrow
(d) Black plus

Ans. (c) Black pointing arrow

16. Which shortkey is used for automatic spell checking?
(a) Shift + Insert (b) Shift + F7
(c) Ctrl + Insert (d) Tab + Insert

Ans. (b) Shift + F7

17. Which shortkey is used to insert table?
(a) Ctrl + F12 (b) Alt + Delete
(c) Ctrl + Delete (d) Tab + Delete

Ans. (a) Ctrl + F12

18. Which of the following is not valid type of data source in mail merge?
(a) Spreadsheet (b) Text files
(c) MySQL (d) CSV file

Ans. (b) Text files

19. The default orientation of a page in Writer is
(a) portrait (b) landscape
(c) book (d) None of these

Ans. (a) portrait

20. Which of the following does not come under page formatting?
(a) Setting margins
(b) Find & replace
(c) Setting header and footer
(d) Page orientation

Ans. (b) Find & replace

21. Saving an existing document with some other name using the Save As option ....
(a) replaces the current document
(b) leaves the current document intact
(c) is not possible
(d) closes the document

Ans. (a) replaces the current document

22. Keyboard shortcut to italicise the selected text is
(a) Ctrl + U (b) Shift + U
(c) Ctrl + I (d) Shift + I

Ans. (c) Ctrl + I

23. Which option should be used to type H_2O, to get 2 at its proper place?
(a) Bold (b) Superscript
(c) Underline (d) Subscript

Ans. (d) Subscript

24. What option should be used to to change the word 'Books' to the word 'Copies' in a document?
(a) Find
(b) Find & Replace
(c) Spell check
(d) Spelling and grammar check

Ans. (b) Find & Replace

25. What is the option to print the document so that the height of the page is less than its width?
(a) Landscape (b) Portrait
(c) Indent (d) Tab setting

Ans. (a) Landscape

B. Fill in the Blanks

1. The sub menu item with three dots '...' just after the sub menu name, denote that it will open the ....

Ans. dialog box

2. The sub menu item with right hand side arrows '▶', means, clicking on it will open ....

Ans. another sub menu

3. Formatting toolbar contains various options for ....

Ans. formatting a document

4. By pressing the Home key you jump to the .... and by pressing the End key you jump to ....

Ans. beginning of the line, end of line

5. After using the Undo command, to go back again to the previous position the, ... option or command is used.

Ans. Redo

6. Double click is used to select the ....

Ans. word

7. Headers appear at the .... and footers appear at the .... of every page.

Ans. top, bottom

8. In the .... page orientation the height of the page is less than its width.

Ans. landscape

9. The .... option is used to see how the document will look like when it will be printed.

Ans. Print preview

10. In Mail Merge the file holding the mailing addresses is called as ....

Ans. data source

C. State whether True or False

1. To open word processor 'Window' menu option is selected.

Ans. False

2. Current file name is shown in Status bar.

Ans. False

3. Open icon for opening a file is part of Standard toolbar.

Ans. True

4. Format Menu contains the options that apply to the whole document.

Ans. True

5. It is possible to open a MS-Word file in LibreOffice Writer.

Ans. True

6. We cannot open LibreOffice Writer file in MS-Word.

Ans. True

7. Writer does not permit to copy a selected text in to another document.

Ans. False

8. It is possible to copy a selected text without using Menu options and keyboard options.

Ans. True

9. To open the 'Find & Replace' dialog box, we have to go to Format menu.

Ans. False

10. We can find all the cities included in a document using 'Find and Replace' feature of Writer.

Ans. True

11. While typing if an incorrect spelling is detected a red line is marked under it. After correcting it, the red line is converted into green line.

Ans. False

12. The text written in Header and Footer is printed on each page of the document.

Ans. True

13. The page number appears with gray background and is printed with background.

Ans. True

14. Writer creates a table as wide as the page area.

Ans. True

15. A new column is created in table by pressing Tab key.

Ans. False

16. Mail Merge is used to prepare multiple copies of the same document.

Ans. False

17. The Form Letter contains the variable information in Mail Merge.

Ans. True

18. The portrait and landscape orientations are set in Paper option under properties.

Ans. True

19. In Print Range by default current page is selected for printing.

Ans. True

20. By default the page size is A4.

Ans. True

D. Short Answer Questions

1. In a document all the occurrences of word "this" have to be changed to "these". Which option is suitable for this and what is the shortcut command used for it?

Ans. Find & Replace option is used for this condition and shortkey is Ctrl + H.

2. Which two documents are essential for Mail Merge?

Ans. Data source and Writer documents are essential for Mail Merge.

3. Explain the concept of Word processing.

Ans. Refer to text on Page 131.

4. List the various softwares available for Word processing.

Ans. The various softwares available for Word processing are:

- AppleWorks
- Microsoft Word
- StarOffice
- WordPerfect
- OpenOffice.org Writer
- LibreOffice Writer

5. Write difference between a text editor and a Word processor software. Write the name of any text editor or Word processor available in market.

Ans. Differences between a text editor and a Word processor software are as follows :

Text Editor	Word Processor
• Text formatting is not available in editors.	• Text formatting is available in Word processors.
• It does not allow automatic spelling and grammar checks.	• It allows automatic spelling and grammar checks.
e.g. Notepad	e.g. Microsoft Word

6. List the various components of LibreOffice suite. Explain each component in one line.

Ans. Components of LirbeOffice Writer are as follows:

- **Title bar** It displays the name of the current document.
- **Ruler** It is used to set tabs, indents and margins for a document.
- **Scroll bar** It is used to view the whole active window.
- **Work area** It is the rectangular area of the document window, where you can type the text.
- **Menu bar** It is located just below the title bar, when you select one of the menus, a sub menu drop down to show further options.

7. Compare the features of manual typewriter, electronic typewriter and Word processing software.

Ans. Comparing the features of manual typewriter, electronic typewriter and Word processing software are as follows:

Manual Typewriter

- It is a mechanical or electro-mechanical machine for writing characters.
- Each one causes a different single character to be produced on the paper, by means of a ribbon with dried ink struck against the paper by a type element.

Electronic Typewriter

- They are automic centering, right margin justifying and hang indenting are available on computer.
- Electric typewriter is more user friendly.

Word Processing Software

- It is used to manipulate text and apply basic design to your pages.
- It includes creating, editing, copying, pasting, moving, saving, formatting text, creating and editing tables etc.

8. Explain the different views to display a document.

Ans. Refer to text on Pages 132 and 133.

9. What are the various methods for selecting the text in a document? Give the steps to select a paragraph.

Ans. Refer to text on Page 136.

10. What are the special characters? How can you insert them in a document?

Ans. Refer to text on Page 145.

11. How will you count the total words of a document?

Ans. Total words in your document are displayed on status bar at the bottom of the workspace.

You can also see the total word by

- Tools tab → Word Count option
- Shortkey Alt + T then Alt + W

12. What are the various menu of Writer GUI?

Ans. Menu provides the list of options to the user provided in a graphical user environment. These menu are categorised according to the tasks they do and it also contains sub menu which in turn has commands to be executed on click. The common menu in GUI are File, Edit, View, Insert.

13. What is the default extension assigned to the document in Writer when you save it? Write down the steps to save the document to Microsoft Word document?

Ans. The default extension assigned to the document in Writer is .odt.

Steps to save the document in Microsoft Word as follows :

- Click the Microsoft Office button.
- Then, click on Save As. The Save As dialog box will appear.
- Select the location, where you want to save the document using the drop down menu.
- Enter the name of the document in File name : box.
- Click on Save button.

14. What is the importance of password in the document? How will you protect the document using password in Writer?

Ans. Refer to text on Pages 149 and 150.

15. What is Mail Merge? Write down the steps to create mailing labels to paste on wedding cards.

Ans. Refer to text on Pages 150 and 152.

16. What are the advantages of table? Prepare your report card of Class VIII in table format.

Ans. The advantages of Table are as follows :

(i) By using the table, we can easily find out the information and it is one of the efficient way for summarise the given information.

(ii) In table, we can add the information in specific way rather than in paragraph.

(iii) Table reduce the complexity of the information or data.

Report Card For Class VIII

Report Card					
Name : Class :			Teacher's Name : Year :		
Subject	1	2	3	Mid term	Final
English					
Hindi					
Math					
Science					
Social Study					
Computer					
ART					
Music					
Remark : Percentage :		Total Marks :		Obtained Marks: Teacher' Sign:	

17. Write an application to your Principal for field visit to any IT Industry.

Ans. Laxmi Nagar

Delhi

July 25, 2020

The Principal

Delhi Public School

M G Road

Delhi

Subject : Visit to an IT Industry

Sir/Madam,

It is a request on behalf of all the students to arrange a field visit to any IT industry to help us understand things better related to technology.

Technology has been advancing at a faster rate. We all need to have a good amount of knowledge regarding the IT industry. It is not only going to help us in our academics but also be fruitful for our future endeavors.

We would be highly obliged if you kindly grant our request and give the permission to our teachers as soon as possible.

Thanking you

Your faithfully,

ABC

(Senior prefect)

SUMMARY

- A document is a paper with written contents and the process of preparing a document is called documentation.
- It is a hand operated mechanical device with which on typing keys can produce printed characters on paper.
- LibreOffice Writer is the free and open source word processor component of the LibreOffice software package you can use it to type letters, newsletters, reports and other documents.
- To permanently store a document on hard disk, you must save the document and assign a name to it.
- The Find and Replace option helps you to search a particular letter, word, phrase or sentence in your document and then replace it, if you want.
- A paragraph in a document can have several sentences, a single sentence, a single word or no words at all.
- Indents are the white space added to the margins and decreasing the text area for paragraph.
- Header and footer generally both contains information such as page number, date, document name, company logo, image etc., which are specified by page styles.
- It is a feature that allows a user to view how a printed version of the document would look like on the screen before printing a hard copy.
- Mail Merge feature enables you to generate a set of forms, letters etc., containing similar information that can be sent to a group of people.

Exam Practice

Multiple Choice Questions

1. .... can be letters, reports, thesis, manuscripts, legal documents, blocks etc.
   (a) Documents (b) Thesis
   (c) Typewriters (d) Processors

Ans. (a) Documents

2. In the year 1974, ... company had introduced an electronic typewriter.
   (a) Microsystems (b) Xerox
   (c) Apple (d) Spreadsheet

Ans. (b) Xerox

3. Components of LibreOffice is/are
   (a) Writer (b) Calc
   (c) Impress (d) All of these

Ans. (d) All of these

4. It shows the name of the currently opened document.
   (a) Title bar (b) Task bar
   (c) Status bar (d) Menu bar

Ans. (a) Title bar

5. Which tab provides options for changing alignment?
   (a) View
   (b) Format
   (c) Preview
   (d) Page Layout

Ans. (b) Format

6. The first tab of LibreOffice Writer is
   (a) File (b) View
   (c) Insert (d) Review

Ans. (a) File

7. Which toolbar is used to cut, copy, paste, undo, redo etc?
   (a) Standard toolbar (b) Formatting toolbar
   (c) Sidebar (d) None of these

Ans. (a) Standard toolbar

8. Which of the following should be used to move a paragraph from one place to another in a writer document?
   (a) Copy and paste (b) Cut and paste
   (c) Delete and retype (d) Find & replace

Ans. (b) Cut and paste

9. What is the overall term for creating, editing, formatting, storing, retrieving and printing a text document?
   (a) Word processing
   (b) Spreadsheet design
   (c) Web design
   (d) Database management

Ans. (a) Word processing

10. For printing a document, you have to put on
   (a) printer (b) monitor
   (c) scanner (d) All of these

Ans. (a) printer

Fill in the Blanks

1. .... is a grid of cells arranged in rows and columns.

Ans. Table

2. .... is a section of the document that appears at the bottom margin of the page.

Ans. Footer

3. To cut the selected text, ... shortkey is used.

Ans. Ctrl + X

4. The mouse is used to control the .... location.

Ans. text cursor

5. In computing ...., anything entered is treated as a character.

Ans. data entry

True/False

1. Word processing is a GUI based software used in the windows environment.

Ans. True

2. Title bar is at the top of the window that bears the name of the window.

Ans. True

3. Scroll bar is available in LibreOffice Writer.

Ans. True

4. Help option allows users to search and find any topic about that program.

Ans. True

5. Formatting toolbar exists above the standard toolbar.

Ans. False

6. Page Style dialog box is used to create table, charts etc.

Ans. False

7. Enter key is used to go to the next line.

Ans. True

8. After typing the text in the document, user can edit that text.

Ans. True

Match the Columns

1. Match the following columns.

	Column I		Column II
A.	← ↑↓ →	1.	Spreadsheet
B.	Default alignment	2.	Cursor control keys
C.	Edit → Cut	3.	Left
D.	Calc	4.	Ctrl + X
E.	Impress	5.	Presentation

Ans. A → 2; B → 3; C → 4; D → 1; E → 5

2. Match the following columns.

	Column I		Column II
A.	Bold	1.	changes the whole selected text in uppercase letters
B.	Tools tab	2.	Ctrl + V
C.	UPPERCASE	3.	Ctrl + B
D.	Superscript	4.	is used to spelling and grammar
E.	Paste	5.	appears slightly above a word or a letter

Ans. A → 3; B → 4; C → 1; D → 5; E → 2

Very Short Answer (VSA) Type Questions

1. How do you locate Writer on your windows computer system?

Ans. Click Start → All Programs → LibreOffice 6.2 → LibreOffice Writer.

2. Write the shortcut keys to format the text style bold, italic and underline.

Ans. Bold - Ctrl+B, Italic - Ctrl+I, Underline - Ctrl+U

3. What is formatted text?

Ans. Formatted text has styling information beyond the minimum of semantic elements: colors, styles (boldface, italic), sizes and special features such as hyperlinks.

4. Write the name of alignments, which are available in Writer.

Ans. Left, Right, Center and Justify.

5. Tanya is working as an assistant manager at Arihant publication. She wants to send diwali greetings to every customer. Which technique can help her in printing address on the envelope of greeting card?

Ans. Mail Merge will help her in printing labels on the bulk of envelopes.

6. Define a table used in Writer.

Ans. A table is a grid of cells arranged in rows and columns. Table can be customised and useful for various tasks such as presenting text information and numerical data.

7. What is the use of bullet styles in our document?

Ans. While working in a document, sometimes we need to highlight some areas of text in the form of lists for summarising key points, so we use the option of creating bulleted and numbered lists.

Short Answer (SA) Type Questions

1. Write the steps to create a new blank document?

Ans. Refer to text on Page 133.

2. What do you understand by merge field while performing Mail Merge?

Ans. Merge field is a placeholder that you insert in the main document. e.g. insert the merge field <city> insert a city name, such as "Paris" that is stored in the city data field.

3. Explain Header and Footer.

Ans. The Header is a section of the document that appears on the top margin.While the Footer is a section of the document that appears on the bottom margin.

Headers and Footers generally contain information such as page number, date, document name etc.

4. What is the difference between the Save and Save As option?

Ans. "Save" means the file gets saved under its current name, in whatever folder it was saved before or in the default folder of that computer whereas "Save As" gives you the opportunity to save the file under a different name and in another folder. "Save As" allows you to name the updated version with a new name and at the same time preserving the old version.

5. How can you remove manual formatting?

Ans. Refer to text on Page 140.

6. Define the merging tables in LibreOffice Writer.

Ans. Refer to text on Page 148.

7. List the variety of modifications that one can make in with the table.

Ans. Using commands on the Layout tab, you can make a variety of modifications to the table such as

- Adding and deleting columns
- Adding and deleting rows
- Changing the cell size
- Aligning cell text
- Changing text direction
- Merging and splitting cells and more.

8. What do you mean by ruler?

Ans. Ruler appears on the top and on the left side of the document window. It allows to format the horizontal or vertical alignment of text in a document.

Two types of rulers are available in Writer as follows:

(i) Horizontal ruler indicates the width of the document.

(ii) Vertical ruler indicates the height of the document.

9. Define the term Mail Merge.

Ans. Mail Merge is a useful tool that allows you to produce multiple letters, labels, envelopes by linking a main (common) document to a set of data or data source. The main document is linked to the data source by common fields of data, called **merge fields.**

You can create your own merge fields, specific to your data source, or you can use a predefined set provided by Writer. e.g. in a form letter, your main document would be the letter informing the person that they have won money, or their car service time has arrived.

10. What is indentation? How can you indent the paragraph in document?

Ans. Refer to text on Page 141.

11. Write the steps to insert the page break in the Writer document.

Ans. Refer to text on Page 144.

Long Answer (LA) Type Questions

1. Explain superscript or subscript.

Ans. Superscript or subscript refers to the number, figure or symbol that is positioned slightly higher or slightly lower than the text on the line. e.g. A footnote or endnote reference number is an example of superscript and a scientific formula might use subscript text.

X_2 Subscript X^2 Superscript

In Writer, select the character that you would like to change and click the Superscript or Subscript symbol from the Text group under the Format tab.

2. Do you think, use of bulleted lists or numbered lists is more appropriate in a Writer document?

Ans. The use of bulleted lists or numbered lists is an effective way to outline or list the items in a Writer document.

By modifying numbered or bulleted lists, you are able to change the way of information that is displayed. Creating an outline list, which can help to organise your document for clear presentations. To customise your eye-catching bullets, Writer provides many different images from which to choose.

Also, Writer gives you the ways of modifying the format of your numeral list.

3. How to Find & Replace the text in Writer?

Ans. Refer to text on Page 137.

4. Explain the different types of tabs available in LibreOffice Writer.

Ans. Refer to text on Page 132.

5. What is the need to modify the spacing of the lines or paragraph of your text?

Ans. An important part of creating effective documents lies in the document design. Line spacing or paragraph spacing is measured in lines or points, which is referred to as leading.
As a part of designing the document and making formatting decisions, you will need to know how to modify the spacing. Just as you can format spacing between lines in your document, you can also choose spacing options between each paragraph.

Typically, extra spaces are added between paragraphs, headings or subheadings. Extra spacing between paragraphs adds emphasis and makes a document easier to read. When you reduce the leading, you automatically bring the lines of text closer together. Increasing the leading will space the lines out, allowing for improved readability.

Self Assessment

Multiple Choice Questions

1. To move the text from its original position to another position without deleting it is called
   (a) scrolling (b) searching (c) moving (d) copying
2. To copy the selected text and put it into clipboard, use
   (a) Copy command from Edit tab (b) Ctrl + C
   (c) mouse right click and select Copy option (d) All of these
3. Which of the following is not a font style?
   (a) Bold (b) Italic (c) Regular (d) Superscript
4. For pasting the cutted text use .... shortkey.
   (a) Edit tab + Paste (b) Ctrl + V (c) Both (a) and (b) (d) Ctrl + C
5. Which of the list is a listing order that is done with numbers?
   (a) Bullet list (b) Number list (c) Order list (d) Both (b) and (c)
6. In LibreOffice Writer, document has text case which help to change the text case. They are
   (a) Sentence case (b) lowercase (c) UPPERCASE (d) All of these
7. It is a section of the document that appears at the top margin of the page.
   (a) Footer (b) Header (c) Head (d) Tail
8. To print a document, press .... shortkey then press Enter.
   (a) Shift + P (b) Ctrl + P (c) Alt + P (d) Esc + P

Fill in the Blanks

1. User can also check the spelling and .... in a document.
2. .... are the white space added to the margins and decreasing the text area for paragraph.
3. .... is a list of items preceded with pictures.
4. To correct or remove any character, text, paragraph, etc, use ....
5. Move to the cursor to the beginning of the document, press the .... key.

True/False

1. Indentation can be done with the help of horizontal ruler also.
2. You can create a nested list in your document.
3. Sentence case command is used to capitalise each first character of every word.
4. You can insert only text as header.
5. A table cannot contain row and column both.
6. Mail Merge is a software function describing the production of single document from a single template form and a structure data source.
7. The first file in mail merge is called the data source file.

Match the Columns

Column I		Column II	
A.	Draw	1.	Pasting
B.	Base	2.	Drawing
C.	Ctrl + V	3.	Open
D.	Number list	4.	Database
E.	Ctrl + O	5.	Styles tab

Very Short Answer (VSA) Type Questions

1. What is a LibreOffice Writer?
2. What all information is displayed on the status bar?
3. What is the use of UPPERCASE text case option in Writer?
4. What is the difference between header and footer?
5. What is the use of various colored line?

Short Answer (SA) Type Questions

1. Write the steps to insert mathematical symbols in a document.
2. Give two advantages of the spelling and grammar check feature of a Writer.
3. Explain the ways to insert a picture.
4. What is the use of menu bar?
5. Define the mouse pointer.
6. Write the features provided by popular Word processors.
7. Give the difference between standard toolbar and formatting toolbar.
8. Write the steps to use synonyms.
9. What are the common text formatting?

Long Answer (LA) Type Questions

1. How can you insert rows and columns?
2. Write the steps to print the Writer document.
3. Define the following terms :

   (i) Text formatting (ii) Page formatting

UNIT

04

Electronic Spreadsheet

Chapter Checklist

- Getting Started with LibreOffice Calc
- Creating a New Spreadsheet
- Mathematical Operators Used in Formulae
- Use of Functions to do Calculations
- Formatting the Worksheet
- Speeding Up Data Entry
- Creating of Charts Using Spreadsheets
- Shortcut Keys for LibreOffice Calc

In science and engineering, scientific calculators are used to perform complex calculations. Spreadsheet application is a tool which is used to perform all kinds of calculations easily and accurately.

Spreadsheet is a long sheet of rows and columns on the computer screen to do data analysis and calculation. It is a grid which interactively manages and organises data in rows and columns. It is also called a electronic spreadsheet.

Spreadsheet is used for managing financial and accounting documents, creating data reports, generating invoices, data analysis from scientific and statistical researches and for doing a variety of calculations on data. It can also store, manipulate and create graphical representations of data.

Spreadsheet packages also provide built-in formulae and functions for common mathematical, financial, statistical and logical operations. Because of these abilities, the spreadsheet packages are used as a universal programme for structured data preparation and processing. To handle the increasing size of the spreadsheet, the concept of a workbook was identified.

LibreOffice suite has a software named Calc which provides the facilities as spreadsheet. LibreOffice Calc is used to perform the following activities:

- Tabulation of data
- Simple mathematical calculations
- Complex calculations using formula and functions
- Arranging data in ascending and descending order (sorting)
- Filtering the required data
- Check the validity of data
- Protection of data using passwords
- Saving for future use

Getting Started with LibreOffice Calc

There are various types of spreadsheet applications developed by various software corporation.

e.g. Lotus 1-2-3, Quattro Pro, Multiplan, MS-Excel, VisiCalc, LibreOffice Calc etc., in which VisiCalc is the oldest spreadsheet software.

Here, we will discuss LibreOffice Calc.

Starting LibreOffice Calc

When installing the operating system Linux (Ubuntu), the LibreOffice gets installed by default along with the icons for each component of LibreOffice (as Writer, Calc, Impress etc.). These icons are then placed on the launcher. In Windows, you need to download LibreOffice from its official website and install it on your computer.

(a) To Start LibreOffice Calc in Windows

- Find the shortcut of LibreOffice on Start menu or on the desktop. Double click to open LibreOffice.
- Click LibreOffice Calc. The Calc spreadsheet window will open.

(b) To Start LibreOffice Calc in Linux

Find the Calc icon on application launcher or search it by clicking on "Show Applications".

Parts of LibreOffice Calc

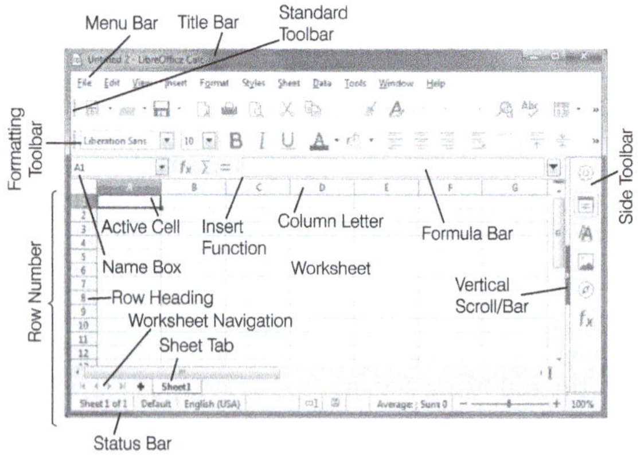

The components of a spreadsheet window are as follows :

(a) Title Bar

The bar located at the top of the window is called title bar. It contains the name of the currently open document. When the spreadsheet is newly created, its name is Untitled X, where X is a number. The first created spreadsheet takes the name as Untitled 1, second is Untitled 2 and so on.

(b) Menu bar

Menu bar is located just below the title bar. It contains the menus with commands for various tasks. Each menu item has a sub-menu called pull-down menu. The various menu items are briefly explain below:

(i) **File Tab** It is found at the top-left corner of the window. It contains options as New, Open, Open Remote, Templates, Save, Save Remote, Save As, Print Preview, Print etc.

(ii) **Edit Tab** It contains options as Undo, Redo, Cut, Copy, Paste, Find & Replace etc.

(iii) **View Tab** It contains options as Normal, Page Break, Formula Bar, Status Bar, Sidebar, Styles, Gallery, Zoom etc.

(iv) **Insert Tab** It contains options as Image, Media, Chart, Object, Function, Date, Time, Comment, Header & Footer etc.

(v) **Format Tab** It contains options as Text, Spacing, Align, Cells, Rows, Page, Conditional, Spreadsheet Theme etc.

(vi) **Styles Tab** It contains options as Footnote, Update Style, New Style, Manage Styles etc.

(vii) **Sheet Tab** It contains options as Insert Cells, Insert Rows, Insert Columns, Delete Cells/Rows/ Columns, Fill Cells, Rename Sheet, Hide Sheet etc.

(viii) **Data Tab** It contains options as Sort , Auto Filter, Select Range, Pivot Table, Subtotals, Form, Data Provider etc.

(ix) **Tools Tab** It contains options as Spelling, Language, AutoCorrect Options, Goal Seek, Forms, Macros, XML Filter Settings etc.

(x) **Window Tab** It contains options as New Window, Close Window etc.

(xi) **Help Tab** It contains options as LibreOffice Help, Send Feedback, Restart in Safe Mode, Donate to LibreOffice, Check for Updates etc.

(c) Toolbar

The Calc opens with the standard and formatting toolbars at the top of the work space by default. These toolbar provide a wide range of common commands and functions. Placing the mouse cursor over any icon displays a small box called a tooltip. It gives a brief explanation of icon function.

(i) **Standard Toolbar** It is located just below the menu bar and contains various options as New, Save, Open, Print etc.

(ii) **Formatting Toolbar** It is located just below the standard toolbar and contains various options as Font Name, Font Size, Bold, Italic etc.

(iii) **Formula Toolbar** It allows entering and editing the formula in the cell. Formula bar consists of the following:

- **Name box** It shows the cell reference, for example B2.
- **Function wizard** It searches the function from the list of available functions.
- **Sum** It is used to total the numbers in the cells above the selected cell. The result of sum is placed in the selected cell.
- **Formula** If you click on Formula icon then it inserts an equal '=' sign into the selected cell and input line allows formula to be entered.
- **Input line** It displays the contents of the selected cell (data, formula or function) and allows editing the cell contents. To edit inside the Input line area, click in the area then type the changes. To edit within the current cell, just double click in the cell.

(d) Worksheet

LibreOffice Calc consists worksheet. Each worksheet can have many individual cells arranged in rows and columns. The sheet tab shows its default name as Sheet1, Sheet2, Sheet3, ... etc.

(e) Rows and Columns

The spreadsheet is divided into vertical columns and horizontal rows. Each sheet can have a maximum of 1, 048, 576 (2^{20}) rows and 1024 (2^{10}) columns. The rows are numbered as 1, 2, 3, 4, ... and columns are numbered as A, B, C, D, ..., Z, AA, AB, AC, ... AZ, BA to BZ, CA, ... AMJ.

(f) Cell and Cell Address

The intersection of a row and column is called a cell. It is the basic element of a numbers, formulas and so on. A cell address is denoted by its column (letter) and row number. e.g. A4, B1, Z89 etc.

(i) **Active cell** In a spreadsheet, cell is the place where we enter the data. Before entering any data in a cell, it has to be first selected by placing a cursor on it. When we position the mouse cursor on a cell, it gets selected and is ready to take data from user. This selected or activated cell is called as active cell. It is always highlighted with a thick border. The address of the active cell is displayed in the name box.

(ii) **Active cell in a worksheet** To enter data in the cell, it should be selected first. Active cell in a worksheet can be moved or selected by the key or a combination of keys.

Key or Key Combination	Result of Key or Combination
Arrow keys (← ↑ → ↓)	Move a single cell in arrow direction
Ctrl + Arrow Keys	Moves the cell to the end of the data range in a particular direction
Home	Moves to column A along the row where the active cell is
Ctrl + Home	Moves the cell to A1 position
Ctrl + End	Moves to bottom right cell of the data range
Page Up	Moves the worksheet one screen up
Page Down	Moves the worksheet one screen down

(iii) **Range of cells** In a worksheet, a block of adjacent cells which is highlighted or selected is called range of cells. Observe the worksheets below:

- **Column range** It is the number of cells spread across the column. The cell address is represented by single column letter and multiple row number in a sequence.

  e.g. The column letter B is constant with rows varying from 3 to 10. The range of cells starts in B3 and ends in B10. This range consists of the cells namely B3, B4, B5, B6, B7, B8, B9 and B10. This ranges is represented by B3: B10.

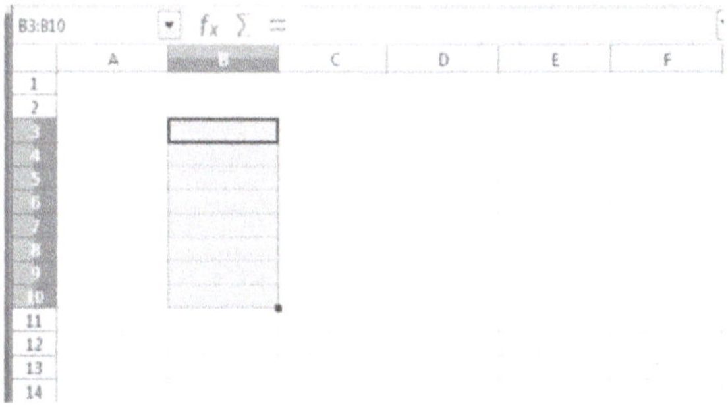

- **Row range** It is the number of cells spread across the row. The cell address is represented by single row number with columns varying from B to E columns.

The range of cells starts in B3 and ends in E3. This range consists of the cells namely B3, C3, D3, E3 and it is represented by B3 : E3.

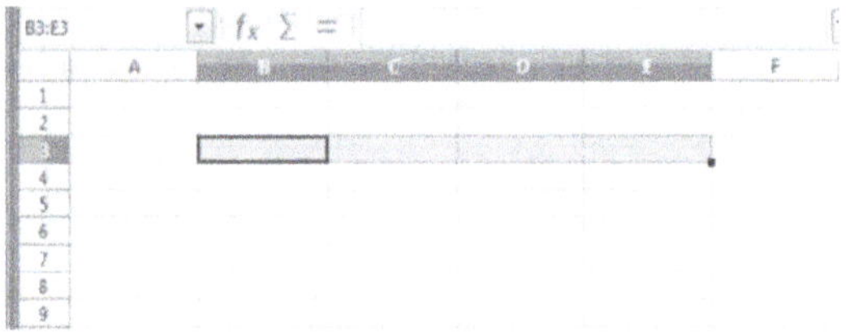

- **Row and column range** It is the number of cells spread across the row and column. This range is a matrix with number of rows and number of columns.

  e.g. The range starts in cell C3 and ends in cell D8. This range consits of the cells from C3 to C8 and cells from D3 to D8. It is represented by C3 : D8.

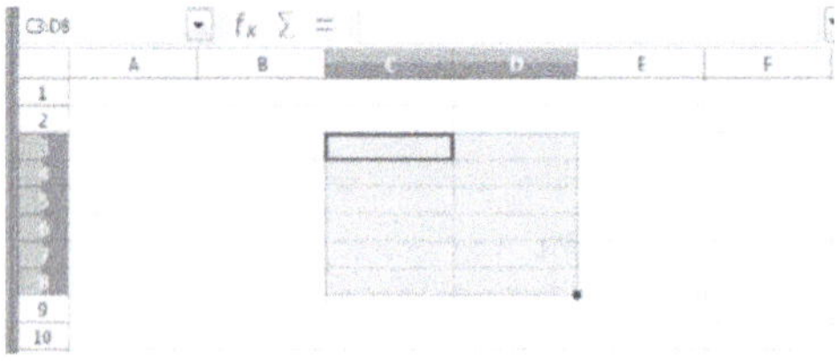

Note *The Ctrl key is used to select more than one 'range of cells' in a worksheet.*

Check Point 01

1. It shows the cell reference.
   (a) Name box (b) Function wizard
   (c) Formula (d) Input line
2. .... is the place where we enter the data.
3. Formula toolbar allows entering and editing the formula in the cell. (True/False)
4. What is cell address?
5. What is the use of Page Up key?

Creating a New Spreadsheet

Steps to create a new spreadsheet are as follows:

Step 1 Click on File tab.

Step 2 Select New option. A context menu will appear.

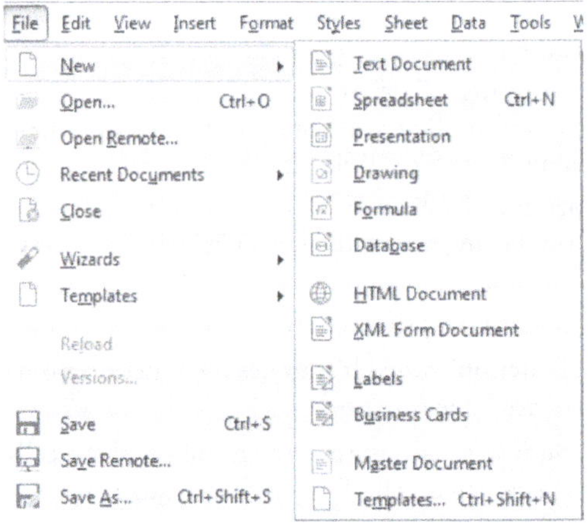

Step 3 Select Spreadsheet. A blank spreadsheet will appear on your screen.

Entering Data

To enter any data in a worksheet, it is required to select the cell. Cell can be selected by positioning the pointer in a cell. The data to be entered can be label, values or formula.

(a) **Label** It is any text entered by using a keyboard. It may combine with letters, numbers and special symbols. By default the labels are left aligned.

(b) **Values** The numerical data consisting of only numbers are called values. By default values are right aligned. There are various forms of values such as integer, decimal, and so on.

(c) **Formulae** Any expressions that begins with an equals '=' is treated as formula. In the expression, the '=' followed by values, cell address and functions are called as formula. When a formula is entered in a cell in a worksheet the value of the equation is displayed in the cell and the formula is shown in formula bar.

e.g.

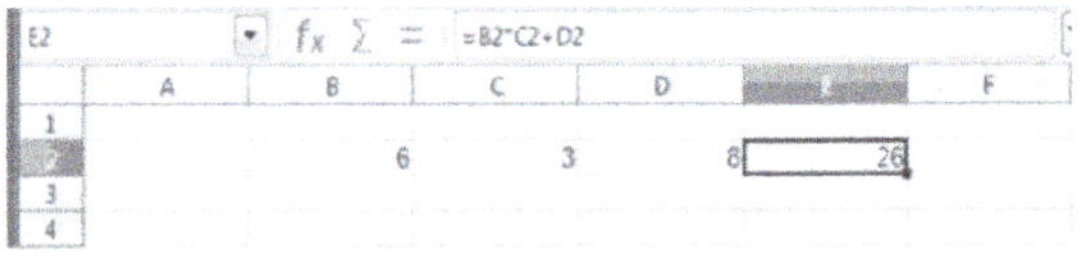

Note *The values do not display the preceding zero. To show the preceding '0', the data type has to be specified as 'Text'.*

Mathematical Operators Used in Formulae

Spreadsheet software has the most powerful features to calculate numerical data using formulae. LibreOffice Calc uses a standard operators for formulae, such as a plus (+), minus (–), multiplication (*), a division (/) for arithmetic operations.

	Mathematical Operators	Operator precedence	
+	addition	First	( )
–	subtraction	Second	^
*	multiplication	Third	/, *
/	division	Fourth	+ , –
^	exponentiation (power)		

Note *The order of evaluation can be changed by using brackets (the expressions with in the brackets are evaluated first).*

Simple Calculations using Values and Operators

More than one mathematical operator can be included in the formula. Below table shows a few formulae:

Writing Simple Formula

Operator	Formula	Result
Addition (+)	= 43 + 2	45
Subtraction (–)	= 23 – 40	–17
Multiplication (*)	= 4 * 6	24
Division (/)	= 4 / 2	2
Exponentiation (^)	= 3^2	9

Use of Brackets in Simple Equations

Formula	Evaluation	Result
= 2 + 4 * 2	= 2 + 8	10
= (2 + 4) * 2	= 6 * 2	12
= 2 * 4 ^3	= 2 * 64	128
= (2 * 4) ^3	= 8 ^ 3	512
= (3 / 3) ^2	= 1 ^2	1
= 13 / (3^2)	= 13 / 9	1.44444

Formulae with Cell Addresses and Operators

The main advantage of entering formula with cell addresses and operators, works just like a variable. When the values of the cells concerned change, the results obtained by the formula also get updated accordingly.

For example, to subtract the values in two cells B1 and B2 and get the subtraction in cell B3. If we position the cursor in cell B3 and simply subtract the values as = 12 – 6, then we will get the correct subtraction in cell B3. But if we change the values in cell B1 to 14 and B2 to 5, then again we have to get the subtraction in the cell B3 by writing = 14 – 5.

But if we write the general form in cell B3 as = B1 – B2. Then we need not to do the subtraction in cell B3. We will get the respective subtraction with the change in values in B1 and B2.

Note *Formula always starts with '=' sign.*

Let us create a simple spreadsheet to prepare a shopping bill of the following items:

Items	Quantity	Unit Price	Total Price
Shoes	1	500	500
T-shirt	2	400	800
Plastic Box	4	50	200
Bed Sheet	1	800	800
Bucket	5	30	150

The steps to create the spreadsheet are as follows:

Step 1 Open the LibreOffice Calc.

Step 2 Give the specific name to the worksheet as 'Shopping Bill'. To do this,

- Select the Menu Sheet→ Rename Sheet. Rename Sheet dialog box will appear.
- Give the name, say Shopping Bill to the worksheet and click OK button.

Step 3 Enter the data that given above. To do this,

- Click on cell A1. Enter the word Items and press Enter key.
- Click on cell B1. Enter the word Quantity and press Enter key.
- Click on cell C1. Enter the word Unit Price and press Enter key.

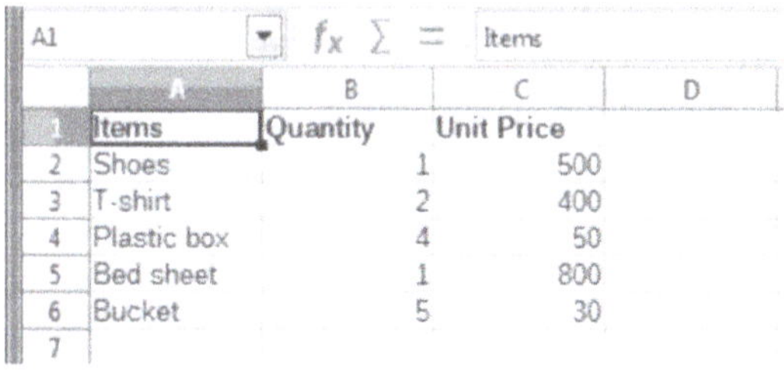

- You may drag the column to resize it. To resize, put the mouse at the edge of the column and drag it to required length.
- Select the heading cells and make them bold using formatting toolbar.

Step 4 Now, save your worksheet with appropriate name. To save the spreadsheet, follow below steps:

- Click on File tab → Save button.
- Save As dialog box will appear.

Step 5 Select the location where you want to save the file and enter file name as Shopping Bill and click on Save button. The file will get saved by default in ODF format with the name Shopping-Bill .ods.

- Now, calculate the Total Price of each item in this worksheet. Enter the heading as we will insert a new column right to the Unit Price and give the heading as 'Total Price' in the cell D1.
- To insert the column before any column, position the cursor on any cell of the column before which you want to insert the column and select:
- Sheet → Insert Columns → Columns Before /Columns After

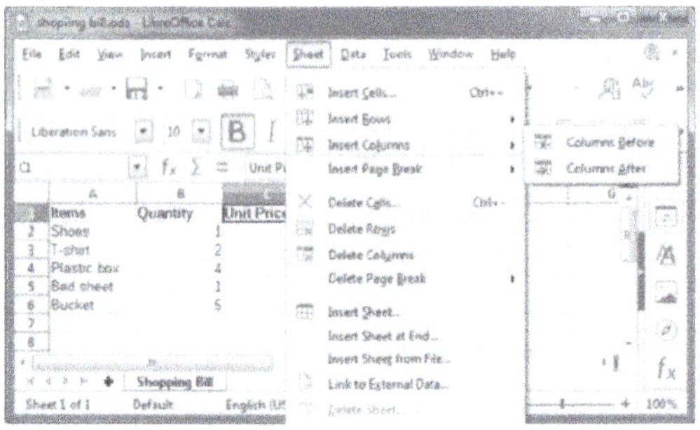

- Now to calculate the Total Price in column D for each item, move the cursor on cell D2 and enter the formula = B2 * C2 to calculate the Total Price for Shoes. We need to apply the same formula for the next items. So instead of writing the formula again and again in the next cell D3 to D6, click on the cell D2, hold and drag it down to D6. The formulas to calculate the total cost will be get copied.

Step 6 Now enter the formula in cell D7 as = D2 + D3 + D4+ D5 + D6 to calculate the Total Price.

Check Point 02

1. .... is any text entered by using a keyboard.
2. By default, values are left aligned. (True/False)
3. Which of the following is/are mathematical operators?
   (a) Addition (b) Subtraction
   (c) Multiplication (d) All of these
4. What is formula?
5. How many cells are there in range A2 : B4 ?

Use of Functions to do Calculations

In the example of Shopping Bill, to calculate the total amount of items, we need to add the price of each item. Position the cursor on the cell D7 and enter the formula = D2 + D3 + D4 +D5 + D6 and get the total in cell D7.

It is possible when you have few number of items but if there are hundreds of items then there will be more chances of error.

In such situation, LibreOffice Calc provides built-in functions. SUM is the function to get the sum of range of cell so, we can use the function = SUM (D4 : D6) in cell D7 to obtain the total amount of all the items.

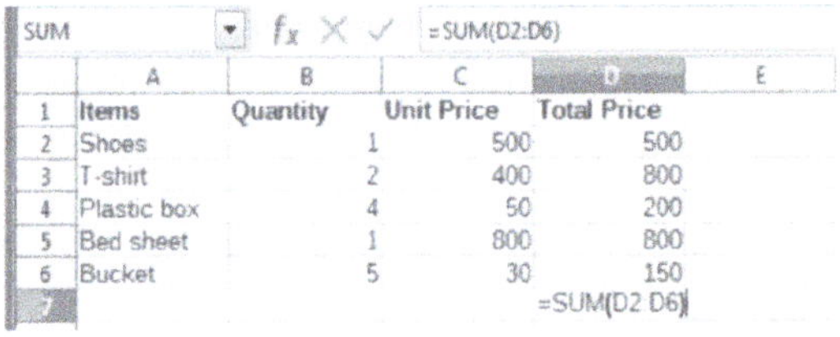

Commonly Used Basic Functions in Calc

Function	Syntax	Use
SUM	=SUM(Number1, Number2,.....)	Adds the values contained in a range of cells.
AVERAGE	=AVERAGE(Number1, Number2,....)	Finds out the average of the values contained in a range of cells.
MAX	=MAX(Number1, Number2,......)	Finds out the largest value contained in a range of cells.
MIN	=MIN(Number1, Number2,......)	Finds out the smallest value contained in a range of cells.
COUNT	=COUNT(Number1, Number2,.....)	Counts the number of cells within a range of cells.

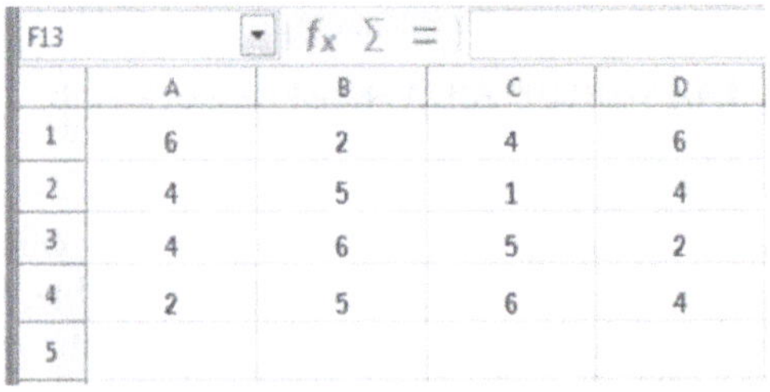

Let us identify the various ways in which a function can be used. Based on the sample data above, the result of the functions are evaluated below:

SUM Function

Formula	Meaning	Result
=SUM (A1,B1,C1)	The sum of cells A1,B1 and C1	12
=SUM(A1:C1)	The sum of cells in the range of cells from A1 to C1	12
=SUM(A1:C1,B2)	The sum of cells in the range of cells from A1 to C1 and B2	17
=SUM(B1:C2)	The sum of cells in the range of cells from B1 to C2	12
=SUM(A1:A3,C1:C3)	The sum of cells in the range of cells from A1 to A3 and C1 to C3	24

AVERAGE Function

Formula	Meaning	Result
=AVERAGE (A1,B1,C1)	The average of cells A1, B1 and C1	4
=AVERAGE (A1:C1)	The average of cells in the range of cells from A1 to C1	4
=AVERAGE (A1:C1,B2)	The average of cells in the range of cells from A1 to C1 and B2	4.25
=AVERAGE (B1:C2)	The average of cells in the range of cells from B1 to C2	3
=AVERAGE (A1:A3,C1:C3)	The average of cells in the range of cells from A1 to A3 and C1 to C3	4

Note *When average is calculated a decimal number with several decimal places may be used.*

MAX Function

Formula	Details	Result
=MAX(A1,B2,C1)	Finds out the largest value among cells A1,B2 and C1	6
=MAX(A2:C2,B3)	Finds out the largest value among the range of cells from A2 to C2 and the cell B3	6
=MAX(A1:C1)	Finds out the largest value among the range of cells from A1 to C1	6
=MAX(A1,B1:C2)	Finds out the largest value among the range of cells from A1 to B1 and the cell C2	6

MIN Function

Formula	Details	Result
=MIN(A1,B2,C1)	Finds out the smallest value among cells A1, B2 and C1	4
=MIN(A2:C2,B3)	Finds out the smallest value among the range of cells from A2 to C2 and the cell B3	1
=MIN(A1:C1)	Finds out the smallest value among the range of cells from A1 to C1	2
=MIN(A1,B1:C2)	Finds out the smallest value among the range of cells from B1 to C2 and the cell A1	1

COUNT Function

Formula	Details	Result
=COUNT(A1,B1)	Counts the number of cells that contain numbers among cells A1, B1	2
=COUNT(A1:C1)	Counts the number of cells that contain numbers in the range of cells from A1 to C1	3
=COUNT(A1:A4)	Counts the number of cells that contain numbers in the range of cells from A1 to A4	4
=COUNT(A1:C1,B2)	Counts the number of cells that contain numbers in the range of cells from A1 to C1 and B2	4
=COUNT(B1:C3)	Counts the number of cells that contain numbers in the range of cells from B1 to C3	6
=COUNT(A1:A3,C1:C3)	Counts the number of cells that contain numbers in the range of cells from A1 to A3 and the range of cells from C1 to C3	6

Formatting the Worksheet

The cell holds any type of data in the spreadsheet. The cell data can be formatted using formatting toolbar or cell formatting window. It is also possible to format the cell using Format Cells dialog box.

To open Formal Cells, follow below steps:

Step 1 Select Format tab, a context menu will open.

Step 2 Click on Cells option. A Format Cells dialog box will appear.

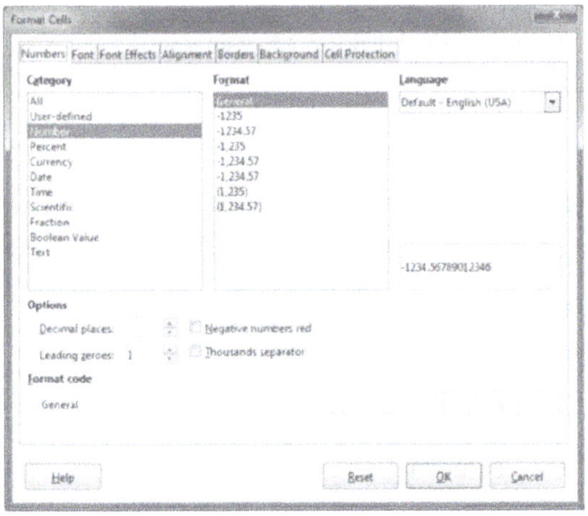

You can change the formatting with the help of this dialog box. Various formatting tools are describe below:

Tool	Details
Font	Apply different font types on a worksheet
Font Size	Apply different font sizes on a worksheet
Bold	the selected text bold
Italic	Italicize the selected text
Underline	Underline the selected text
Left Alignment	Align text in a cell to the left
Center Alignment	Align text in a cell to the center
Right Alignment	Align text in a cell to the right
Increase decimal places	Show more precise value by showing more decimal places
Decreased decimal places	Show less precise decimal places

Use of Dialog Boxes to Format Values

The Format Cells dialog box in the toolbar can be used to find more about formatting a cell or range of cell. Format Cells can also be open by Ctrl+1 shortkey.

Formatting a Range of Cells with Decimal Places

The division of different numbers may result in varied decimal places in the quotient. In such cases, it is necessary to format the number to a fixed number of decimal places.

Follow the below steps to format a cell to the required number of decimal places:

Step 1 Select the range of cells.

Step 2 Open Format Cells dialog box.

Step 3 Click on Numbers tab.

Step 4 Select the Number category.

Step 5 Change the Decimal places option.

Step 6 Click OK button.

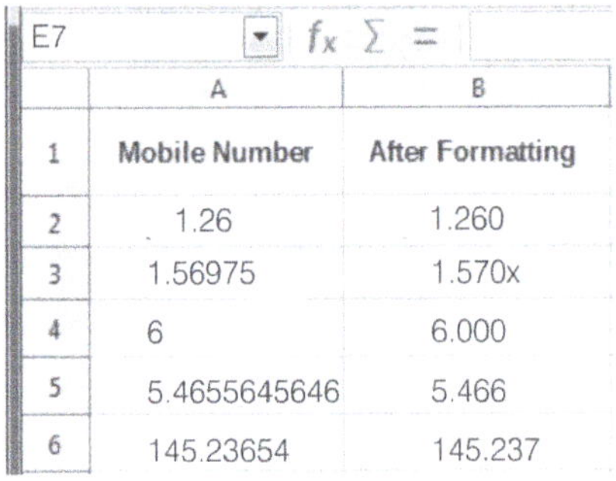

E7

	A	B
1	Mobile Number	After Formatting
2	1.26	1.260
3	1.56975	1.570x
4	6	6.000
5	5.4655645646	5.466
6	145.23654	145.237

Formatting a Range of Cells to be Seen as Labels

In a telephone number, the STD code starts with 0. But while entering the telephone number with the STD code the first digit zero '0', disappears from the telephone number. This is because the telephone number is stored as a numeric value.

If you make these numeric values as text, then the complete telephone number will appear with a preceding zero.

Follow the steps below in order to format a range of cells as text:

Step 1 Select the range of cells.

Step 2 Open the Format Cells dialog box.

Step 3 Click the Numbers tab.

Step 4 Select Text under category.

Step 5 Click OK button.

Step 6 Enter number which you want to change as text.

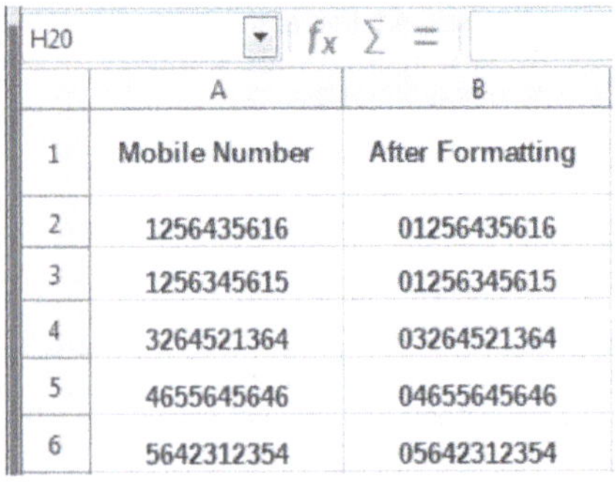

H20

	A	B
1	Mobile Number	After Formatting
2	1256435616	01256435616
3	1256345615	01256345615
4	3264521364	03264521364
5	4655645646	04655645646
6	5642312354	05642312354

Formatting a Cell Range as Scientific

In a spreadsheet, by default the date format is in American Format ; (mm/dd/yyyy). Here, mm means month, dd means date and yyyy means year.

The date 10/25/2019 means that it is the 25th day of October 2019. In a spreadsheet, the user can change this date in many different formats.

Follow the below steps to do this:

Step 1 Select the range of cells.
Step 2 Open the Format Cells dialog box.
Step 3 Click on Numbers tab.
Step 4 Select the Date category.
Step 5 Select the date format.
Step 6 Click OK button.

10/25/2019
25. Oct. 2019
Friday, October 25, 2019
25. October 2019
Oct 25

Formatting a Range of Cells to Display Time

Time is indicated in a computer as 09:25:46 AM. The common format of this is HH:MM:SS AM/PM. Here, HH means hours, MM means minutes and SS means second. Follow the below steps to format the cells to display the time:

Step 1 Select the cell range.
Step 2 Open the Format Cells dialog box.
Step 3 Click the Numbers tab.
Step 4 Select the Time category.
Step 5 Select any time format.
Step 6 Click OK button.

Display time as different formats

25 : 46 : 00
09 : 25 : 46 AM
09 : 25 : 46
09 : 25 AM
09 : 25

Formatting Alignment of a Cell Range

The labels and values can be aligned to the left, center, or right of a cell range by using the alignment icons, on the standard toolbar.

Follow the below steps to aligned the text in cell :

Step 1 Select the range of cells.
Step 2 Open the Format Cells dialog box.
Step 3 Click the Alignment tab.
Step 4 Select any option from Horizontal category as Left, Center, Right, Justified etc.
Step 5 Click OK button.

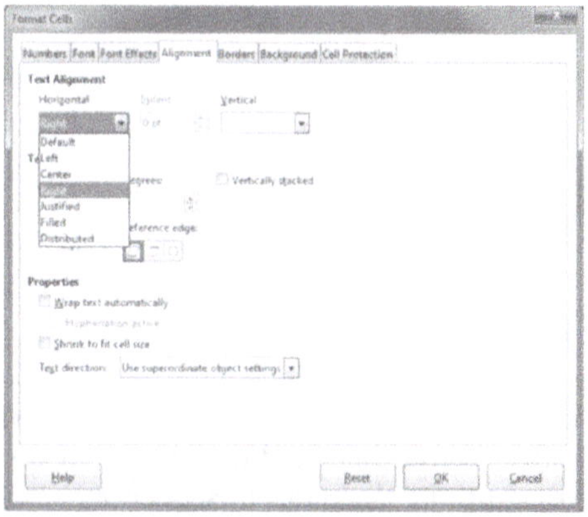

Create the worksheet as below using formatting tools and formulae:

	A	B	C	D	E	F
1		Marks of Students Class 9th				
2	Students	Hindi	English	Computer	Mathematics	Average
3	*Riya*	45	86	69	78	69.5
4	*Rohit*	85	65	75	86	77.75
5	*Kiaan*	64	58	76	84	70.5
6	*Disha*	77	86	63	87	78.25
7	Average	67.75	73.75	70.75	83.75	

- Center align row 1.
- Make row 1 and row 2 Bold.
- Italicise cells A3, A4, A5 and A6.
- Use function Average in cell F3 to calculate the average of Marks scored by Riya in Hindi (B3), English (C3), Computer (D3) and Mathematics (E3).
- Copy this formula by dragging it from F3 to F6.
- Use function Average and write a formula in B7 to calculate the average of Marks scored by Riya, Rohit, Kiaan, Disha for subject Hindi.
- Copy this formula by dragging it from B7 to E7 and use them to calculate the average for English, Computer and Mathematics.

Check Point 03

1. ……… adds the values contained in a range of cells.
2. The cells hold any type of data in the spreadsheet. (True/False)
3. What is the use of Average () function?
4. Give one difference between MAX () and MIN ().
5. Format Cells can also be open by .... shortkey.
   (a) Ctrl + 1 (b) Ctrl + 2 (c) Ctrl + 3 (d) Ctrl + 4

Speeding Up Data Entry

The most important ability of a spreadsheet is to drag and drop the contents of one cell to another by using a mouse. Calc includes several other tools for automating input, especially of a repetitive task.

They include the fill tool, selection lists and the ability to input information into multiple sheets of the same document.

Using the Fill Handle

The Calc Fill Handle tool is used to fill the next cells till you drag it with the next predefined value.

e.g. If you want to fill the numbers in sequence of 2, 4, 6, ... or name of months as January, February ..., enter the first two values, select them and drag to the next cells till you want to continue the series in sequence.

(a) For Number Series

Type the numbers 2, 4 in two consecutive cells and select them using a mouse. Click on the right down corner of the selected cells, hold down the left button of mouse and drag downward till you want to continue.

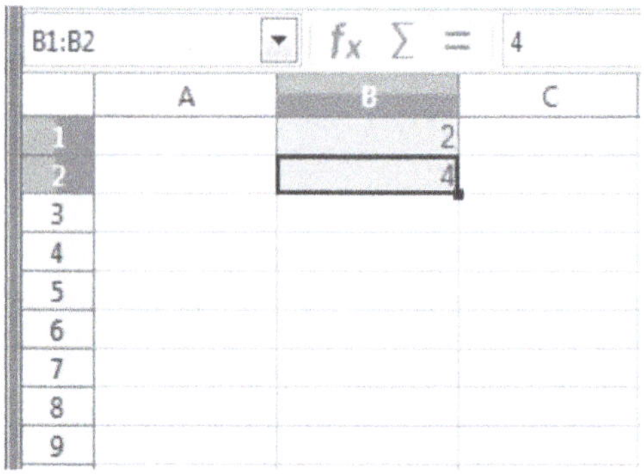

(b) Copying a Formula

If you want to apply the same formula to the number of cells in the rows or columns, you need not enter the formula again and again in each cell.

A formula can be copied that saves the time and efforts in case of long and complex formulae to reduce chances of errors.

There are two ways to copy a formula as below

(i) **Use of Copy and Paste commands** To do this, follow the below steps:

Step 1 Select the cell.

Step 2 Copy the contents of the selected cell by shortcut key Ctrl + C.

Step 3 Select the cell in which the formula is to be pasted.

Step 4 Paste the contents in the selected cell by shortcut key Ctrl + V.

The small black square in the bottom right corner of the selected cell or range is called a **fill handle**.

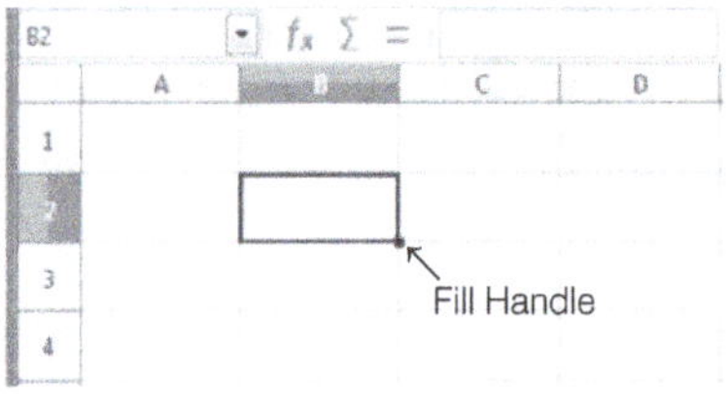

(ii) **Use of fill handle** To do this, follow the below steps:

Step 1 Select the cell which contains the formula.

Step 2 Click the small black square in the bottom right corner of the selected cell.

Step 3 Drag the fill handle up to the required cell.

Referencing

It is the way to refer the formula or function from one cell to the next cell along the row or column.

There are three types of addressing or referencing as follows:

(a) Relative Referencing

When you drag any formula in any row or column in any direction, the formula gets copied in new cell with the relative reference. Almost all spreadsheet applications use relative referencing by default.

When we drag the formula downwards in columns, the row number of the cell address gets one added. In same way, when you drag the formula horizontally from the left to right, the column name of the cell address is added on to the next column letter.

	A	B	C	D	E
1	S. No.	Items	QTY	Unit Price	Total Price
2	1	T-Shirt	3	350	= C2 * D2
3	2	Bed Sheet	2	700	= C3 * D3
4	3	Bucket	5	40	= C4 * D4
5	4	Shoes	1	1200	= C5 * D5
6		Total	= SUM (C2:C5)	= SUM (D2:D5)	= SUM (E2:E5)

Fig. 1

	A	B	C	D	E
1	S. No.	Items	QTY	Unit Price	Total Price
2	1	T-Shirt	3	350	1050
3	2	Bed Sheet	2	700	1400
4	3	Bucket	5	40	200
5	4	Shoes	1	1200	1200
6		Total	11	2290	3850

Fig. 2.

In Fig 1, in cell E2, the formula = C2 * D2 has been used to calculate the total price of T-Shirt.

In cell C6, the formula = SUM (C2 : C5) has been used to calculate total quantity of all items. Now drag the formula from E2 to E5 vertically and from C6 to E6 horizontally.

As you drag formula from C6 to E6, the formula gets changed to = SUM (E2 : E5) from = SUM (C2 : C5). The columns names get changed, while row numbers will remain same.

Note *To see the formula after dragging, select from menu View → Show Formula*

(b) Absolute Referencing

In this referencing, a $ symbol is used before the column name as well as row number to make it constant in any formula.

e.g. $A $5 * B4 etc. In this case, even if you drag your formula in any direction, the cell name with dollar sign remains constant. This type of referencing is used in higher classes.

(c) Mixed Referencing

It is a combination of absolute and relative cell referencing. In this referencing, the $ sign is used before row number or column name to make it constant.

e.g. In $A5 * B$4, only relative part will change when it copy into another cell.

	A	B	C
1			
2			
3		= $A5 * B$2	= $A5 * C$2
4		= $A6 * B$2	= $A6*C$2
5			

Thumb Rule for Referencing

Types of cell reference

Example	Types of reference
A1	Relative reference
$A1	Mixed Reference (Column letter is absolute)
A$1	Mixed Reference (Row number is absolute)
$A$1	Absolute reference (No change)

Creation of Charts Using Spreadsheets

These are the graphical and pictorial representation of worksheet data.

In Calc, charts are created by using Insert tab. LibreOffice Calc supports charts, graphs or histograms generated from specified group of cells. The generated graphical component can either be embedded within the current sheet, or added as a separate object.

Different Types of Charts

Different types of charts are as follows :

- **Column Chart** Values are display in the form of vertical columns in this chart. Many different data series and their values are display on X-axis and Y-axis, respectively.
- **Bar Chart** Categories are listed vertically, so that bars appear on the horizontal, thus there is less emphasis on time flow.
- **Line Chart** Line chart tends to emphasize the rate of change rather than volume of change over time.
- **Scatter Chart** They are useful, if the data on the X-axis represent uneven intervals of time or increments of measurement.
- **Area Chart** They are used to compare the changes in volume of a data series over time, emphasizing the amount of change rather than the rate of change.
- **Pie Chart** Only one data series can be plotted, making up 100%. They are used to compare the size of the parts with the whole.

Components of a Chart

A sample chart and its components is given below :

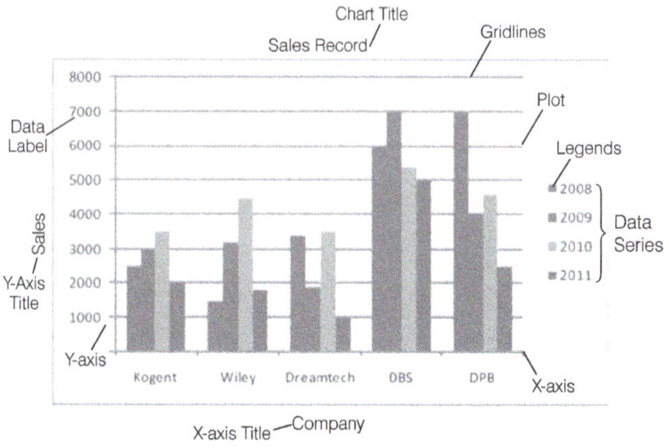

Now, components of a chart in detail are as follow :

- **X-axis** is a horizontal axis known as category axis.
- **Y-axis** is a vertical axis known as value axis.
- **Data Series** is the set of values you want to plot in the chart.
- **Chart Area** is the total area of the chart.
- **Legends** is a unique color or pattern, which helps you to identify an individual data series.
- **Chart Title** is the descriptive text aimed at helping user to identify the chart.
- **Axis Titles** are the titles given to three axis i.e. X, Y, Z.
- **Gridlines** are horizontal and vertical lines which are inserted in the chart.
- **Data Label** provides additional information about a data marker.

Creating Chart

Steps to create a chart are as follows :

Step 1 Select the data you want to summarise visually and then click on the Insert tab.
A context menu will appear.

Step 2 Choose Chart option. Chart Wizard dialog box will appear.

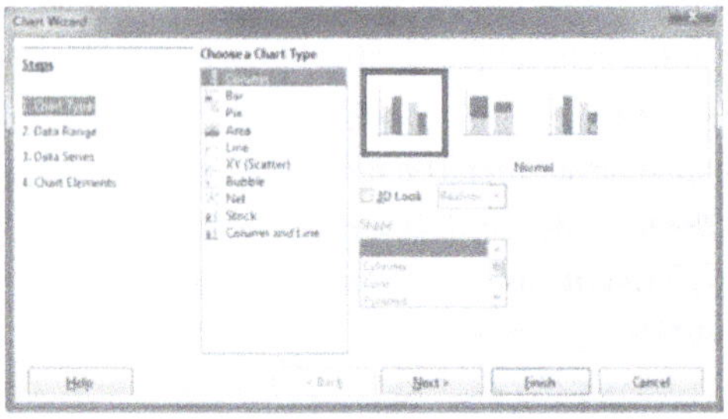

Step 3 Select Chart Type as Column, Bar, etc., and choose the desired option in Normal. Click on Next button.

Step 4 Select a Data Range and click on Next button.

Step 5 Change the order of data using Add or Remove button. Click on Next button.

Step 6 Choose Title, legend and grid settings and click on Finish button.

Shortcut Keys for LibreOffice Calc

Shortcut Keys	Effect
Ctrl+X	Cuts out the selected elements
Ctrl+C	Copies the selected items
Ctrl+V	Paste from the clipboard
Ctrl+Alt+Shift+V	Paste unformatted text from the clipboard. The text is pasted using the fomat that exists at the insertion point
Ctrl+Shift+V	Opens the Paste Special dialog box
Ctrl+A	Selects all
Ctrl+Z	Undoes last action
Ctrl+Y	Redoes last action
Ctrl+Shift+Y	Repeats last command
Ctrl+I	The Italic attribute is applied to the selected area. If the cursor is positioned in a word, this word is also marked in italic.
Ctrl+B	The Bold attribute is applied to the selected area. If the cursor is positioned in a word, this word is also put in bold.
Ctrl+U	The Underlined attribute is applied to the selected area. If the cursor is positioned in a word, this word is also underlined.
Spacebar	Toggles row selection, except when the row is in edit mode.
Ctrl+Spacebar	Selects the current column
Shift+Spacebar	Selects the current row
Ctrl+O	Opens a document
Ctrl+S	Saves the current document
Ctrl+N	Creates a new document
Ctrl+Shift+N	Opens Templates and Documents dialog box
Ctrl+P	Prints document
Ctrl+F	Activates the Find toolbar
Ctrl+H	Opens the Find & Replace dialog box
Ctrl+Shift+F	Searches for the last entered search term
F1	Starts the LibreOffice Help In the LibreOffice Help: Jumps to main help page
F10	Activates the first menu (File menu)
Shift+F10	Opens the context menu
Ctrl+Q	Exits application
Ctrl+Home	Moves the cursor to the first cell in the sheet (A1)
Ctrl+End	Moves the cursor to the last cell in the sheet that contains data
Home	Moves the cursor to the first cell of the current row.
End	Moves the cursor to the last cell of the current row.
Shift+Home	Selects cells from the current cell to the first cell of the current row.
Shift+End	Selects cells from the current cell to the last cell of the current row.
Shift+Page Up	Selects cells from the current cell up to one page in the current column or extends the existing selection one page up.
Shift+Page Down	Selects cells from the current cell down to one page in the current column or extends the existing selection one page down.

Check Point 04

1. .... is the total area of the area.
2. Data label provides additional information about a data marker (True/False).
3. $A$6 is an example of
   (a) Relative referencing (b) Absolute referencing (c) Mixed referencing (d) None of these
4. Define line chart.
5. Which shortcut key is used to start LibreOffice Help?

NCERT FOLDER

Check Your Progress

Pg 130-134

A. Multiple Choice Questions

Read the questions carefully and circle the letter (a), (b), (c) or (d) that best answers the questions.

1. Which of the following technique can be used to allow only date value in cell?
   (a) Data formatting (b) Data sorting
   (c) Data filtering (d) Data validation

Ans. (a) Data formatting

2. Which of the following options when selected deletes all data validation?
   (a) Delete formatting (b) Delete all
   (c) Delete formula (d) Delete me

Ans. (a) Delete formatting

3. We can replace multiple occurrences of a word using which of the following facilities of Calc?
   (a) Find & Replace
   (b) By replace only
   (c) By copy command
   (d) By preview command

Ans. (a) Find & Replace

4. What is the name of mechanism to arrange the data in a particular order?
   (a) Sorting (b) Searching
   (c) Filtering (d) Validating

Ans. (a) Sorting

5. What is the name of mechanism to filter out unnecessary data?
   (a) Sorting (b) Searching
   (c) Filtering (d) Validating

Ans. (c) Filtering

6. Which of the following type of package does Calc refer to?
   (a) Spreadsheet (b) Double sheet
   (c) Multi-sheet (d) Cannot determine

Ans. (a) Spreadsheet

7. Which of the following is an extension of a worksheet created in Calc?
   (a) .ods (b) .odd
   (c) .xls (d) .obj

Ans. (a) .ods

8. How can one calculate the total of values entered in a worksheet column of?
   (a) By manual entry (b) By auto-sum
   (c) By formula (d) By sum function

Ans. (d) By sum function

9. If we move a cell containing a formula having reference to another cell in the worksheet what will happen to the cell numbers used in the formula?
   (a) The cell row and columns are changed at destination.
   (b) The cell row change at destination.
   (c) The cell columns are changed at destination.
   (d) No change will scour.

Ans. (a) The cell row and columns are changed at destination.

10. What is the correct way to enter a function in Calc?
   (a) Directly typing function name in a cell
   (b) Using function wizard or selecting from toolbar
   (c) Both (a) and (b)
   (d) Depends on the function

Ans. (d) Depends on the function

11. A function should start with

(a) '=' sign (b) alphabets

(c) numbers (d) All of these

Ans. (a) '=' sign

12. Which of the following option is used to print a chart?

(a) Insert . Chart (b) File . View

(c) File . Print (d) View . Chart

Ans. (c) File . Print

13. How many axes does charts in Calc have?

(a) Two (b) Three

(c) Two or three (d) Four

Ans. (a) Two

14. The chart preview can be seen in

(a) Page preview (b) Chart preview

(c) Export chart (d) All of these

Ans. (d) All of these

B. Fill in the blanks

1. The column immediately next to column "Z" is ....

Ans. AA

2. The default extension of a workbook created using a LibreOffice Calc spreadsheet is ....

Ans. .ods

3. The spreadsheet feature used to continue the series is called as ....

Ans. fill handle

4. The formula "=MIN(C1:C5)" stored in cell C6 when copied to cell D6 changes to ....

Ans. = M1N (D1 : D5)

5. The formula in cell A2 is =B2+C3. On copying this formula to cell C2, C2 will change to ....

Ans. = D2 + E3

6. The cell address of the cell formed by the intersection of the ninth column and the eighth row will be ....

Ans. I8

7. $A1$B2 is an example of .... referencing in spreadsheet software.

Ans. mixed

8. Numbers entered into a cell are automatically .... aligned.

Ans. right

9. If A1:A5 contain the numbers 16, 10, 3, 25 and 6 then =Average(A1:A5;60) will display ....

Ans. 20

10. In .... referencing, the reference changes rows and columns automatically when it is copied to a new cell.

Ans. relative

C. State whether True or False.

1. A cell is a combination of row and column.

Ans. False

2. A spreadsheet is also called as worksheet.

Ans. True

3. There are 'n' number of sheets in a spreadsheet.

Ans. False

4. In a spreadsheet, we can change the column width and row height.

Ans. True

5. $A1$B2 is an example of mixed referencing.

Ans. True

D. Solve the following in a Spreadsheet.

1. Cell A1 contains the number 10 and B1 contains 5. What will be the contents of cell C1, if the formula =A1+B1*2^3 is entered in cell C1?

Ans. 50

2. The contents of Cell A1, B1, C1 and D1 are 5, –25, 30 and –35, respectively. What will be the value displayed in cell E1 which contains the formula =MIN(A1:D1).

Ans. –35

3. Cell D5 contains the formula =$B$5+C5 and this formula is copied to cell E5, what will be the copied formula in cell E5?

Ans. = $B$5 + D5

4. Cell D5 contains the formula =$B5 + C5 and this formula is copied to cell E5, what will be the copied formula in cell E5?

Ans. = $B5 + D5

5. Cell D5 contains the formula =$B5 + C$5 and this formula is copied to cell E6, what will be the copied formula in cell E6?

Ans. = $B6 + D$5

E. Short Answer Questions.

1. What do you call the document created in a spreadsheet application?

Ans. Worksheet

2. What are the steps to create a new spreadsheet?

Ans. Refer to text on Page 166.

3. What is the difference between spreadsheet and worksheet ?

Ans. Differences between Spreadsheet and worksheet are as follows:

Spreadsheet	Worksheet
A spreadsheet is an Calc file with one or more worksheets.	A worksheet is a single spreadsheet of data.
A spreadsheet would be the entire binder, with everything in it.	A worksheet would be like one section in that binder.

4. What is the default name of the worksheet? How can it be renamed?

Ans. The default name of worksheet is Untitled X, where X is a number. It can be renamed by saving this worksheet with another name.

5. Write the steps to insert and delete the worksheet in Calc.

Ans. Step to insert worksheet in Calc:

- .Click right mouse button on the Sheet tab and choose Insert sheet.

Step to delete worksheet in Calc:

- In the Sheet tab, clicks the right mouse button and chooses Delete from the pop-up menu.

6. What is an active cell? How to delete the contents of an active cell?

Ans. In a spreadsheet, cell is the place where we enter the data. Before entering any data in the cell, it has to be first selected by placing a cursor on it. When we position the mouse cursor on a cell, it gets selected and is ready to take data from the user. This selected or activated cell is called as active cell.

To delete the contents of an active cell, right click on active cell and choose Clear Contents option from context menu.

7. What is relative and absolute cell address in the spreadsheet?

Ans. Refer to text on Pages 172 and 173.

8. Explain any two operations performed on data in a spreadsheet.

Ans. Formulas and functions are two main operations performed on data in a Spreadsheet.

- **Formulas** These are equations that perform calculations on values in worksheet. It is an order of values, names, cell references, functions and operations in a cell that together give a new value.
- **Functions** These are predefined formulas that perform calculations using specific values in a particular order.

9. How do formulae work in a spreadsheet?

Ans. Refer to text on Page 167.

10. Can you include more than one mathematical operators in a formula?

Ans. Yes, more than one mathematical operators in a formula can be included.

e.g. Suppose cells A1, B1 and C1 contain the values 10, 5 and 6 respectively. Cell D1 has formula = A1 * B1 + C1, which include two mathematical operators * and +. The result of cell D1 will be 56.

11. How to make visible the desired toolbar a spreadsheet?

Ans. To make visible the desired toolbar a spreadsheet, use keyboard shortcut Ctrl + F1.

12. Give the syntax and example of any three mathematical functions in spreadsheet.

Ans. (i) SUM ()

It adds the values contained in a range of cells.

Syntax = Sum (Number 1, Number 2 , ...)

e.g. If cells A1 = 5, B1 = 5 and C1 = 5 then function = SUM (A1, B1, C1) will give the result 15.

(ii) Average ( )

It finds out the average of the values contained in a range of cell.

Syntax = AVERAGE (Number 1, Number 2, ...)

e.g. If cells A1 = 6, B1 = 4 and C1 = 2 then function = AVERAGE (A1, B1, C1) will give result 4.

(iii) COUNT ( )

It counts the number of cells within a range of cells.

Syntax = COUNT (Number 1, Number 2, ...)

e.g. If cells A1 = 2, B1 = 4 and C1 = 1 then function = COUNT (A1, B1, C1) will give result 3.

13*. Give the syntax and example of any three statistical functions in spreadsheet.

Ans. (i) **AVERAGE function** This function calculates the average of all the values provided as argument to this function.

Syntax = AVERAGE (number1, number2, ...)

e.g. to calculate the average of the values of range starting from Al to A5 in cell B9, you need to simply write = AVERAGE(A1:A5) in cell B9.

(ii) **MAX function** This function is used to return maximum value from a list of arguments.

Syntax = MAX(number1, number2, ...)

e.g. if the values contained in cells A1,A2, A3 and A4 are 5,7, 2 and 10 respectively then

= MAX(A1:A4) will return 10.

(iii) **MIN function** This function is used to return minimum value from a list of arguments.

Syntax = MIN (number1, number2,......)

e.g. if the values contained in cells A1, A2, A3 and A4 are 5, 7, 2 and 10 respectively then

= MIN(A1:A4) will return 2.

14*. Give the syntax and example of any three decision making functions in spreadsheet.

Ans. Decision making functions in spreadsheet are as follows:

(i) **IF** This function verifies whether a condition is met or not. If the condition is met returns true. If the condition is not met returns false.

Syntax = IF (condition, [value if true], [value if false])

e.g. = IF (ISNUMBER (100), "Yes", "No")

If the number is 22, it will return Yes.

(ii) **IFERROR** This function returns the expression value if no error occurs otherwise returns the error value.

Syntax = IFERROR (expression, [error value])

e.g. = IFERROR (1/0, "Divide by zero error")

It will return the text "Divide by zero error".

(iii) **AND** This function checks multiple conditions and returns true if all the conditions are true.

Syntax = AND (condition 1, condition 2)

e.g. = AND (1 > 0, 2 < 5)

As, both the conditions are true, it will return true.

15*. Give the syntax and example of any three date and time functions in spreadsheet.

Ans. Date and time functions in spreadsheet are as follows:

(i) **TODAY** This function returns the current system date. The value is updated when you reopen the document or modify the values of the document.

Syntax = TODAY ()

e.g. = TODAY ()

returns as 5/29/2020

(ii) **TIME** This function returns the current time value from values for hours, minutes and seconds. This function can be used to convert a time based on these three elements to a document time value.

Syntax = TIME (Hour; Minute; Second)

e.g. = TIME (4; 20; 4)

returns 04 : 20 : 04

(iii) **NOW** This function returns the system date and time. The value is updated when you recalculate the document or each time a cell value is modified.

Syntax = NOW ()

e.g. = NOW () returns 5/29/2020 17 : 16

16*. Give the syntax and example of any three logical functions in spreadsheet.

Ans. Logical functions in spreadsheet are as follows:

(i) **OR** This function returns TRUE if atleast one argument is True. OR function returns the value False, if all the arguments have the logical value False.

Syntax = OR (Logicalvalue1; Logicalvalue2 ...N)

Logicalvalue1 ...N are conditions to be checked. All conditions can be either True or False. If a range is entered as a parameter, the function uses all values of the range.

e.g. = OR (12 < 11;13 > 22; 45 = 45) returns True

= OR (False; True) returns True

(ii) **NOT** This function complements (inverts) a logical value.

Syntax = NOT (Logicalvalue)

Logicalvalue is any value to be complemented.

e.g. = NOT (A)

If A = True, then NOT (A) will evaluate False.

(iii) **FALSE** This function returns the logical value False. The FALSE () function does not require any arguments and always returns the logical value False.

Syntax = FALSE ()

e.g. = FALSE () returns False

= NOT (FALSE ()) returns True.

17*. Give the syntax and example of any three string functions in spreadsheet.

Ans. String functions in spreadsheet are as follows:

(i) **CONCATENATE** This function combines several text strings into one string.

Syntax = CONCATENATE ("Text1"; ...N)

where Text1...N represent text passages, which are to be combined into one string.

e.g. = CANCATENATE ("Good"; "Morning"; "Mrs") returns GoodMorningMrs.

** Not in syllabus.*

(ii) **LEFT** This function returns the first character or characters of a text.
Syntax = LEFT ("Text"; Number)
where,
Text is the text where the initial partial words are to be determined.
Number (optional) specifies the number or characters for the start text. If this parameter is not defined, one character is returned.
e.g. = LEFT ("Output"; 3) returns "out".

(iii) **LEN** This function returns the length of a string including spaces.
Syntax = LEN ("Text")
where,
Text is the text whose length is to be determined.
e.g. = LEN ("Good Afternoon") returns 14.

18. Explain the advantages of drawing a chart in Calc.

Ans. Advantage of drawing a chart in Calc are as follows:

- It is easy to use
- It shows the data in a very sophisticated manner.
- Charts help to forecast the trends on the basis of comparisons done.
- It is easy for the users to compare the information.

19. Explain in one line each the various types of charts.

Ans. Refer to text on Page 173.

20. Write the steps to creating a chart in Calc.

Ans. Refer to text on Page 174.

21. Name and explain any five components of a chart in a spreadsheet package.

Ans. Refer to text on Pages 173 and 174.

SUMMARY

- Spreadsheet is used for managing financial and accounting documents, creating data reports, generating invoices, data analysis from scientific and statistical researches and for doing a variety of calculations on data.
- The bar located at the top of the window is called title bar. It contains the name of the currently open document.
- The intersection of a row and column is called a cell.
- Any expressions that begins with an equals '=' is treated as formula.
- Spreadsheet software has the most powerful features to calculate numerical data using formulae.
- The cell data can be formatted using formatting toolbar or cell formatting window.
- It is the way to refer the formula or function from one cell to the next cell along the row or column.
- When you drag any formula in any row or column in any direction, the formula gets copied in new cell with the relative reference.
- In this referencing, a $ symbol is used before the column name as well as row number to make it constant in any formula.
- It is a combination of absolute and relative cell referencing. In this referencing, the $ sign is used before row number or column name to make it constant.
- These are the graphical and pictorial representation of worksheet data.

Exam Practice

Multiple Choice Questions

1. A worksheet is a
(a) collection of workbooks
(b) processing software
(c) combination of rows and columns
(d) None of the above

Ans. (c) combination of rows and columns

2. The simplest way to move data from one location to another in Calc is
(a) by Quick Access toolbar
(b) using Cut and Paste
(c) by the drag and drop method
(d) Both (b) and (c)

Ans. (d) Both (b) and (c)

3. The AutoFill can apply from
(a) left to right (b) right to left
(c) up to down (d) All of these

Ans. (d) All of these

4. The default page orientation in Calc is
(a) Landscape (b) Horizontal
(c) Portrait (d) None of these

Ans. (c) Portrait

5. Cell address $B$5 in a formula means
(a) it is a mixed reference
(b) it is an absolute reference
(c) it is a relative reference
(d) None of the above

Ans. (b) it is an absolute reference

6. While entering a formula, cell address B$5 represents
(a) Absolute Referencing (b) Mixed Referencing
(c) Relative Referencing (d) All of these

Ans. (b) Mixed Referencing

7. A cell range starting from first row, first column to fourth row and fifth column can be represented as
(a) [A1 : E4] (b) [A0 : E3]
(c) [E4 : A1] (d) [E3 : A0]

Ans. (a) [A1 : E4]

8. A cell range always has the .... symbol between the cell references.
(a) ;(semicolon) (b) .(full stop)
(c) ,(comma) (d) :(colon)

Ans. (d) :(colon)

9. If cell range A1 : A5 contain the numbers 20, 16, 5, 35 and 7 then = AVERAGE(A1 : A5, 50) will display.
(a) 22.167 (b) 27.167 (c) 10 (d) 40

Ans. (a) 22.167

10 =COUNTA (4, 78, False, 18) will return ....
(a) 2 (b) 3 (c) 4 (d) 5

Ans. (c) 4

11. If you type =2 * (6-4) in cell A1, what value will be display?
(a) 2 (b) 4 (c) 6 (d) 8

Ans. (b) 4

12. You can place the chart legend in the chart at
(a) Bottom (b) Corner
(c) Top, Right and Left (d) All of these

Ans. (d) All of these

13. In Calc chart, text displayed at data points to indicate the specific category is called
(a) data point (b) data series
(c) data label (d) legends

Ans. (c) data label

14. You have used a spreadsheet to calculate the average marks of a class in Mathematics. Which input is essential to find the average marks?
(a) Marks of each student of class in Science
(b) Marks of each student of class in Mathematics
(c) Average marks in Mathematics of each student of class
(d) Names and roll numbers of each student of class

Ans. (b) Marks of each student of class in Mathematics.

15. A chart is created on the basis of values in
(a) mail merge (b) database
(c) spreadsheet (d) document

Ans. (c) spreadsheet

16. Which of the following charts is used for comparing the changes in data over a period of time?
(a) Bar chart (b) Area chart
(c) Scatter chart (d) Line chart

Ans. (d) Line chart

17. Which of the following chart selects only one range of the data series?
(a) Line chart (b) Pie chart
(c) Scatter Chart (d) Bar chart

Ans. (b) Pie chart

18. The another name for the XY chart is
(a) Column chart (b) Net chart
(c) Bar chart (d) Scatter chart

Ans. (d) Scatter chart

19. Which of the following shortcut keys brings the cursor to the last cell on the sheet that contains data?
(a) Ctrl+Home (b) Ctrl+End
(c) Ctrl+Page down (d) Ctrl+down arrow

Ans. (b) Ctrl+End

20. For selecting a non-continuous range of cells, you need to do what?
(a) Press Alt key (b) Press Shift key
(c) Press Esc key (d) Press Ctrl key

Ans. (d) Press Ctrl key

21. For selecting the entire worksheet in Calc, you need to press
(a) Alt + Shift + Spacebar
(b) Ctrl + Shift + Spacebar
(c) Shift + Spacebar
(d) None of the above

Ans. (b) Ctrl + Shift + Spacebar

22. The sample of a Calc worksheet on the screen can be seen by
(a) Print preview
(b) Print
(c) Review
(d) None of the above

Ans. (a) Print preview

Fill in the Blanks

1. Calc is a .... software package.

Ans. spreadsheet

2. When you .... or .... , the selected range gets surrounded by a moving border.

Ans. copy, cut

3. The .... and .... operations copies data from source range to target range and erases it from the source range.

Ans. cut, paste

4. Address of the cell at 10th column and 30th row is ....

Ans. J30

5. The cell having bold boundary is the ....

Ans. active cell

6. Any formula in Calc starts with an ....

Ans. equal (=) sign

7. The keyboard shortcut for copy is .... and for paste is ....

Ans. Ctrl + C, Ctrl + V

8. In .... referencing, the relative address of the cell gets adjust with respect to the current cell.

Ans. relative

9. For absolute referencing, ... sign is used before the parts of formula.

Ans. $

10. If you enter 15 + 30 in a cell, Calc will display ....

Ans. 15 + 30

11. To specify the number of decimal places in a cell the .... tab of the Format Cells dialog is used.

Ans. Numbers

12. The .... tool is used in speadsheet that creates a growth series, wherein subsequent values follow an increasing or a decreasing geometric pattern.

Ans. Fill series

True/False

1. You cannot open two different workbooks in Calc simultaneously.

Ans. False

2. When a cell containing a formula is moved, the cells referring the moved cell show an error value.

Ans. False

3. A cell entry can be edited either in the cell or in the formula bar.

Ans. True

4. If the data entered in a cell is 546Z then, Calc will treat it as a number because it starts with a digit.

Ans. False

5. We cannot enter the date/time in a cell.

Ans. False

6. The Fill handle tool is used for labour intensive entering data in a spreadsheet.

Ans. True

7. The title of the chart tells the type of the chart.

Ans. False

8. A chart is a graphical representation of worksheet data.

Ans. True

9. The contents of a cell can be changed by pressing F2 key on keyboard.

Ans. True

Match the Columns

1. Match the following columns.

Column I		Column II	
A.	Ctrl + End	1.	Moves to worksheet one screen up
B.	Page Up	2.	Moves the cursor to the last cell of the current row
C.	Page Down	3.	Moves to bottom right cell of the data range
D.	Home	4.	Moves the worksheet one screen down
E.	End	5.	Moves the column A along the row where the active cell is

Ans. A → 3; B → 1; C → 4; D → 5; E → 2

Very Short Answer (VSA) Type Questions

1. Reena is new to Calc. Her instructor has asked her to open Calc on her PC and questioned about active cell. Help Reena in identifying the active cell on her screen.

Ans. An active cell is a cell with heavy black color boundary.

2. What is the default alignment of number, text and formula in a spreadsheet?

Ans. Default alignment of text or label entry is left alignment and for numbers and formula it is right alignment.

3. Soham has clicked on the cell residing at the intersection of first row and ninth column. What will be the address of the selected cell?

Ans. First row and ninth column address will be I1.

4. How many ways are there for adding a new worksheet in a Calc workbook?

Ans. There are two methods of adding a new worksheet in a Calc workbook; Insert worksheet tab at the bottom and Insert Sheet option under Sheet tab.

5. In Calc, how many ways are there to express/format a number?

Ans. Numbers in Calc can be expressed in many different formats like date, time, percentage or decimals.

6. What do you mean by relative referencing?

Ans. Cell referencing in which the cells are referred by their relative position in the worksheet relative to a particular cell is called relative referencing.

7. How many cells would be there in the cell range [A1 : B2]?

Ans. There would be 4 cells in the given cell range.

8. The cell A1 has value Monday. If you are asked to click and drag the Fill handle of A1 downside then what will be the contents of cell A2, A3, A4 and A5?

Ans. Cells A2, A3, A4 and A5 will contain Tuesday, Wednesday, Thursday and Friday respectively.

9. If = 6 – 5 * 2 is entered in a cell, then what will be the cell content?

Ans. –4 will be contained in cell as a result.

10. In a spreadsheet software, the formula =A1+$A$2 was entered in cell A3 and then copied into cell B3.

What is the formula copied into B3?

Ans. =B1+$A$2 will be copied into B3.

11. Write down the formula for adding values of cells A1 to A5.

Ans. Formula for adding values of cells A1 to A5 would be =SUM(A1 : A5).

12. What will be the column names of the below statement?

(i) 26th column

(ii) 28th column

Ans. (i) Z (ii) AB

Short Answer (SA) Type Questions

1. Write down the significance of electronic spreadsheets.

Ans. Using electronic spreadsheets, large volume of data can be stored in worksheets. Worksheets can be managed, edited, viewed, retrieved and printed easily in desired format. Electronic spreadsheets support charts, which represent data pictorically.

2. Sana has entered 49+30 in a cell. The worksheet is not displaying 79 in the cell. Instead, 49+30 is getting displayed. Help, Sana in rectifying the problem.

Ans. In Calc, every formula must start with an = (equal) sign. Since, Sana has not put = sign before 49+30, thus she is not able to see the desired value. Result will be displayed if she will use = (49 + 30) formula.

3. What is the use of the COUNT( ) function in Calc?

Ans. Calc COUNT( ) function can be used to total the number of cells in a selected range. The COUNT( ) function will add up the number of cells in a selected range that contains numbers.

4. Suggest the appropriate function for the following situations:

(i) Selecting the maximum value out of a range A1 to B20.

(ii) Calculating average of marks entered in cells E5, F5, G5, H5 and I5.

Ans. (i) = MAX(A1 : B20)

(ii) = AVERAGE(E5: I5)

5. Define the meaning of formula.

Ans. Formula plays a major role in spreadsheet making. If we all needed to do is to put text and numbers in rows and columns, just about any Word processing program would fill the bill. Formula allows us to perform calculations using values from any cells to have the result appear in the formula cell.

6. For what purpose pie charts are useful?

Ans. Pie charts are useful for the following purposes:

(i) They convey approximate propositional relationship at a point in time.

(ii) They compare part of a whole at a given point in time.

(iii) Exploded portion of a pie chart emphasize a small proportion of parts.

7. Explain formula toolbar.

Ans. Refer to text on Page 165.

4. Write command for the operations (*i*) to (*iii*) based on the spreadsheet below:

	A	B	C	D	E	F	G
1	Item Code	Item Desc	Type	Unit Price	Qty	Amount	Rebate
2	101	Pen	Consumable	150	1500		
3	102	Photo Copier	Non-consumable	240000	24		
4	103	Photocopy Machine	Non-consumable	6400	70		
5	104	Eraser	Consumable	108	8400		

Sheet1 Sheet2 Sheet3

(i) To calculate the Amount as Unit Price*Qty for each item in Column F.
(ii) To calculate the sum of Amount and display in cell F6.
(iii) To calculate total Rebate across all items in cell G6.

Ans. (i) At cell F2, type =D2*E2 and then copy this formula using mouse Fill handle onto range F3 : F5.
(ii) At cell F6, type = SUM (F2 : F5)
(iii) At cell G6, type =SUM(G2 : G5).

5. Arihant stationery keeps stock of various stationeries in his shop. The proprietor wants to maintain a stock value and reorder level for following items as given in a spreadsheet. Write formulas for the operations (*i*) to (*ii*) and answer the question (*iii*) based on the spreadsheet given below alongwith the relevant cell address:

	A	B	C	D	E	F	G	H
1	Item Code	Item Name	Minimum Stock Quantity	Quantity in Stock (Unit)	Rate (₹)	Stock Value (₹)	Quantity to Order (Unit)	Order Value
2	101	P. Holder	200	500	35			
3	123	Whitner	450	150	25			
4	113	Steppler Pin	250	450	5			
5	156	Paper cutter	300	600	10			

Sheet1 Sheet2 Sheet3

(i) To calculate the Stock Value as product of 'Quantity in Stock' and 'Rate' for each item present in the spreadsheet.
(ii) To calculate the 'Quantity to Order' as 'Minimum Stock Quantity'-'Quantity in Stock' for each item.
(iii) Proprietor wants to graphically represent his stationery stock. Suggest him the most appropriate feature of Calc.

Ans. (i) At cell F2, type = D2*E2 and then copy this formula using Fill handle in range F3 : F5.
(ii) At cell G2, type = C2 – D2 and then copy this formula using Fill handle in range G3 : G5.
(iii) He should create chart of any type to graphically represent his data.

Long Answer (LA) Type Questions

1. Explain the concept of cell referencing alongwith its various types.

Ans. Calc supports three types of cell referencing, which are as follows:

(i) **Relative** Every relative cell reference in formula automatically changes when the formula is copied down a column or across a row. As the example illustrated here shows, when the formula is entered (= B4 – C4) in Cell D4 then this formula copied in D5 then it will change into (= B5 – C5) related to cell.

(ii) **Absolute** An absolute cell reference is fixed. Absolute references do not change if you copy a formula from one cell to another. Absolute references have dollar sign ($) like $S$9. As the shows, when the formula =C4*$D$9 is copied from row, the absolute cell reference remains as $D$9.

(iii) **Mixed** A mixed cell reference has either an absolute column and a relative row, or an absolute row and a relative column. e.g. $A1 is an absolute reference to column A and a relative reference to row 1. As a mixed reference is copied from one cell to another, the absolute reference stays the same but the relative reference changes.

2. Explain any five functions that can be used in a worksheet.

Ans. Refer to text on Pages 168 and 169.

3. Define the following terms

(i) row and column range (ii) Active cell in worksheet

Ans. (i) Refer to text on Page 166. (ii) Refer to text on Page 165.

4. What is spreadsheet? Also define its menu bar.

Ans. Refer to text on Pages 163 and 164.

Self Assessment

Multiple Choice Questions

1. A .... compares pieces of data using horizontal stacks.
   (a) pie chart (b) scattered chart (c) area chart (d) bar chart
2. The cell labeled F5 refers to
   (a) row F column 5 (b) column F row 5
   (c) function available in cells (d) function key F5
3. Which key is used to edit contents of the active cell?
   (a) F2 (b) F3 (c) F5 (d) F9
4. Absolute cell referencing occurs when
   (a) formula is dragged but the cell references do not adjust.
   (b) spreadsheet is saved with "absolute" as file name.
   (c) formula is dragged and the cell reference adjusts automatically.
   (d) $ symbol is automatically added with each cell value.
5. Find out the odd one
   (a) Absolute (b) Relative (c) Mixed (d) AutoFill
6. The default alignment of text in a cell is
   (a) Left (b) Right (c) Centered (d) Justified

Fill in the Blanks

1. The .... features automatically calculates the sum of the selected cells in the last blank cell.
2. The .... symbol is used to designate an absolute cell reference.
3. .... is the extension of Calc files.
4. To close a workbook .... is used.

True/False

1. A formula must begin with + sign.
2. There is only one type of chart in Calc.
3. You can insert a cell using Insert tab.
4. You can enter data in a cell.

Match the Columns

1. Match the following columns.

Column I		Column II	
A.	Ctrl + Home	1.	Cells spread across the row
B.	Values	2.	Cells spread across the column
C.	Home	3.	Moves the cell to A1 position
D.	Row range	4.	Numbers
E.	Column range	5.	Moves to column A along the row where the active cell is

Very Short Answer (VSA) Type Questions

1. Define an active cell.
2. Briefly explain the AutoFill feature of Calc.
3. How is MIN() function useful in spreadsheet?
4. What is column range?

Short Answer (SA) Type Questions

1. What do you mean by Formulae?
2. What are the differences between column range and row range?
3. Explain the = SUM ( ) function in brief.
4. Define formatting of a cell range as scientific.
5. Differentiate between MAX( ) and MAXA( ) functions.
6. What do you mean by copying and moving a range?
7. What are the row headings and column headings in spreadsheet?
8. Define formatting a range of cells to display time.

Long Answer (LA) Type Questions

1. Define the following terms:
   (i) Embedded chart
   (ii) Chart sheet
2. What are the different types of data that can be entered in Calc?
3. Differentiate between mixed referencing and absolute referencing by giving suitable examples.

UNIT

05

Digital Presentation

Chapter Checklist

- Characteristics of a Good Quality Presentation
- Getting Started with LibreOffice Impress
- Creating a Presentation
- Copying, Moving and Deleting Content
- Workspace Views
- Running a Slide Show
- Formatting the Text
- Bullets and Numbering
- Paragraph Spacing
- Working with Tables
- Adding and Formatting Images
- Managing Graphic Objects
- Working with Slide Masters
- Adding Transitions

Presenting information clearly and effectively is a key skill to get your message or opinion across the audience. Today, presentation skills are highly required in almost every field. Presentation skills include content as well as flow of presentation. A presentation includes regular text, list items, table, graphics elements, sound, video and animation.

Presentation is used to present the project proposal in business organisations. Presentation is highly used in teaching and training. Some examples of presentation software are Adobe Acrobat, K Presenter, OpenOffice.org Impress, MS PowerPoint, LibreOffice Impress etc. Impress is one of the important components of Libreoffice suite from the Document Foundation. It is free, open source and widely used by large community to create presentation.

In LibreOffice Impress, an effective presentation can be created by using different multimedia elements. The text editing and formatting, such as bold, colors, text alignment, borders, drawing etc of presentation in Impress uses the same commands and options as that of writer and Calc.

Characteristics of a Good Quality Presentation

A good quality presentation is required to convey the message clearly to the audience.

The following points or guidelines have to be taken care of while preparing a good quality presentation:

(i) **Number of lines** On one page or slide try to include 5 to 8 lines. Adding more number of lines or a paragraph may take more time to read as the font size may become too small.

(ii) **Font size** Accordingly the font size of the texts in the presentation may be decided. It will be appropriate to keep the font size at 32 points or more, so that the audience can easily read the contents.

(iii) **Correct use of grammar and language** The grammar and language should be correct in your presentation, because if you make a mistake that will replicate to the number of persons in the audience. So, you must present the contents error free in terms of grammar and spellings of language by reading the slides carefully.

(iv) **Inserting images, drawings, tables or graphs** Try to avoid inserting more than two graphics (images, drawings, tables or charts) in any slide. Inserting too many graphics becomes confusing for the audience.

(v) **Use of colors** Try to use dark colors, bold letters with different fonts to highlight certain points. Use fair or silent background colors and dark colors for fonts. Use of dark-colored fonts over a dark background or taking only one color red throughout the whole presentation is not a good practice. Consider the factor that which color will be more comfortable for the human eyes to see. Use different colors somewhere in between the presentation to show the importance of words.

(vi) **Animation and video** Do not include more than one animation or video in one slide. Including more than one, will overlap the sounds and may cause confusion to the audience.

(vii) **Pay attention to target group** While creating the presentation, give attention to meet the requirements of the target audience. Focus on the contents, sequence of the topics in such a way that it makes a flow to attract the attention of the audience from the objectives. Otherwise, the audience might be lost.

Getting started with LibreOffice Impress

The process to start LibreOffice Impress may slightly differ according to the operating system (Windows or Linux) that you are using.

To start LibreOffice Impress in Windows, double click its shortcut icon on the desktop.

Or click on the Start button or Windows button, select LibreOffice 6.2 → LibreOffice Impress from application window.

In Ubuntu Linux, open the LibreOffice Impress by any of the following options:

(i) Find the LibreOffice Impress icon on the application launcher and click it to start the application.

(ii) Find the LibreOffice Impress icon through search your computer icon on the launcher. To search enter the word Impress and select LibreOffice Impress from the search results.

After starting Impress, its initial window will open as shown in figure:

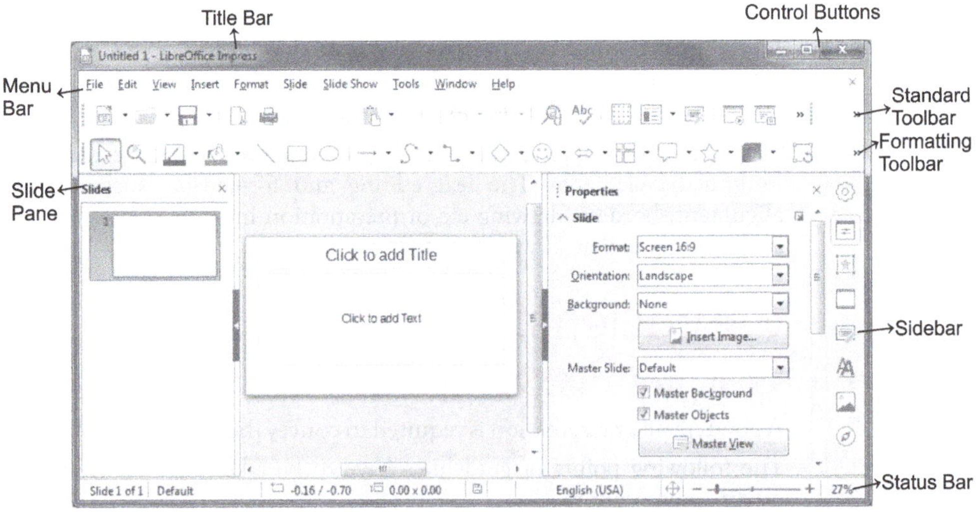

Parts of Impress Window

The parts of a Impress window are as follows

(i) **Title bar** It contains the name of presentation file with extension (.odp) and presentation application as LibreOffice Impress. It is always of the top of the LibreOffice Impress window.

Window manipulation buttons or control buttons are located in the right corner. These are minimize, maximize/restore and close buttons.

(ii) **Menu bar** It contains the menus with logically grouped commands. All the commands required to create the presentation are found here. The various menus are as follows:

- **File** This menu is used to perform basic operations on the presentation (saving, opening and existing one, creating a new one, etc.)
- **Edit** This menu contains functions for copying, cutting and pasting text segments.
- **View** It is used for window view adjustment (different view types are selected, zooming etc) and for adding toolbars.
- **Insert** This menu is used to insert various objects like tables, shapes, textbox and charts into a presentation.
- **Format** It contains functions for text formatting.
- **Slide** It is used to insert new slide, duplicate slide or delete slide.
- **Slide Show** It is a tool for viewing presentations.
- **Tools** They are used to control spelling in a presentation.
- **Window** It is used for viewing already opened presentations.
- **Help** It is used to see the help of any topic on Impress.

(iii) **Various toolbar** There are various toolbars to manage GUI of Impress. You can use these toolbars as and when required for various tasks.

- **Standard toolbar** Each command of the menu bar is placed here as icons for easy operations.
- **Slide pane** It is a vertical pane to see the slide in small size to navigate on any slide easily. As you click on particular slide, that slide will be displayed in the larger size in middle of the window. Now, you can modify and make required changes, add or remove effects to complete the slide.
- **Workspace** This is the central part of the window, where the presentation slides are created, text is entered, images and other objects are inserted.
- **Side bar** It is located by default on the right side of the Impress window. But if it is not displaying on the window, you can show this by click on View menu → select Sidebar option from the drop-down that appears. Impress sidebar contains 7 decks as Properties, Slide Transition, Animation, Master Slides, Styles, Gallery, Navigator which show by clicking on its icon.
- **Master pages** You can modify the base architecture of slide. You can make the presentation base and the common style for all slides using this. There are a few default slide master pages available in Impress.
- **Layouts** You can prepare your own layouts and keep these safe for future use. You can select any of these and modify it or use it as required.
- **Table design** This gives styles for creating tables. Anyone can modify the style according to his or her own choice.
- **Custom animation** There are many animation features for the texts, drawings etc, in a slide. Using this feature you can add, change or remove animation features.
- **Slide transition** Using slide transition, you can set the way, how the slide will appear during presentation. There are too many ready-made alternatives available. You can also modify features like speed of transition, sound effects, automated transition etc.
- **Drawing toolbar** Using drawing toolbar, you can make various artistic works in the presentation to make your presentation effective.
- **Insertion point** It is a location of the cursor where your text will appear as you type anything (means location where the cursor is blinking.)
- **Status bar** It displays information about the active presentation, the current position of the cursor and the zoom slider. It can be adjusted according to user preferences. Status bar can be turned off in the view menu by selecting the status bar command.
- **Zoom control** This tool is used to zoom in or zoom out the slide.

Closing LibreOffice Impress

To close the Impress application directly, select the control button close (X) or select the File menu → Exit command or use the keyboard shortcut Ctrl + Q.

Check Point 01

1. Write the name of presentation software.
2. Title bar of Impress window contains the name of presentation file. State True/False.
3. Which of the following operation is used in File tab?
   (a) Saving (b) Copying (c) Cutting (d) Pasting
4. .... gives styles for creating tables.

Creating a Presentation

Creating a Presentation using Template

(i) To create a new blank presentation, select the File menu → New or click on the icon New or use the combination of keys Ctrl + N.

(ii) A window Select a Template will appear. Choose a template as per your choice by clicking on the template as shown in figure to start preparing the presentation.

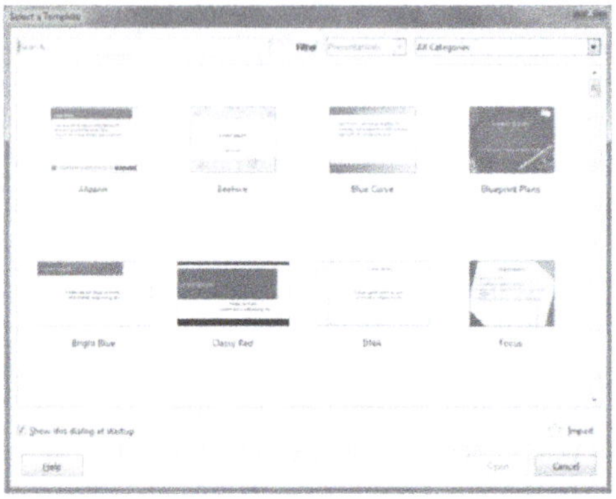

(iii) Prepare your presentation using template. The selected template appears in the form of title slide layout as shown in figure.

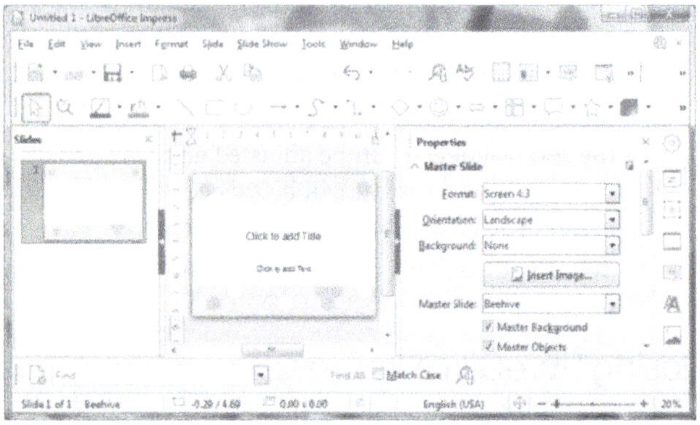

(iv) When creating a presentation, the first slide is normally the title slide. You can use either a blank layout or one of the title layouts as per your title slide.

Now, enter the title text in this slide as shown in figure.

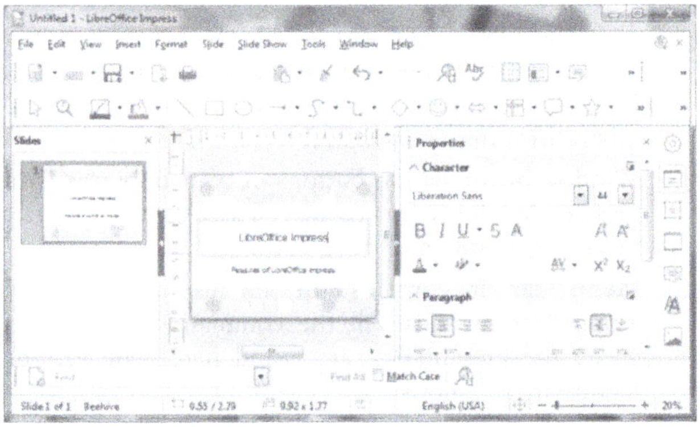

Adding Text

To add text to a slide that contains text frame, click on Click to add text in the text frame and then type your text. The outline styles are automatically applied to the text as you insert it.

Selecting Slide Layout

The appropriate layout can be selected from Layouts section in the Properties window. The layouts included in LibreOffice range from a blank slide to a slide with six content boxes and a title as shown in figure.

You can also select a slide layout by using menu, Slide → Layout → Title Slide as shown in below figure.

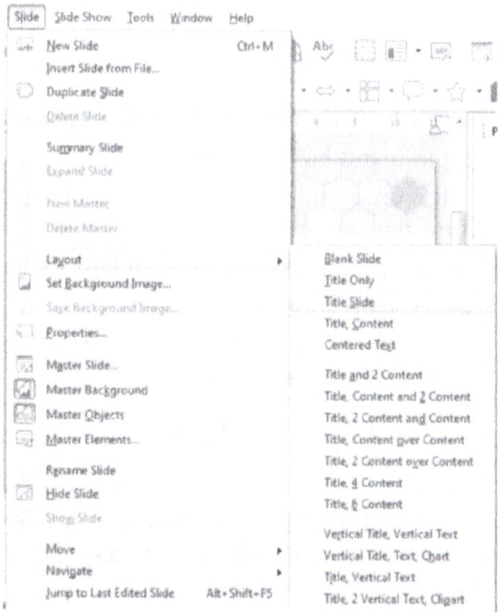

The layout you have selected will be applicable in the right side of the window. Alternatively, you can select the slide in the slide pane, it will appear in the workspace and here you can select the required layout from the Layouts section in the sidebar.

Saving a Presentation

To save the presentation, you are working on, follow the steps as given below:

(i) Select the File menu → Save, or use the shortcut key combination Ctrl + S, or click on the Save button on the standard toolbar.

(ii) This will open the Save As dialog box as shown in figure, which allows to select the location on the disk and assign the name to save the presentation.

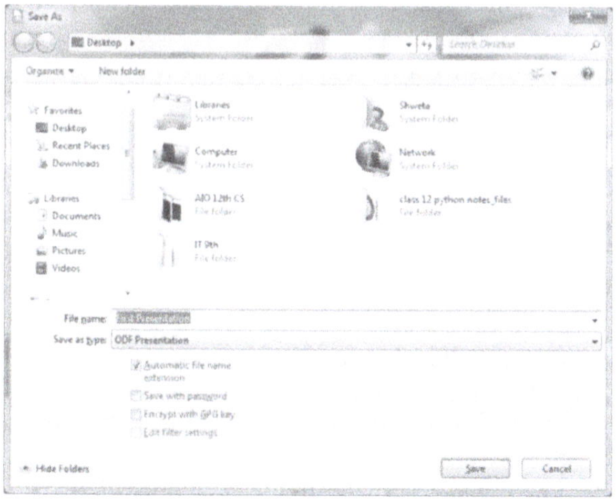

(iii) To change the location in drive, open the directory in which you want to save the file.

(iv) Enter a name of presentation file.

(v) Click Save button.

(vi) If the presentation is already saved, the contents will be updated in that presentation file.

Saving a Presentation with Different Name

To save the presentation with a different name, select File → Save As or use the shortcut key combination Ctrl + Shift + S. In Save As dialog box, a new file name can be entered in File name field. Saving is finished by using the Save button.

Saving a Presentation with a Different Format

By default, the presentation is saved with .odp extension. To save a presentation as another file type, select File → Save As. In the Save As dialog box, click on Save as type drop-down menu and select the choice from the offered programs as per your requirement.

Saving a Presentation as HTML

To publish the presentation on the Web or to open the presentation in the Web browser, save it in HTML (Hypertext Markup Language) format, which could be opened in any Web browser. To save the presentation as HTML, follow below steps:

(i) Click on File → Export

(ii) Select the directory in which you want to save the file.

(iii) Enter a file name.

(iv) Click Save button.

Save a File in PDF Format

A Portable Document Format (PDF) of the presentation can be created by saving a file in the PDF format, which can be viewed with the free Adobe Acrobat Reader. However, it cannot be edited. To save a file in the PDF format:

(i) Click on File → Export as PDF. PDF options dialog box will appear.

(ii) Click Export. Export dialog box will appear.

(iii) Enter the presentation name in File name.

(iv) Click on Save button.

Closing a Presentation

To close a presentation, select File → Close or use the keyboard shortcut keys Ctrl + W.

Opening an Existing Presentation

When you want to open an existing presentation, follow the given steps:

(i) To open a presentation again, select File → Open command or use the keyboard shortcut key Ctrl + O.

(ii) It will open the Open dialog box. Specify the location of the file that is to be opened in the look in field, select the files and open it with the Open command.

Using Help

Help function is located in the Help menu. By selecting the LibreOffice Help tab, a window is opened with a list of available help topics.

In the Search terms text box, you can enter a term to explore. The quickest way to open the Help function is by using the F1 function key.

Working with Slides

Now to carry forward the presentation work, the next slide has to be added. The new slide can be inserted into the presentation by inserting a new slide as well as inserting a duplicate slide. Inserting a duplicate slide will insert the copy of the existing or current slide into the presentation.

Inserting a Duplicate Slide

Sometimes, you may wish to insert the same slide as the previous ones just like the first page of the book has the title of the book and the same title also appears on the cover page of the book. In such a case, you may copy the slide to the next slide. In simple words, you want to duplicate an already created slide.

To insert the duplicate slide, follow below steps:

(i) Select the slide you want to duplicate from the slides pane.

(ii) Select from the menu Slide → Duplicate Slide.

Or Right click on the slide in slide pane and select Duplicate Slide from the menu.

Or Click the Duplicate Slide icon in the standard toolbar.

(iii) You can insert the duplicate slide in your presentation by using one of the above options.

Inserting New Slides

To insert a new slide, use any of the following way:

(i) Select from menu bar Slide → New Slide.

Or Right click on a slide in slide pane and select New Slide from the context menu.

Or Click the New Slide icon in the standard toolbar.

Or Use the keyboard shortcut Ctrl + M.

(ii) You can insert the new slide in your presentation by using one of the above options.

Copying and Moving Slides

The slides once created can be reused within the presentation or in another presentation. To move the slide to another location use cut and paste process. To copy the slide, use the process of copy and paste.

(a) Cut and Paste/Copy and Paste

To cut and paste/copy and paste something in a presentation follow the given steps:

(i) Select the slide by making it in the slide shorter view, or on the left side of the screen in the normal view.

(ii) Click on the right mouse button and select the Cut option (if you want to move it) or Copy option (if you want to copy), from the context menu.

(iii) Place the cursor in the presentation where you want to move or copy the slide.

(iv) Right click the mouse button, select the Paste option from the context menu.

(b) Using Keyboard Shortcuts

Cut, copy and paste operations can also be performed by the combination of keys:

(i) Cut → Ctrl + X

(ii) Copy → Ctrl + C

(iii) Paste → Ctrl + V

(c) Drag and Drop Copying and Moving Method

The copy, cut and paste operations can also be performed by drag and drop method.

(i) Select the slide that you want to copy.

(ii) Click and hold the left mouse button on the marked slide and at the same time press and hold the Ctrl button.

(iii) Move the mouse cursor to the desired location.

(iv) Release the left mouse button and then release the Ctrl button. The copied slide is pasted to another location.

(v) Moving the text or slide via drag and drop method can be done in the same way like copying, but without using the Ctrl button.

Deleting Slides

To delete any slide from a presentation first it should be selected. To delete one or more slides, follow the given steps:

(i) Select the slide(s) by marking them in the slide pane.

(ii) Right click the mouse button on the selected slide.

(iii) Select the Delete Slide option in the context menu.

(iv) Another quick way to delete the slide is just select the slide and press the Delete button from the keyboard.

Renaming a Slide

The slides are named as Slide 1, Slide 2, ... by default. It is possible to give the name to the slide by renaming it.

To rename a slide, follow the given steps:

(i) Select the slide by marking them in the slide pane.

(ii) Right click the mouse button on the selected slide.

(iii) Select the Rename Slide option in the context menu.

(iv) A Rename Slide dialog box will appear where you can assign the new name to the slide

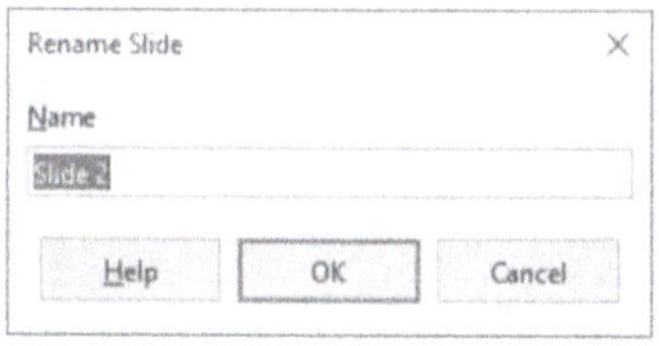

Check Point 02

1. Which shortcut key is used to create a presentation?
2. To save the presentation with a different name, Save As option will be used. State True/False.
3. Inserting the same slide as the previous ones is called ....

Copying, Moving and Deleting Content

Impress is the component of LibreOffice. So, you can use the same commands and options that of LibreOffice Writer for text editing in LibreOffice Impress. To copy or move some text or an object in the presentation to another location (in the same presentation or another presentation), it is necessary to first select the text, and then follow the below steps:

(i) Select the text and click the right mouse button.

(ii) Select the Copy option from the context menu (keyboard shortcut : Ctrl + C) for copying or cut option (keyboard shortcut : Ctrl + X) to cut.

(iii) Position the cursor on the location of the slide, to which you want to move or copy the content.

(iv) Press the right mouse button and select the Paste option from the context menu (keyboard shortcut : Ctrl + V).

Deleting the Text

It is easy to delete the text of the slides. The Delete and Backspace keys on keyboard is used to delete the text. The Delete key deletes the character on the right of the cursor and the Backspace key deletes the character on the left of the cursor. Pressing Delete key or Backspace key deletes one character at a time. To delete the line or paragraph of text, first select the text and then press the Delete key. Alternately you can use the Cut option to delete the text.

Undoing and Returning the Changes

Impress keeps the history of recent changes made. When we execute a command on some text, for example delete the text, we are able to reverse what we have done. This is known as the undo function. It is also possible after having undone the change, get it back. This is called the redo function. These options are located in the standard toolbar and can also be performed using keyboard shortcut keys Ctrl + Z is used for undo and Ctrl + Y is used for Redo.

- Alternately, use Edit → Undo. Using this method, the menu will indicate what type of operation you will be undoing. Another way to do this is to press the Undo icon on the standard toolbar.
- Redo function is used to revert the result of the undo function. It can be used many times, as the undo function was used. To use this function use Edit → Redo.

If you want to rollback your undo command, you can use redo. You can also execute the redo function by pressing the Redo icon on the standard toolbar.

View a Presentation

The presentation created in Impress can be viewed in a number of ways. One may wish to view the presentation in larger or smaller or in medium size. It is possible to view the presentation as per the user's requirement.

Controlling the Size of the View

Zoom & View Layout dialog box opens in the View tab. It is possible to select among the proposed values to increase zoom, or enter your own value, which must be a whole number.

Other ways to zoom are:

(i) Use of the Zoom slider on the status bar.

(ii) Use of the Zoom button on the formatting toolbar.

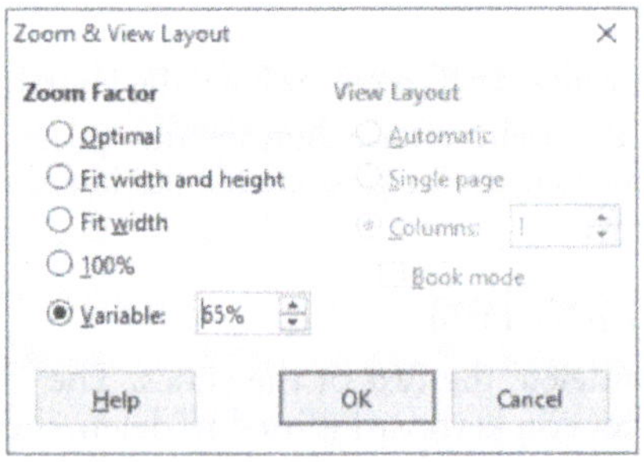

Zoom Slider

On the status bar has two marked sections. If you are positioned in the first highlighted section, the entire slide will display within the workspace. If you position yourself to the second one, the increase of 100% of the slide, will be displayed.

Workspace Views

The various workspace views are in the drop-down list of the View menu. These views are Normal, Outline, Notes, Slide Sorter, Slide Master, Notes Master, Handout Master. The appropriate view can be selected from the View menu. Different views of presentation are given below:

(i) **Normal View** It is shown in given figure. It is the main view for working with individual slides. This view is used to format and design and to add text, graphics and animation effects. In this view, the slide is displayed in the middle of the window. On the left side of the window, the pane with slides thumbnails (slides) is displayed (if the slide pane is selected from the View menu).

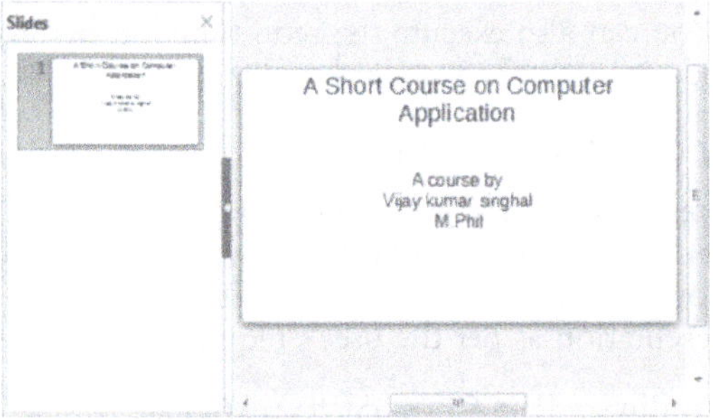

(ii) **Outline View** It contains all the slides of the presentation in a sequence. It shows each slide in the outline format. Only the text contained in each slide is displayed inside the workspace. It displays slide text in the form of a structure. This view is shown in given figure:

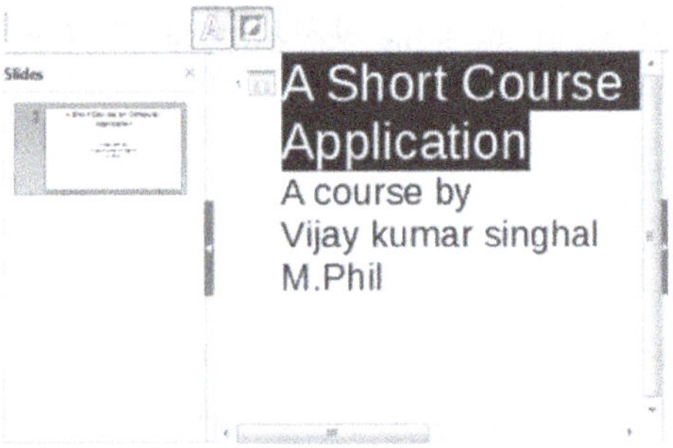

(iii) **Notes View** It is used to add notes to a slide for the information of presenter. It is not seen by the audience while showing the presentation. It displays the area in which the notes, are used to help during the presentation. This view is shown in given figure

(iv) **Slide Sorter view** It contains all of the slides thumbnails. It is suitable for rearranging the slide order. It is used to sort slides with the drag and drop method. Use this view to work with a group of slides or with only one slide. This view is shown in given figure.

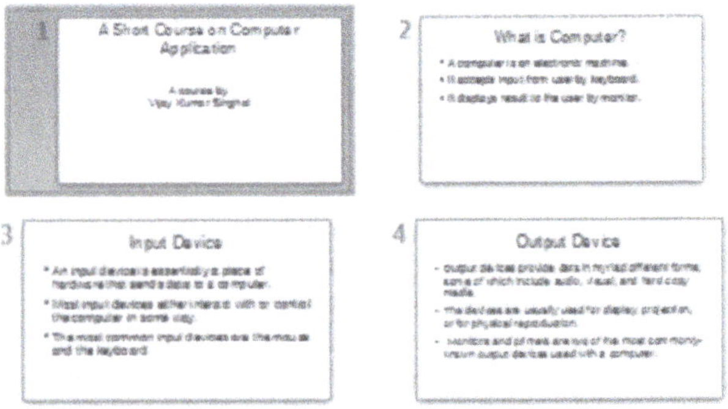

Running a Slide Show

(i) To run the slide show, click Slide Show → Start from First Slide on the main menu bar or click the Start from First Slide icon on the standard toolbar or press F5. The slide show starts to run.

(ii) By clicking the mouse button, you can move to the next slide or you can use the arrow keys on the keyboard to go to the next slide or the previous one. You can also press the spacebar key on the keyboard to proceed to the next slide.

(iii) Right click anywhere on the screen to open a menu for navigating the slides and set other options.

(iv) In the last slide, you will get a message Click to exit presentation. Just click the mouse button or press any key on the keyboard to exit the presentation.

(v) It you want to exit the slide show at any time, just press the Esc key.

Formatting the Text

The contents of the slides can be formatted in various ways. The most common way is to use the formatting icons on the formatting toolbar. Another way is by selecting Format → Text from the menu bar and the third way is by using the keyboard shortcuts. The various formatting options are explained below and shown in the figure:

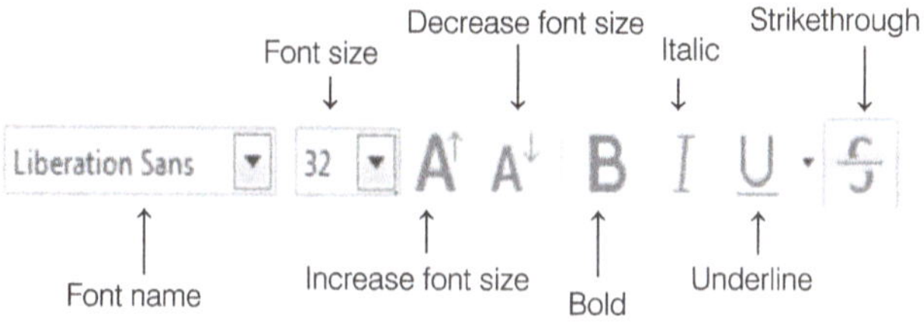

(i) **Font name** Click on the Font name drop-down to see the list of fonts and select a font name.

(ii) **Font size** Click on the font size drop-down to see the list of font size from where you can select the font size.

(iii) **Increase font size** Clicking on A with upward arrow will increase the size of the text (keyboard shortcut-Ctrl +]).

(iv) **Decrease font size** Clicking on A with downward arrow, will decrease the size of the text (keyboard shortcut - Ctrl + [ ).

(v) **Bold** Clicking on Bold (**B**) to change the text as bold (keyboard shortcut - Ctrl + B)

(vi) **Italic** Clicking on Italic (*I*) to change the text as italic (keyboard shortcut-Ctrl + I).

(vii) **Underline** Clicking on Underline (U) to change the text as underline (keyboard shortcut - Ctrl + U).

(viii) **Strikethrough** Clicking on strikethrough (S) to draw a line through the selected text.

(ix) **Superscript** Clicking on Superscript (X^2) raises the selected text above baseline (keyboard shortcut - Ctrl + Shift + P).

(x) **Subscript** Clicking on Subscript (X_2) lowers the selected text below baseline (keyboard shortcut - Ctrl + Shift + B).

(xi) **Font color** Clicking on font color drop-down box (▼) to the right of font color icon opens the color pallet from where you can change the font color.

(xii) **Highlighting** Clicking on Highlight color drop-down box (▼) to the right of highlight color icon opens the color pallet from where you can change the highlight color.

Aligning the Text

The Align left (≡), Align center (≡), Align Right (≡) and Justify (≡) icons are used to align the text to the left, center, right and justify respectively. Align Top, Center vertically and Align Bottom are used to align the selected text to the top, center or bottom of the text box.

Check Point 03

1. Which shortcut key is used for cut operation?
2. How backspace key is used to delete the text from the slide?
3. .... is the main view for working with individual slides.
4. Esc key is used to exit the slide show at any time. State True/False.

Bullets and Numbering

Bullets and numbering creates a bulleted or numbered list from selected paragraphs. Select first all list items and click the arrow on the Toggle Bulleted List or Toggle Numbered List icon. A drop-down menu will appear. In the drop-down panel, choose the format for bullets or numbers.

Bulleted List Format

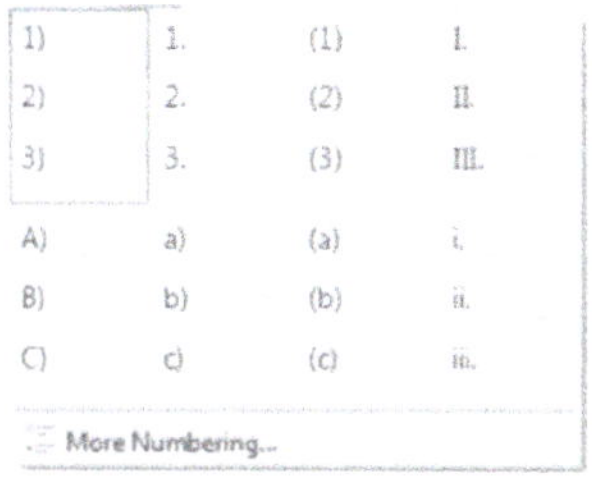

Numbered List Format

Click More Bullets or More Numbering option at the bottom of these drop-down lists open the Bullets and Numbering dialog box as shown in figure

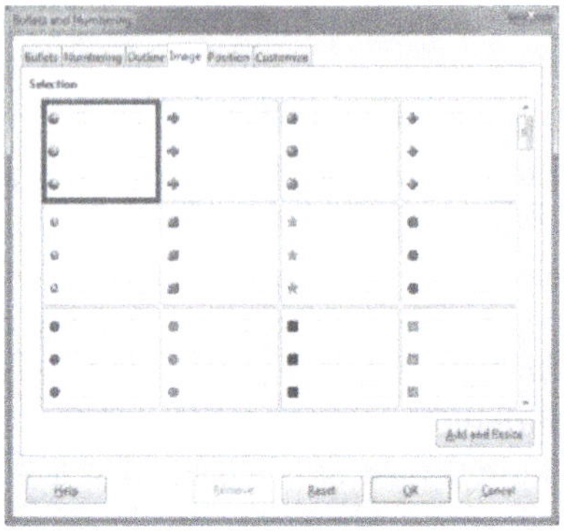

In this dialog box, select Image tab to set an image for the bullets.

Paragraph Spacing

Increase Paragraph Spacing and Decrease Paragraph Spacing options are used to increase or decrease the spacing above and below the selected paragraphs.

These options are located in the formatting toolbar.

Line Spacing in Text Paragraph

Adjust the spacing between the lines of a selected paragraph. Click on the small triangle to the right of the Line Spacing icon, which is given under the spacing section in the Properties task pane. Select the type of line spacing from the drop-down list shown in figure.

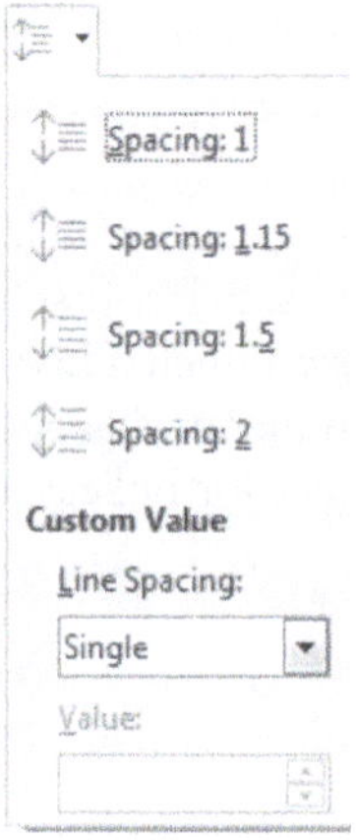

Working with Tables

Inserting Tables

Tables are inserted by selecting the Table icon on the standard toolbar, or by selecting the Table command on the Insert tab. A Insert Table dialog box will appear.

In the Insert Table dialog box, the Number of columns and the Number of rows are specified.

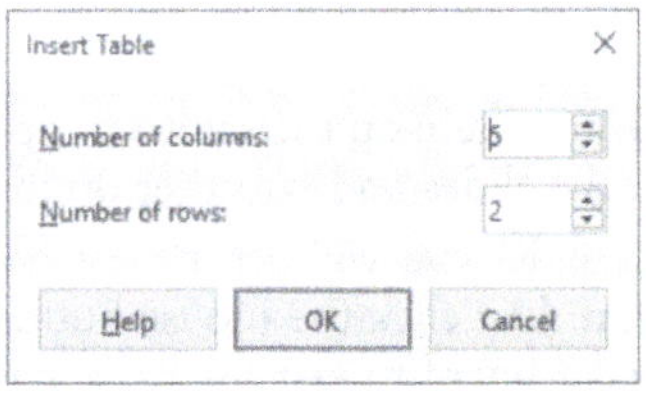

We have already seen that when we insert a blank slide in the presentation, we can create a table by clicking on the Table icon.

By clicking on the arrow next to the Table icon, the table drop-down menu opens, by dragging the cursor, the desired number of rows or columns can be selected.

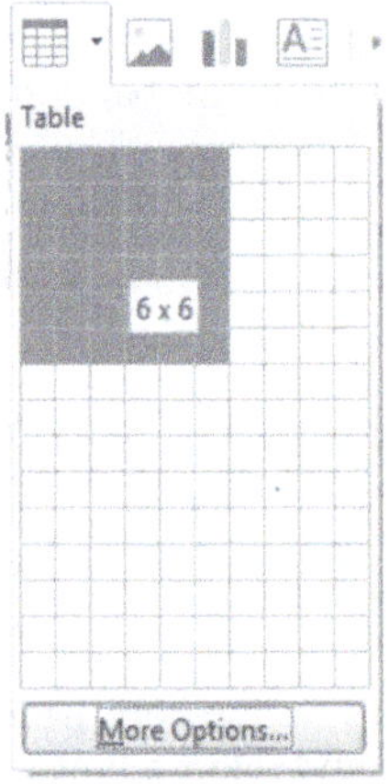

Entering and Editing Data in a Table

The content is put in table by placing the insertion point in a table cell and entering text moving the insertion point in a table can be done in three ways:

(i) By pressing the left mouse button.

(ii) By pressing the Tab key on a keyboard.

(iii) By using arrow keys on the keyboard.

Selecting a Cell

To select a cell within a table, position the mouse cursor along its left edge and when the cursor changes to a sloped white arrow, press left mouse button as show in figure.

Selecting a Row/Column

To select a row or column in a table, position the row or column to select and when the mouse cursor changes to a sloped white arrow, press the left mouse button and drag it to the end of row or column.

Selecting a Table

To select an entire table, first click on its edge. When the mouse cursor changes to a sloped white arrow, click on the left mouse button. To move the table, position on its edge, and when the cursor changes to a sloped white arrow, drag the table to a specified location.

Adjusting Column Width and Row Height using the Mouse

To change the width of the column, position on the border line between the two columns, and when the cursor changes to a (↔) sign, press the left mouse button, hold and drag it until the column achieves the desired width. The same can be done for adjusting the row height.

Table Borders and Background

The various table formatting options can be applied on the table just like writer. The borders and background can be assigned to the table. To do this, right click on the table border, the Table Properties dialog box will open as shown in figure, from where you can change the borders and background of the table.

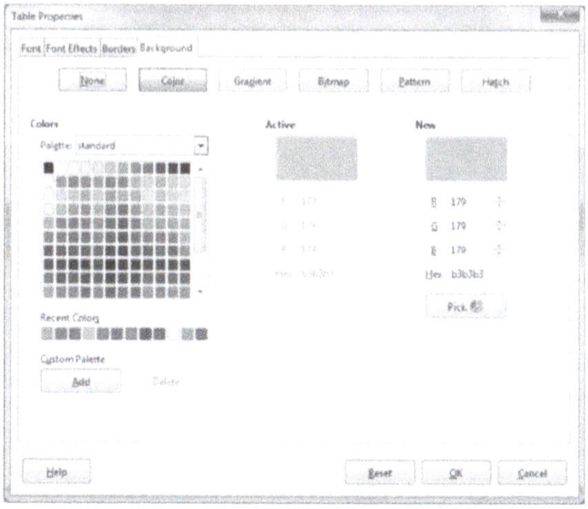

Adding and Formatting Images

Graphics can be inserted in the presentation for giving more information. Images can be inserted from the gallery and files stored in the computer.

Inserting an Image from a File

To insert an image in a slide, do the following:

(i) To insert an image into presentation, select Insert → Image on the menu bar or click on the Insert Image icon located on the standard toolbar. The Insert Image dialog box will open.

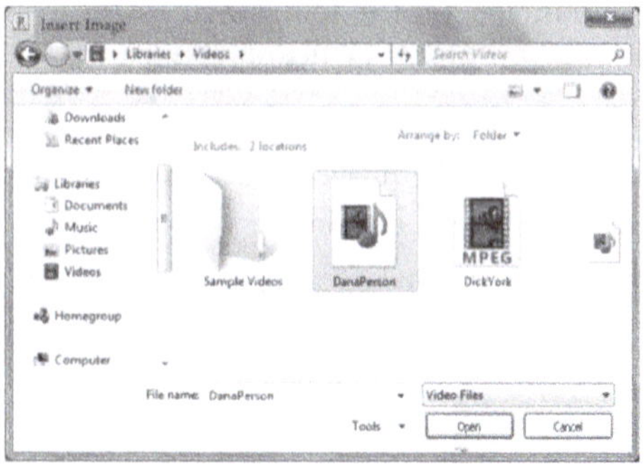

(ii) Select the file from the desired directory. By selecting the preview option, a thumbnail of the selected image will be displayed in the preview pane on the right.

Inserting an Image from the Gallery

The gallery contains the images that can be used in a presentation. To insert an image from the gallery, follow below steps:

(i) Select Insert → Media → Gallery from the menu. The gallery displays the available themes with images.

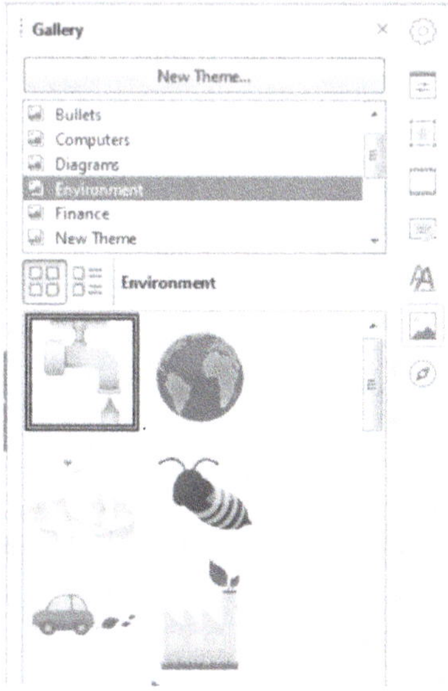

(ii) Select a theme and scroll to find a suitable image.
(iii) Click on the image and drag it onto the workspace.
(iv) Release the mouse button and the image will be placed into your slide.

Formatting Images

Formatting an image includes moving, resizing, rotating an image. The image inserted into presentation can be formatted.

Moving Images

To move the image, do the following:

(i) To move the image in the slide, click on an image, observe that the cursor changes to ✥.
(ii) Click and drag the image to the desired position.
(iii) Release the mouse button.

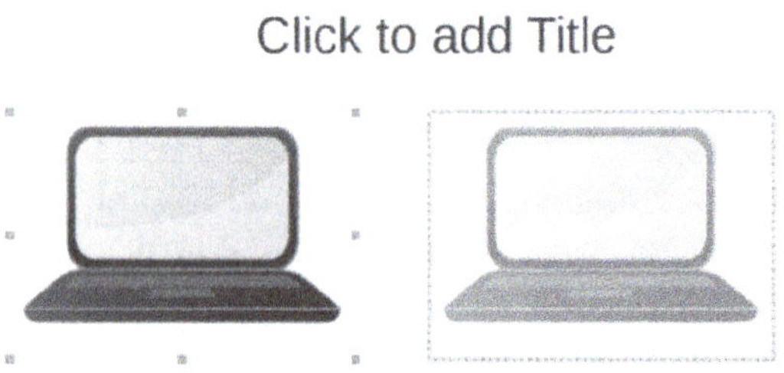

Resizing images

To resize the image, do the following:

(i) Select the image by clicking on it. Observe that selection handles displayed.
(ii) Position the cursor over one of the selection handles. The cursor changes the shape giving a graphical representation of the direction of the resizing.
(iii) Click and drag to resize the image as shown in figure.

(iv) Release the mouse button when satisfied with the new size.

Rotating images

The image can be rotated in any direction using the Rotate icon. To manually rotate an image, do the following

(i) Select the image to display the selection handles.
(ii) Click the Rotate icon on formatting toolbar.
(iii) Click again on the selected image and the selection handles change shape and color.
(iv) Click the mouse and move in the direction in which you want to rotate the image.
(v) When satisfied, release the mouse button.

Formatting using the Image Toolbar

When an image is selected, the Image toolbar becomes available under the Properties window as shown in figure

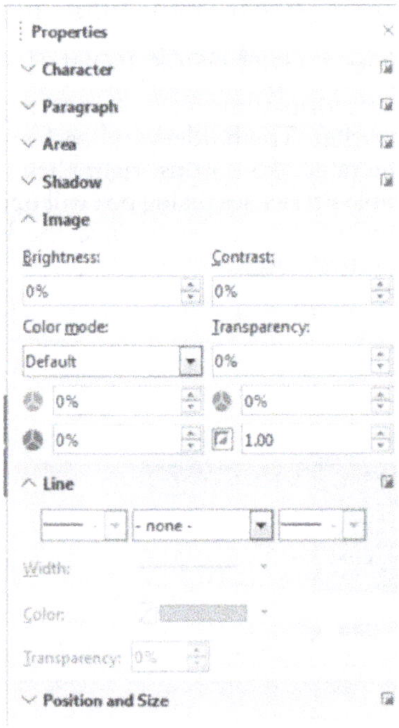

This toolbar provides a number of formatting options. The Image toolbar can also be displayed by selecting View → Toolbars → Image from the menu bar.

Managing Graphic Objects

Drawing Tools

Impress provides various drawing tools. The Drawing toolbar having the majority of the tools used to create graphical objects as shown in figure.

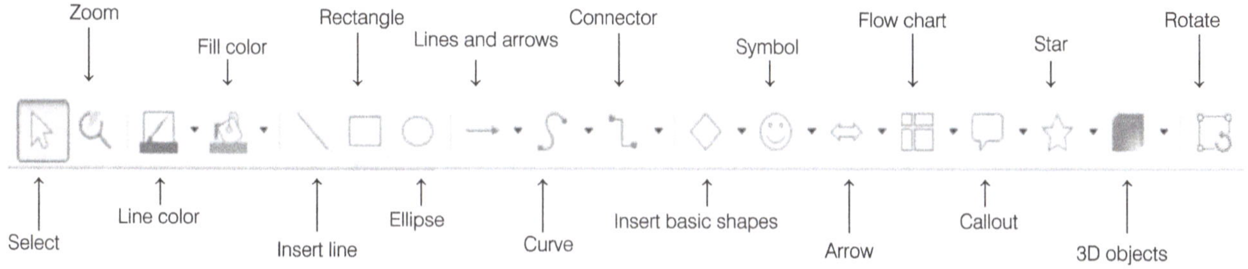

To activate this toolbar, select View → Toolbars → Drawing from the main menu bar.

(a) Drawing Lines

To draw a line, follow the below procedure:

(i) Click on the small triangle to the right of the Lines and Arrows tool and select the desired line from the available selection.

(ii) Click and drag on the slide to create the line or shape and release the mouse button.

(b) Drawing Shape

As similar to drawing a line, you can draw shapes by selecting the desired shapes from the available section and clicking and dragging on the slide. An example of drawing the shape has been illustrated in figure.

Grouping Objects

More than one objects can be grouped together and treated as a single object. A group formed by grouping the objects can be formatted as a single object, moved, rotated, deleted and so on.

To group objects together

(i) Select the objects to be grouped using select tool on the Drawing toolbar or hold down the Shift key and click on each object. To select all the objects, go to Edit → Select All on the main menu bar or use the keyboard combination Ctrl + A.

(ii) When the selection handles are displayed, go to Format → Group on the main menu bar or use the keyboard combination Ctrl + Shift + G or right-click on an object within the selected group and select Group from the context menu.

Ungrouping Objects

To ungroup objects follow the below given procedure :

(i) Select the group by clicking on any one of the objects in the group.

(ii) When the selection handles are displayed, go to Format → Group → Ungroup on the menu bar or use the keyboard combination Ctrl + Atl + Shift + G or right click on the group and select the Ungroup from the context menu.

Working with Slide Masters

Impress comes with various slide masters (master slides). These slide masters are available in the master slides section of the sidebar. There are three subsection, namely Used in this Presentation, Recently Used and Available for Use.

Click the expand marker next to the name to expand it.

It will show thumbnails of the slides. Just click the collapse marker to collapse the subsection to hide the thumbnails. Every slide masters shown in the Available for Use, lists form templates with the same name.

Adding Transitions

To apply transition effects on a slide, follow these steps:

(i) In the sidebar, select the Slide Transition icon to open the Slide Transition section.

(ii) In the Slides Pane or Slide Sorter view, select the slides to apply the transition. If you want to apply the transition to all the slides, do not select any slides.

(iii) In the Transition Gallery list, select a transition.

(iv) Modify the selected transition by changing the speed or adding a sound, in the Modify Transition section. To play a sound during transitions, select a sound from the sound list.

(v) If a sound is selected, the Loop until next sound option becomes active. Select this option to play the sound repeatedly until another sound starts.

(vi) Select how to advance to the next slide: Manually (On mouse click) or automatically (Automatically after). To select an automatically advance, you will have to specify how long the slide should remain visible before it automatically advances to the next slide.

(vii) To apply transition to all slides, click Apply Transition to All Slides.

(viii) To start the slide show from the current slide, check transitions, click Slide Show.

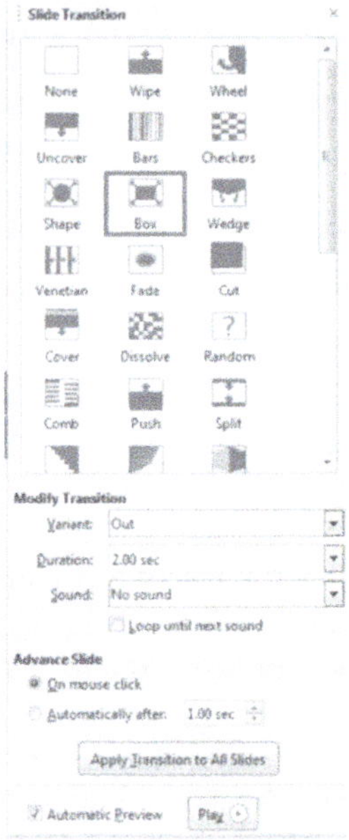

Slide Transition

Check Point 04

1. Clicking on *I* changes the text to ....
2. How many alignment options are available in Impress to align the text?
3. Which tab is used to insert an image into presentation?
4. Which options are available to format an image?

NCERT FOLDER

Check Your Progress

Pg 169-172

A. Multiple Choice Questions

Read the questions carefully and circle the letter (a), (b), (c) or (d) that best answers the questions.

1. Which of the following option is not available on Presentation Wizard?
   (a) Empty presentation
   (b) Form template
   (c) Open new presentation
   (d) Open existing presentation

Ans. (c) Empty presentation, form template, open existing presentation options are available on Presentation wizard.

2. Which of the following is not a part of main Impress window?
   (a) Slides pane (b) Workspace
   (c) Work pane (d) Task pane

Ans. (c) Slides pane, Workspace and Task pane are the parts of main Impress window.

3. Which of the following is not a section of task pane?
   (a) Master pages (b) Layouts
   (c) Custom View (d) Custom animation

Ans. (c) Task pane or side bar is located by default on the right side of the Impress window. It contains master pages, layouts, custom animation, slide transition etc.

4. Which view button listed below is not one of those available in the workspace?
   (a) Normal view (b) Outline view
   (c) Thumbnail view (d) Notes

Ans. (c) The various workspace views are available in Impress as Normal view, Outline view, Notes view, Slide sorter view, Notes master view, Handout master view, Slide master view.

5. Which view is generally used for creating, formatting and designing slides?
   (a) Normal view (b) Outline view
   (c) Notes (d) Slide Sorter view

Ans. (a) Normal view is the main view for working with individual slides. This view is generally used for creating, formatting and designing slides.

6. The slide show can be exited at any time during the slide show by pressing which of the following keys?
   (a) Space bar (b) End key
   (c) Break key (d) Esc key

Ans. (d) The slide show can be exited at any time during the presentation by pressing the Esc key.

7. Which of the following features is used to create a new slide show with the current slides but presented in a different order?
   (a) Rehearsal (b) Custom Slide Show
   (c) Slide Show Setup (d) Slide Show view

Ans. (b) Custom slide show feature is used to create a new slide show with the current slides. In this, user can set his/her desired settings.

8. Which of the following feature is used to progress the slide show automatically while speaking on the topic?
   (a) Custom Animation (b) Rehearse Timing
   (c) Slide Transition (d) Either (a) or (b)

Ans. (c) Slide Transition is used to progress the slide show automatically while speaking on the topic. It occurs in slide show view while moving from one slide to the next during on screen presentation.

B. Fill in the blanks

1. .... is used to maintain consistency in design and color in the presentation.

Ans. Master slide

2. .... view is used to view all the slides simultaneously.

Ans. Slide sorter

3. .... is used to perform basic operations on the presentation.

Ans. File menu

4. Master Page is used to modify the .... of the slide.

Ans. base architecture

5. To create a new blank presentation, use the key combination ....

Ans. Ctrl + N

6. In every presentation, first slide should be ....

Ans. Title slide

7. To save a presentation, we can use key combination ……… .

Ans. Ctrl + S

8. In LibreOffice Impress, by default the presentation is saved with ……… extension.

Ans. .odp

9. The keyboard shortcut key for slide show is ……… .

Ans. F5

10. The shortcut key to close the LibreOffice impress is ……… .

Ans. Ctrl + W

11. The shortcut key to insert a new slide is ………… .

Ans. Ctrl + M

12. The ……… view is used to apply animation on the content of slide.

Ans. Normal

13. A paper copy of presentation given to the audience is known as ……… .

Ans. handouts

14. To play a sound during transitions, select a sound from the ……… list.

Ans. Sound

15. To play the sound repeatedly, the ……… is used.

Ans. Loop until next sound

C. State whether True or False

1. The order of the slides cannot be changed in slides pane.

Ans. True; The order of the slides cannot be changed in slides pane. It displays presentation slides in the thumbnail form.

2. Slide design or layout can be changed for multiple slides simultaneously.

Ans. True; Slide design or layout can be changed for multiple slides simultaneously, which can be selected from layouts section in the Properties window.

3. Every slide in a presentation has exactly one slide master.

Ans. True; Every slide in a presentation has exactly one slide.

4. Animations once applied can be changed but cannot be removed.

Ans. False; Animations are applied to individual elements in a single slide : title, chart, shape or individual bullet point and also removed from custom Animation section on the task pane.

5. Slide names are included in outline view.

Ans. False; Outline view contains all the slides of the presentation in a sequence. Only the text contained in each slide is displayed inside the workspace.

6. The notes added to slides can be seen during the presentation.

Ans. False; The notes added to slides cannot be seen during the presentation. Notes are used to help the presenter for the information.

7. A presentation can have multiple slide masters.

Ans. True; A presentation can have multiple slide master. Therefore, to change the appearance of a presentation. You must change or edit the slide master.

8. A user can create his/her own slide master.

Ans. True; A user can create his/her own slide master. A slide master is a slide that is used as the starting point for other slides.

9. Once a pre-defined slide master is selected, the background of slide cannot be changed.

Ans. False; Once a pre-defined slide master is selected, to change the appearance of a presentation, you must change or edit the slide master.

10. The text added to the header is displayed on the first slide only.

Ans. False; The text added to the header is displayed on every slide or first slide. If user wants to put date and time in header, click on this option.

11. The text added to the footer is displayed on the last slide only.

Ans. False; The text added to the footer is displayed on the last slide or every slide such as page number.

12. User can create his/her own template and use it in the Presentation Wizard.

Ans. True; User can create his/her own template and use it in the Presentation wizard. A template is called a design of presentation slides.

13. The Notes View is used for the audience.

Ans. False; Notes view is not seen by the audience while showing the presentation. It displays the area in which the notes are used to help during the presentation.

14. It is not possible to insert audio or video clips in the presentation.

Ans. False; To enhance the effectiveness of presentation, a user can add audio or video clips in the presentation.

15. Header and footer can be inserted in the presentation.

Ans. True; Headers and footers are respectively printed on the top and bottom of the slide. They can include both text and pictures.

D. Short Answer Questions

1. List the possible multimedia contents that are included while creating a presentation.

Ans. The possible multimedia content that are included while creating a presentation as follows:

- image
- audio
- video
- cartoon characters

A multimedia presentation is a standalone presentation that includes information presented with images, video, or digital representation and includes sound which might be a narrative, music or sound effects. Such effects are used to present content because it makes the content interesting as well as entertaining.

2. List the important points to be considered while making an effective presentation.

Ans. Refer to text on Page 190.

3. What are the advantages of using a presentation?

Ans. Advantages of using a presentation are as follows:

(i) The presentation provides an opportunity to meet customers face to face.

(ii) Presentation makes it easier to engage the audience.

(iii) It provides flexibility to make changes in the content.

(iv) It provides an effective way to share your thoughts, product/service in front of the audience more clearly.

(v) It is a versatile tool for communication that can be used in meetings and viewing the content more clearly on a laptop or computer.

4. What objects can be inserted to slides in Impress?

Ans. Impress offers the capacity of inserting various types of objects such as picture, clipart, drawing, photograph and so on. To insert an object, click on Insert tab then select object from the drop down menu what type of object you want to insert.

5. What are the steps to add picture or object to the slide?

Ans. Refer to text on Page 197.

6. How can text be added to header or footer on the sliders?

Ans. You can add text object as header or footer anywhere in the master slide:

(i) Choose View → Master slide.

(ii) On the Drawing toolbar, select the Text icon.

(iii) Drag in the master slide to draw a text object, and then type or paste your text.

7. Describe the use of fields available in header and footer.

Ans. Headers and footers are respectively printed on the top and bottom of the slide. They can include both text and pictures. e.g. You can add page number, date, company's logo, title of presentation, etc in header and footer.

The use of fields available in Header and footer

- **Date and time** If user wants to put date and time in header, click on this option. By doing so, two radio buttons will activate. Click on Variable button to automatically update the date and click on Fixed to fix the date.
- **Footer** To insert some text in the footer part of the slide, check this option and enter the text.
- **Slide number** If user wants to put serial number on each slide, click on this check box.

Apart from this, if user wants to add notes or handouts on header and footer, click on Notes and Handouts tab from Header and Footer dialog box.

8. Write the steps to create a template.

Ans. In Impress, a template is called a design of presentation slide. To create a template, do the following.

(i) Open a new or existing presentation.

(ii) Add the predefined content (text and images) of the presentation template that you want to appear in every slide created from this template.

(iii) Format, create or modify any styles that you want to use in the new template.

(iv) From the menu bar, choose File → Templates → Save as Template

(v) The Save as Template dialog Box will open, displaying the existing categories and a Template name text box to enter a name for the new template.

(vi) Select the My Templates folder.

(vii) Click the Save button. The template is saved and the dialog box will close.

9. Write down the steps to add slide transition in your presentation.

Ans. Refer to text on Page 200.

10. How will you add the slide number at the bottom of each slide?

Ans. To add slide number at the bottom of each slide, do the following

(i) The slide number can be displayed by using the Slide number option in Header and Footer.

(ii) If user wants to add slide number only on single slide, then click Apply button otherwise click on Apply to All.

11. How will you insert a company's logo (picture) in first slide of your presentation?

Ans. To insert a company's logo (picture) in first slide, do the following.

(i) Select the first slide in which you want to add a company's logo.
(ii) Click Insert tab → Image option
(iii) The Insert Image dialog box will appear
(iv) Find the image that you want to insert as company's logo and click the image to select it.
(v) Click the Open button. Selected image will add to the slide screen.
(vi) Adjust the size of the image as per your requirement.
(vii) To send the image at the back of the slide, click on the Send to Back option.

12. How will you add the name of the company on the top of the each slide?

Ans. To add the name of the company on the top of each slide, do the following:

(i) Select View → Master slide.
(ii) To add text to the main area of the slide, select the Text icon on the Drawing toolbar.
(iii) Click once in the master page and drag to draw a text object, then type or paste your text into the text object.
(iv) Click Close Master view on the master view toolbar or go to View → Normal on the main menu bar when you are finished.

13. Write down the steps to insert a table in a presentation.

Ans. Refer to text on Page 196.

14. Write down the steps to insert a chart in slide.

Ans. Steps to insert a chart are as follows

(i) Select the data you want to summarise visually and then click on the Insert tab.
(ii) A chart appears containing selected data.
(iii) Select chart type from standard toolbar.
(iv) Chart Type dialog box will appear.
(v) Select chart type as column, bar, etc and choose the desired option in Normal.
(vi) Click on Ok button.
(vii) Choose Title, Legend, Grid and Axis from standard toolbar.

15. What are the five views of presentation?

Ans. In Impress, to view the presentation of slides, various views are used. These views are as follows:

(i) **Normal view** It is the main view for working with individual slides. This view is used to format and design and to add text, graphics and animation effects. In this view, the slide is displayed in the middle of the window.

On the left side of the window, the pane with slides thumbnails is displayed.

(ii) **Outline view** It contains all the slides of the presentation in a sequence. It shows each slide in the outline format. Only the text contained in each slide is displayed inside the workspace. It displays slide text in the form of a structure.

(iii) **Notes view** It is used to add notes to a slide for the information of presenter. It is not seen by the audience while showing the presentation. It displays the area in which the notes are used to help during the presentation.

(iv) **Slide Sorter view** It contains all of the slides thumbnails. It is suitable for rearranging the slide in order. It is used to sort slides with the drag and drop method. Use this view to work with a group of slides or with only one slide.

(v) **Slide show view** In this view, the computer screen is completely filled by a single slide. This view is used for the rehearsal or actual slide show and user cannot make any changes during this view. For this view, press F5 key from keyboard.

SUMMARY

- In LibreOffice Impress, an effective presentation can be created by using different multimedia elements.
- A good quality presentation is required to convey the message clearly to the audience.
- By default, the presentation is saved with .odp extension.
- A Portable Document Format (PDF) of the presentation can be created by saving a file in the PDF format, which can be viewed with the free Adobe Acrobat Reader.
- Outline View contains all the slides of the presentation in a sequence. It shows each slide in the outline format.
- Slide Sorter view contains all of the slides thumbnails. It is suitable for rearranging the slide order.
- Increase Paragraph Spacing and Decrease Paragraph Spacing options are used to increase or decrease the spacing above and below the selected paragraphs.
- Graphics can be inserted in the presentation for giving more information. Images can be inserted from the gallery and files stored in the computer.
- Formatting an image includes moving, resizing, rotating an image.

Exam Practice

Multiple Choice Questions

1. Impress presentation is a collection of
(a) slides and handouts (b) speaker's notes
(c) outlines (d) All of these

Ans. (d) Impress presentation is a collection of slides, handouts, speaker's notes, outlines.

2. Which of the following is an example of presentation software?
(a) K presenter (b) LibreOffice Impress
(c) Both (a) and (b) (d) K word

Ans. (c) Some examples of presentation software are K presenter, openoffice .org Impress, MS-Powerpoint, Libreoffice Impress etc.

3. Which of the following component contains the name of presentation file?
(a) Tool bar (b) Title bar
(c) Menu bar (d) Status bar

Ans. (b) Title bar contains the name of presentation file with extension (.odp) and presentation application as LibreOffice Impress.

4. How many decks are available in Impress sidebar?
(a) 3 (b) 4
(c) 7 (d) 5

Ans. (c) Impress sidebar contains 7 decks as Properties, Slide Transition, Animation, Master slides, styles, Gallery, Navigator which shown by its icon.

5. By which menu, you can create blank presentation?
(a) View (b) File
(c) Insert (d) Format

Ans. (b) To create a new blank presentation, select the file menu → New.

6. Which shortcut key is used to save the presentation?
(a) Ctrl + S (b) Ctrl + P
(c) Alt + S (d) None of these

Ans. (a) To save the presentation, select the File menu → Save or use the shortcut key combination Ctrl + S or click on the Save button on the standard toolbar.

7. Which key is used to erase characters to the right of the cursor?
(a) Delete (b) Backspace
(c) Both (a) and (b) (d) Shift

Ans. (a) Delete key deletes the character on the right of the cursor and the backspace key deletes the character on the left of the cursor.

8. Which Impress view displays miniature version of slides are arranged on the screen and is useful record them and see more slides at one time?
(a) Slide show
(b) Slide master
(c) Notes Page
(d) Slide sorter

Ans. (d) In slide sorter view, miniature version of slides are arranged on the screen. You can reorder them and see more slide at one time.

9. What is the shortcut key to start the LibreOffice Impress presentation from the beginning?
(a) F8 (b) F5
(c) F11 (d) F10

Ans. (b) To start the LibreOffice Impress presentation from the beginning, click Slide Show → Start from first slide on the main menu or Press F5.

10. Text can be formatted like
(a) Bold (b) italic
(c) underline (d) All of these

Ans. (d) The various text formatting options are bold, italic, underline, font size, font name etc.

11. Which step is used to insert a table in a slide?
(a) Insert tab → Table
(b) Insert tab → New Table
(c) View tab → Table
(d) None of the above

Ans. (d) Tables are inserted by selecting the Table icon on the standard toolbar, or by selecting the Table command on the Insert tab.

12. Which shortcut key is used to ungroup the object?
(a) Ctrl + Shift + G
(b) Ctrl + Alt + Shift + G
(c) All + Shift + G
(d) None of the above

Ans. (b) Ctrl + Alt + Shift + G shortcut key is used to ungroup the object or right click on the group and select ungroup from the content menu.

Fill in the Blanks

1. .... contains the menus with logically grouped commands.

Ans. Menu bar

2. In Impress, a .... is called a design of presentation slide.

Ans. template

3. By default, the presentation is saved with .... extension.

Ans. .odp

4. To open the presentation in the web browser, save it in .... format.

Ans. HTML

5. The keyboard shortcut .... is used for copy operation.

Ans. Ctrl + C

6. In .... view, the slide is displayed in the middle of the window.

Ans. Normal

7. Clicking on .... changes the text to bold.

Ans. B

8. To insert an image into presentation, select .... on the menu bar.

Ans. Insert → Image

9. More than one objects can be grouped together and treated as a ....

Ans. Single object

10. .... will show thumbnails of the slides.

Ans. Slide master

True/False

1. All pages of a Impress presentation is also called a slide.

Ans. True; All pages of a Impress presentation is also called a slide. Each slide contains the information or data that can include text, pictures, chart and more.

2. It will not be appropriate to keep the font size at 32 points in presentation.

Ans. False; It will be appropriate to keep the font size at 32 points or more, so that the audience can easily read the contents in presentation.

3. Edit menu contains functions for copying.

Ans. True; Edit menu contains functions for coping, cutting and pasting text segments.

4. Impress can not be started from Start button.

Ans. False; To start LibreOffce Impress in Windows, double click its shortcut icon on the desktop or click on the Start button.

5. Status bar displays information about the active presentation,

Ans. True; Status bar displays information about the active presentation, the current position of the cursor and the zoom slider.

6. The appropriate layout can be selected from Layouts section in the Properties window.

Ans. True; The appropriate layout can be selected from Layouts section in the Properties window. The layouts included in LibreOffice range from a blank slide to a slide with six content boxes.

7. If you want to save the presentation file with different name, you can use Save button.

Ans. False; To save the presentation with a different name, select File → Save As or use the shortcut key combination Ctrl + Shift + S.

8. The slides once created can be reused within the personation.

Ans. True; The slides once created can be reused within the presentation or in another presentation.

9. It is not possible after having undone the change, get it back.

Ans. False; It is also possible after having undone the change, get it back. This is called the redo function.

10. Notes view contains all the slides of the presentation in a sequence.

Ans. False; Outline view contains all the slides of the presentation in a sequence, which shows each slide in the outline format.

11. The content is put in table by placing the insertion point in a table cell.

Ans. True; The content is put in table by placing the insertion point in a table cell and entering text.

12. Slide masters are available in the master section of the sidebar.

Ans. False; Slide masters are available in the master slides section of the sidebar. There are three subsection, namely Used in this Presentation, Recently Use and Available for Use.

Match the Columns

1. Match the following columns.

Column I		Column II	
A.	Impress	1.	By using the F1 function key.
B.	Slide show	2.	is located by default on the right side of the window
C.	Side bar	3.	is a free, open source and widely used presentation software.
D.	A PDF of the presentation	4.	is a tool for viewing presentation
E.	Open the Help function	5.	can be created by saving a file in the PDF format

Ans. A → 3; B → 4; C → 2; D → 5; E → 1

Very Short Answer (VSA) Type Questions

1. What is a presentation?

Ans. A presentation is a collection of individual slides that contain information on a topic. A presentation is like a notebook that contains multiple pages in the form of slides.

2. What is meant by slide pane?

Ans. Slide pane is a vertical pane to see the slide in small size to navigate on any slide easily.

3. How will you close the presentation?

Ans. To close a presentation, select File → Close or use the keyboard shortcut keys Ctrl + W.

4. Write the keyboard shortcut for paste operation.

Ans. Ctrl + V

5. What do you understand by undo?

Ans. After delete the text, we are able to reverse what we have done. This is known as the undo function.

6. Write the use of notes view in presentation.

Ans. Notes view is used to add notes to a slide for the information of presenter.

7. What is the use of Superscript icon?

Ans. Superscript (X^2) icon raises the selected text above baseline.

8. How will you select a row/column in table?

Ans. To select a row or column in a table, position the row or column to select and when the mouse cursor changes to a slopped white arrow, press the left mouse button and drag it to the end of row or column.

Short Answer (SA) Type Questions

1. How will you open LibreOffice Impress in Ubuntu Linux?

Ans. In Ubuntu Linux, open the LibreOffice Impress by any of the following options:

(i) Find the LibreOffice Impress icon on the application launcher and click it to start the application launcher.

(ii) Find the LibreOffice Impress icon through Search your computer icon on the launcher. To search, enter the word Impress and select LibreOffice Impress from the search results.

2. Write the steps to save a file in the PDF format.

Ans. Refer to text on Page 191.

3. How will you rename a slide in Impress?

Ans. Refer to text on Page 193.

4. Write the procedure to delete the text of the slide.

Ans. It is easy to delete the text of the slides. The Delete and Backspace keys on keyboard is used to delete the text. The Delete key deletes the character on the right of the cursor and the Backspace key deletes the character on the left of the cursor. Pressing Delete key or Backspace key deletes one character at a time. To delete the line or paragraph of text, first select the text and then press the Delete key. Alternately you can use the Cut option to delete the text.

5. Explain the slide sorter view in brief.

Ans. Slide sorter view contains all of the slides thumbnails. It is suitable for rearranging the slide order. It is used to sort slides with the drag and drop method. Use this view to work with a group of slides or with only one slide.

6. Write the steps to create a presentation using template

Ans. Refer to text on Page 190.

7. How will you insert a new slide in presentation?

Ans. Refer to text on Page 192.

8. How will you copy the text in the presentation?

Ans. To copy some text or an object in the presentation to another location (in the same presentation or another presentation), follow the below steps:

(i) Select the text and click the right mouse button

(ii) Select the Copy option from the context menu (keyboard shortcut : Ctrl + C) for copying.

(iii) Position the cursor on the location of the slide, to which you want to copy the content.

(iv) Press the right mouse button and select the Paste option from the context menu (keyboard shortcut-Ctrl + V)

9. Write the steps to run a slide show.

Ans. To run a slide show, do the following:

(i) To run the slide show click Slide Show—Start from first slide on the main menu bar or click the Start from first slide icon on the standard toolbar or press F5. The slide show starts to run.

(ii) By clicking the mouse button, you can move to the next slide or you can use the arrow keys on the keyboard to go to the next slide or the previous one you can also press the spacebar key on the keyboard to proceed to the next slide.

(iii) Right click anywhere on the screen to open a menu for navigating the slides and set other options.

(iv) In the last slide, you will get a message, click to exit presentation. Just click the mouse button or press any key on the keyboard to exit the presentation.

(v) If you want to exit the slide show at any time, just press the Esc key.

Long Answer (LA) Type Questions

1. Explain the characteristics of good quality presentation.

Ans. Refer to text on Page 187 and 188.

2. How will you insert and delete the slide in presentation?

Ans. To insert a slide, use any of the following way

(i) Select from menu bar Slide → New Slide.

Or Right click on a Slide in slide pane and select New Slide from the context menu.

Or Click the New Slide icon in the standard toolbar.

Or Use the keyboard shortcut Ctrl + M.

(ii) You can insert the new slide in your presentation by using any of the above options.

To delete any slide from a presentation, first it should be selected. To delete one or more slides, follow the given steps.

(i) Select the slide(s) by marking them in the slide pane.

(ii) Right click the mouse button on the selected slide.

(iii) Select the Delete Slide option in the context menu.

(iv) Another quick way to delete the slide is just select the slide and press the Delete button from the keyboard.

3. Describe the workspace views in detail.

Ans. Refer to text on Page 194.

Self Assessment

Multiple Choice Questions

1. Which of the following menu contains functions for copying, cutting and pasting text segments?
   (a) File (b) Edit (c) Insert (d) Format
2. Which tool is used to zoom in or zoom out the slide?
   (a) Drawing toolbar (b) Status bar (c) Zoom Control (d) None of these
3. What is the step to save the presentation as HTML?
   (a) File → Export (b) File → Export as PDF
   (c) Edit → Export (d) None of these
4. Which shortcut key is used to open an existing presentation?
   (a) Ctrl + N (b) Ctrl + S (c) Alt + O (d) Ctrl + O
5. Which of the following option is used to increase the size of the text?
   (a) A↓ (b) A↑ (c) B↑ (d) None of these

Fill in the Blanks

1. Presenting information clearly and effectively is a key skill to get your message or opinion across the ....
2. Impress sidebar contains .... decks.
3. When creating a presentation, first slide is normally the ....
4. Inserting a .... will insert the copy of the existing slide into the presentation.
5. The slides are named as .... by default.

True/False

1. The grammar and language should be correct in your presentation.
2. Window menu is used to control spelling in a presentation.
3. The appropriate layout can be selected from Insert section in the properties window.
4. The various workspace views are in the drop-down list of view.
5. The borders and background can be assigned to the table.

Match the Columns

1. Match the following columns.

Column I	Column II
A. Presentation	1. is used to add notes to a slide
B. Format menu	2. is used to present the project proposal in business organisation.
C. Impress	3. displays the list of fonts.
D. Notes view	4. contains functions for text formatting
E. Font name	5. is the component of LibreOffice presentation.

Very Short Answer (VSA) Type Questions

1. Explain any one characteristic of a presentation.
2. What do you mean by Insert menu?
3. What is meant by status bar?
4. Explain the redo function.
5. How will you align a text in presentation?

Short Answer (SA) Type Questions

1. How will you open LibreOffice Impress?
2. What is meant by side bar?
3. Explain the steps to select a slide layout.
4. Write the steps to open existing presentation.
5. How will you insert a duplicate slide?
6. Write the steps for undo and redo functions.

Long Answer (LA) Type Questions

1. Explain the components of Impress Window.
2. Explain the copying and moving slides in detail.
3. How will you format the text in Impress presentation?

SAMPLE QUESTION PAPER 1

A Sample Question Paper for CBSE Class 9

Information Technology

General Instructions

1. Please read the instructions carefully.
2. This Question Paper consists of **21 questions** in two sections: Section A & Section B.
3. Section A has Objective Type Questions whereas Section B contains Subjective Type Questions.
4. **Out of the given (5 + 16 =) 21 questions, a candidate has to answer (5 + 10 =) 15 questions in the allotted (maximum) time of 2 hours.**
5. All questions of a particular section must be attempted in the correct order.
6. **Section A : Objective Type Questions (24 Marks)**
   (i) This section has 5 questions.
   (ii) Marks allotted are mentioned against each question/part.
   (iii) There is no negative marking.
   (iv) Do as per the instructions given.
7. **Section B : Subjective Type Questions (26 Marks)**
   (i) This section has 16 questions.
   (ii) A candidate has to do 10 questions.
   (iii) Do as per the instructions given.
   (iv) Marks allotted are mentioned against each question/part.

Time : 2 hours | ***Max. Marks : 50***

FULLY SOLVED

Section A (Objective Type Questions)

1. *Answer any 4 out of the given 6 questions based on Employability Skills* $(1 \times 4 = 4)$

(i) Ramesh is chai wala selling tea near a busy bus stop. He is a .... (1)
(a) Business man (b) Employee (c) Employer (d) None of these

(ii) Resources that produce heat, power that can be used as energy to produce electricity are called .... (1)
(a) Natural resources (b) Energy resources (c) Artificial resources (d) None of these

(iii) .... is the means by which the message is sent. (1)
(a) Media (b) Channel (c) Communicate (d) All of these

(iv) An input device is a .... device that sends data into the computer system. (1)
(a) Software (b) Hardware (c) Both (a) and (b) (d) None of these

(v) .... is an acquired or natural capacity that enables an individual to perform a particular job or task with considerable proficiency. (1)
(a) knowledge (b) Talent (c) Ability (d) Courage

(vi) Heating of the Earth because of burning of fossil fuels is due to .... (1)
(a) Global warming (b) Harmful radiation (c) Green house effect (d) None of these

2. ***Answer any 5 out of the given 6 questions*** **(1 × 5 = 5)**

(i) You have used a spreadsheet to calculate the average marks of a class in Mathematics. Which input is essential to find the average marks? (1)
 (a) Marks of each student of class in Science
 (b) Marks of each student of class in Mathematics
 (c) Average marks in Mathematics of each student of class
 (d) Names and roll numbers of each student of class

(ii) A document is a paper with written contents and the process of preparing a document is called .... (1)
 (a) documentation (b) presentation (c) workbook (d) worksheet

(iii) .... is a tool for viewing presentation. (1)
 (a) Transition (b) Animation (c) Slide show (d) All of these

(iv) The bar located at the top of the spreadsheet window is called .... (1)
 (a) Menu bar (b) Title bar (c) Status bar (d) None of these

(v) BPO services follow .... to ensure error free and exceptional free. (1)
 (a) Improvement (b) Encourage (c) Quality checks (d) All of these

(vi) Master Page is used to modify the .... of the slide. (1)
 (a) Base Architecture (b) Super Architecture (c) Both (a) and (b) (d) None of these

FULLY SOLVED

3. ***Answer any 5 out of the given 6 questions*** **(1 × 5 = 5)**

(i) .... option is used to move some content from one place to another. (1)
 (a) Cut (b) Copy (c) Move (d) Insert

(ii) The spreadsheet feature used to continue the series is called as .... (1)
 (a) Fill series (b) Fill handle (c) Either (a) or (b) (d) None of these

(iii) .... is the way to refer the formula or function from one cell to the next cell along the row or column. (1)
 (a) Referencing (b) Macros (c) Automation (d) Animation

(iv) .... are firms with their headquarters in India. (1)
 (a) ISP (b) MNC (c) HSP (d) NSP

(v) A paper copy of presentation given to the audience is known as .... (1)
 (a) Normal (b) Sorter (c) Transition (d) Handouts

(vi) The formula in cell A2 is = B2 + C3. On copying this formula to cell C2, it will change to .... (1)
 (a) = D3 + E2 (b) = D2 + E3 (c) = D2 + E2 (d) = D3 + E3

4. ***Answer any 5 out of the given 6 questions*** **(1 × 5 = 5)**

(i) A table has a number of .... (1)
 (a) rows (b) columns (c) Both (a) and (b) (d) None of these

(ii) In Writer, which tab is used to spelling and grammar, language, macros etc? (1)
 (a) Window tab (b) Tools tab (c) Help tab (d) Form tab

(iii) Which bar is located just below the menu bar? (1)
 (a) Standard toolbar (b) Formatting toolbar (c) Status bar (d) None of these

(iv) Which tool is used to apply different font sizes on a worksheet? (1)
 (a) Font (b) Font size (c) Bold (d) Left alignment

(v) Help function is by using the which function key? (1)
 (a) F1 (b) F2 (c) F3 (d) F4

(vi) .... can be inserted in the presentation for giving more information. (1)
 (a) Pictures (b) Images (c) Shapes (d) Graphics

5. ***Answer any 5 out of the given 6 questions*** **(1 × 5 = 5)**

(i) .... comes with various slide masters. (1)
 (a) Writer (b) Spreadsheet (c) Impress (d) Base

(ii) Which view displays slide text in the form of a structure? (1)
(a) Normal (b) Outline (c) Notes (d) Slide sorter

(iii) In a spreadsheet, by default the date format is in .... (1)
(a) Australian format (b) Britain format (c) American format (d) Indian format

(iv) How many types of referencing in spreadsheet? (1)
(a) Two (b) Three (c) Four (d) Five

(v) In Writer, which tab is used to insert text box, check box, option button etc? (1)
(a) Form (b) Table (c) Window (d) Help

(vi) To jump to the end of a document, press .... (1)
(a) Shift + End (b) Delete (c) Alt + End (d) Ctrl + End

Section B (Subjective Type Questions)

Answer any 3 out of the given 5 questions based on Employability Skills. Answer each question in 20-30 words (2 × 3 = 6)

6. Explain, the types of questions in brief. (2)

7. List any two comparison of activities between entrepreneurship and employment. (2)

8. What is the use of scanner? (2)

9. What do you mean by positive thinking? Write about the importance of positive thinking. (2)

10. Write the purpose for biodiversity. (2)

Answer any 4 out of the given 6 questions in 20-30 words each (2 × 4 = 8)

11. How will you type the capital letters? (2)

12. How will you add the text in the slide? (2)

13. What is Global In-house Centres? Write any two Global In-house Centres. (2)

14. Write the steps to start LibreOffice Calc in Windows. (2)

15. What is the use of Help tab and Tools tab in Writer document? (2)

16. (i) How will you save a presentation with a different format? (2)
(ii) How will you ungroup the objects?

Answer any 3 out of the given 5 questions in 50-80 words each (4 × 3 = 12)

17. What precautions are required to ensure that ICT use is safe? (4)

18. (i) Describe any two factors which are included in typing ergonomics. (4)
(ii) How can you add a new lesson in the RapidTyping software?

19. List the various components of LibreOffice Writer. (4)

20. Give the syntax and example of any five mathematical functions in spreadsheet. (4)

21. (i) List the possible multimedia contents that are included while creating a presentation. (4)
(ii) Define the following views of presentation:
(a) Outline View (ii) Slide Show View

Answers

1. (i) (a) Business man (ii) (b) Energy resources (iii) (b) Channel
(iv) (b) Hardware (v) (c) Ability (vi) (c) Green house effect
2. (i) (b) Marks of each student of class in Mathematics
(ii) (a) Documentation (iii) (c) Slide show (iv) (b) Title bar
(v) (c) Quality checks (vi) (a) Base architecture
3. (i) (a) Cut (ii) (b) Fill handle (iii) (a) Referencing
(iv) (b) MNC (v) (d) Handouts (vi) (b) = D2 + E3
4. (i) (c) Both (a) and (b) (ii) (b) Tools tab (iii) (a) Standard toolbar
(iv) (b) Font size (v) (a) F1 (vi) (d) Graphics
5. (i) (c) Impress (ii) (b) Outline (iii) (c) American format
(iv) (b) three (v) (a) Form (vi) (d) Ctrl + End
6. There are two types of questions as discussed below :
   - **Close Ended Questions** Such questions are those which can be answered with a 'Yes' or a 'No'. Their answers are limited to a 'Yes' or a 'No' and no other detail is required.
     For example, Did he go to the temple?
     Yes
   - **Open Ended Questions** Those questions that requires answer in detail are open ended questions. The option of answers to such questions are unlimited.
     For example, What is your favourite memory from childhood?
     The answer to such a question could be unlimited and will be described in detail.
7. Two comparison of activities between entrepreneurship and employment are :
   (i) The job done by the person is decided by himself or herself. But in employment, the job done is decided by employer.
   (ii) Use personal knowledge and interest to make money for oneself is possible in entrepreneurship but not in employment.
8. Scanner is an input device that makes copies and reproduces text and images and convert it into a digital file, allowing the computer to read or display the scanned object. Scanners can be used for storing the documents in their original form that can be modified and manipulated later on. It is mainly used to convert a scanned document in a digital format. Scanners come in a variety of sizes from hand held models to desktop models as Handheld scanners, Flatbed scanners and Drum scanners.
9. Positive thinking is a positive approach that looks towards life's challenges with a positive outlook or finds positivity in everything around us. It requires a person to look at the good in things, observe, understand and works for improving them.
   The importance of positive thinking are :
   (i) It overcomes challenges.
   (ii) It makes us do well by making us energetic.
   (iii) It helps us better at work.
   (iv) It makes us and people around us happy.
10. Biodiversity is essential for the following purposes :
    - Preserving ecological processes such as fixing, recycling of nutrients
    - Soil formation
    - Circulation and cleansing of air and water
    - In maintaining global life support systems such as plants giving out O_2 and absorbing CO_2
    - Maintaining the water balance within ecosystems
    - Watershed protection
    - Maintaining stream and river flows throughout the year
    - Erosion control
    - Local flood reduction

11. To type capital letters, switch ON the Caps Lock by pressing the key before typing. A light will shine on the top right side corner of the keyboard that shows Caps Lock is ON. To switch it OFF, again press the Caps Lock key before typing.
12. To add text to a slide that contains text frame, click on Click to add text in the text frame and then type your text. The outline styles are automatically applied to the text as you insert it.
13. Global In-house Centres (GICs) include both MNC owned units that undertake work for the parent's global operations and ISPs owned units of domestic companies. e.g. Barclays Technology Center India, Honeywell.
14. • Find the shortcut of LibreOffice on Start menu or on the desktop. Double click to open LibreOffice.
    • Click LibreOffice Calc. The Calc spreadsheet window will open.
15. **Help tab** is used to allow users to search and find any topic about that program, send feedback, know about license information, etc.
    Tools tab is used to spelling and grammar, language, word count, bibliography database, macros, etc.
16. (i) By default, the presentation is saved with .odp extension.
    To save a presentation as another file type, follow below steps :
    Step 1 Select File → Save As. The Save As dialog box will appear.
    Step 2 In the Save As dialog box, click on Save as type drop-down menu and select the choice from the offered programs as per your requirement.
    (ii) To ungroup objects, follow the below given procedure:
    • Select the group by clicking on any one of the objects in the group.
    • When the selection handles are displayed, go to Format → Group → Ungroup on the menu bar or use the keyboard combination Ctrl + Alt + Shift + G or right click on the group and select the ungroup from the context menu.
17. The precautions may be
    • By keeping the use of ICT safe, we need to make sure that we do not overuse it.
    • One should install protective softwares which can help to reduce any damage to the data present in the computer, from malware function, data erasing etc.
    • Almost every type of content is available on the Internet these days, but we need to avoid getting manipulated with violent, pornographic or harmful content and make best use of useful content.
18. (i) Some of the factors that are included in typing ergonomics :
    1. **Sitting posture** While operating the computer keyboard, sit straight, slightly bending your neck forward. Check your comfort and sitting position of body. Touch the lower portion of your back to the lower portion of the back rest of the chair. Touch both the feet to the floor. While typing, you should not cross your legs. There should be a distance of approx 15 cm between two knees.
    2. **Position of Hands** A good position of hands is either parallel or slightly below the elbow. Your forearms should be at level with the keyboard and palms down. Keep your wrists straight. The shoulders and elbows should hang naturally. The elbows should neither touch the body nor be too far away from the body. Elbows should also be bent at 90° angle.

    (ii) Perform the following steps to customise a new lesson in the Lesson Editor :
    Step 1 Click on the Lesson menu button on the taskbar, a drop-down menu will appear. Select the Create new lesson option from the menu.
    Step 2 Select a course in the Navigation tree in which you want to add the lesson such as Beginner.
    Step 3 Click on the Lesson type option, a drop-down menu will appear. Click on the main pad option to select the lesson types.
    Step 4 Type the text in the text area that you want to add in the lesson.
    Step 5 After typing the text, go to the Lesson properties pane.
    Step 6 Click in the text box under the Title section and give the lesson a name such as My Lesson.
19. Components of LibreOffice Writer are as follows :
    • **Title Bar** It is located at the top of the window and displays the document name. The format of the name displayed on the title bar is document name - LibreOffice Writer.
    • **Menu Bar** It is located just below the title bar. When you select one of the menus, a sub menu drop down to show further options.
    • **Toolbars** Toolbars are the horizontal bars that contains icons representing various tools and commands. They provide a quick access to common functions, allowing you to format text, insert image, create tables and much more.

- **Status Bar** It is displayed on the bottom of the window and used to view the information such as page number, current page, current template, etc.
- **Scroll Bar** It is used to view the whole active window. There are two types of scroll bars, i.e. horizontal scroll bar and vertical scroll bar.
- **Zoom Control** Lets you zoom in for a closer look at your text. The zoom control consists of a slider. You can slide it left or right to zoom in or out, to increase or decrease the zoom factor.

20. The syntax and example of any five mathematical functions in spreadsheet are as follows :

(i) **SUM ( )** It adds the values contained in a range of cells.

Syntax = SUM (Number1, Number2 , ...)

e.g. If cells A1 = 5, B1 = 5 and C1 = 5 then function = SUM (A1, B1, C1) will give result 15.

(ii) **AVERAGE ( )** It finds the average of the values contained in a range of cell.

Syntax = AVERAGE (Number1, Number2, ...)

e.g. If cells A1 = 6, B1 = 4 and C1 = 2 then function = AVERAGE (A1, B1, C1) will give result 4.

(iii) **COUNT ( )** It counts the number of cells within a range of cells.

Syntax = COUNT (Number1, Number2, ...)

e.g. If cells A1 = 2, B1 = 4 and C1 = 1 then function = COUNT (A1, B1, C1) will give result 3.

(iv) **MAX ( )** It finds out the largest value contained in a range of cells.

Syntax = MAX (Number1, Number2, ...)

e.g. If cells A1 = 5, B1 = 7 and C1 = 6 then function = MAX (A1, B1, C1) will give result 7.

(v) **MIN ( )** It finds out the smallest value contained in a range of cells.

Syntax = MIN (Number1, Number2, ...)

e.g. If cells A1 = 5, B1 = 7 and C1 = 6 then function = MIN (A1, B1, C1) will give result 5.

21. (i) The possible multimedia content that are included while creating a presentation as follows:

- image
- audio
- video
- cartoon characters

A multimedia presentation is a standalone presentation that includes information presented with images, video, or digital representation and includes sound which might be a narrative, music or sound effects. Such effects are used to present content because it makes the content interesting as well as entertaining.

(ii) (a) **Outline view** It contains all the slides of the presentation in a sequence. It shows each slide in the outline format. Only the text contained in each slide is displayed inside the workspace. It displays slide text in the form of a structure.

(b) **Slide Show view** In this view, the computer screen is completely filled by a single slide. This view is used for the rehearsal or actual slide show and user cannot make any changes during this view. For this view, press F5 key from keyboard.

SAMPLE QUESTION PAPER 2

A Sample Question Paper for CBSE Class 9

Information Technology

General Instructions

See Sample Question Paper 1.

Time : 2 hours ***Max. Marks : 50***

Section A (Objective Type Questions)

1. ***Answer any 4 out of the given 6 questions based on Employability Skills*** (1 × 4 = 4)

(i) .... is a pointing device that allows to control the movement of pointer. (1)

(a) Mouse (b) Joystick (c) Touch screen (d) Touch pad

(ii) Clearance of trees for agriculture and non-agriculture uses is .... (1)

(a) Mining (b) Deforestation (c) Pollution (d) Over exploitation

(iii) In written type of communication, the written .... is used to convey the message. (1)

(a) mark (b) image (c) symbol (d) None of these

(iv) Sushma kept working for two years before success came her way. This quality of Sushma came under .... (1)

(a) knowledge (b) patience (c) commitment (d) comment

(v) .... help us to create a good image of ourselves. (1)

(a) Personal hygiene (b) Acknowledgement (c) Knowledge (d) All of these

(vi) To view a web page, you need a .... on your computer. (1)

(a) server (b) web browser (c) notepad (d) paint

2. ***Answer any 5 out of the given 6 questions*** (1 × 5 = 5)

(i) How can one calculate the total of values entered in a worksheet column? (1)

(a) By manual entry (b) By auto-sum (c) By formula (d) By sum function

(ii) .... option allows you to setup a connection to an FTP, Google Drive and several other services. (1)

(a) Save Remote (b) Cut Remote (c) Copy Remote (d) All of these

(iii) .... is the main view for working with individual slides. (1)

(a) Outline view (b) Normal view (c) Slide sorter view (d) None of these

(iv) In ...., the $ sign is used before row number or column name to make it constant. (1)

(a) Mixed referencing (b) Absolute referencing (c) Relative referencing (d) All of these

(v) .... is also called web-enabled services. (1)

(a) IT (b) ICT (c) ITeS (d) None of these

(vi) More than one objects can be .... together and treated as a single object. (1)

(a) Individual (b) Grouped (c) Both (a) and (b) (d) None of these

3. ***Answer any 5 out of the given 6 questions*** (1 × 5 = 5)

(i) The .... text will be highlighted. (1)

(a) Selected (b) Corrected (c) Edited (d) All of these

(ii) The column immediately next to column "Z" is .... (1)

(a) AZ (b) ZA (c) AA (d) None of these

FULLY SOLVED

(iii) The keyboard shortcut for copy is .... and for paste is .... (1)
(a) Ctrl + V, Ctrl + C (b) Ctrl + C, Ctrl + V (c) Ctrl + C, Ctrl + C (d) Any of these

(iv) Students can also contact a teacher or a trainer via Internet to use .... (1)
(a) IBT (b) CBT (c) WBT (d) All of these

(v) .... deletes the character on the left of the cursor. (1)
(a) Delete (b) Backspace (c) Insert (d) Arrow

(vi) .... is any text entered by using a keyboard. (1)
(a) Symbol (b) Space (c) Label (d) None of these

4. *Answer any 5 out of the given 6 questions* (1 × 5 = 5)

(i) You can insert .... in a document. (1)
(a) image (b) shape (c) symbol (d) All of these

(ii) .... is very important in the document for proper authorization. (1)
(a) Password (b) Login (c) Login name (d) None of these

(iii) In LibreOffice writer document, every paragraph has a paragraph .... (1)
(a) change (b) edit (c) style (d) All of these

(iv) In spreadsheet, which tab contains options as Sort, AutoFilter, Select Range? (1)
(a) Sheet (b) Data (c) Tools (d) Edit

(v) .odp is the extension of .... (1)
(a) Writer (b) Spreadsheet (c) Impress (d) None of these

(vi) To delete any slide from a presentation, first it should be .... (1)
(a) Selected (b) Corrected (c) Editing (d) All of these

5. *Answer any 5 out of the given 6 questions* (1 × 5 = 5)

(i) .... is used to sort slides with drag and drop method. (1)
(a) Slide Sorter view (b) Notes view (c) Outline view (d) Normal view

(ii) Clicking on .... with downward arrow, will decrease the size of the text. (1)
(a) Z (b) X (c) A (d) +

(iii) Which of the following is/are mathematical operator(s)? (1)
(a) Addition (b) Subtraction (c) Multiplication (d) All of these

(iv) Almost all spreadsheet applications use .... referencing by default. (1)
(a) Relative (b) Mixed (c) Absolute (d) None of these

(v) Formatting a document allows to select paper format as .... (1)
(a) A 4 (b) A 5 (c) B 4 (d) All of these

(vi) The paragraph style settings have a .... (1)
(a) menu (b) pop down window (c) commands (d) None of these

FULLY SOLVED

Section B (Subjective Type Questions)

Answer any 3 out of the given 5 questions based on Employability Skills. Answer each question in 20-30 words (2 × 3 = 6)

6. What are green skills? (2)

7. What is the effect of language in communication? (2)

8. Describe the role of patience and hardworking for achieving goals. (2)

9. Suggest any two qualities of a self-confident person. (2)

10. What do you understand by output device? (2)

Answer any 4 out of the given 6 questions in 20-30 words each (2 × 4 = 8)

11. What is the use of numeric keypad in keyboard? (2)

12. Explain, the term slide transition in brief. (2)

13. List the various uses of IT in a banking system. (2)

14. Write a short note on formula in spreadsheet. (2)

15. List the variety of modifications that one can make in the table. (2)

16. (i) How will you save a presentation? (2)
(ii) What do you understand by Undo in presentation?

Answer any 3 out of the given 5 questions in 50-80 words each (4 × 3 = 12)

17. Write the differences between IT and ITeS. (4)

18. Define the following terms: (4)
(i) MAX () (ii) Label

19. What do you mean by group objects in presentation? (4)

20. What is touch typing technique? Also, explain the various stages of touch typing technique. (4)

21. (i) Explain, any five different types of tabs available in LibreOffice Writer. (4)
(ii) (a) Define the term mail merge.
(b) What is the importance of password in the document?

Answers

1. (i) (a) Mouse (ii) (b) Deforestation (iii) (d) None of these
(iv) (b) patience (v) (d) All of these (vi) (b) Web browser

2. (i) (d) By sum function (ii) (a) Save Remote (iii) (b) Normal view
(iv) (b) Absolute reference (v) (c) ITeS (vi) (b) Grouped

3. (i) (a) Selected (ii) (c) AA (iii) (b) Ctrl + C, Ctrl + V
(iv) (d) All of these (v) (b) Backspace (vi) (a) Symbol

4. (i) (d) All of these (ii) (a) Password (iii) (c) style
(iv) (b) Data (v) (c) Impress (vi) (a) Selected

5. (i) (a) Slide Sorter view (ii) (c) A (iii) (d) All of these
(iv) (a) Relative (v) (d) All of these (vi) (b) pop down window

6. Green skills are those skills required to adapt processes, services and products to climate change and the environmental rules and necessities related to it. These skills are used to promote green economy.

7. The process of communication is both verbal and written. Language plays main role in all the types of communication. The same words can have very different meanings depending on how we interpret them.

In case of use of incorrect words, unfamiliar language and lack of detail, language can act as a barrier to communicate what one wishes to convey.

i.e. Language can act as a barrier when an Indian who knows only Hindi and a Chinese who has the knowledge of Mandarin only want to interact with each other.

8. Success may not be achieved quickly. It is important for an entrepreneur to have patience while running the business. Every new business goes through failures and therefore, an entrepreneur needs to work hard till it becomes successful. It is necessary for an entrepreneur to continuously work hard to achieve his company's goal.

9. Two qualities of a self-confident person are :
(i) **Self-Belief** It is confidence in our own abilities or judgement. People learn from their own mistake and achieve success.
(ii) **Positive Attitude** It is focusing on the positive side of an event in the time of adversily. The situation of losing a game can be perceived as an opportunity to review the game.

10. An output device is a part of computer hardware equipment, used to communicate the results of data processing which are carried out by the information processing system (such as a computer), to the outside world. Output devices carry the results of various operations performed by the user. Output device makes it possible to view or print data.

11. Numeric keypad is used when enormous numeric data is to be entered. This keypad is just like a simple calculator. It is normally located on the right hand side of computer keyboard.

    Numeric keypad contains numbers 0 to 9, addition (+), subtraction (–), multiplication (*), division (/), a decimal point (.), Num Lock and Enter keys.

12. Using slide transition, you can set the way, how the slide will appear during presentation. There are too many ready-made alternatives available. You can also modify features like speed of transition, sound effects, automated transition etc.

13. In modern banking system, computer is an essential part. Every activity of a bank is now online. All the work of bank like record the customer's data, transaction etc, done by computers. Recurring deposits (e-RD), Fixed deposits (e-FD), money transfer from one account to another (NEFT, RTGS), online transactions etc, are done using Internet.

14. Any expression that begins with an equals '=' is treated as formula. In the expression, the '=' followed by values, cell address and functions are called as formula. When a formula is entered in a cell in a worksheet, the value of the equation is displayed in the cell and the formula is shown in formula bar.

15. Using commands on the Layout tab, you can make a variety of modifications to the table such as
    - Adding and deleting columns
    - Adding and deleting rows
    - Changing the cell size
    - Aligning cell text
    - Changing text direction
    - Merging and splitting cells and more

16. (i) To save the presentation, you are working on, follow the steps as given below :

    ***Step* 1** Select the File menu→ Save, or use the shortcut key combination Ctrl + S, or click on the Save button on the standard toolbar.

    ***Step* 2** This will open the Save As dialog box, which allows to select the location on the disk and assign the name to save the presentation.

    ***Step* 3** To change the location in drive, open the directory in which you want to save the file.

    ***Step* 4** Enter a name of presentation file.

    ***Step* 5** Click Save button. If the presentation is already saved, the contents will be updated in that presentation file.

    (ii) Impress keeps the history of recent changes made. When we execute a command on some text, for example delete the text, we are able to reverse what we have done. This is known as the undo function. It is also possible after having undone the change, get it back. This is called the redo function. These options are located in the standard toolbar and can also be performed using keyboard shortcut keys Ctrl + Z is used for Undo and Ctrl + Y is used for Redo.

17. Differences between IT and ITeS are as follows :

IT	*ITeS*
IT stands for Information Technology.	ITeS stands for Information Technology enabled Services.
It is the study of design, management, development, implementation and support of computer based information systems.	It is the study of outsourced service which has arisen due to involvement in various fields of IT.
It includes hardware and software industry and even IT telecom.	It includes call center, BPO, KPO, RPO, etc.

18. (i) **MAX ( )** This function is used to return maximum value from a list of arguments.

    Syntax = MAX(Number1, Number2, ...)

    e.g. If the values contained in cells A1,A2, A3 and A4 are 5,7, 2 and 10 respectively, then

    = MAX(A1:A4) will return 10.

    (ii) **Label** It is any text entered by using a keyboard. It may combine with letters, numbers and special symbols. By default, the labels are left aligned.

FULLY SOLVED

19. More than one objects can be grouped together and treated as a single object. A group formed by grouping the objects can be formatted as a single object, moved, rotated, deleted and so on.

Grouping Objects To group objects, follow the below given procedure :

(i) Select the objects to be grouped using select tool on the Drawing toolbar or hold down the Shift key and click on each object. To select all the objects, go to Edit→ Select All on the menu bar or use the keyboard combination Ctrl + A.

(ii) When the selection handles are displayed, go to Format→ Group on the menu bar or use the keyboard combination Ctrl + Shift + G or right-click on an object within the selected group and select Group from the context menu.

20. Touch typing improves speed and accuracy. A touch typist never looks at the keyboard. The fingers hit the right keys by habit. The typist is entirely focused on the text being typed, reading the words and phrases as the fingers type the text reflexively.

There are three stages involved in touch typing technique :

***Stage* 1** This stage of the process begins with learning the home row of the keyboard (the row beginning with the Caps Lock key). Looking at the keyboard is strictly forbidden. This is followed by learning the lower and upper rows, the number row, uppercase letters and special symbols.

***Stage* 2** In this stage, a touch typing learner starts memorising frequently used syllables and typing words containing these syllables.

***Stage* 3** This stage involves typing actual text to perfect the skills acquired.

21. (i) Five different types of bars/tabs in LibreOffice Writer are as follows :

- **File Tab** It is found in the top-left corner of LibreOffice Writer window. It is used to open existing document, create new document, save, export, send, close, print, etc.
- **Edit Tab** It is used to cut, copy, paste, redo, find, select all, etc.
- **View Tab** It is used for web layout, text boundaries, data sources, navigator, etc.
- **Insert Tab** It is used to insert header, footer, bookmark, frame, page break, chart, movie and sound, footnote/ endnote, etc.
- **Format Tab** It is used to bullets and numbering, page, title page, wrap, alignment, arrange, flip, rotate, group, etc.

(ii) (a) Mail Merge is a useful tool that allows you to produce multiple letters, labels, envelopes by linking a main (common) document to a set of data or data source. The main document is linked to the data source by common fields of data, called **merge fields**.

You can create your own merge fields, specific to your data source, or you can use a predefined set provided by Writer. e.g. in a form letter, your main document would be the letter informing the person that they have won money, or their car service time has arrived.

(b) Password is very important in the document for proper authorisation. Only authorised users can open their accounts or can access their documents using the password option. LibreOffice Writer provides the feature to protect the document.

SAMPLE QUESTION PAPER 3

A Sample Question Paper for CBSE Class 9

Information Technology

General Instructions

See Sample Question Paper 1.

Time : 2 hours ***Max. Marks : 50***

UNSOLVED

Section A (Objective Type Questions)

1. *Answer any 4 out of the given 6 questions based on Employability Skills* (1 × 4 = 4)

(i) Sports academy is .... (1)

(a) analog business (b) hybrid business (c) digital business (d) None of these

(ii) ...... is the process in which the receiver interprets and understands the message. (1)

(a) Decoding (b) Encoding (c) Sender (d) Communication

(iii) Mouse also includes a ...... between these two buttons to scroll down the application window and their contents also. (1)

(a) left wheel (b) right wheel (c) scroll wheel (d) None of these

(iv) ...... gases occur naturally through decomposition of organic matter and through human activity. (1)

(a) Natural (b) Green house (c) Fossil fuel (d) None of these

(v) Expressing certainty or affirmation even in tough situation is known as .... (1)

(a) Positive thinking (b) Negative thinking (c) Both (a) and (b) (d) None of these

(vi) An ...... is the business owner and an ...... is the worker and get a salary. (1)

(a) employee, entrepreneur (b) entrepreneur, employee

(c) employee, citizen (d) None of these

2. *Answer any 5 out of the given 6 questions* (1 × 5 = 5)

(i) .... is a tightly integrated part of business. (1)

(a) ICT (b) IT (c) ITC (d) None of these

(ii) More than one objects can be .... together and treated as a single object. (1)

(a) Ungrouped (b) grouped (c) Both (a) and (b) (d) None of these

(iii) The format of the name displayed on the title bar in writer is .... (1)

(a) Document name-LibreOffice Writer (b) LibreOffice Writer

(c) Document Name (d) None of these

(iv) After using the UNDO command,to go back again to the previous position, the .... option or command is used. (1)

(a) cut (b) paste (c) redo (d) None of these

(v) The cell address of the cell formed by the interaction of the ninth column and eight row will be .... (1)

(a) 8I (b) I8 (c) I7 (d) None of these

(vi) Which shortcut key is used to insert table? (1)

(a) Ctrl + F12 (b) Alt + Delete (c) Ctrl + Delete (d) Tab + Delete